# THE QUEST FOR
# THE IRISH CELT

*For Fiach and Aoife*

# THE QUEST FOR THE IRISH CELT

## THE HARVARD ARCHAEOLOGICAL MISSION TO IRELAND, 1932–1936

MAIRÉAD CAREW

IRISH ACADEMIC PRESS

First published in 2018 by
Irish Academic Press
10 George's Street
Newbridge
Co. Kildare
Ireland
www.iap.ie

9781788550093 (Cloth)
9781788550109 (Kindle)
978178855016 (Epub)
9781788550123 (PDF)

British Library Cataloguing in Publication Data
An entry can be found on request

Library of Congress Cataloging in Publication Data
An entry can be found on request

Interior design by www.jminfotechindia.com
Typeset in Minion Pro 11/14 pt
Printed in Great Britain by TJ International Ltd, Padstow, Cornwall

Cover design by edit+ www.stuartcoughlan.com
Jacket front: Harvard anthropologist Earnest Albert Hooton standing with skulls
used in his research, *Life* magazine, 1 January 1936.
Jacket back: top: Mesolithic site at Cushendun, Co. Antrim (Peabody Museum
of Archaeology and Ethnology, Harvard University);  bottom left: Adolf Mahr
(National Museum of Ireland); bottom right: Dr. Hugh O'Neill Hencken (centre)
with unidentified American Anthropologists, 1933 (Peabody Museum of
Archaeology and Ethnology, Harvard University).

# Contents

# Acknowledgements

M uch of the research for this publication was carried out during the course of my PhD thesis, completed in 2011, under the supervision of Professor Mary Daly and funded by the Irish Research Council. I would like to thank the archivists and librarians of the following institutions who helped me with my research: the Peabody Museum of Archaeology and Ethnology, Harvard University; UCD Archives; the National Museum of Ireland; the Royal Irish Academy; the National Archives of Ireland; the National Library of Ireland and the Royal Society of Antiquaries of Ireland.

I would also like to thank the Tyrone Guthrie Centre, Annaghmakerrig, for providing the space and beautiful surroundings in which I completed this book.

✑

# Introduction

This is the first full-length book on the history of the Harvard Archaeological Mission to Ireland, between the years 1932 and 1936. The Harvard Mission was one of the most important cultural undertakings in the history of the Irish Free State. It included three strands of study: excavations, physical anthropology and social anthropology. While the social anthropology strand has been explored in a comprehensive article by Anne Byrne,[1] there have not been similar publications on the archaeological strand or the complementary physical examinations of thousands of Irish people during the thirties.

This eugenic anthropological survey was important in the context of Irish-American history. The Rockefeller Foundation, wealthy Irish Americans and the Irish Free State Government were involved in the funding of it as it was deemed politically and economically important to establish the identity of the Irish as white, Celtic and Northern European during this period. This book will explore why the American anthropologists came to Ireland at the time and why the project was considered to be important to Harvard University. It will place the Harvard Mission initiative in the context of the broader cultural regeneration projects driven by nationalism and Irish-Ireland ideology in the Irish Free State after independence. This study will explore what sites were excavated, who chose them and why, and how the disciplines of archaeology and physical anthropology were used to scientifically validate the identity of the Irish. The stereotype of Ireland as isolationist and culturally barren during the 1930s is challenged by this work. In the 1930s the study and celebration of native Celtic culture in a European and global context was both modernist and internationalist. The Harvard Mission can be considered as a cultural case study in the context of other cultural initiatives of the first two nationalist governments of the Irish Free State.

Chapter 1 places the Harvard Mission to Ireland in the context of the cultural republic of the 1920s and 1930s. The role of the Harvard Mission, as part of the revitalisation project of the Irish Free State which involved the institutionalisation of native culture and a repositioning of Ireland in terms of Europe and the diaspora, is examined. The role which archaeology, in particular, plays in this nation-building project is discussed. Themes of regeneration, anthropological modernism, race, nationalist cultural ideology and the writing of cultural history in Ireland are explored. Chapter 2 examines the reconnaissance trip undertaken in 1931 by the Harvard Mission anthropologists to evaluate the possibilities of their forthcoming survey and research, including the excavation strand. At that time the National Museum of Ireland (NMI) was at the centre of archaeological research and the role of amateur archaeologists and antiquarians was still important. The primary research question for the Harvard Mission archaeologists, influenced by the Director of the NMI, the Austrian archaeologist and Nazi, Adolf Mahr, was about the origin of the Celtic Race in Ireland.

Chapter 3 attempts to answer the question posed by the Irish archaeologist, R.A.S. Macalister, in 1937: 'Why should Harvard University thus concern itself with Ireland?'[1] An exploration of why the Harvard Mission came to Ireland and the political ideology underpinning its archaeological work, dominated by eugenic and racialist concerns, is examined. This work fitted easily with Irish nationalist aspirations for a proven scientific Celtic identity. American and Irish perspectives on Celtic Ireland will be included and their respective initiatives with regard to the study of Celtic Ireland examined. Chapter 4 explores the pragmatic and political reasons why the Harvard Mission undertook crannóg research at Ballinderry 1, Ballinderry 2 and Lagore. The establishment of an American school of archaeology was considered at Ballinderry. Chapter 5 explores the large-scale excavations at Lagore and how the interpretations and dating of the site by the leader of the Harvard Archaeological Mission, Hugh O'Neill Hencken and his team were influenced by the intellectual framework employed within a historical, social, political and racial context. It is examined as a case study of the influence of politics on the creation of archaeological knowledge by the Harvard Mission.

Chapter 6 explores what was meant by Irish prehistory in the 1930s and what was the motivation of the Harvard Mission in the excavation of Mesolithic sites in Northern Ireland. The politics of Irish prehistory in the 1930s was in the context of the focus on the recovery of archaeological evidence for the earliest Irishman. Did it matter if the Harvard Mission recovered this evidence in Northern Ireland or in the Irish Free State, and what, if any, were the political implications of that? Chapter 7 discusses the Unemployment Schemes for archaeological research inaugurated in 1934 by Éamon de Valera in an effort to help solve the social problem of rife unemployment in the 1930s. Cultural and economic protectionism included state-controlled excavations to retrieve knowledge that was crucial as scientific evidence for the cultural identity of the state as Celtic and Christian. Some of the Harvard

Mission sites were excavated under these schemes. They also served as an important training ground for scientific archaeologists, where talented Irish archaeologists such as Seán P. Ó Ríordáin emerged.

Chapter 8 explores how classification and chronological concepts in archaeology affect interpretation of data and how political ideas are embedded in the methodology employed. The academic and personal background of Hugh O'Neill Hencken and his assistant Director, Hallam L. Movius, as well as employees and volunteers, are also relevant to this process. The Harvard Mission were to influence the subsequent development of a school of scientific archaeological research in Ireland where new excavation techniques were employed and specialised scientific reports commissioned in order to interpret the data. Chapter 9 explores the importance of the media to Celtic identity with particular reference to Celtic Art and 'Celtic' and 'Christian' archaeological sites excavated by the Harvard Mission and under the auspices of the Unemployment Schemes. The media reports in the American press helped to disseminate ideas about Irish Celts within the diaspora. *The Pageant of the Celt* was a re-enactment in 1934 of 'Celtic' history at the Chicago World Fair. Artefacts recovered by the Harvard Mission archaeologists were displayed at the fair in a special Irish Free State exhibition which centred on the National Museum collections.

# 1 THE HARVARD ARCHAEOLOGICAL MISSION IN THE IRISH CULTURAL REPUBLIC

The outstanding feature of Ireland's cultural development and of her position in the civilised world may be stated thus: she is not the cradle of the Celtic stock, but she was its foremost stronghold at the time of the decline of the Celts elsewhere; she is the most wonderful artistic province of the Celtic spirit, its centre of missionary enterprise, its last refuge; pre-eminently *the* Celtic country. Ireland is now the only self-governing State with an uninterrupted Celtic tradition, and has the duty of becoming *the* country for Celtic Studies.[1]

– Adolf Mahr, 1927

## Archaeology and Politics in the Irish Free State

The Harvard Mission to Ireland[2] was a large-scale anthropological study of the Celtic race in Ireland, funded mainly through grants and donations administered by the Peabody Museum of Archaeology and Ethnology, Harvard University.[3] The Irish Free State made funding available for the archaeological strand from 1934 by defraying the costs of labour through Unemployment Schemes.[4] While the project contained three strands: social anthropology, physical anthropology and archaeology, the focus of this chapter and the book as a whole is the archaeological strand and the corroborating evidence from physical anthropology.[5] In America in the 1930s the academic discipline of anthropology was sub-divided into four topics for study: archaeology, physical anthropology, ethnology and linguistics. The Harvard School specialised in archaeology and physical anthropology.[6] The aim of the Harvard Mission was to study the origin and development of the races and cultures of Ireland.[7] Large-scale scientific excavations were carried out between the years 1932 and 1936 and the physical examinations of thousands of Irish people became part of the nation-building project of the Irish Free State, focussing on cultural revitalisation programmes (between 1922 and 1948) under the auspices of nationalist governments.[8] The Harvard Mission archaeologists included Northern Ireland in their survey of the Irish Free State. This was because, as the Director of the archaeological strand, Hugh O'Neill Hencken asserted, 'the territory was an integral part of Ireland' prior to the seventeenth century.[9] Excavations were carried out on both sides of the border. Academic journals such as the *Journal of the Royal Society of Antiquaries of Ireland* and *Proceedings of the Royal Irish Academy* welcomed articles on Irish archaeology from all over the island. Neither organisation changed this policy after the establishment of the border. In contrast, *The Ulster Journal of Archaeology* had a regionalist policy and papers were primarily focussed on Ulster archaeological research.[10] The Harvard Mission to Ireland included three years of fieldwork and two years of analysis and preparation of reports.

The Harvard Mission became part of the essentialist drive of the de Valera government to establish a cultural republic in the 1930s. The institutionalisation and professionalisation of native cultural endeavour began after 1922. It included archaeological initiatives as antiquities were considered crucial in the process of imagining the nation.[11] The 'imagined community' envisaged by Benedict Anderson[12] was given visual and tactile expression through material culture. Monuments and artefacts applied a sense of concreteness, permanence and longevity to the abstract concept of the nation. The Harvard Mission was also an expression of diaspora nationalism which saw an attempt to improve the social and economic circumstances of the Irish in America through Celtic cultural endeavour.[13] Irish-Americans contributed financially to the Harvard research: this was facilitated by Judge Daniel O'Connell and his brother, the ex-Congressman Joseph O'Connell, who organised the Friends of the Harvard Anthropological Survey of Ireland.[14]

Hugh O'Neill Hencken, the leader of the archaeological strand, was of Irish and German extraction. His grandfather, also called Hugh O'Neill, left Newtownards, County Down in 1854 to travel to Belfast, where he sailed for New York. He became a well-known dry-goods merchant in New York and served as Patron of the Metropolitan Museum of Art and the Natural History Museum.[15] Hencken was educated at Princeton University in America and Cambridge University in England. By 1931 he was Assistant Curator of European Archaeology at the Peabody Museum in Harvard. This success reflected the rising fortunes in social and economic terms of the Irish in America in the early decades of the twentieth century. In 1934, the early Irish historian, Eoin MacNeill, expressed the view that 'a right appreciation of Ireland's place in history disseminated in America must contribute to the cultural and spiritual upbuilding of America'.[16] Indeed, it was following MacNeill's successful tour of universities in the United States in 1930 that the Harvard Mission began its work in Ireland in 1932.[17]

## Irish Archaeology: The Playground of the Politician?

Irish-Ireland ideology and anthropological modernism underpinned the cultural regeneration of the nation-state between 1922 and 1948.[18] De Valera sent the *Saorstát Éireann Official Handbook of the Irish Free State*, edited by Bulmer Hobson, and commissioned by the Cosgrave government, to the Chicago World Fair (1933–4) to accompany an Irish Free State cultural exhibition. It was intended to provide 'a survey of the progress made' by 'the end of the first decade of national freedom' and included essays on Irish history, archaeology, folklore, literature, Irish language, art, industries, geology and tourism.[19] Despite this progress, R.A.S. Macalister, professor of Celtic Archaeology at UCD from 1909 to 1943, continued to worry about the intertwining of archaeology and politics, and expressed the view that 'the archaeology of Ireland is worthy of a better fate than to become the playground of the politician'.[20] However, in Ireland between the years 1922 and 1948 it was virtually impossible to disentangle archaeology from political influence. This was because archaeology as a discipline does not function independently of the societies in which it is practised and has a value for the present.[21] In order to understand the rise of archaeology as a discipline it must be examined in a socio-cultural and political context.[22] This is important in the interpretation of the work of the Harvard Mission to Ireland, which began with a trip by American archaeologists to Ireland in 1931 in order to determine which archaeological sites would be selected for excavation as part of a five-year project.

The Harvard Mission excavations took place during a period, described by the Cambridge archaeologist, Grahame Clark, of 'intense archaeological activity' following the establishment of the Irish Free State.[23] However, while this comment is correct it is made without elaboration. Other important initiatives which could be included were the development of a native school of Irish scientific archaeology and the setting up of the Unemployment Schemes for archaeological research in 1934. These initiatives, driven by nationalist ideals, placed Ireland at the forefront of European archaeology in the 1930s. The Harvard Mission excavations were central to this development. After independence, Clark noted that the state continued to strive for a separate national identity through the medium of archaeology and described the process as the 'nationalisation of archaeological activities'.[24] He points out that this intense activity did not fully survive the attainment of political objectives. Waddell agrees that 'the bright promise of the 1930s is hard to discern in the following two decades'.[25] However, the important fact remains that Irish archaeology was a necessary ingredient to the attainment of political objectives as cultural activity often presages or acts as a catalyst for political activity. It was hugely important to the nation-building project during this period as it was then scientifically possible, through the practice and methods of archaeology, to recover proof of the antiquity of the Irish Celtic race. This cultural authority of science consolidated and validated political identity. The discipline of archaeology was rooted in the landscape and, therefore, the territory defined as the homeland, the definition of which was essential to the nationalist agenda. Attempts were also made in the 1930s to establish an American School of Celtic Studies at the National Museum of Ireland.[26] While this did not materialise, de Valera included a School of Celtic Studies in the Dublin Institute for Advanced Studies in 1940, an idea initially mooted by Eoin MacNeill.[27]

## The Harvard Mission and Irish–Ireland Ideology

In the Irish Free State the native expression of cultural activity was the consolidation of the doctrine of Douglas Hyde when he pleaded for an Irish nation 'upon Irish lines' in his famous speech 'The Necessity for De-

Anglicising Ireland', delivered to the National Literary Society in Dublin on 25 November 1892.[28] Hyde (later to become the first President of the Irish Free State in 1938) postulated that it was 'our Gaelic past' which prevented the Irish from becoming 'citizens of the Empire'.[29] He exhorted all Irishmen to speak the Irish language, revive Irish customs, buy Irish goods, and play Irish music and Irish sports. Hyde believed that '*our* antiquities can best throw light upon the pre-Romanised inhabitants of half Europe'.[30] This was important to the creation of an Irish national identity because it was believed that Ireland, unlike many other European nations, had developed independently and was, therefore, free of Roman influence. This belief, which the Harvard archaeologists shared, influenced their interpretations of the crannóg excavations.[31] Archaeology was necessary to demonstrate the material culture of a nation which Hyde described as 'the descendant of the Ireland of the seventh century, then the school of Europe and the torch of learning'.[32]

With independence came the prioritisation of native cultural expression. There was also an impetus to institutionalise the cultural endeavours which had previously been the preserve of the educated middle and, particularly, the upper classes, such as the collection of antiquities and folktales. In his discussion of the Gaelic League Tom Garvin argues that politicians of independent Ireland 'had imbibed versions of its ideology of cultural revitalisation'.[33] Archaeology became the material expression of this 'cultural revitalisation' in the 1920s and 1930s. These ideas were also reflected in D.P. Moran's book *The Philosophy of Irish Ireland,* published in 1905. Eoin MacNeill expressed a similar view in the *Irish Statesman* on 17 October 1925 and commented that 'if Irish nationality were not to mean a distinctive Irish civilisation, I would attach no very great value to Irish national independence'.[34]

## Archaeology, Modernism and the Celtic Revival

In his book *Modernism and the Celtic Revival,* Gregory Castle refers to 'the increasing cultural pessimism of the late nineteenth century and the claim that not only the population of cities but the world itself, that is the West, was degenerating'.[35] This resulted in an idealisation of rural life which is evident in the writings of W.B. Yeats and others from the Cultural Revival period. This was a rejection of urban culture with its associated side effects of industrialisation, including poverty and social problems. Hyde's version of the nation, emphasising the soil, the Irish race and the Irish language was the vision of deAnglicisation which de Valera promoted. Eugen Weber discusses similar ideas in French culture in his book *Peasants into Frenchmen*. He explores how land, the soil, physical activity and health were essential to ruralist conservatism in France. This was interpreted as an expression of the nation's soul with its hostility to modernity, urban life and cultural diversity.[36] de Valera's much derided 1943 speech, broadcast on the fiftieth anniversary of the founding of the Gaelic League, expressing ideas of rural romanticism, youthful health and racial purity, can also be seen in this light.[37]

In his book Castle explores what he terms, 'an underlying affinity between anthropology and modernism'.[38] He explains that anthropological observations and the study of the past was an essential part of the modernist agenda. The Harvard Mission to Ireland could be placed in this context whereby modern physical and social problems could be solved through the medium of science in the 1930s. Castle notes that 'the desire to revive an authentic, indigenous Irish folk culture is the effect of an ethnographic imagination that emerges in the interplay of native cultural aspirations and an array of practices associated with the disciplines of anthropology, ethnography, archaeology, folklore, comparative mythology, and travel writing'.[39] In the 1890s anthropology, archaeology and ethnography were emerging scientific disciplines. The West of Ireland became important to the Celtic Revivalist and anthropologist alike. For example, J.M. Synge, author of *The Aran Islands*, was educated in continental Celticism and studied under the French Celtic scholar, Henri D'Arbois de Jubainville. Synge attended lectures on Celtic culture and mythology, philology and cultural anthropology at the Sorbonne in Paris.[40] Revivalists and anthropologists attempted to reclaim traditions, histories, and cultures from imperialism and 'to reclaim, rename, and reinhabit the land'.[41] This pivotal role of anthropology in the Celtic Revival resulted in 'autoethnography', as native intellectuals attempted to represent themselves to the coloniser using the language and methodology of the colonial discipline of anthropology.[42]

In the Irish Free State's programme of native cultural revitalisation, anthropology, archaeology, Irish language, folklore and native traditions became important in themselves rather than as motifs illustrating Irish literature in the English language. The Harvard Mission as part of this revitalisation programme can be described as a modernist project in the sense that it was an anthropological survey to study scientifically a society in transition between tradition and modernity. John Brannigan, in his book *Race in Modern Irish Literature and Culture*, explains that 'the Harvard study should be contextualised as an important moment in the evolution of the modernist state, in which social and physical sciences were understood to be strategic instruments vital to the bio-political ambitions of the state.[43] The scientific establishment of the credentials of the Celtic race by international archaeological and anthropological expertise was essential to these political aspirations.

The combined native and internationalist dimensions to cultural production fitted de Valera's anthropological cultural vision, emphasising cultural heritage as a pathway to the future for an independent republic. Nicholas Allen, in his paper 'States of Mind: Science, Culture and the Irish Intellectual Revival, 1900–1930', makes the point that 'Immediately after the Anglo-Irish and Civil Wars, we find the discourse of science applied widely in support of cultural, political, and economic development in the new state'.[44] While Allen doesn't refer to archaeology in his article, his ideas can also be applied to the Harvard Mission's work as the Harvard academics applied scientific techniques of American archaeology to their work in Ireland. American archaeology had become increasingly scientised in the early decades of the twentieth century.[45]

## Irish: The Language of the Celts

Albert Earnest Hooton[46], the American physical anthropologist and manager of the Harvard Mission, wrote about the importance of the Irish Free State, citing that one of the reasons for choosing it for a Harvard survey was because of 'the Celtic tongue, an archaic Aryan language once spoken over a large part of Europe'.[47] Hugh O'Neill Hencken, like his contemporaries, took an interest in Celtic, an Indo-European language. He was later to publish a book entitled *Indo-European Languages and Archaeology* as a volume of the *American Anthropologist* in 1955.[48] According to G.R. Isaac in his paper 'The Origins of the Celtic Languages: Language Spread from East to West', it is still impossible to discuss the origin of the Celts without reference to the Celtic language. He argues that 'without language, there are no Celts, ancient or modern, but only populations bearing certain genetic markers or carriers of certain Bronze Age and Iron Age material cultures. The origin of the Celts therefore is the prehistory and protohistory of the Celtic languages'.[49] The Irish language, therefore, as well as the material culture of the Celts, were deemed important areas of study in Irish universities in the nineteenth century and this continued after independence in 1922.

In 1854, Eugene O'Curry had been appointed to the first Chair of Celtic Archaeology at the Catholic University. R.A.S. Macalister became the first Professor of Celtic Archaeology at University College Dublin in 1909. Douglas Hyde, president of the Gaelic League from its foundation in 1893 to his resignation in 1915 for political reasons, campaigned for and succeeded in making Irish a compulsory subject for matriculation to the newly established National University of Ireland in 1908.[50] The state took over the Gaelic League's educational function by including Irish as a compulsory subject in the educational system and by setting up the special Government Publications Office, *An Gúm*, in 1926.[51] The Irish language was established as the national language in Cosgrave's 1922 constitution and was also given this status in de Valera's 1937 constitution. By 1934, in his keynote speech at the International Celtic Congress held in Dublin from 9–12 July, Douglas Hyde was still advocating for the preservation and propagation of the Irish language. At this stage, Éamon de Valera, who was in the audience together with Maud Gonne, Agnes O'Farrelly and delegates from Brittany, Scotland, Wales and the Isle of Man, had pledged his backing for a permanent research institute where all the Celtic languages might be studied'.[52]

Patrick Pearse, who had served as the editor of the League's journal, *An Claidheamh Soluis* (1903-1909), aimed to create 'a modernist literature in Irish'.[53] He argued that 'Irish literature if it is to live and grow, must get into contact on the one hand with its own past and on the other with the mind of contemporary Europe'.[54] By the 1930s literary works of 'an indigenous tradition of amateur self-ethnography' appeared.[55] These included books such as Maurice O'Sullivan's *Twenty years A-Growing*, *The Autobiography of Peig Sayers of the Great Blasket Island*, Tomás Ó Crohan's *The Islandman*, and Pat Mullen's *Man of Aran*. Irish-speaking islanders were regarded in this period as pre-industrial and pre-modern. Ideas about degeneration in cultural and racial terms, a common discourse in the 1930s, fed into the need for regeneration through cultural, economic, political and moral projects in the Irish Free State. One of the most influential cultural critics in the interwar period in Ireland, the writer Seán O'Faoláin, criticised the Irish language revival, referring to 'the poverty and degenerate nature' of Gaeltacht culture'.[56] This rhetoric is similar to that of the nineteenth-century colonialist writers on Ireland. The use of the word *degenerate* is disingenuous as the impetus of the Irish language revival and native cultural regeneration in general was an attempt to address the perceived degenerate nature of culture, race and society at that time.[57] Comhdháil Náisiúnta na Gaeilge (a new umbrella co-ordinating body for Irish-language organisations) was established in 1943.

The 1930s can be seen as the apogée of a native cultural revitalisation programme which began with Hyde's speech and served as the cultural blueprint for the independent state. The Irish Free State, under Cosgrave in the 1920s and de Valera in the 1930s, favoured cultural activity which fitted into this ideological framework. Unfortunately, Irish-Ireland ideology got a bad name because of the vitriolic outpourings of journalists such as D.P. Moran.[58] The impetus for regeneration in the Irish Free State was part of a wider European project where nation-states across Europe defined their nationhood in terms of race, culture, language and purity. These modernist regeneration projects included the enactment of laws which institutionalised concepts of national culture, and embedded it in the political agenda of the state. The nationalist governments of Cosgrave and de Valera shared a similar Irish-Ireland cultural ideology. Attempts to establish the racial credentials of the Irish as Celtic dovetailed neatly with the American agenda of the Harvard anthropologists and archaeologists. They concentrated on rural dwellers for their anthropometric survey as they believed that 'the country people were perhaps more truly representative of Irish racial types and less likely to be mixed with recent foreign blood than would be the city dwellers'.[59]

## From Hyde to Lithberg

As part of the deAnglicisation project Douglas Hyde had written about the importance to the Irish nation of the collections of a national museum and the necessity of gathering antiquities and 'enshrining' each one of them in 'the temple that shall be raised to the godhead of Irish nationhood'.[60] When Hyde penned these words, no doubt, he was not referring to all vestiges of the past but to selected items from what he perceived to be a Celtic, Irish and Christian past. The idea that 'relics' of the Gaelic past should be displayed or contained in a sacred building such as a temple expresses the veneration of an idyllic past, or Golden Age, which was a central tenet of the doctrine of Irish nationalism. The raising of this building to 'the godhead of Irish nationhood' further expands on the idea that the past and how its interpretation was controlled through museum display became important in terms of imagining and defining the nation.[61] These museum exhibits were a means of transmitting ideas about national territory, history and homeland, and reflect the nation in microcosm. The selection process itself was part of this nationalist endeavour. The Dublin Museum of Science and Art was opened in 1890 and was formally renamed the 'National Museum of Science and Art, Dublin' by its Director, George Noble Count Plunkett,

in 1908. Count Plunkett, a cultural nationalist and Home Ruler, was father
of the executed 1916 leader Joseph Mary Plunkett. The new title, according
to Plunkett, was 'more appropriate for the institution having regard to its
representative position in the capital as the Museum of Ireland and the
treasury of Celtic antiquities.'[62]

## A State Framework for Irish Archaeology

Archaeology, as a useful political tool, underpinned visually the identity of the
state as Celtic and Catholic. The process whereby 'culture became a surrogate
for politics' applied to the discipline.[63] It is described by Gearóid Ó Tuathaigh
as a 'cultural vision of decolonisation.'[64] This decolonisation process, involving
the reclamation, culturally and politically, of archaeological monuments and
artefacts, had already begun in the nineteenth century. This is exemplified
in the media furore over the British Israelite excavations for the Ark of the
Covenant at the Hill of Tara in 1899–1902. Cultural nationalists, including
Arthur Griffith, Douglas Hyde, W.B. Yeats, Maud Gonne and George Moore
were involved in the protests to get the digging stopped as they regarded it as
a 'desecration' of Tara, the capital of an ancient and independent Ireland. At
the time, British Israelites regarded Tara as a royal site in the British Empire.
They wished to recover the Ark and present it first to Queen Victoria and
later to her son Edward VII.[65]

Another controversy of note at the end of the nineteenth century was
the contested ownership of the Broighter hoard, discovered in 1896 in Co.
Derry. The hoard, deposited some time after 100 BC consisted of gold objects,
including two bar torcs, two necklaces, a bowl, a buffer torc and a beautiful
model boat with oars and a mast. The objects were sold to a Derry jeweller,
who sold them to Robert Day, an antiquarian, who sold them to the British
Museum. The prominent Unionist, Edward Carson, represented the Royal
Irish Academy (RIA) at a subsequent court case. The hoard was deemed to
be 'treasure trove' and handed over to King Edward VII, who gave it to the
RIA and the hoard later became part of the celebrated gold collection of the
National Museum of Ireland.[66]

After independence the dominant cultural vision of nationalist elites
was embedded into the discipline, reflected in the policies and practices
of Irish archaeology. In 1927 the creation of a state framework for Irish
archaeology was achieved by the provision of a new cultural policy
document for the National Museum of Ireland: the 1927 Lithberg Report,

prioritising Celtic and Christian artefacts; and the framing of the National Monuments Act, 1930, which defined a 'National Monument' for the first time. These important initiatives not only provided the framework within which Irish archaeology was practised under state control but also reflected the influence of Gaelic League ideology. Professor Nils Lithberg of the Northern Museum of Stockholm was commissioned to write a report on the purpose of the National Museum by the Irish Government. He was chosen for the task because the Northern Museum of Stockholm was 'one of the most notable national museums in Europe'.[67] Lithberg had been appointed as the first holder of the position of Professor of Nordic and Comparative Folklife Research there in 1918. The Northern Museum of Stockholm was described by Barbro Klein as a 'culture-historical museum'.[68] Culture-historical archaeology became popular towards the end of the nineteenth century. It was influenced by nationalist political agendas and used to prove a direct cultural or ethnic link from prehistoric peoples to modern nation-states. Growing nationalism and racism, according to Bruce Trigger 'made ethnicity appear to be the most important factor shaping human history'.[69] The Lithberg Report was the blueprint for a culture-historical museum in Ireland. It was very important in the context of the politics of museum display and was a key document in the nationalisation policy of the government for Irish archaeology.[70] It was recommended that the collections should be 'firmly based on Ireland's native culture' and that the gold ornaments from the Early Bronze Age, the artefacts from the pre-Roman Iron Age and the Early Christian Period should be kept separate so that 'the collections will receive the glamour of ancient greatness to which they are entitled'.[71] In the process, as Elizabeth Crooke put it, 'The Museum and the Irish nation was reinventing itself'.[72]

The Lithberg Report was also important in the context of European identity. The American involvement in Irish Free State archaeology gave it a global resonance and satisfied an American desire in the 1930s for roots in old Europe. Thousands of artefacts recovered by the Harvard Mission archaeologists during their five-year project in Ireland were deposited in the National Museum. How the past was packaged for the viewer and how selected artefacts were displayed in the museum illustrated the official narrative of the nation's history. This reflects Ernest Gellner's view of the political principle of nationalism that 'the political and the national unit should be congruent'.[73] Culture, as represented by archaeology in the Irish Free State and its strategic display in a national institution was a politically aspirational endeavour. The emphasis on archaeology in the National

Museum was heavily criticised by Sir Thomas Bodkin. He blamed this on the two former directors of the National Museum, the prehistorians Walther Bremer and Adolf Mahr, writing that 'neither of them professed interest in the Fine Arts, and their well-nigh exclusive preoccupation with archaeology worked to the great disadvantage of the Museum'.[74]

The introduction of new legislation for the protection of archaeological heritage was also politically aspirational. In an address delivered to the Royal Irish Academy in 1927, R.A.S. Macalister, President of the Royal Society of Antiquaries, stated that 'Ireland must remember that she holds in trust for Europe a large number of ancient monuments of unique importance: and the sooner legislation is obtained to facilitate the nationalisation of these monuments, the better it will be for the national credit of the Free State'.[75]

In the legislation enacted finally in 1930, a 'National Monument' was defined as 'a monument or the remains of a monument the preservation of which is a matter of national importance by reason of the historical, architectural, traditional, artistic, or archaeological interest attaching thereto'.[76] The word 'national' was a political rather than a cultural designation.[77] The definition of 'national monument' caused difficulty because if politicians decided that the preservation of particular monuments was not a matter of 'national' importance, in theory at least, they didn't have to be protected. The Dáil debates surrounding the National Monuments Bill give an insight into the political opinions involved in the interpretation of key concepts contained in the legislation. The embeddedness of a desired identity, reflected in the type of monument deemed to need protection, served the cultural and political needs of the state at that time.[78]

The debate about the validity of protecting Big Houses, seen as a vestige of Protestant identity, also surfaced. According to Terence Dooley, this was because the landed class 'had come to symbolise colonial rule and their houses were symbols of an old order'.[79] Apart from the symbolic and political difficulties inherent in their preservation there was also the prohibitive cost to consider'.[80] For example, Coole Park, the residence of Lady Gregory, was sold to the Department of Lands in 1927 and demolished in 1941. There was some disquiet about its demolition expressed in newspaper coverage of the time because of Lady Gregory's association with the Irish Literary Revival, W.B. Yeats and the founding of the Abbey Theatre. At the time, Lady Gregory and Coole Park were not seen as culturally valuable from an Irish-Ireland perspective.[81] The Chairman of the Board of Works expressed the view that 'no one is going to deny Lady Gregory's claim to a place of honour in Anglo-Irish literature but it is straining it somewhat to suggest that her home should be preserved as a National Monument on that account'.[82] If money was spent on preserving such buildings, it was argued, the excessive cost might affect the preservation of 'real national monuments'.[83] Examples of 'real national monuments' included Newgrange, round towers, churches at Glendalough and the Rock of Cashel. If the meaning of the monument was contested, its 'national' essence was not secure, resulting in the structure not being covered under the definition in the legislation. Similar legislation to protect national monuments was enacted in France, Germany, Italy, Greece, Austria, Belgium, Holland, Switzerland, Sweden, Denmark, Norway, Spain, Portugal, Russia, Turkey, Palestine and Great Britain.[84]

The law against unlicensed excavations and the unauthorised export of antiquities was very important as prior to this, archaeological expeditions, carried out by America and Britain to Egypt and other countries, had resulted in the looting of archaeological material and the export of it to the country of origin of the archaeologists. This was something which worried Macalister with regard to the Harvard Mission. A concern among archaeologists had been reported in an article published in the *Irish Press* in 1932 'that a wealth of Irish antiquities may find their way across the Atlantic instead of being preserved at home'.[85] Hugh O'Neill Hencken and Hallam L. Movius Jr. made a statement in 1934 that 'It is the policy of Harvard University that the objects found during excavations should become the property of the National Museum of Ireland'.[86] Unlike the strict legislation in the Irish Free State, the Ancient Monuments Acts (Northern Ireland) of 1926 and 1937 did not make illegal the export of archaeological material which resulted in the shipment of material to America.[87]

While Douglas Hyde's ideas about embracing all Irish cultural activity were adopted by the government of the Irish Free State, this did not include archaeological manifestations of Protestant identity. Síghle Bhreathnach-Lynch expresses this idea succinctly:

> In keeping with other nations emerging from colonial rule, not surprisingly, the new Irish state was anxious to establish as soon as possible a distinctive national character, one that was as different as possible from that of its erstwhile ruler. Great Britain was perceived as urban, English-speaking and Protestant. Ireland would go to endless lengths to prove itself to be the opposite: rural, Irish-speaking and Catholic. A significant aspect of this construct of identity was the belief that Ireland's national identity was rooted in a Golden Age, that is the ancient Celtic past.[88]

Culture-historical ideas were embedded in the Lithberg Report and the National Monuments Act as the cultural value of artefacts and archaeological monuments were established within this framework. The parameters of the selection process of sites excavated by the Harvard Mission and under the Unemployment Schemes and the subsequent interpretative paradigm used was also defined by this. It enabled the state to control the creation of archaeological knowledge and to make political claims to disputed territory though the medium of archaeological discourse (see Chapter 6).

## Archaeology and Folklife

The Harvard Mission archaeologists included reports on local folklore in their scientific papers.[89] Archaeology in this period was directly linked with the life of ordinary people. This was part of a democratisation of culture, a European phenomenon, and an expression of anthropological modernism. In the Lithberg Report, for example, it was recommended that 'on these two principles, that is, the knowledge of Ireland's earlier culture and of the present day life of the people, should in my opinion, an Irish National Museum be based'.[90] To this end it recommended the creation of a folklife section in the National Museum. The Folklore of Ireland Society was created in 1926. The Irish Folklore Institute was formed in 1930 and received finance by way of a Cumann na nGael government grant and a Rockefeller Foundation grant of £500. Within five years the institute had built up a collection of over 100 manuscript volumes. This important work was continued by the de Valera government with the establishment of the Irish Folklore Commission in 1935 and in 1937–8 the innovative Schools Collection was carried out. Séamus Ó Duillearga, who was involved in the setting up of the Irish Folklore Commission, travelled extensively in Scandinavia and established strong academic and cultural ties there.[91] Micheál Briody notes that the Irish Folkore Commission was the first such organisation devoted solely to the collection of folklore in any country and succeeded in 'assembling one of the finest and most extensive collections of folk tradition in the world'.[92] In 1936, at the inaugural meeting of the Historical Society of UCD, Ó Duillearga, then director of the Folklore Commission, pointed out that scholars on the continent and in America were taking particular interest in its work. In a letter dated 2 November 1938 from the Department of External Affairs to Maurice Moynihan, Secretary, Department of the Taoiseach, it was noted that 'Ó Duillearga was going to deliver a series of lectures on folklore in the American Universities in the Spring and that Ó Duillearga desired 'to

extend the operations of the Folklore Commission to the Six county area.[93]
Ó Duilleargas's UCD address in 1936 on the oral tradition was entitled 'An
Untapped Source of Irish History'. He described the work of the Folklore
Commission as embracing 'everything of a traditional character which could
throw light on the social and cultural life of the Irish people of past times'.[94]
In his book, Briody observed that 'The Irish Folklore Commission achieved
international status by bypassing England and going to, what it considered,
the fountainhead of folklore scholarship',[95] the northern countries of
Europe. The establishment of a folklife collection at the National Museum
became more important after political independence. In 1935 the Folklore
Commission invited Ake Campbell and Albert Nilsson, two Swedish
ethnologists, to come to Ireland on a 'Folk-Life Mission' to make a survey of
Irish rural farmhouses.[96]

Adolf Mahr, a friend of Ó Duilleargas's, and board member of the
Irish Folklore Commission, was also involved in the Quaternary Research
Committee, set up in 1934, which brought the Danish mission to Ireland;
their work on the bogs had important scientific implications for Irish
archaeology.[97]

## Archaeology and the Democratic Ideal

It was explained in the Lithberg Report that the object of a Historical
Museum was not to collect objects of artistic and monetary value as these
objects have 'an intrinsic capacity of preserving themselves' but to collect
'more simple objects which have a small market value and for this reason
are threatened with destruction'.[98] The ideal of a National Museum should be
'to give a consecutive representation of the native civilisation of the country
from the time when the human mind first showed its creative power until
the present day, and it should embrace all classes which have been or still
are components of its society'.[99] This sentiment reflects the democratic ideal
of the independent nation-state. It also reflects the fact that archaeology was
no longer the preserve of the monied and leisured classes but was a state-
sponsored activity.

Malcolm Chapman has noted that the 'Celts' and the 'folk' often seem
'virtually conterminous categories' because 'folklore' like the idea of the Celts
had become romanticised.[100] This idea of the idyllic life of the peasantry
was a throwback to the nineteenth-century cultural-nationalist idea of the
pure, native, Gaelic-speaking, rural-dwelling Irishman. According to Joep
Leerssen, a sense of Irish cultural identity came to be located in antiquity

and peasantry in the nineteenth century.[101] This trend of glorifying 'past and peasant' continued into the twentieth century and was given material expression in the nationalist museums of Europe in their folk-life collections. The recommendations for the folklife section contained in the Lithberg Report were based on the open-air museum at Skansen in Stockholm.[102]

One of the Harvard Mission anthropologists, Conrad M. Arensberg, commented in his book *The Irish Countryman* that: 'The folklorist has discovered Ireland, and today the Free State Government subsidises the preservation of folklore as a monument to national greatness'.[103] Folklore and superstition were also important in the preservation of archaeological monuments. Macalister lamented the fact that superstitions were 'once potent in preserving the ancient monuments'. He worried that 'unless something intervenes to stay the damage, the world will lose many of the lessons that Ireland, and Ireland alone, can teach'.[104] But these superstitions lingered and local people were sometimes suspicious of the scientific work of the Harvard archaeologists, with their emphasis on physical anthropology. For example, Rev. L.P. Murray, editor of the *County Louth Archaeological Journal* was worried that the respect shown for burial grounds by ordinary people would be diminished by the work of the Harvard Misssion and would lead inevitably to the destruction of more monuments in the future. He criticised the methods used in excavating the Bronze Age burial site at Knockast, Co. Westmeath. He did not agree with disturbing the remains of the dead and he questioned the use of bone measurements to acquire useful archaeological data.[105] He described their work at burial-sites as 'ghoulish performances' and posed the question: 'If it is permissible, today, to rifle a Bronze Age cemetery, will it not also be permissible, in the years to come, to excavate the consecrated burial grounds of today?'[106]

## The Irish Free State in a Global Cultural Context

The Harvard Mission work took place during a time when, Terence Brown asserts, the Irish Free State, was 'notable for a stultifying lack of social, cultural, and economic ambition'.[107] This popular idea of cultural barrenness has persisted despite being challenged in a collection of essays edited by Joost Augusteijn entitled *Ireland in the 1930s*.[108] Auguesteijn argues that, in this decade when Fianna Fáil came to power, attempts were made to develop the Free State into 'an entity which was not only politically but also socially, culturally and economically independent and which dealt with its citizens in a purely Irish manner'.[109] This theme is explored in a diverse range of papers whose topics include the Irish language revival, the cottage schemes for agricultural labourers and the centenary celebrations for Catholic Emancipation. While archaeological initiatives are not included in his book, they can also be considered as part of this wider cultural continuum.

Native cultural achievements in the early decades of independence, including the work of the Harvard Mission, are often not recognised by cultural historians as there has been a tendency to view cultural history through the lens of the censorship laws. In Brown's opinion, the relationship between Irish-Ireland ideology and 'exclusivist' cultural and social pressures culminated in the Censorship of Publications Act, 1929.[110] There was also the enactment of the Censorship of Films Act, 1923. In Brian Fallon's opinion the importance of the censorship laws has been 'much overplayed'.[111] Indeed, the analysis of native cultural achievement celebrating archaeology, literature, ancient manuscripts written in the Irish language, oral traditions, folklore, the rural way of Irish life and Catholicism has been severely limited by this methodology and has resulted in a skewed view of this period as culturally underachieving and stagnant. The placing of 'Anglo-Irish' literature on a pedestal as the defining Irish cultural expression of this period means that the intellectual movement of this era, which was not purely a literary one, has not been fully analysed to date. Ian Morris, an archaeologist and historian at the Stanford Department of Classics, wrote that archaeology is 'cultural history or it is nothing'.[112] The history of other forms of successful native Irish cultural endeavour likewise are essential in the writing of Irish cultural history in the early decades of independence.

According to Paul Delaney, the post-colonialist writer, Seán O'Faoláin, 'helped to shape the ways in which subsequent generations of readers viewed the cultural history of the Free State'.[113] O'Faoláin, who was not a trained historian, eschewed native achievements in favour of what he considered to be an internationalist agenda in an English-speaking world.[114] The interpretation of culture through a broader lens shows how native cultural achievement was also internationalist in its scope. Cultural ideologues such as Douglas Hyde and Eoin MacNeill were very influential in the creation of a cultural identity for the independent state and the institutionalisation of native forms of cultural expression. Hyde's ideas about cultural revitalisation in his speech was later developed by MacNeill in his own writings and in his work as a public intellectual.[115] However, in a recent book, *Histories of the Irish Future* by Bryan Fanning (2015), exploring intellectual history through the writings of Irish thinkers, cultural nationalists such as Eoin MacNeill and Douglas Hyde are omitted. The impact of Hyde's speech, 'The

Necessity for deAnglicising Ireland' on the intellectual and cultural life of twentieth-century Ireland has been underestimated. The ideas contained in it were essential to the cultural underpinnings of the nationalist state. Eoin MacNeill's academic work, as a cultural activist in the public sphere and in his cultural work abroad, was also essential to the process of state formation. His leadership of cultural institutions such as the Irish Manuscripts Commission which he cofounded in 1928, serving as its first president, was crucial to the post-colonial writing of Irish history and its establishment as a viable academic discipline in Irish universities. After the destruction of the Public Records Office at the Four Courts on 30 June 1922 during the Civil War, the importance of an organisation dedicated to the publication of original historical source materials in English and Irish was crucial.[116] State cultural institutions were based on and validated by the important writings and ideas of Hyde and MacNeill, and very important cultural and scientific work such as that of the Harvard Mission was also facilitated during this period of cultural renewal.

## Cultural Protectionism and Diaspora Nationalism

The much criticised censorship laws can also be interpreted as a form of cultural protectionism in this period. Peter Martin points out that Irish nationalists combined ideas about censorship with their objections to British and Anglo-American culture.[117] This combination of ideas about social, cultural and racial purity of the Irish was to underpin nationalist ideology It was also an expression of fears about the degeneracy of the race reflected in social problems and a perceived decline in the physical quality of the race and in the quality of cultural production. It is also worth noting that censorship in the 1920s and 1930s was not peculiar to Ireland and can be placed in an international context.[118] The agenda of the Harvard Mission to Ireland merged with the nationalist, Celtic agenda of the Irish Free State Government. Paradoxically, while Ireland was culturally and economically protectionist, her sights were fixed firmly on Europe and, to a lesser extent America, for cultural sustenance. However, native Irish cultural institutions and projects held their own in European and global cultural contexts. The Harvard Mission, which itself was an expression of Irish diaspora nationalism, involved American academics at the height of their professions, bringing international expertise to the discipline of Irish archaeology. The popular idea of insular self-obsession is belied by the fact that international expertise was actively sought by the Irish Free State Government. Examples of this include the seeking of a keeper of Irish Antiquities with European archaeological expertise, such as the German, Walther Bremer, an expert in German archaeology and Celtic culture who was appointed in 1926; Adolf Mahr, the Austrian Celtic archaeologist, succeeded Bremer in 1927 as Keeper of Irish Antiquities and was later appointed to the position of Director of the National Museum in 1934; American/Harvard expertise in archaeological methodology and physical anthropology was embraced with enthusiasm; Danish expertise was acquired for the Quaternary Research Committee; and Scandinavian expertise was sought for the establishment of the Folklore Commission. Some important senior state jobs in the economic and cultural sector in the Irish Free State were held by Germans during the 1930s. Heinz Meking was the chief adviser with the Turf Development Board; Ludwig Mühlhausen was a Professor of Celtic Studies; Colonel Fritz Brase was head of the Irish Army's School of Music; Otto Reinhard was Director of Forestry in the Department of Lands; Robert Stumpf was a radiologist at Baggot Street; Friedrich Herkner was Professor of Sculpture at the National College of Art; Friedrich Weckler was chief accountant of the ESB from 1930 to 1943; and Oswald Muller Dubrow was Director of the Siemens-Schuckert Group, which built the Shannon Hydroelectric Scheme.[119] A dam and power station was constructed at Ardnacrusha, Co. Limerick on the River Shannon and the first national electrification grid in Europe was created. It was opened by W.T. Cosgrave in 1929. Trips to the Shannon development were offered by Great Southern Railways.[120] This massive undertaking cost the state £5.2 million, an astronomical sum at the time.[121]

Political progress was expressed through scientific and technological progress and the scheme became 'a potent symbol of a new post-Treaty Ireland, as an indigenous source of energy to power industrial development'.[122] The view was expressed in the *Irish Statesman* that this project reflected the 'attitude of mind proper to a self-governing nation'[123] This attitude of mind was also evident in the paintings of the artist, Seán Keating. Keating was commissioned to create a series of paintings on the theme of 'the dawn of a new Ireland', to celebrate this industrial achievement. One of the most famous of these paintings was *Night's Candles are Burnt Out*, first exhibited at the Royal Academy in London in 1929.[124] Some of Keating's paintings were also sent as part of a cultural package which centred on the collections of the National Museum of Ireland to the Chicago World Fair in 1933 and 1934.[125] In a *New York Times Magazine* article, 'The Shannon stirs new hope in Ireland', it was noted that it was 'the outward sign of transforming forces liberated by the Treaty settlement that are destined to create an Ireland that need no longer turn wistfully to the past for its golden age'.[126] However, nationalist governments in Ireland continued to look to the future through the perceived achievements of the Irish nation expressed through cultural production during its past golden ages, Celtic and Christian. During the construction of the Hydroelectric Scheme there was much contemporary debate about the preservation of national monuments. One example was the contested treatment of St. Lua's Oratory, a medieval ruin which was moved from Friar's Island to the grounds of St. Flannan's Roman Catholic Church in Killaloe.[127]

## Catholic Identity and Material Culture

The identity of the Irish Free State as Celtic and Catholic was important to the first two nationalist governments. The Cosgrave government organised the centenary of Catholic Emancipation in 1929. The de Valera government oversaw the Eucharistic Congress of 1932, described in the *Round Table* journal as 'a hosting of the Gael from every country under the sun'. There was much appropriation of material culture for Catholic purposes in the celebrations of the Eucharistic Congress in 1932. The congress became 'a culminating event in the Irish national struggle', in which images of the past played an important role.[128] For example, replicas of round towers were erected at College Green and St. Stephen's Green. St. Patrick's bell was borrowed from the National Museum for use in the Pontifical High Mass on 26 June 1932.[129] The sound of St. Patrick's bell at the event was described by the Catholic writer, G.K. Chesterton, as follows:

> It was as if it came out of the Stone Age; when even musical instruments might be made of stone. It was the bell of St. Patrick, which had been silent for 1,500 years. I know of no poetical parallel to the effect of that little noise in that huge presence. From far away in the most forgotten of the centuries, as if down avenues that were colonnades of corpses, one dead man had spoken. It was St. Patrick; and he only said: 'My master is here.'[130]

The association of St. Patrick's bell exclusively with Catholicism in this way was an appropriation of an archaeological artefact for use in the construction of an identity for Ireland which was different culturally and socially from their Anglo-Saxon neighbours. In his address at the Eucharistic Congress at a state reception at Dublin Castle in honour of the Cardinal Legate, de Valera stated that 'At this time when we welcome to Ireland this latest Legation from the Eternal City, we are commemorating the Apostolic Mission to Ireland, given fifteen centuries ago to St. Patrick, Apostle of our Nation'.[131]

The Eucharistic Congress was described as 'a flashpoint in the formation of a specific Irish Catholic identity'.[132] More than a million people attended masses in the Phoenix Park over five days. Adolf Mahr was commissioned to write a book, *Christian Art in Ancient Ireland: Selected Objects Illustrated and Described*, for the event. It was presented by de Valera to the Cardinal Legate at Government Buildings on 23 June 1932.[133] Volume II of the book was completed by Mahr's successor, the archaeologist Joseph Raftery, in 1941. In his review of Mahr's book, Cyril Fox wrote in 1932, that 'we warmly congratulate the Government of Saorstát Éireann on this new evidence of their appreciation of "the vital function which art has in the life of a nation."'[134] This viewpoint about art and the nation provides an interesting counterpoint to that espoused by Brian P. Kennedy on the importance of art in independent Ireland.[135] The cultural revival, prior to 1922, was infused with the Protestant ethos of W.B. Yeats, Lady Gregory and others but was supplanted by a catholicisation of culture in the newly independent state where 'Celtic' was assumed to be synonymous with Catholic. Indeed, Celtic Art was a politically hot topic as it was considered essential to the identity of the state and the prospect of discovering valuable Celtic objects was a core ambition of the Harvard archaeologists. While Hyde advocated an inclusive religious ethos, the cultural vision of the first two nationalist governments under Cosgrave and de Valera was a Catholic one. As modernist thinking did not necessarily take the form of secularism in the interwar period, expressions of Catholicism fitted the broader cultural regenerative model, driven by nationalist ideology.

This cultural blossoming became imbued with the catholicity of the newly independent State. The 'Early Christian Period', in archaeology, for example, came to be seen as exclusively Catholic. This is also reflected in the setting up of the Academy of Christian Art in 1929 which was under the patronage of Saints Patrick, Brigid and Columcille. Article iv of its constitution stated that 'For reasons of doctrine and ritual the academy shall include none but Catholics'.[136] In 1922, the Central Catholic Library in Dublin was established.[137] It was de Valera's view that 'the Irish genius has always stressed spiritual and intellectual values rather than material ones'.[138] This emphasis on the spiritual was also expressed in the foreword to the catalogue, *The Pageant of the Celt*, performed at the Chicago World Fair in 1934. One example of this type of sentiment included the statement: 'We who have seen our world wrecked on the reefs of material philosophy must seek our own rebirth and the salvation of our heirs in the beacon light of that Celtic philosophy which in other days saved the world for Christian ideals'.[139] *The Pageant of the Celt*, narrated by Micheál MacLiammóir, covered a 3,500-year period of Irish history in nine scenes, from the arrival of the 'Milesians' in prehistory to the 1916 Rising.[140] It was reported in the *Chicago Herald* that John V. Ryan, President of Irish Historical Productions, Inc., and a Chicago attorney, composed the 'richly poetic version of Ireland's history'.[141] The objective of the pageant was 'to present a spectacle worthy of their Celtic past, and reveal to Americans of Celtic tradition a glimpse of their rich racial heritage'.[142]

## A Century of Progress in Irish Archaeology

An official Irish Free State exhibition was displayed in the modernist Travel and Transport building at the Chicago World Fair in 1934, the theme of which was 'A Century of Progress'.[143] This was organised by Daniel J. McGrath, the Irish Consul-General in Chicago and centred around antiquities in the National Museum. An 'impressive effort' involved the collaboration of the National Museum of Ireland, the Royal Irish Academy and the Royal Society of Antiquaries of Ireland to present 'A Century of Progress in Irish Archaeology'.[144] Artefacts and copies of them included 'Celtic' cultural items from the Early Christian Period and 'Celtic' cultural items from the Early Bronze Age. Artefacts discovered by the Harvard Mission archaeologists included a cast of the Viking gaming board and an electrotype of a bronze hanging bowl from Ballinderry 1 Crannóg, Co. Westmeath. The antiquities were considered at the time to be very important because of 'the all-European and indeed, universal importance of Irish archaeology'.[145] Editions of the *Journal of the Royal Society of Antiquaries of Ireland* and the *Journal of the Co. Louth Archaeological Journal* were displayed. Also exhibited were popular guides on archaeological sites; a copy of the National Monuments Act, 1930; the 'List of scheduled monuments in the care of the Commissioners of Public Works'; and some Office of Public Works (OPW) Annual Reports with descriptions of famous sites such as Glendalough, Clonmacnoise and the Rock of Cashel. A photographic album compiled by the Dublin optician and antiquarian Thomas Holmes Mason, MRIA, contained photographs of the well-known archaeological monuments in their natural settings including Newgrange, Dowth, Dun Aengus, the Skelligs, Glendalough, Monasterboice and Clonmacnoise. The archaeological exhibit was part of a wider cultural package which reflected the ideas and values and aspirations of the Irish Free State. Included were facsimiles of the Book of Kells and the Book of Durrow; stills from the film *Man of Aran*, paintings by Jack B. Yeats, Paul Henry and George Russell (AE), books and cards from the Cuala Press, tapestries from the Dún Emer Guild and books in the Irish language.[146]

The correlation of race, religion and cultural expression was typical of the period. The idea that a pure race would produce a pure cultural product was an idea common in archaeological discourse. MacNeill's academic tour of universities in the United States in 1930 not only attracted the Harvard Mission to Ireland, but the Mission's work in turn gave scientific credence to Irish archaeological and medieval historical scholarship. MacNeill, who can be seen as a cultural ambassador for Ireland, was working hard to encourage the development of Celtic Studies in the United States.[147] Celtic Studies became an important conduit for the post-colonial desire to re-establish cultural connections within the diaspora as a way of gaining a cultural and, therefore, economic, foothold on the world stage.

## A World Centre of Celtic Culture

Douglas Hyde had expressed his gratitude for the interest of American academics in 'everything concerned with us – history, archaeology and language'.[148] He corresponded regularly with the American Celticists including Fred Norris Robinson, Arthur L.C. Brown and Roger Sherman Loomis. He also kept an autographed photograph of Theodore Roosevelt, a Celtophile, on the wall in his study.[149] In 1930, Eoin MacNeill was invited to tour some American universities by Professor Arthur L.C. Brown, of Northwestern University; Professor J. Peet Cross, of Chicago University and Professor Robert D. Scott, of the University of Nebraska.[150] He described these scholars as 'of the highest reputation on both sides of the Atlantic as authorities on the mediaeval literatures of Northern and Western Europe'.[151] During his tour, he visited Harvard, Columbia, New York, Yale, Fordham, Notre Dame, and Northwestern University in Chicago. At that time Harvard and the Catholic University of America were the two institutions at the forefront of the development and promotion of Celtic Studies in the United States. Fred Robinson of Harvard was central to the development of Celtic Studies at Harvard and its increasing importance in the cultural life of North America.[152] When he arrived in New York on 2 April 1930 MacNeill was met by detectives and the police as political threats had been made against him.[153] His first lecture was on early Celtic institutions and law which was delivered at New York University (NYU) on 2 April 1930. A dinner was hosted in his honour by the American Irish Historical Society of New York and the Law School of New York University. The American Irish Historical Society (AIHS) was founded in 1897 for the purpose of correcting the perception of Ireland's role in American history.[154] By the 1930s this perception was beginning to change. Other speakers at the dinner included Daniel F. Cohalan, who took an active role in the AIHS. Cohalan was the son of an Irish immigrant who left Cork at the height of the Famine in 1847. He had a lot of political influence and was regarded as the 'leader of the Irish race in America'.[155] Prior to his meeting with Eoin MacNeill, Cohalan had met with important cultural and political figures including Douglas Hyde, Patrick Pearse and Roger Casement. He served as President of the Board of Directors of the influential Irish-American newspaper, the *Gaelic American* from 1903 and was co-founder of the Sinn Féin League of New York with John Devoy in 1907. Cohalan was leader of the Irish-American organisation Friends of Irish Freedom (FOIF) which was launched a few weeks prior to the 1916 Rising. He supported the Irish Treaty of 1921. MacNeill revealed in his speech in the NYU Law School that 'he did not believe in impartial national histories' and that he was 'willing frankly to admit his inability to write an impartial history of Ireland'.[156] This admission gives an insight into his philosophy of history, his nationalist perspective of the past and the expectations of his Irish-American audience.

In 1931 Professor John L. Gerig announced a plan that Harvard and Columbia universities would join together to establish a university in the Scottish Highlands 'to serve as a world centre of Celtic culture and to preserve the Scottish and Irish dialects from the extinction threatened by the rapid advance of English as a world tongue'.[157] Gerig taught Celtic for many years at Columbia University and had been a student of d'Arbois de Jubainville, the famous nineteenth-century French Celticist.[158] He wrote to E.J. Gwynn, Provost of Trinity College Dublin, that the plans for the university should 'emphasise to the Scots and the Irish the role of America in world culture'. E.J. Gwynn replied that 'The real centre of Celtic studies, ought, of course, to be [....] in Dublin'.[159]

In the *Gaelic American* of 27 June 1931 it was reported that Gerig bemoaned the lack of endowments and special chairs for Gaelic studies and the fact that there were 'no special professors to devote their whole time to the racial heritage of the Gael'.[160] For many years the *Gaelic American* newspaper had highlighted 'the neglect of Americans of Irish blood in safeguarding their cultural heritage and their backwardness in this respect as compared with other races that make up the cosmopolitan population of America'.[161]

Gerig's 'arresting plea' for a campaign to stimulate interest in Celtic culture in America was discussed in an article published in the *Irish Independent* on 6 June 1931. The view was expressed by the author that 'Ireland was once the centre of learning for Europe. There is no reason why it should not again become the fountain of culture at least for the children of her own race'.[162] In the *Gaelic American* newspaper, 27 June 1931, it was reported that the quality of research work was recognised by leading Irish scholars and colleges, and that this had 'inspired the hope that America will take the place of Germany in this field of endeavour'. E.J. Gwynn strongly approved of American interest in Celtic Studies. He wrote to Gerig on 10 November 1930 that 'it is a great satisfaction to know that the decline of Celtic scholarship in France and Germany is being counterbalanced to some extent by the increasing interest shown in the universities of U.S.A'.[163] James McGurrin, President-General of the AIHS of New York, in a letter published in *The Irish Times*, 21 June 1934, acknowledged the fact that the growing interest in things Celtic had produced a large body of research work, 'and its highest practical expression is seen in the work of the Harvard University Archaeological Mission'.[164] After his American tour, Eoin MacNeill suggested that in order to promote a knowledge of Irish national culture, both past and present, special Irish cultural sections in US public libraries and in the libraries of schools, colleges and universities should be set up.[165] J.P. Walshe, Secretary at the Department of External Affairs, advised de Valera on 5 October 1937 that 'the time has come to interest ourselves directly as a Government in what we might call, for want of a better expression, cultural propaganda in the United States'.[166] It was his view that it would be money well spent as it would increase the number of tourists. In 1936, a proposal was made to establish in the US an institute similar to the American-Scandinavian Foundation.[167]

In 1940, a School of Celtic Studies and a School of Theoretical Physics were combined in de Valera's modernist project – the Institute for Advanced Studies in Dublin. It was de Valera's ambition that the institute would be a world centre for Celtic Studies and he modelled it on the Institute for Advanced Studies at Princeton University. In a Dáil debate on the Institute for Advanced Studies Bill, 1939, de Valera had explained that 'at the moment we have the leadership of the Celtic nations in so far as we alone of these have a government which can foster, with special interest, the prosecution of such studies'.[168] The purpose of the school was to edit and publish material relating to early modern Irish and to produce grammars and dictionaries. De Valera explained what he meant by the term 'Celtic':

> By 'Celtic,' I want it to be clearly understood, we mean more than merely Irish studies. We are thinking of the related Celtic nations and we are anxious to hold our place, as I indicated at the start, as the chief centre for Celtic Studies. There was a time when the centre for Celtic Studies was outside this country but, as time goes on, it is becoming more and more apparent that this country is the natural centre for Celtic studies and we have the men for the work.[169]

Timothy Linehan of Fine Gael objected to the expenditure on the proposed institute and the abuse of the term 'Celtic', stating that 'you can justify any expenditure of money in this country, you can justify anything in this country by making it Celtic, Gaelic, Irish or national. Anybody who would attack this Bill probably would be attacked all over the country as anti-national and anti-Celtic'.[170] The School of Celtic Studies at the Dublin Institute for Advanced Studies did not include archaeology among its disciplines. It is likely that there were political reasons for this.

Daniel A. Binchy, a scholar of Irish linguistics and early Irish law, and later a member of the American Academy of Arts and Sciences, had been appointed as the first Chairman of the Governing Board of the School of Celtic Studies in 1940. He had served on the Board of the Irish Folklore Commission with Adolf Mahr. Binchy and Mahr had 'diametrically opposed views on Nazism'.[171] These political tensions had affected Binchy's attendance at meetings of the Board. He had served as an Irish diplomat in Germany between 1929 and 1932 and later wrote articles which were very critical of Hitler and the Nazis.[172] The study of prehistory was getting a bad name in Germany because of the abuse of the discipline by the state.[173] Binchy, no doubt, feared that something similar could happen in Ireland considering that an influential Nazi had been director of the National Museum until 1939. By 1946, the Professor of Celtic Archaeology at UCD, Seán P. Ó Ríordáin was complaining about the 'limited number engaged in the pursuit of archaeology' in Ireland and made an appeal for financial aid for research, 'whether it be provided through the Universities or through a special research institute. It is hoped that the State will prove as generous in this as it has been to other intellectual disciplines'.[174] However, this was not to be and no archaeological institute was established.

# 2 ADOLF MAHR AND THE POSSIBILITIES OF HARVARD ARCHAEOLOGICAL RESEARCH

The collection is not a matter of mere local interest; it is of international importance. It contains the key of many problems in the past history of Europe at large. The Free State holds it in trust for the entire world, and it cannot be adequately controlled except by a scholar of European reputation.[1]

– R.A.S. Macalister (1928)

The rise of archaeology as a scientific discipline in nineteenth-century Ireland, according to John Hutchinson was 'strongly driven by a nationalist desire to establish Irish descent from the ancient Celts, and thereby Irish claims to be one of the original civilizations of Europe'.[2] In the twentieth century, after independence, this was still the case. Reference was made in a Hooton manuscript to 'the peculiar importance

of Irish archaeology' and to the idea that 'the traditions and beliefs of
the prehistoric and ancient historic populations have been to a great
extent perpetuated in their living descendants'.[3] In his privately published
memoir Hugh O'Neill Hencken described how he went to the Western
Union office near Harvard Square and wrote out a long cablegram to
Adolf Mahr at the National Museum of Ireland about the possibilities
of Harvard excavating in Ireland. He received an 'enthusiastic reply but
with some reservations'.[4] Mahr, an expert in European Celtic archaeology,
strongly influenced the selection of archaeological sites for excavation by
the Harvard Mission. He was convinced of the importance of Ireland to
America and his enthusiasm for the work of the Americans was essential
to their success. In his view Ireland's 'real world importance' was its
archaeological heritage, with its bearing on the formation of European
civilisation. He wrote that 'Irish archaeology is the only thing which
can give us a status in European learning'.[5] The shared understanding of
Mahr and the American anthropologists and archaeologists was that the
identity of the Irish was 'Celtic' and this belief underpinned the selection
of sites for excavation. The initial Harvard proposal was to scientifically
excavate archaeological sites for every prehistoric and proto-historic
period, to study the monuments and artefacts discovered, to determine
racial affinities of skeletal remains excavated and to collect folklore about
ancient remains.[6]

## Transitions: Archaeology and Society

Irish society in the 1930s was, the Harvard academics believed, a society in
transition between traditional and modern and, therefore, ideal for study.
Irish archaeology itself was going through a transition from traditional
antiquarianism to modern archaeology. The gradual professionalisation of
archaeology in Ireland resulted in scientific archaeologists taking the place
of antiquarians over the course of the 1920s and 1930s. There were still
debates and controversies raging in the 1930s in Britain between 'scientific
archaeologists' and 'antiquarians' and the question of who had the right to
control interpretation of the past, a debate which had been ongoing there since
the nineteenth century.[7] Adolf Mahr and the Harvard archaeologists were
central to the process of change in Ireland. Amateur archaeologists played a
key role in showing the Americans around during their reconnaissance trip
in 1931 and in sharing their unique knowledge about local areas. The Harvard
archaeologists were seen as objectivists who would rescue Irish archaeology

from the narrow parochialism and speculative mire of antiquarianism, and give it a global resonance.

During the 1930s the National Museum of Ireland used antiquarians who were described as having 'archaeological leanings' and 'correspondents' in various parts of the country as opposed to university- or museum-trained archaeologists. These amateurs or antiquarians were not qualified as archaeologists, but they acquired antiquities for the museum and helped in the discovery of new archaeological monuments and the protection of existing ones. Some of them even undertook excavations at the behest of Mahr. This was simply a pragmatic solution as the number of professionally trained archaeologists in the state was miniscule. Seán P. Ó Ríordáin pointed out, in 1931, 'the great dearth of trained workers in archaeology in Ireland', and 'the lack of opportunities for their training'.[8] In the 1930s and 1940s there was the gradual phasing out of the use of unqualified individuals to direct archaeological excavations. The more important sites were left to trained archaeologists and museum staff.

However, the public perception of both archaeologists and antiquarians was often negative in character. When Myles na gCopaleen wrote in his *Irish Times* column 'Cruiskeen Lawn' on 29 May 1942 about 'Irish Iberian flint-snouted morons (c.6000 B.C.), who practised the queer inverted craft of devising posterity's antiquities', he was perhaps reflecting contemporary Irish society's suspicion of archaeology and the 'scholarly dirt-shovellers' who practised it. Considering the fact that the Professor of Archaeology at UCC, Canon Patrick Power had the following to say about the discipline in 1925, this is hardly surprising: 'For long Irish Archaeology had in fact been left to charlatans and dabblers, whence it acquired a rather dubious reputation which, to a certain extent, perhaps adheres to it still'.[9] Eoin MacNeill noted that 'the study of the prehistoric got a bad name, and deserved it'.[10]

Mahr was ambivalent in his attitude to antiquarians. He lamented the fact that many megalithic monuments in Ireland had been destroyed and 'used as quarries' and had served as 'a happy hunting ground for members of field clubs and other people whom one can call only glorified stamp-collectors'.[11] However, he continued to use those whom he regarded as having 'archaeological leanings'. Trigger observed that antiquarians, did not employ a coherent methodology and 'did little deliberate digging and had no sense of chronology'.[12] This echoes Piggott's view of antiquarians which was that they produced literary collections that included genealogical material, heraldic imagery and folk tales, along with occasional descriptions of artefacts.[13]

The collection's focus of antiquarian pursuits during the nineteenth century and in the early decades of the twentieth century had also resulted in the damaging of archaeological monuments. This particularly affected the collection of 'Celtic' objects, usually associated with the La Tène Period of the Iron Age. Much of this material did not come from stratified contexts and it did not have a provenance. [14]

Brian Fagan described archaeology in nineteenth-century Ireland as being the preserve of the monied upper class, as 'a gentleman's pursuit, and often a country gentleman's calling'.[15] The transfer of power from an Anglo-Irish dilettante amateur elite to Irish Free State professional employees happened during the transition of Irish archaeology from a tool of colonialist endeavour to that of Free State nation-building. This gradual transition was reflected in the main personalities involved, from R.A.S Macalister, who served as Professor of Celtic Archaeology at UCD between the years 1909 to 1943, to S.P. Ó Riordáin who succeeded him, and their widely differing social and religious backgrounds. To many, Macalister was of the old school. Both he, and Harold G. Leask, were dubbed 'ascendancy archaeologists' by the archaeologist H.E. Kilbride Jones.[16] Leask, the founder of the study of Irish medieval architecture, was the author of *Irish Castles and Castellated Houses*, published in 1941. There was a general lack of interest in this type of work as castles were seen as vestiges of colonial power and 'an unwelcome guest at the academic feast in the new Irish state'.[17] Indeed, Macalister had described medieval archaeology in 1928 as 'a sad decline from the achievements of Celtic Ireland'.[18] Not surprisingly, castles were not included in the research programme of the Harvard Mission. Before his appointment to UCD, Macalister, a Presbyterian of Scottish descent and son of Dublin-born Cambridge anatomist Alexander Macalister, had been Director of the Palestine Exploration Fund from 1900 to 1909. During this period he excavated at Tell el-Jazari, the biblical city of Gezer. In the late nineteenth and early twentieth century he was regarded as the most distinguished archaeologist in Ireland. O'Sullivan describes Macalister, in his position as Professor of Celtic Archaeology at UCD, as 'the pioneer whose interpretation of the role set an ambitious standard for those who followed'.[19]

## Adolf Mahr: 'The foremost archaeologist in the country'

After independence, the Irish Free State Government brought in expertise from abroad for leadership in important economic and cultural institutions.

When the position of Keeper of Irish Antiquities became vacant in 1926, Macalister suggested himself for the post in a letter to William T. Cosgrave, President of the Executive Council.[20] The government, however, awarded the position to the German Prehistorian Professor Walter Bremer of Marburg in 1926.[21] Following the premature death of Bremer, the Irish Government advertised the position of Keeper of Irish Antiquities all over Europe in an effort to find a scholar of European reputation. Adolf Mahr, an Austrian archaeologist, applied for the position and his was one of the last of thirteen applications received. He was appointed Keeper of Irish Antiquities on 29 September 1927.

Macalister approved of Mahr's appointment and in 1928 expressed the view that: 'The authorities of the Free State Government showed to the world that they fully realised their responsibility in the matter of the appointment of a successor'.[22] Hencken regarded Mahr as 'the foremost archaeologist in the country'.[23] Mahr had been trained in the subjects of anthropology and ethnology and specialised in prehistory at the University of Vienna. He became an expert in the Iron Age and was awarded a Doctor of Philosophy degree in Prehistoric Archaeology in July 1912. His doctoral thesis was on the La Tène Period in Upper Austria, which was later published as *Die La Tène – Periode in Oberosterreich*.[24] He worked at the Museum of Linz in 1912 for approximately two years, reorganised the prehistoric collections and introduced a new Register of Acquisitions in 1919. At that time he also worked on an inventory of artefacts in the Museum of Hallstatt and wrote a book on this collection, *Die Prahistorischen Sammlungen des Museums zu Hallstatt*, which was published in 1914.[25] Mahr was employed at the Natural History and Prehistoric Museum in Vienna from 1912 and held positions as Assistant Curator, Curator and Deputy Director of the Anthropological-Ethnological Department. In 1918, he took part in excavations in Montenegro and Albania and participated in excavations in Holland during the period 1919 to 1920. In 1926 he excavated the Grunerwerk salt mine at Hallstatt in Austria.

On 17 July 1934, de Valera appointed Mahr to the position of Director of the National Museum of Ireland, despite the fact that he was not an Irish citizen.[26] He was enabled to do so as the nationality clause included in the regulations governing the filling of technical and professional posts had been omitted since February 1934.[27] A permit under the Aliens Order 1935 was received in respect of his employment as Director.[28] It appears that no other candidates were considered for this position despite E. Estyn Evans's claim that there were 'excellent applicants for the post from Britain'.[29]

An Englishman of Welsh parentage, Evans held the position of lecturer in geography at Queen's University, Belfast from 1927. He was of the view that Mahr's appointment was an illustration of 'the strength of the hatred of all things British prevailing in Éire in the years following Partition'.[30] But it was unlikely that applications were received from Britain as it seems that the post of Director of the National Museum was not advertised. Seósamh Ó Néill, Secretary at the Department of Education, suggested that 'in the interests of this important National Institution, that an appointment should be made to the Directorship without delay'.[31]

Adolf Mahr has been described by Irish historians as a possible Nazi spy and was, according to John P. Duggan, 'handily placed' in the National Museum.[32] Mahr became a member of the Nazi party on 1 April 1933, a year before his appointment as Director of the National Museum. It seems that de Valera was aware of Mahr's links with Nazism in the 1930s but it is not known if he had this information prior to making the appointment. Frederick Boland, the Assistant Secretary of the Department of External Affairs, described Mahr in 1939 as 'the most active and fanatical National Socialist in the German colony here'.[33] Mahr had communicated his decision to resign as leader of the Nazi party in Ireland to the government in July 1938.[34] He was not hiding his allegiance to the Nazi party and had corresponded in friendly and open terms with one of the Harvard team, the prehistorian Hallam L. Movius, about his political views.[35] According to Dermot Keogh, Mahr, as Director of the National Museum was in a position 'to observe as an insider Irish politics and society'.[36] But Mahr wasn't simply an observer. As Director of the most important cultural institution in the Irish Free State his position allowed him to influence the direction of Irish archaeology at a very important time culturally, politically and economically. O'Donoghue's view was that it was Mahr's position as a Nazi leader during the 1930s which gave him influence that he would otherwise not have wielded as a 'humble museum director'[37] is incorrect. The 'humble museum director' working under a nationalist government was the custodian of the past of a nation struggling to define itself as non-British, Irish and European within a global Celtic context. The Nazi regime did not consider its archaeologists to be 'humble'. In Germany, the Nazis took over many institutions and generously funded research in prehistoric archaeology. They also controlled archaeological institutions in countries after occupation.[38] Mahr was a founder member, along with Seamus Ó Duillearga and others, of the German Society for Celtic Studies, established in Berlin on 25 January 1937.[39] The society was described in the *Irish Times* as 'non-political and non-sectarian'; its aim was 'to spread the knowledge of Celtic culture and languages in Germany, and to establish cultural and social relations between the Germanic and Celtic peoples'.[40]

The arrival of the Harvard Mission to Ireland was a godsend for Mahr, who was suddenly in the position to excavate a myriad of sites for which he previously would simply not have had the financial resources. He could see an opportunity for gaining knowledge about Irish archaeology and training Irish archaeologists in innovative techniques. There was also the possibility of self-aggrandisement as he could claim the credit for this massive cultural project. Mahr's own eugenic thinking, which was the basis for Nazi ideology, would have made him partial to the anthropological views of Hooton and the Harvard team, explained in more detail in the next chapter.[41] Irish archaeologists including Joseph Raftery, S.P. Ó Ríordáin and Michael V. Duignan were all trained at the National Museum under the tutelage of Adolf Mahr.[42] They were given opportunities such as travelling studentships abroad and received scientific training on the Harvard and Unemployment Scheme sites. Joseph Raftery was appointed Keeper of Irish Antiquities at the National Museum in 1949 and later became Director in 1976.

Ó Ríordáin, a Catholic, had worked as a dockyard apprentice and earned a qualification as a teacher. While teaching in Cork he studied archaeology under Canon Patrick Power at UCC and took other courses in Celtic Studies.[43] Canon Power, 'whose competence was in the field of modern Irish, not archaeology', had lectured on Celtic Archaeology at St. Patrick's College, Maynooth between 1910 and 1931, becoming Professor of Celtic Archaeology at UCC in 1915'.[44] Ó Ríordáin, one of Mahr's protégés, was awarded a National University of Ireland (NUI) travelling studentship in 1931 and subsequently carried out research at universities and museums in Britain, Germany, Switzerland, France and Scandinavia. His study tour was co-ordinated by Adolf Mahr who advised him where to go and provided him with letters of introduction. When Ó Ríordáin returned to Ireland he took up a position at the National Museum of Ireland, where he received further training.[45] In 1936, he was appointed to the position of Professor of Celtic Archaeology at UCC. On Macalister's retirement in 1943 Ó Ríordáin was appointed to the chair of Celtic Archaeology at UCD. According to Kilbride Jones, Ó Ríordáin 'liked to regard himself as the doyen of Irish archaeologists'.[46] He influenced M.J. O'Kelly who was trained on Unemployment Scheme sites and who later went on to be the first curator of the Cork Public Museum in

1944. O'Kelly succeeded Ó Ríordáin as Professor of Celtic Archaeology at University College Cork in 1946.

In 1945 Michael V. Duignan replaced Monsignor John Hynes at UCG.[47] Hynes, 'a popular administrator and minor historian'[48] and the first Catholic to hold the position of Dean of Residence, had been appointed as Professor of Archaeology in 1924. He was described by Joseph Raftery, however, as 'completely untrained in archaeological research and methods'.[49] All of these appointments in the 1930s and 1940s reflect the gradual democratisation and professionalisation of Irish archaeology – its 'coming of age'.[50]

Mahr's own ambition for the National Museum to take the place of universities in the training of future archaeologists seemed to have been temporarily achieved in the decades prior to the Second World War. With the appointment of Mahr as Keeper of Irish Antiquities at the National Museum of Ireland in 1927, a battle began for control of the interpretation of the Irish past between the National Museum of Ireland and Irish universities. This battle for intellectual supremacy was played out between Mahr and his museum allies on the one hand and the university men R.A.S Macalister and Eoin MacNeill on the other. The gradual change in attitude of younger archaeologists towards Macalister was, perhaps, fuelled by political and religious reasons, rather than professional ones. This was reflected, for example, in Macalister's hesitation, when requested to deliver an address to the Royal Irish Academy in 1927. His choice of subject was 'a matter of some difficulty, owing to the catholicity of the Academy's interests'.[51]

When Ó Riordáin was promoted to the Chair of Celtic Archaeology at UCC, Mahr boasted that he had reason 'to be proud that it was a pupil of mine who won this distinction, because it shows that the Museum is not only doing normal museum work but is even fulfilling the functions of a university'.[52] Hencken, perhaps influenced by Mahr whom he described as 'an old friend',[53] dismissed Macalister as 'a nineteenth century antiquary', commenting that:

> Professor Macalister, it should be explained is British in origin rather than Irish and has the dislike of Americans common among the middle-class British combined with an unhealthy interest in American money. As the name of the chair which he holds might suggest, he is not an archaeologist in the modern sense but a 19th century antiquary. His British origin and lack of ability combined with his small stature and

strict Methodism have put him at so grave a disadvantage in Dublin, at least in his own eyes, that he guards his position with the utmost jealousy.[54]

Macalister, as a scholarly and scientific man of his time, was very open to learning new archaeological techniques as they came into vogue and it is only in recent years that Macalister's contribution to Irish archaeology has been fully recognised.[55] Emphasis is often placed on Macalister's lack of expertise. For example, Tarlach Ó Raifeartaigh dismissed Macalister's reading of the ogham inscriptions in Kerry, stating that they 'often owed more to imagination than observation'.[56] Macalister's excavation techniques were described as being 'those of Schliemann rather than of Pitt Rivers'.[57] However, Macalister was a prolific writer and produced over 350 texts, which included notes, articles and books. He was also involved in setting up the Archaeological Exploration Committee at the Royal Irish Academy. The derogatory description by Hencken does not fit with the fact that Macalister was pushing for an anthropological committee in the Royal Irish Academy in 1927 and the establishment of an Archaeological School within the universities.[58] The archaeological work of the Harvard Mission, with its emphasis on extremely rich archaeological sites such as crannógs, which resulted in the retrieval of thousands of artefacts, allowed Mahr to reign supreme and to sideline the universities, who were not invited to participate. It also means that the Harvard Mission project became essentially a collections-driven exercise at that time. The reports produced were empiricist and descriptive while analysis and interpretation of archaeological data was limited. These ideas will be explored in more detail in subsequent chapters.

## Harvard Mission Research Questions

By the time of the arrival of the Harvard Mission, the idea that Ireland was a Celtic country was deeply embedded. In 1920, Éamon de Valera, in an open letter to President Woodrow Wilson of the United States of America, stated 'that the people of Ireland constitute a distinct and separate nation, ethnically, historically and tested by every standard of political science – entitled, therefore, to self-determination'.[59] The question of when the Celts came to Ireland became an important research question for the Harvard Archaeological Expeditions. As Adolf Mahr was their main adviser and archaeological contact in Ireland his views on this matter were paramount.

He did not agree with MacNeill's and Macalister's views that the Celts first came to Ireland in the Iron Age.[60] He was convinced that the Late Bronze Age in Ireland represented 'the conquest, by the Indogermanic world, of a very important stronghold of the pre-Aryans.'[61] The idea of Guidels or Gaels, of Celtic origin, who introduced the Bronze Age in Ireland and Britain was popularised by Sir John Rhys in the nineteenth century with the publication of his book *Celtic Britain*.[62] George Coffey was the first Irish archaeologist to suggest that the Celts came directly from the continent, bypassing Britain.[63] Mahr expressed the views of Rhys in a lecture which he gave to the Royal Archaeological Institute of Great Britain and Ireland in 1929 under the title 'The Archaeological Aspect of the Goidelic Question: a critical survey of the Bronze Age and Early Iron Age of Ireland'. The ideas expressed were not new and had been previously discussed by writers including R.A. Smith, O.G.S. Crawford and Henri Hubert.[64] Mahr referred to Ireland as '*the* Goidelic country', a term which Eoin MacNeill apparently abhorred.[65] In 1919, MacNeill had dismissed the idea of a Celtic invasion during the Bronze Age, stating that 'There is, then, no evidence from archaeology, history, or language, sufficient to establish even a moderate degree of probability for the theory of a Celtic occupation of Ireland or Britain during the Bronze Age.'[66] The 'Celticization' of Ireland remained a research question for many decades to follow despite the fact that Ireland's archaeological record, according to John Waddell, 'offers no clear evidence for the Celtic settlements so often postulated.'[67]

In the 1930s the Harvard Archaeological Expeditions and the corresponding excavations undertaken under the Unemployment Schemes enabled Mahr to test his hypothesis of a Celtic invasion occurring in the Bronze Age. Numerous sites potentially dating to the Bronze Age were scientifically excavated. The main question which needed to be answered, in Mahr's opinion, was whether the megaliths represented new cultural types and religious notions, or whether they represented 'a wave of racial invasion and presumably, conquest'.[68] V. Gordon Childe, in his paper 'Scottish Megalithic Tombs and their Affinities', published in 1933, plays down the colonising aspect of the megalithic phenomenon in favour of cultural diffusion.[69] In the 1930s cultural diffusion was an antidote to the more militaristic explanation of cultural change involving invasions, with a superior race armed with its more sophisticated cultural products conquering an inferior one. In *The Prehistory of Scotland* published in 1935, Childe stresses the aristocratic character of the megaliths.[70] In 1931 Christopher Hawkes had published his ideas about the ABC of the British

Iron Age, which he explained in terms of continental Celtic invaders.[71] Mahr's own view was that the megalith-building was more than a cultural innovation and that 'there was also racial immigration involved'.[72] Mahr's theories on Bronze Age Celts may have had a more practical dimension also. He observed that the La Tène material from Ireland hardly filled more than one or two average-sized museum cases in comparison with the 50 or more that could be filled with Bronze Age finds.[73] Perhaps this pragmatic approach to acquiring large numbers of artefacts for his museum influenced Mahr's choice of sites. Mahr, probably because he believed that the Celts arrived in the Bronze Age and the fact that he knew that there was a 'mystifying scarcity' of Iron Age settlement sites, did not give any Iron Age sites to the Harvard Team to excavate.

Hencken and Movius cautioned in their report on the Bronze Age cemetery cairn at Knockast, Co. Westmeath, that 'an association of racial type with cultural diffusion must be regarded, however, as hypothetical until we have further evidence on which to base such a claim'.[74] The cultural diffusionism of the American anthropologists perhaps reflects the cultural imperialism of America in the 1930s, achieved by peaceful means through philanthrophy, the funding of cultural global projects, global media and the spread of capitalism. Ireland's relationship with America (and in particular Irish-America), was played out on Irish archaeological sites, north and south, during the period 1932 to 1936. This reflects Bruce Trigger's idea that archaeological research is 'shaped to a significant degree by the roles that particular nation states play, economically, politically, and culturally, as interdependent parts of the modern world-system'.[75]

## Museum Display and the Creation of Archaeological Knowledge

Adolf Mahr, in his role at the National Museum, presided over the selection and display of artefacts. This invention of the nation through selective museum display was conditioned by the climate and thought of the day and was in turn influenced by social, political and ideological factors. Museums can be used as 'instruments of state regulation'.[76] For example, many totalitarian governments have sought to control the interpretation of archaeological data.[77] This was the case with Germany and Italy, but democratic nation-states like Ireland were also involved in this process. The notion of studying archaeology as a way of gaining information about human history was accompanied by the development of modern nationalism.[78] Nationalism influences the interpretation of culture and 'sometimes takes pre-existing cultures and turns them into nations, sometimes invents them, and often obliterates pre-existing cultures'.[79]

The commissioning of the Lithberg Report in 1927 was the first step in the direction of the control of interpretation of artefact assemblages.[80] The focus of the Harvard Mission and the Unemployment Scheme archaeologists, under advice from Adolf Mahr, was to recover objects dating to the Early Christian Period and the Bronze Age, the two 'Golden Ages' of Irish History. The focus of the collections was Ireland's important place in the history of Europe. This was to be reflected in the display of European comparative material.

British comparative material was not suggested in the Lithberg Report despite the geographical and cultural proximity of Britain to Ireland. With regard to the subject of political perspective in relation to the Irish past, Macalister commented with insight in 1925:

> The Anglophile looks back to the dim ages of the past [...] and he can describe nothing but hordes of naked savages, living mere animal lives, and expending their whole time and energies in devastating tribal wars: a savagery from which England has raised us. The Anglophobe scans the same horizon and sees the cloud-clapped towers, the gorgeous palaces, the solemn temples, of a cast and imposing civilisation, devoted to letters and learning: a civilisation which England has destroyed.[81]

This provenancing of Irish material culture within a European context set the scene for future interpretations of archaeological sites, artefacts, the writing of archaeology and, therefore, the writing of cultural history. Lithberg also recommended the removal of casts of non-Irish architectural monuments and copies of objects to storage.

The partition of Ireland came with the passing of the Government of Ireland Act (1920). However, the collections of the National Gallery and the National Museum were not divided. Therefore, the National Museum collections represented the past of all of the island of Ireland and not just the Irish Free State. This was cultural aspiration reflecting political aspiration of a united Ireland, the past in essence becoming an aspirational future. The political nation-state, considered incomplete by those aspiring to a United Ireland, was identified with the cultural nation-state which encompassed the whole island. The Museum exhibitions, therefore, no longer reflected the greatness of the British Empire and Ireland's place within it. Instead, the artefacts symbolising the greatness of an ancient independent nation with roots deep within a broad European Celtic culture were displayed. The work of the Harvard Mission contributed on a grand scale to this nationalist project.

The arrangement of artefacts can serve to visually articulate the power, identity and tradition of the ruling elite, and the creation of archaeological knowledge in the process. This is because 'all archaeology is interpretation'.[82] For as long as it is acceptable to view Ireland's past as heroic, independent, creative, prehistoric and Celtic, it is acceptable to have items which visualise these concepts on prominent display. This is based on the premise that culture is political and a conduit for change, often reflecting or even foreshadowing political change. The establishing of a unique, utopian culture associated with a defined territorial space is the essence of nationalism. The interpretative process within the museum reflected the shifting paradigm of historical, political and cultural forces outside it.

Collections, exhibitions and individual displays of artefacts cannot be isolated from the larger cultural contexts of national identity formation. Artefacts can be appropriated as symbols of specific group identities which become fixed through the National Museum's handling of them. In the Western model of national identity, nations were seen as 'culture communities, whose members were united, if not made homogeneous, by common historical memories, myths, symbols and traditions'.[83] The National Museum acted as a mirror of the nation-state with its assumptions of ethnic, linguistic and cultural hegemony, and became a microcosm of the culture community. Trigger explains that the main function of nationalist archaeology is 'to bolster the pride and morale of nations or ethnic groups'.[84] Museums serve as a repository for visual expressions of memory. They act as an aid to remembering an agreed-upon past.[85] The National Museum of Ireland became the powerhouse of nationalist archaeology after 1922, the act of appropriation of the past being a political one. Cultural and political nationalism were interwoven and political ideas were embedded in cultural ideology.[86] As a cultural tentacle of the independent Irish Free State Government, the National Museum was in the privileged position of being able not only to reflect change but to act as an agent or catalyst for it. The Lithberg Report resulted in the National Museum of Ireland being effectively transformed into a strong state-sponsored visual statement about national aspirations and became an important symbol of the independent state.

## American Reconnaissance Trip, 1931

The American academics believed that Ireland played a leading role in the cultural development of Northern and Western Europe. Reasons for choosing the Irish Free State included the 'extremely meagre' knowledge of Stone Age peoples and the 'comparatively ill-known' archaeology of Ireland.[87] The Harvard anthropologist L. Lloyd Warner made the relevant contacts in Ireland to pave the way for the work of the Harvard Mission anthropologists and archaeologists. He directed the work in social anthropology but was also responsible for all three strands in Ireland until the work was complete. In 1931, Hencken and Warner arrived on a reconnaissance trip to determine what sites they would excavate and where they would carry out their anthropological surveys. They also made a second visit. A preliminary survey of the country was carried out to see if the proposed research was practical. They met with Cardinal MacRory, Catholic Primate of all Ireland; Eoin MacNeill and his brother, the Governor-General, James MacNeill (served 1928–32); Professor George O'Brien, Professor of National Economics and Professor of Political Economy at UCD; Séamus Ó Duillearga, then lecturer at University College Dublin and editor of *Béaloideas*, the journal of the Folklore of Ireland Society; and Adolf Mahr. Hooton noted in his manuscript that all of these people approved of his proposed project and some helped with the preliminary survey.[88]

In 1931, Mahr was first approached about the Harvard Archaeological Mission and agreed to meet Hencken on 3 July 1931, where Mahr extended 'a most cordial and enthusiastic welcome' to him'.[89] They spent the day discussing the proposed project and the only difficulty which Mahr foresaw was the attitude of Macalister. Hencken assessed Mahr as 'a thoroughly up-to-date archaeologist in the very best sense, and, except when he lapses into his feud with Macalister, is a man of the broadest vision'. He believed that the antagonism between Mahr and Macalister was because 'each feels that by virtue of his position he is State Archaeologist of Saorstát Éireann'.[90] It would seem that the Irish Free State Government also wanted to sideline Macalister and place the National Museum at the centre of cultural endeavour. It was Mahr and not Macalister who was commissioned by the state to write a book to coincide with the hosting of the thirty-first International Eucharistic Congress, which took place in Dublin in June 1932.[91] However, Hencken was pragmatic enough to remember that the point of view of both Mahr and Macalister had to be respected when dealing with Irish archaeology, as Macalister was Chairman and Mahr Secretary of the Standing Committee of the influential National Monuments Advisory Council (NMAC), established under the National Monuments Act, 1930.

On the morning of 3 July 1931, Macalister came to the National Museum to speak to Hencken. Before their meeting Macalister had a private meeting with Mahr. Mahr later told Hencken that he had tried to persuade Macalister of the benefits of the proposed Harvard Expeditions to Irish archaeology. Afterwards Hencken and Macalister had lunch to discuss the matter. On 7 July 1931 the machiavellian Mahr took advantage of Macalister's absence from Dublin to hold a meeting in his house between the Standing Committee of the NMAC, Hencken and Warner. Sir Philip Hanson, the Chairman of the Board of Works and Harold J. Leask, the Inspector of National Monuments, were present. Hencken concluded that those assembled were 'enthusiastic' about the project. Justice Liam Price suggested that General O'Hara of the Irish Air Force might arrange for some aerial photography. After this meeting Hencken was satisfied that he had all the necessary support of the Irish officials and specially Mahr. Mahr had suggested that the Royal Irish Academy might cooperate with the Harvard expeditions. Macalister was President of the Royal Irish Academy at that time and Hencken was hopeful that he might be persuaded.[92]

Hencken stressed to Macalister at their meeting that Harvard did not have a special interest in forming an Irish archaeological collection and only wanted a representative sample of material. He also emphasised that they would not interfere in sites that Irish archaeologists were planning to dig. As Hencken knew that Macalister had planned to dig both Newgrange and Tara, these would not be included in Harvard's programme. At the end of the lunch Hencken felt that Macalister 'was prepared to help rather than to hinder'. When Mahr was informed about their successful meeting he replied that 'we could then be assured of a license to dig anywhere except at Tara and New Grange in twenty-four hours'.[93]

It was suggested in a Hooton manuscript that the Irish authorities were most anxious that copper mines in the south of Ireland be excavated by the Harvard Mission.[94] These included six early mine shafts for copper working at Derrycarhoon, County Cork and others in Killarney, County Kerry. Grooved hammers dating to the Bronze Age had been found at Killarney. As Irish copper was important on the continent during the Early Bronze Age, these sites, which had never been excavated, might reveal very important information about metal-working. It was Hooton's view that one of the mining sites in the south should be excavated as soon as possible because 'this is an undertaking that Macalister, Mahr, and indeed every other British archaeologist would welcome with enthusiasm'.[95] However, Hencken and his team did not act on Hooton's suggestions.

During the 1931 trip, attempts were made to find a county which would fit the criteria of the social and anthropological requirements of the Harvard Mission while also being suitable from an archaeological point of view. The counties which were of immediate interest to Hencken were counties Clare, Sligo and Antrim. Hencken considered these counties and Co. Meath to have the best and greatest variety of archaeological sites suitable for excavation.[96] Hencken was also very interested in Rathcroghan, in County Roscommon, the seat of Ailill and Maeve, which he believed to have been occupied in the first centuries of the Christian era. Hencken considered Meath an unsuitable county from the point of view of a social and anthropological survey but did not explain the reasons for this view in his report. In any event he considered Tara to be 'a labor far beyond the scope of the expedition at present contemplated, and Meath without Tara would be unsatisfactory'.[97] In his report Hencken noted that Mahr placed particular emphasis on County Sligo being the 'best single archaeological area in the Free State'.[98]

When Hencken and his team arrived in Ireland in 1931 the site selection process would have been very difficult without the assistance of amateur archaeologists. On 3 July 1931, Mahr wired Henry Morris in Sligo of Hencken's impending arrival there the following day. Morris, an Irish scholar and schools inspector, was an amateur archaeologist.[99] He drove Hencken to approximately thirty-five sites over the course of two days, 4–5 July 1931. Hencken described Sligo as 'a veritable Carnac and as yet awaits detailed exploration'.[100] Hencken returned to Ireland on 17 July 1931 and travelled to Limerick. Mahr arranged for him to be met there by a local amateur archaeologist, J.N.A. Wallace, who had contributed a number of papers on Irish silver to the *North Munster Antiquarian Journal*.[101] He was described by Hencken as an 'eminent Limerick archaeologist'.[102] Hencken and Wallace spent two days travelling around Clare and visited a total of twenty-four sites. The attention of the Harvard Mission archaeologists had been drawn to the Bronze Age burial site at Carrownacon, Ballyglass, County Mayo by one of the museum 'correspondents', Sean Langan of University College, Galway, who made arrangements to carry out the work. Movius explained that when the Harvard archaeologists expressed an interest in digging the site, 'Mr. Langan kindly had it located by men sounding in the field with bars'.[103] It was subsequently excavated by the Second Harvard Archaeological Mission. Hencken was shown the site at Lagore, County

Meath by Patrick Ward of Dunshaughlin in 1933. The following year he excavated it under the auspices of the Third Harvard Archaeological Expedition to Ireland.

Adolf Mahr and the Harvard archaeologists were interested in extending the Irish Free State archaeological programme to Northern Ireland. County Antrim was considered to be unsuitable for a social and physical anthropological survey because of its history of colonisation. Antrim was rich archaeologically with plenty of forts, 'dolmens' and lake-dwellings. In Hencken's view its main importance was that there were 'a series of sites which have produced evidences of post-Palaeolithic stone cultures, said to be Asturian and Campignian' providing 'the earliest traces of man in the island'.[104] He believed that these early inhabitants of Ireland 'had made their way into Northern Ireland from the Continent when both Ireland and Great Britain were joined together and to the rest of Europe by land-bridges'.[105] Hencken considered that it would be easy to excavate in the North without prejudicing Harvard's work in the Irish Free State. Also, they would be likely to discover more finds which they could export to the United States. Movius carried out an examination of the lithic sites in Northern Ireland between 18 July and 1 August 1933.[106] This work was facilitated by the Ancient Monuments Advisory Council, whose chairman, William Patrick Carmody, the Dean of Down, extended to them 'every hospitality and facilitated our work in every possible way'.[107] Excavations in Northern Ireland commenced during the Third Harvard Archaeological Expedition in 1934.

Adolf Mahr could see how potentially useful the archaeologist Claude Blake Whelan's knowledge and assistance would be to the Harvard Expedition in Northern Ireland. Blake Whelan was later credited by Hencken as 'the only archaeologist in Ireland who has any real knowledge of the Irish Stone Age'.[108] In 1933, Blake Whelan brought Movius on a guided tour of the lithic sites in Northern Ireland. He was from Belfast and worked for the Electricity Board of Northern Ireland and was a member of the Royal Irish Academy. Hencken noted that it was often hard to discern the places where Stone Age man lived as 'his graves are largely unknown and his presence can only be detected by the well-trained eye in the small pieces of flint and other stones that he shaped into tools'.[109] According to him, local archaeologists who were familiar with such sites were unlikely to guide foreign excavators to them. This was not the case in Ireland as they had 'an excellent and unselfish supporter' in Blake Whelan, who had 'an unrivalled knowledge of the homes of prehistoric hunters of the Irish Stone Age'.[110] Hencken admitted that without Blake Whelan's help their work 'could not have been accomplished'.[111] Mahr made the suggestion that Blake Whelan should be encouraged to carry out an excavation with Hencken and Movius, which should be subsequently published under Blake Whelan's name. This was to be financed by the Harvard Mission.[112] Movius and Blake Whelan dug at Rathlin Island, in 1934.[113] This was a site which had been found by Blake Whelan some years previously but it had not been excavated or published. Blake Whelan was elected a delegate for Northern Ireland to the Prehistoric Society of France in 1932, on the proposal of Dr Marcel Baudouin, the honorary president of the society, with whom Whelan had collaborated on a paper on the diorite axes of Rathlin Island.[114]

The sites which Blake Whelan showed Movius included the Mesolithic raised beach site of Larne; Island Magee with its lower estuarine deposits 'containing probably the oldest cultural horizon in Ireland'; the raised beach at Glenarm; the raised beach at Cushendun, below which 'is an industry possibly allied to Azilian'; Bronze Age middens at Whitepark Bay; the Bann Valley with its Neolithic stone industries; and Lough Neagh.[115] A Mesolithic site at Glenarm, County Antrim, which had been discovered by Blake Whelan, was excavated between 5–25 July 1934 by Movius and his team. Hooton was informed that, except for Larne, this was the first Irish raised beach section ever examined; it provided important chronological information'.[116] Over a ton of flint tools were sent to the Belfast Museum. In Movius's report, published in the *Journal of the Royal Society of Antiquaries of Ireland* in 1937, the author commended Blake Whelan because he had 'noted the stratigraphy and photographed the exposed section'.[117]

The Harvard Mission archaeologists wished to excavate some megalithic tombs, which they believed were introduced to Ireland from Spain, and accordingly they identified some undisturbed tombs they wished to dig. They were interested in excavating Rathcroghan which they believed was built by the Celts who had arrived in Ireland from the continent about the fourth century BC. Hencken expressed an interest in the Moytirra megalithic cemetery as it was the only site in Ireland which had produced Breton bell beakers at that time. These highly decorated pots date from the Late Neolithic period through to the Bronze Age (c.2900–1800 BC) and were found over large areas of central and western Europe. He was also interested in monuments such as the stone tumuli visible on the summits of Keishcorran, Slieve Deane and Ox Mountains, a lake-dwelling near Ballymote, numerous forts, and the monastic settlement on Inismurray.

However, despite its archaeological riches, Sligo was considered to be unsuitable for a social and anthropological survey. The reason for this, as Warner pointed out, was that 'Sligo has always been one of the gateways of Ireland'. Hencken considered that:

> It is unfortunate that this very factor, which helps to render Sligo useless from the point of view of social anthropology, makes it of extreme archaeological significance, especially at the beginning of the Metal Ages, when the dolmens were being built and when Ireland played a leading role in the cultural development of Northern and Western Europe. At only one other time, the early Christian period, has Irish civilization been of comparable importance.[118]

Hencken registered his interest in the Carrowkeel passage-tomb cemetery as it 'closely resembled architecturally 'the best cupola tombs of the Iberian peninsula'. He was also fascinated by the passage tomb complex at Carrowmore in Sligo.[119] Morris showed him the megalithic monument known as Leac Chon Mhic Ruis, 'an immense cairn upon which is a megalithic monument 100 feet long consisting of a courtyard upon which open three double-chambered galleries'. Morris also showed him other similar tombs.[120]

Hencken came to the conclusion that if Clare was decided upon for the full survey – social, physical and archaeological – it would be best to do an archaeological survey based on published materials. Sites could be planned, photographed and some selected for excavation. As he regarded few sites to be suitable for excavation in Clare, other forts, lake-dwellings and tumuli could be excavated around the country in an effort to throw light on Clare in particular and on Ireland in general. As Clare formed part of the old kingdom of Connaught he thought it advisable that other sites selected should be in this area. This would include the dolmens of Sligo and Rathcroghan. Warner subsequently wrote to Hencken and expressed the view that County Clare was better from his point of view. Hencken was not as enthusiastic about excavating sites in Clare as he had been about those in Sligo as the former 'has only a few of much interest to the excavator'. He regarded the numerous dolmens of Clare to 'belong to the family of large cists, the least interesting and instructive type'. He was also disappointed at the number of them that were 'badly wrecked' and were therefore unlikely to conceal undisturbed prehistoric burials. He was convinced that 'although Clare is not the richest archaeological area in Ireland, the Irish field as a whole, which is a largely untouched one, promises amply to repay the work now contemplated'.[121] In 1931, Hencken's attention was drawn to a large Bronze Age mound at Poulawack, and a cliff fort at Cahercommaun, both in County Clare.[122] Both of these sites were to be excavated by the Harvard Mission in 1934.[123]

Hencken expressed a preference for excavating in Sligo because it was less costly than Clare where workmen were paid 4/- a day before the change from the gold standard. This linked a currency's value to that of gold and a country on the gold standard could not increase the amount of money in circulation without also increasing its gold reserves. America abandoned the gold standard in 1933. Hencken came to the conclusion that 'it cannot be said that Clare is a very hopeful area for excavating, though there are a few sites worth trying'.[124] He also noted that 'Much excavation could be done in Sligo for comparatively little money, since workmen could be hired for 3/- or 3/6 a day before the abandonment of the gold standard and probably no question of compensation would arise'.[125] When Hencken and Movius visited the Bronze Age burial site at Ballyglass, County Mayo, to organise the excavations, they found to their dismay that the locals demanded exorbitant wages of a pound a day and landowners expected expensive compensation. They were unwilling to pay wages of this amount as it would set a precedent for future excavations. Mahr travelled to the area on their behalf and managed to renegotiate the terms so that workmen accepted ten shillings a day. He was unable to reduce the level of compensation due to 'superstitious fears'. Compensation of £5 was expected for a small burial compared with a similar amount paid to a farmer for a large crannóg in the Midlands.[126] The excavation only took one day. A cremated burial was discovered and artefacts included a rare type of bronze axe and several flint implements.[127]

Hencken was interested in historic sites, reflecting his multidisciplinary training by Hector Munro Chadwick, the English philologist and historian who founded the 'Archaeology and Anthropology Tripos Section B', at the University of Cambridge. Hencken believed that the numerous forts in County Clare 'probably began with the Celtic invasion of the Iron Age'.[128] He was interested in one called Cahermacnaughten because it was the seat of the O'Davorens. This stone ring fort was inhabited by the O'Davoren family and their law school until the end of the seventeenth century. However, he thought that it was unlikely that many artefacts would be discovered from the stone forts as there was so little soil above the native limestone. Also, the problem of shifting a large amount of stones from the interior of these forts before excavation could begin would be costly. There were some forts suitable for excavation, including the very large Cahermoghan fort with its triple fortification. This was of interest because the Bronze Age 'great Clare gold hoard' had been found nearby at Mooghaun in 1854. Hencken considered that 'the place looks more promising than any other in the county'.[129] Among other historical sites in County Clare which aroused Hencken's curiosity was Magh Adhair, a flat-topped mound surrounded by a fosse, and the inauguration place of the Kings of Thomond; and the monastic site of Inis Cealtra. In 1931, the Harvard Mission archaeologists were of the opinion that the Celts built the crannógs and were interested in tracing evidence for Celtic continuity in the archaeological record. In his report, Hencken wrote that 'both the forts and the crannógs were occupied in Early Christian times, and indeed, some of the oldest monasteries were closely patterned after the former. It was at this time that Ireland produced its celebrated Celtic Art which probably represents one of the highest cultural levels ever attained by the early peoples of western Europe'.[130]

The crannógs selected by Mahr and Hencken for excavation proved to have very rich artefactual assemblages. Approximately two thirds of the work programme of the five Harvard Missions was devoted to carrying out excavations on three crannóg sites – Ballinderry 1 in County Westmeath, Ballinderry 2 in County Offaly and Lagore in County Meath.[131]

## De Valera and the Harvard Mission

County Clare was chosen as a representative county for the detailed anthropological survey. No doubt this decision pleased Éamon de Valera who represented East Clare in the Dáil. Warner wrote to de Valera on 25 July 1932 explaining the nature of the proposed project and promising that it would be financed by the Harvard School of Business Administration:

> The proposed research in County Clare by Harvard University will study the socio-economic life of the people and will excavate and survey several archaeological sites. We will be particularly concerned with the study of market areas, the relation of farm holding to market areas and family life, the interplay of social relations between town and county, and in general the total economic structure and life of the town of Ennis and the county.[132]

Warner believed that they could add to the fund of economic knowledge that they were obtaining in America by a similar research in Ireland, so that the results of the work 'will be of value to the Irish political economist, industrialist, and business man and will not be of mere academic interest'. He stated that 'our whole approach will be entirely objective and we will feel that we have failed if any prejudice or bias comes into our results in any way whatever'.[133] De Valera sent a positive reply to this letter stating that, as he understood it, 'it will be a scientific study of the socio-economic life of the Irish people and a research into the archaeological sites of the ancient Irish and in no way will be political but only interested in obtaining the objective truth through careful collection of the facts'.[134]

Warner had a meeting with de Valera whom he described as 'a very fine man who is intelligent and grasped what I was talking about immediately'. Warner had also to persuade Bishop Fogarty of Killaloe to give him permission to carry out the survey work in Clare. Bishop Fogarty and de Valera were not on good personal terms. Fogarty disapproved of de Valera's politics and had referred to him as a 'Dictator'.[135] The Harvard team was sensitive to the political and cultural conditions in Ireland during their research and were therefore anxious to obtain permission and support from senior political and religious figures. Warner received his letter of introduction from de Valera and the Harvard Mission began its work shortly afterwards. Warner continued to be worried about the political situation in Ireland and wrote to Hooton on 26 July 1932 to express his fears: 'The possibilities of civil war are ever present and it is generally understood that I.R.A. gunmen are quietly organising and importing arms and ammunition from America to start a revolution if de Valera's policies fail, or if de Valera becomes more moderate'.[136]

One of the reasons Clare was chosen by the American anthropologists was because they considered it to be 'in transition' between a modern and traditional society.[137] The 'Harvard University Social and Economic Survey' was led by Conrad Maynadier Arensberg and Solon Toothaker Kimball. Warner had supervised the PhD theses of both men. Arensberg, who was a graduate student in anthropology came to Ireland on a Sheldon Travelling Fellowship. He studied at Trinity College Dublin and at UCD under George O'Brien, Professor of National Economics and Political Economy, and under Professor Eoin McNeill. He also acquired a knowledge of the Irish language.[138] Arensberg made other useful contacts in the academic community in Ireland, including the folklorist Séamus Ó Duillearga. Arensberg and Kimball credited Ó Duillearga with 'paving our way among the country folk'[139] as it was he who had encouraged the locals in North Clare to cooperate and share their knowledge of traditional songs and stories with the Americans. Arensberg and Kimball studied the country people of North Clare and the inhabitants of Ennis, observing the way of life of the small farmer class and the townspeople, their relationships and their traditions. They used innovative ethnographic research methods for examining the way of life of ordinary people using an interdisciplinary approach. The results of this work were published in two books, *The Irish Countryman* and *Family and Community in Ireland*.[140] Hooton expressed the view that 'Ultimately all of this material will contribute to a single unified anthropological history and analyses of this gifted and virile nation'.[141]

# 'IRELAND BELONGS TO THE WORLD': CELTIC ORIGINS, ANTHROPOLOGY AND EUGENICS

We believe that the mysticism, artistry, and other peculiar gifts of the modern Irish can be understood only by fitting their prehistory into their modern civilization, and by establishing the continuity of their ancient culture in their life of today.[1]

– Earnest A. Hooton

## Why should Harvard University concern itself with Ireland?

In 1937, R.A.S. Macalister posed the pertinent question 'Why should Harvard University thus concern itself with Ireland?'[2] The reasons why the Harvard Mission came to Ireland and the political ideology underpinning its archaeological work was dominated by eugenic and racialist concerns.[3] This work fitted easily with Irish nationalist aspirations for a proven scientific Celtic identity. The academic framework which was used for interpretative purposes and the academic backgrounds of the protagonists helps to explain how and why particular results were obtained about the Celtic race. Macalister believed that the answer to his question on the reasons for Harvard concerning itself with a study of the Irish was 'the fact that Ireland belongs to the world'. He wrote that:

> Here, at the remote end of Europe, but little disturbed by the stream of Time which tore the rest of the Continent to pieces over and over again, Ireland went on in her own old way, and kept alive primeval cultures, arts, beliefs, which were elsewhere submerged. Only in Ireland can we get down to the foundations upon which European civilisation is based; and as the whole world is interested in European civilisation, the whole world calls upon Ireland to solve problems that can be solved nowhere else.[4]

Macalister was probably referring in an oblique way to the problematic issues associated with the mixing of races, which were being debated around the world in the 1920s and 1930s. Themes of cultural and racial purity were expressed through the disciplines of archaeology and anthropology and were an essential part of a cultural vision reflecting the 'underlying affinity between anthropology and modernism'.[5]

The Harvard Archaeological Mission was organised and managed by Earnest A. Hooton and was under the direction of an executive committee of the Division of Anthropology of Harvard University. The members of this committee included Hooton, Alfred Marston Tozzer and Roland Burrage Dixon. Tozzer served as Director of the International School of American Archaeology in Mexico from 1914 and was appointed chair of the Department of Anthropology at Harvard in 1921. He also became a faculty member of the Department of Sociology at Harvard in 1930. In 1946, he was appointed John E. Hudson Professor of Archaeology at Harvard.[6] Roland Burrage Dixon formed 'an integral part of the archaeological heritage of the Peabody Museum' at Harvard.[7] He made significant contributions and publications in the fields of archaeology, linguistics, physical anthropology and sociocultural anthropology, eventually becoming a professor of anthropology at Harvard in 1916.[8] He also had an interest in folklore and served as the Secretary-Treasurer of the Harvard Folk-Lore Club (founded 1894).[9] Among Dixon's important books was *The Racial History of Man*, published in New York in 1923.

One of the reasons that Ireland was selected for a co-operative study by social and biological scientists from the Division of Anthropology of

Harvard University was that it was 'politically new but culturally old' and that it was 'the country of origin of more than one-fifth of the population of the United States'. The Harvard team proposed to investigate the social, political, economic and industrial institutions in Ireland and to examine the Irish people. Their physical characteristics would be measured to determine their 'racial affinities'.[10] Excavations would be carried out in an effort to connect prehistoric cultures with early historic and modern Irish civilisation. The relationship of social and material culture to race and environment would be analysed.

## The Harvard Mission and Eugenics

Another reason, cited by Hooton, for choosing Ireland for the Harvard survey was because the Celtic language was 'an archaic Aryan language'.[11] For an emerging European, independent nation-state prior to the Second World War, being identified as a white European Celt (possibly an offshoot of the Aryan race) was economically and culturally advantageous. Cultural imperialism was also associated with biological determinism during this period.

Hooton was a member of the American Eugenics Society (AES) and served as Chairman of the Sub-Committee on Anthropometry. The AES was founded a year after the Second International Conference on Eugenics which was held in New York in 1921. Among the founders were the 'premier racial theorist' Madison Grant, Vice-President of the Immigration Restriction League and author of *The Passing of the Great Race: Or the Racial Basis of European History* published in New York in 1918; and the 'doyen of American archaeology', Henry Fairfield Osborn, who penned the preface to Grant's book. The AES became the 'key advocacy and propaganda wing of the Eugenics movement'.[12] The advisory council of this society included William Welch, the Rockefeller Foundation's medical director.[13] The Rockefeller Foundation funded medical research in Ireland and in Europe in the 1920s and 1930s. It also funded various anthropological surveys, including the work of the Harvard Mission to Ireland. Practical social problems relating to race and immigration influenced the focus of American anthropology in the 1920s and this was reflected in the interest of the National Research Council and the Social Science Research Council in such projects.[14] In the 1930s biological determinism in anthropology was hotly debated in academic circles. This followed the Social Darwinian ideas and eugenic discourse on race prevalent at the end of the nineteenth and beginning of the twentieth century in America and Europe. In the nineteenth century, inferiority based on racial classification was used to justify colonialism, slavery and dispossession. A similar classification through the medium of physical anthropology in the 1920s and 1930s could be used to justify harsh immigration laws in the United States, discrimination and segregation laws.

One of the aims of the American eugenics movement was to 'create an American eugenic presence throughout the world'. To this end a 'network of eugenic investigators' was installed in Belgium, Great Britain, Norway, Sweden, Denmark, Czechoslovakia, Italy, Holland, Poland, Germany and the Irish Free State. Potential immigrants to the United States were 'eugenically inspected'.[15] This ideology drove the Harvard Mission to Ireland. Hooton stated that the purpose of the physical anthropological work conducted in Ireland, which involved measuring and observing the bodily features of thousands of Irish men and women, was 'to determine their racial affinities and their constitutional proclivities'.[16] At that time it was believed that proclivities for drunkenness, criminality, laziness or other socially deviant behaviour could be ascertained through the examination of physical attributes. Equally, more positive attributes of those deemed to be superior races could be ascertained.

Edwin Black claims in his book *War Against the Weak Eugenics and America's Campaign to Create a Master Race*, that the AES supported Germany's eugenic programme.[17] However, Hooton was staunchly anti-Nazi in his writings in the late 1930s.[18] Hooton, it seems, could not see the inherent paradoxes in his own beliefs and wrote of his disapproval of Nazi distortion of anthropological ideas:

> There is a rapidly growing aspect of Physical Anthropology which is nothing less than a malignancy. Unless it is excised, it will destroy the science. I refer to the perversion of racial studies, and of the investigation of human heredity to political uses and to class advantage. Man has long sought to excuse his disregard of others' rights by alleging certain biological differences which determine the superiority of his own race or nationality and the inferiority of others. The allegation of racial superiority or inferiority previously dismissed as a mere sophistry now assumes the nature of a valid reason for wholesale acts of injustice.[19]

Hooton's apparently contradictory views on race and eugenics were commonplace at that time. He was appalled at the 'national sadism and sheer suicidal lunacy as impels the present German government to destroy that minority element which has been responsible for some of its most brilliant cultural achievements'.[20] Christopher Hale described Hooton as 'a fervent eugenicist' and a 'disciple of the Italian criminologist Cesare Lombroso' who had 'disliked blacks and Jews'.[21] Hooton was disciplined by the President of Harvard for his 'inhuman' teachings.[22] However, despite being a eugenicist who advocated better breeding for the human race and the removal of those deemed unfit for human society such as the disabled, the insane, the criminal and the economically unviable, Hooton was not overtly racist in the sense that he believed that the unfit from all races, including the white race, should be removed from society. He proposed the establishing of 'an America national breeding bureau that would determine who could reproduce with whom'.[23] It was no coincidence, however, that in America, those who fitted many eugenic categories also fitted the category of poor immigrants including 'Negroid', Italian, Mexican and poor rural Americans. Indeed Black's definition of the eugenic movement was 'It was a movement against non-Nordics regardless of their skin color, language or national origin'.[24] Germany's eugenic programme was getting a very bad press by the late 1930s in the United States.[25] Prior to that there was much support for Hitler among eugenic societies and in universities. A Nazi eugenics exhibit, organised by the Deutsches Hygiene Museum in Dresden, was shown across American between the years 1934 and 1943. It was sponsored by the American Public Health Association. It was hoped that it would 'make the case that eugenics provided an economically viable and scientifically valid alternative to the social welfare programs initiated by Franklin D. Roosevelt'.[26] Roosevelt's New Deal included unemployment schemes for archaeological research which, in turn, influenced a similar scheme in Ireland. (See Chapter 7)

## The Study of the Celts in Ireland

The quest for the recovery of scientific evidence for the long-headed Celt and ancestor of the European white man was pursued by Hooton through the work of the Harvard Mission. By the time the American academics arrived in Ireland in 1932 to study the Celtic race, using new archaeological science and physical anthropology, academic interest in Celtic origins and identity was well established. While the idea of a Celtic race was fixed in literature, attempts were made initially in the nineteenth century to classify it scientifically. The inhabitants of the Aran Islands were a case in point. They were deemed to be primitive and therefore an uncontaminated race. The traditional belief was that the Aran islanders were descended from the Celts. Samuel Ferguson had written about them in 1852: 'If any portion of the existing population of Ireland can with propriety be termed Celts, they are this race'.[27] William Wilde, the polymath, eye-surgeon, archaeologist and father of Oscar, led the Ethnological Section of the British Association to Aran in 1857.[28] The famous archaeologist, George Petrie, was also interested in the islands and wrote that 'In the Island of Innishmain alone, then, the character of the Aran islander has hitherto wholly escaped contamination, and there it still retains all its delightful pristine purity'.[29] The so-called purity of race and culture of the inhabitants were viewed in nationalistic terms by some writers and was described by Scott Ashley as follows:

> The Aran Islands were being invented as bastions of the ancient sublime, so the islanders themselves were endowed with nationalist and racial significance. They were modern primitives, insulated from the deadening hand of progress and Anglicization, true Irishmen and women, models for an Ireland freed from British dominion. They were a pure Gaelic stock uncorrupted by infusions of degenerate blood from the mainland; they were perhaps, the last true descendants of the Fir-Bolgs, the primeval inhabitants of Ireland.[30]

A.C. Haddon and Dr C.R. Browne, who carried out a scientific survey of the Aran Islanders in 1892, were also influenced by the work of J.T. O'Flaherty who published 'A Sketch of the History and Antiquities of the Southern Islands of Aran, lying off the West Coast of Ireland; with Observations on the Religion of the Celtic Nations, Pagan Monuments of the early Irish, Druidic Rites, & Co' in *Transactions of the Royal Irish Academy* for 1825. O'Flaherty in his paper asserted that 'In no part of the Celtic regions are the Celtic habits, feelings, and language better preserved than in the southern Isles of Aran'.[31] Like other nineteenth-century romantics writers, he believed that Aran was a microcosm of Ireland which in turn was a microcosm of Celtic Europe. He pointed out that Gaul, Spain, Britain and the other Celtic States had lost all their records of remote antiquity but that Ireland had preserved historic evidence 'illustrative not only of her own antiquities, but, in a great measure, of those of Europe'.[32] The Aran Islands survey was carried out by the Anthropometric Committee of the Royal Irish Academy. A study of the ethnography of the Aran Islands was to be the first in the series of such studies to be undertaken around the country by the committee. The emphasis was on the routine observations made in the Anthropometric Laboratory and in researches in country districts.

Eoin MacNeill got his own anthropometric chart completed at the Dublin Anthropometric Laboratory in the Museum of Comparative

Anatomy, Trinity College Dublin.[33] It was dated 11 February 1893 and signed by Professor A.C. Haddon. Haddon, described by H.J. Fleure as 'a pioneer of modern anthropology', and a 'keen and vigorous evolutionist' was a demonstrator in zoology at Cambridge from 1879 until he left his position to take up a Professorship at the Royal College of Science in Dublin in 1880.[34] Haddon co-founded the Anthropometric Laboratory at Trinity College which was modelled on the London Laboratory of Francis Galton, a cousin of Charles Darwin's. Galton set up his laboratory in 1884, a year after he had first coined the term 'eugenics'. The aim of the work conducted at the Dublin Anthropometric Laboratory was to gain an 'understanding [of] the racial characteristics of the Irish people'.[35] Haddon and Browne expressed the opinion that 'the ethnical characteristics of a people are to be found in their arts, habits, language, and beliefs as well as in their physical characters'.[36] However, this survey was not undertaken under the auspices of any specific eugenics society even though the direction of the research had eugenic overtones. There was no eugenics society established in Dublin but one was set up in Belfast in 1911, and eugenic ideas permeated the social sciences of the late nineteenth and early twentieth century in Ireland.[37]

Race could be scientised by categorising it using instruments of measurement common in physical anthropology.[38] There was in turn the scientising of social status by correlating it with race. The methods employed in the examination of the physical characteristics of the Aran natives were based on those employed by John Beddoe, outlined in his influential book, *The Races of Britain*, published in 1885. Beddoe had paid a visit to Inis Mór in 1861. Haddon and Browne also made use of Beddoe's 'Index of Nigrescence' which worked out the degree of prognathism (protrusion of the lower jaw) of each skull. John Messenger described the conflicting results between literary and scientific interpretations of cultural reality in the Aran Islands. One of the reasons for this, he argued, was primitivism, a type of utopianism and nativism which was influenced by nationalism. This led to beliefs about the Aran Islanders which 'run counter to scientific opinion' and included the idea that they were 'direct descendants of Celts;' that the Irish were a 'pure Celtic race' and that 'Celtic civilization developed long before and was superior to Greek and Roman civilizations'.[39] The racial aspect of Celtic identity was expounded by Douglas Hyde in his 1893 speech, 'The Necessity for de-Anglicising Ireland': 'We must strive to cultivate everything that is most racial, most smacking of the soil, most Gaelic, most Irish, because in spite of the little admixture of Saxon blood in the north-east corner, this island is and will ever remain Celtic at the core'.[40] Eoin MacNeill developed this idea, writing in 1921 that: 'In ancient Ireland alone we find the autobiography of a people of European white men who come into history not moulded into the mould of the complex East nor forced to accept the law of imperial Rome'.[41] The previous year, de Valera, during his fundraising tour of the United States, attempted to get political recognition for the Irish Republic by arguing that 'Ireland is now the last white nation that is deprived of its liberty'.[42]

Macalister asserted in 1927 that Ireland and Scandinavia were the most important European countries to the ethnologist and social historian because 'all the rest have been forced into a Roman mould which has distorted or destroyed the native institutions'.[43] When Eoin MacNeill published *Celtic Ireland* in 1921, the author had clearly accepted the premise that Ireland was indeed a Celtic country, explaining that he had 'sought to establish the foundations of our early historical polity on a supposed Celtic colonisation coincident with the Roman conquest of Britain. [44] MacNeill was wary of the misuse of historical sources for political reasons and warned that 'superficial methods of expounding history are perhaps the main cause of modern race-delusions'.[45] As archaeology was interpreted as scientific evidence for historical events, MacNeill was satisfied that Macalister, whom he described as 'the highest Irish archaeological authority', believed that the Celtic colonisation of Britain and Ireland began in the Late Celtic or La Tène Period of the Iron Age.[46] Macalister expressed the view in an address delivered to the RIA in 1927 that 'on the current, and most probable, hypothesis, the Celtic culture was introduced into this country by a body of invaders – or, rather, a succession of invaders – who came at some time during the course of the European Iron Age'.[47]

Archaeology as a discipline is intimately connected with the political and social context in which it is interpreted. The author of the interpretation is invariably influenced by his/her own social background and education. As Christopher Evans explained it, 'the practice of archaeology is never divorced from its times'.[48] Macalister, for example, was of the view that the putative invaders of Ireland abstained from intermarriage with the natives and that: 'The fair-complexioned and the dark-complexioned people are rigorously kept apart: the former are the aristocrats, with the attributes, physical and mental, of nobility, while the latter are the serfs'.[49] Macalister's idea of aristocrats and serfs is an observation based more on social prejudice than scientific fact. Macalister wrote in his book *Ireland in Pre-Celtic Times* (1921) that there was evidence for two stocks in Ireland 'separated from one another by social position running parallel with racial character'.[50] This correlation between race and social position was a common eugenic notion. Greta Jones has described how eugenic societies 'showed a clear bias toward seeing eugenic worth as reflected in superior social status'.[51] In the United States there was also a belief in the eugenic superiority of the North European.[52] Macalister's belief that 'the distinction was maintained by obstacles to intermarriage' may reflect the global debates about miscegenation that were current in the 1920s. He was also of the opinion 'that the ruling classes were an importation, a tribe of conquerers, who had subdued and reduced the original inhabitants to a subordinate position, if not to actual serfdom'.[53] This view reflected the nineteenth-century colonialist attitude of archaeologists to wards human progress. Macalister was aware of the problems associated with the issue of race in physical anthropological surveys, noting that 'Mankind is scientifically divided into races, a term too often misused'.[54] He defined *race* as follows:

> It must be clearly understood that Race depends simply and solely on physical characteristics, and on psychical and temperamental idiosyncrasies: the peculiarities with which a man is born. It has nothing to do with religion, language, political and social connexions or sympathies, or with any other of the peculiarities which a man acquires from his environment as he grows up.[55]

## Macalister and Eugenics

Race was integral to nineteenth-century archaeological scholarship and continued to be important in the twentieth century, particularly in the interwar period. The 1930's Harvard eugenic survey of the Celtic/Irish race side by side with the archaeological study of human remains was an example of this. In his address to the Royal Irish Academy in 1927 Macalister had expressed the view that 'there is the greatest need' for an Anthropological Committee, commenting that 'there are few countries in the world of whose ethnology we know less than we do of Ireland'.[56] He had also observed in his book, *Ireland in Pre-Celtic Times*, that 'the subject of Irish craniology, both ancient and modern, is as yet an almost untilled field'.[57] He was familiar with the physical anthropologist's use of the cephalic index which was used to determine skull type and explained the cephalic index as a figure which 'expresses the breadth of the head as a percentage of the length'.[58] A Swedish professor of anatomy, Anders Retzius, was first to use the cephalic index in physical anthropology in the nineteenth century, to classify ancient human remains found in Europe. He classified brains into three main categories, 'dolichocephalic' which were long and thin, 'brachycephalic' which were short and broad and 'mesocephalic' which were of intermediate length and width. These ideas were later used by the eugenic theorist Georges Vacher de Lapouge who in *L'Aryan et Son Role Social* (1899) divided humans into hierarchical races with the Aryan white dolichocephalic at the top.

It was Macalister's opinion that these physical measurements of Irish skeletons showed that the Bronze Age culture was introduced into Ireland by trade and not by conquest or invasion and that, 'until the process of contamination began after the Anglo-Norman conquest, no brachycephalic race found a footing in the country'.[59] Similar classifications had been used by the American anthropologist William Z. Ripley in *The Races of Europe* in 1899. Ripley's book was rewritten in 1939 by Carleton S. Coon, a student of Hooton's.[60] Coon believed that Caucasians had followed a separate evolutionary path from other humans and that the earliest Homo Sapiens were long-headed white men. Coon attempted to use Darwinian adaptation to explain the physical characteristics of race.[61]

Macalister expressed disappointment that the study of the Irish race was hampered by the limited amount of skeletons available for examination. This was because most of the burials found were cremations. There was also the problem of excavations being carried out 'either by ignorant labourers dreaming of treasure, or by equally ignorant and far more reprehensible collectors, in search of curiosities for their cabinets'.[62] The main collection available for study was a number of crania dug up from a 'charnel mound' near Donnybrook in south Dublin in 1880.[63] Other than this collection Macalister acknowledged that he could 'discover nothing but isolated measurements of individual bones, scattered through books and the proceedings of societies'.[64] Despite this lack of evidence he concluded that the results showed that 'the pre-Norman population of Ireland was dolichocephalic, this belonging either to the Nordic or the Mediterranean Race'.[65] In a supplementary examination of descriptions from the literature, Macalister deducted from a section which he selected specifically for the purpose that 'all persons of importance native to Ireland are described as having golden hair' and that 'there is evidence that the superior classes had light-coloured eyes'.[66] He acknowledged that this assertion was made despite the fact that while measurements of stature and of head-shape can be obtained from skeletons 'the test of coloration cannot be applied except to a living person'.[67] He was very much in favour of this new anthropological approach to Irish archaeology.

## Ireland as a Microcosm of Celtic Europe

The notion of Ireland as a microcosm of Celtic Europe was explored by the Harvard Mission. The Aran Islands Survey itself could be seen as the precursor, in microcosm, of the Harvard Mission project with its three-stranded approach to the study of the Irish Celt. Apart from the difference in scale there was also a difference in political and cultural perspective. Haddon and Browne fused the old colonialist approach of a study of exotic natives on tiny secluded islands with the increasingly nationalistic outlook of the Royal Irish Academy. Previous work such as that by Beddoe reflects a nineteenth century colonialist perspective and the use of anthropology as an instrument of government information to control inferior, subject races. Liam S. Gogan, Assistant Keeper of Irish Antiquities at the National Museum of Ireland, dismissed Beddoe in 1933 as 'that old fool Beddoe who for the satisfaction of Victorian Britain demonstrated that a large section of our population was negroid'.[68] The idea of the Celt in the 1930s was that of a noble, tall, blue-eyed and fair-haired warrior. The Harvard Mission represented an Irish-American rediscovery of the noble Celt of antiquity, which had a European and global resonance. In his privately published memoir Hugh O'Neill Hencken remembered Hooton saying to him 'I think the Department should do something about Ireland and I think the Boston Irish would support it'.[69] Wealthy Irish-Americans contributed to the funding of the project.[70]

## The American Anthropologists and their Theoretical Framework

An understanding of the intellectual background and politics of the Harvard anthropologists is essential to the academic framework and the political context within which the Harvard Mission carried out its work. Hooton is best known for his anthropological work on human evolution, racial differentiation, the description and classification of human populations and criminal behaviour.[71] He believed that 'Physical anthropology is properly the working mate of cultural anthropology' and in turn physical anthropology was 'the hand-maiden of human anatomy'.[72] A biological determinist, Hooton expressed admiration for the work of scholars engaged in scientific racism in the late nineteenth and early twentieth century.[73] He obtained a PhD in Classics at Harvard in 1911 and went to study under Sir Arthur Keith while he was on a Rhodes Scholarship to Oxford. There, he developed his interest in human palaeontology and in particular palaeoanthropic fossils from England and Europe. He also studied classical archaeology, Iron Age and Viking archaeology and was involved in the excavation of Viking boat burials. In 1912 he took a diploma in anthropology under R.R. Marrett, an ethnologist who had established a Department of Social Anthropology at Oxford in 1914.[74] In 1913, Marrett had helped Hooton to get a job as an instructor in anthropology at Harvard. It was noted in *Life* Magazine in 1939 that Marrett was one of the men at Oxford 'who helped to mold Earnest Albert Hooton into what Hooton is today'.[75] Before he embarked on his work in Ireland Hooton had gained extensive professional experience in organising large surveys, training personnel for field work, and the analysis of results obtained.[76] During the 1930s he organised large-scale anthropometric surveys of human beings – students attending Harvard University and attendees at the Chicago and New York World Fairs.[77] His statistical laboratory was located over the Peabody Museum at Harvard. The bone lab, over which he presided, held extensive collections of human skeletons from all over the world. For thirty years between 1920 and 1950 he was eminent in American anthropology and many students of physical anthropology came under his influence. This ultimately changed the composition of the American Association of Physical Anthropologists.[78]

In the 1930s American anthropology came under the influence of British anthropologists who espoused theories of functionalism. This idea was that all structures and institutions of a social group work in a sort of physiological manner and to understand society the functional relationship of its component parts need to be understood.[79] Those most associated with this school were the Cambridge anthropologists, A.R. Radcliffe-Brown who spent six years at Chicago and Bronislaw Malinowski who spent three years at Yale. Lloyd Warner, who was responsible for the social anthropological strand of the Harvard Mission's work in Ireland, came under Radcliffe-Brown's influence and was himself influential at Harvard in the early 1930s.[80] At Cambridge in the 1930s the functionalist school of anthropologists, under Malinowski and Radcliffe-Brown, wished to remove themselves from the discipline of archaeology because that discipline had more in common with history. Malinowski believed that anthropology needed to discard 'the purely antiquarian associations with archaeology and even pre-history'.[81] Radcliffe-Brown was of the opinion that archaeology had a natural affinity with history.[82] Hooton's view was that 'archaeology shares with history the function of interpreting the present through knowledge of the past'.[83]

Warner wanted to design a research framework which allowed the researcher to see 'society as a total system of interdependent, inter-related statuses'.[84] At that time Warner was working as a tutor and instructor in the Anthropology Division of Harvard University where he was an Assistant Professor of Social Anthropology. He had carried out extensive studies in the social anthropology of primitive peoples and directed a survey of the social structure and functioning of a large New England town. He had previously carried out fieldwork among the Aborigines in Australia. He was also collaborating in anthropological research in the industrial field with the Harvard School of Business Administration. His job in Ireland was to participate in the sociological field work and to personally train and supervise the workers.[85]

Warner's ideas reflect Hooton's understanding that: 'The function of the anthropologist is to interpret man in his entirety – not piecemeal'.[86] Warner sought to study communities in the New World rather than in exotic locations. He was instrumental in bringing to American anthropology the ideas of the social scientist, Emile Durkheim.[87] Hooton's difficulty with social anthropology was that 'they wilfully abstract social phenomena and divorce man's activities as a social animal from man himself'. He believed that it was possible 'to predict from the physical type of racial hybrid his occupational, educational, and social status'.[88] This reflected his own view that biology was the main predictor of man's place in the world and not environment or education. This idea is the essence of scientific racism. According to Stocking this 'scientizing trend' in American anthropology during the 1930s was a 'renewal of Morganian tradition'.[89] Lewis Henry Morgan was a lawyer, statesman and ethnologist who earned himself the title 'Father of American Anthropology' for his scientific work on social anthropology, which was heavily influenced by the ideas of Darwin.[90] In 1875 he was responsible for forming the section of anthropology in the American Association for the Advancement of Science.

The physical anthropological expedition was the last strand of the Harvard Mission to start work in Ireland. At first it consisted of only one man, C.W. Dupertuis, who was an advanced student of Physical Anthropology at Harvard. In his lecture to the Experimental Science Association of Dublin University on 26 February 1935 entitled 'Notes and Observations of Recent Anthropometric Investigations', Dupertuis explained that for the first time in history an attempt had been made to make a racial survey of the population of a whole country. In an *Irish Times* article the following day it was reported that Dupertuis believed that the survey 'would go a long way towards clearing up the racial problems of Europe'. The reasons given for the expression of this eugenic ideal were as follows:

Ireland being more or less an isolated country, was probably not so mixed racially as Continental countries, and he [Dupertuis] felt that in certain parts of this country the descendants of more or less pure racial types which came in from across the waters would be found. He hoped to be able, at the end of the survey, to answer such questions as who were the Celts, and what was their racial type or types, and what element in the present day population represented the descendants of the earliest inhabitants of this island and just where they were to be found today.[91]

Dupertuis spent a lot of time in many districts of Ireland and grants were put at his disposal by the Irish Free State Government to help him during the later stages of his work. He already had two years of experience in anthropometry at the Century of Progress International Exposition, 1933–4, in Chicago, where he organised the Harvard Anthropometric Laboratory, which measured and observed visitors to the fair. After the first year of anthropometric work in Ireland Dupertuis returned to America. The following year he came back to Ireland accompanied by his wife, Helen Dawson. She worked as his recorder and collaborator in the Irish survey. She held a National Research Council Fellowship in Anthropology and used this to study Irish women of the West Coast. She collected an anthropometric sample of some 1,800 women for analysis in an effort to establish the characteristics of the Celtic race.[92]

Hooton acknowledged that Seosamh Ó Néill, Secretary of the Department of Education for the Irish Free State was very cooperative with the physical survey of the Harvard Mission. Ó Néill was instrumental in coaxing members of his and other government departments to submit themselves to an anthropometric examination. He was also responsible for administrating the grant of £40 given by the Government for the work towards defraying of expenses incurred during the collection of data.[93] De Valera not only manifested keen interest in the anthropometric survey, but also offered helpful suggestions, and Sir Richard Dawson Bates, the Home Secretary for Northern Ireland, also gave his official sanction to the work there.[94] Dupertuis interviewed Major-General W.R.E. Murphy, the Deputy Commissioner of the Garda Síochána, who agreed to provide letters of introduction to the superintendents of the Civic Guard in various parts of the country. This was approved by the Commissioner of the Garda Síochána, Colonel Éamon Broy. The Gardaí therefore became, 'active co-workers in the gathering of anthropometric material'. The cooperation of the Royal Ulster Constabulary of Northern Ireland was also acquired and their members helped in collecting or facilitating the collection of anthropometric data.

Bishops and parish priests around the country were useful to the survey and 'helped round up subjects' for examination.[95]

## Measuring Celtic Skulls

To ascertain the race to which skulls recovered during archaeological excavations belonged, the Harvard Mission anthropologists employed the discredited nineteenth-century technique of mustard seed measurement. This technique, used to assess cranial capacity, was designed by a physician from Philadelphia, Samuel George Morton (who died in 1851), to find out the average size of human brains. Morton attempted to rank races according to the sizes of their brains. Stephen Jay Gould describes Morton's technique and his abandonment of it in his book *The Mismeasure of Man*:

> He [Morton] filled the cranial cavity with sifted white mustard seed, poured the seed back into a graduated cylinder and read the skulls' volume in cubic inches. Later on, he became dissatisfied with mustard seed because he could not obtain consistent results. The seeds did not pack well, for they were too light and still varied too much in size, despite sieving. Re-measurements of single skulls might differ by more than 5 per cent, or 4 cubic inches. Consequently, he switched to one-eighth-inch-diameter lead shot 'of the size called BB' and achieved consistent results that never varied by more than a single cubic inch for the same skull.[96]

The physical anthropological examinations conducted by the Harvard team on skeletons from archaeological sites showed whether the skeletons had large brow ridges, pronounced prognathism or very long arms. Simian-type stereotyping of the Irish Celt, with negroid features, had been popular in American and British newspapers published in the nineteenth century.[97] Scientific results obtained by the Harvard academics rivalled these imaginative and discriminatory depictions.

Hooton made helpful suggestions with regard to the reconstruction of the skeletons at the Bronze Age cemetery-cairn at Knockast in County Westmeath, excavated by the Harvard archaeologists, and collaborated with them in the preparation of the site report. Aleš Hrdlička also assisted in the examination of the bones.[98] Hrdlička, a physical anthropologist, served on the anthropometric sub-committee of the American Eugenics Society (AES) with Hooton. They were both also on the Committee of the Negro with the leading American eugenicist Charles Davenport. This committee was established in

1926 by the American Association of Physical Anthropology and the National Research Council. Classifications of skulls at Knockast were deemed by the Harvard team to be significant as a large skull contained a brain which 'from point of size is well above the average for modern Europeans'.[99] The skull was described as dolichocephalic and orthognathous and the cranial capacity was established using mustard seed measurement.[100] The archaeologists interpreted some skeletons at Knockast to be of a type which 'one would normally expect on the basis of the present data with respect to Bronze Age man in Ireland' a type which had been identified by Professor Shea of University College Galway. Professor Shea compared this type with that of the 'short-cist people of Scotland'.[101] The Harvard archaeologists believed that they could identify different races of people in the archaeological record based on physical anthropology, which they associated with differentiated cultural activities. For example, the 'small cremating people' identified at Knockast were deemed to represent a different physical type to those contained in the inhumation burials at the site.[102] It was extrapolated from this that they represented an intrusive element at Knockast. The cairn was considered to have affinities with similar Late Bronze Age types in Britain. The conclusion was made that 'the Late Bronze Age in Ireland must be considered intrusive, and Knockast the result of these new elements mingling with indigenous Bronze Age culture'.[103]

The idea that the cremating people were a different race, based largely on their different funerary practices, was contradicted by other evidence from Knockast where cremation and inhumation were for a time at least, contemporary rites. Bones from a cremated burial of a young woman were mixed with the skeleton of a child and some cremated remains were found under the child's skull.[104] These difficulties associated with correlating racial types with particular cultural assemblages or practices were acknowledged by the excavators.[105] But, despite the limitations, much interesting information from an archaeological viewpoint was gleaned from physical anthropology about the lifestyle and health of the inhabitants of the site. For example, one male individual at Knockast had been badly crippled by arthritis and had recovered from a bad ear infection, leading Hooton to muse that 'his recuperative powers must have been extraordinary'. There was also evidence for right-handedness and squatting.[106] Sir Arthur Keith wrote about the skeleton found in the flexed position in the cairn at Knockast that it 'may have Round Barrow (or beaker) blood in him'.[107] The concept of equating a particular race with a specific artefact, pottery type, or monument type was popular in 1930s archaeological discourse.

Most of the human remains found in the Harvard excavations were sent to America for examination by physical anthropologists. A huge survey of skeletal remains was undertaken by the Harvard Mission at Gallen Priory, County Offaly in 1934 and 1935. T.D. Kendrick[108] from the British Museum directed the excavation. He was assisted by Michael V. Duignan[109] of the National Museum and the site was excavated under the Unemployment Schemes. Kendrick had invited the Harvard anthropologists to examine the site as 'such quantities came to light that he felt the anthropological opportunities should not be wasted'.[110] Gallen Priory was included in Harold G. Leask's report on the more important archaeological results obtained from the Unemployment Schemes in 1935.[111] Hooton along with William White Howells[112] undertook the examination of the skeletons. They were both members of the Anthropometry sub-committee of the AES. Howells was Research Associate in Physical Anthropology at the American Museum of Natural History, New York (and later became a director of the AES in 1954). He pioneered cranial measurements in world population studies. In his study of the skeletons at Gallen Priory he observed that 'the series has been described by the ordinary methods of craniometry'.[113] Craniometry was a technique employed by Harvard anthropologists on the Irish sites and was 'the leading numerical science of biological determinism during the nineteenth century'.[114] Howells accepted the limitations of this technique, acknowledging that the examination of morphological features were sometimes subjective, such as the measurement of the 'degree of prognathism'. Two observers may differ in their personal perceptions of a classification, and, in his opinion, it was 'difficult for a single observer to maintain a constant standard when he has no 'standard' outside of his own mind to which to refer'.[115] Hooton remarked that 'if they are somewhat unsatisfactory they are at least better than nothing at all'. He advocated that the standard should be 'the typical development in the adult male cranium of the north of Europe'.[116] Howells, despite using the technique was not convinced of its accuracy and wrote prophetically that 'these conclusions with regard to the prehistoric people have been arrived at on the basis of craniology alone. Therefore, even though archaeology may in the future show them to be wrong, the cranial evidence will have been given its full weight'.[117]

The study of the Gallen skeletons was published in the *Proceedings of the Royal Irish Academy* in 1941.[118] Hooton referred to the work as an 'admirable study'. Howells's work was used as a basis for comparison of the modern Irish population as it was the largest skeletal series of the Irish that had ever been available for examination.[119] Adolf Mahr was satisfied that the Gallen skeletons 'will provide a welcome body of information, from which to draw conclusions also as to the racial characteristics of the population in the period immediately preceding the Early Christian centuries'.[120] Howells observes in his study of the skeletal remains that three quarters of the Gallen skulls can be described as orthognathous, 'as is to be expected among Europeans'.[121]

The comparative material used included Aleš Hrdlička's work on the Irish in the USA, included in a general discussion on the white race, published in the *American Journal of Physical Anthropology* in 1932.[122] Howells also based his work on that of G.M. Morant, who examined crania in England and Scotland and compiled series of cranial types for Neolithic, Bronze and Iron Age peoples.[123] Howells described the Neolithic type as 'homogeneous, purely dolichocephalic, narrow-nosed and short-faced'. However, this changes in the Early Bronze Age 'due to the incursion of a well-defined brachycephalic type'.[124] Howells suggested that 'the true time-sequence be violated' and that the larger collections of Iron Age crania should be compared with those of later times.[125] These larger collections included the Anglo-Saxons and seventeenth-century Londoners. He observed that 'The evidence which the later groups afford has led Hooke and Morant, and Keith also, to conclude that the Iron Age folk, whatever their own origins, form the basis of the modern population without influences from the Anglo-Saxons'.[126] Howells concluded that the Gallen type 'can only be descended directly from the Irish Iron Age'.[127] He ascertained that the skeletons represented an 'homogeneous blend' of dolicocephalic Neolithic and brachycephalic Bronze Age stock.[128] This anthropological blending allowed for a solid continuity without compromising the purity of the stock.

In 1935, C.P. Martin, Chief Demonstrator of Anatomy at Trinity College Dublin, wrote that 'The Iron age passes almost imperceptibly into the early Christian era so far as archaeology is concerned'.[129] C.P. Martin's work was dismissed by Howells because Martin had 'published measurements on all of the known Irish crania of early and recent times, but without reaching any significant conclusions'.[130] Martin himself conceded in his book *Prehistoric Man in Ireland* that his series of skulls was 'small as a basis for compiling reliable statistics'.[131] Howells saw similarities between the Iron Age, Crannóg and Early Christian skulls, arguing that 'the Iron Age and crannóg skulls approach the Gallen type; the Iron Age skulls are very much like the British Iron Age series, or between this and the Gallen type; while the Crannóg skulls are near to the Gallen series, and the Early Christians [ …] are practically identical with it'.[132] While Howells acknowledged that 'archaeology makes it clear that in England the advent of iron was accompanied by invaders' he also accepts Adolf Mahr's theory that 'in point of numbers the Iron Age immigration to Ireland was small and unimportant'.[133] Howells corroborated Mahr's stance, stating that the Gallen skeletons 'gives a cranial type which calls for no Iron Age invasion'.[134] Hooton published a paper entitled 'Stature, head form and pigmentation of adult male Irish' in 1940.[135] In MacNeill's view 'the anthropometric statistics in this paper are deeply interesting and must have great significance. They should form a basis and give a stimulus for a more complete study'. However, MacNeill dismissed remarks made in Hooton's paper which connected the Irish language with physical racial features.[136]

## The Racial Celts: Modernist Fantasy or Scientific Fact?

The Australian prehistorian, V. Gordon Childe, described in Sally Green's biography, as 'the most eminent and influential scholar of European prehistory in the twentieth century',[137] influenced a generation of British and Irish archaeologists, including Macalister.

Childe was influenced by the racial ideology of the times, reflecting the pervasiveness of eugenic ideas and the nineteenth-century ranking of races which was still in vogue in the 1920s and 1930s. In 1926, he published a book *The Aryans*, expressing the view that the Aryans were 'the linguistic ancestors' of the Celts.[138] He commented that the Aryans bequeathed to their linguistic heirs 'if not skull-types and bodily characteristics, at least something of this more subtle and more precious spiritual identity'.[139] This reference to the Celtic language reflected Childe's interest in philology and Indo-European origins.[140] He asserted that 'it was the linguistic heirs of this people who played the leading part in Europe from the dawn of history and in Western Asia during the last millennium before our era'.[141] While he was later to dismiss this tome and exclude it from his 'Retrospect',[142] published towards the end of his life, it is worth noting that he too, came under the influence of prevailing political ideologies. Childe described the physical attributes of the Aryans as follows:

> The physical qualities of that stock did enable them by the bare fact of superior strength to conquer even more advanced peoples and so to impose their language on areas from which their bodily type has almost completely vanished. This is the truth underlying the panegyrics of the Germanists: the Nordics' superiority in physique fitted them to be the vehicles of a superior language.[143]

This physical description could equally be applied to the story of the Celtic invasion of Ireland. In 1935, Macalister described the Iron Age 'invasion' in terms of 'the flashing iron blades of the tall, fair-haired newcomers, who landed one fateful day in or about the fourth century BC'.[144] This white supremacist, Eurocentric worldview allowed for the Irish to be classified as European stock, with the implication of a Nordic dolichocephalic heritage. Andrew P. Fitzpatrick made the point that studies of the Celts creates 'an essentially modernist fantasy'.[145]

Childe described the way 'Aryan speech and cult was carried from the "cradle land" to regions previously un-Aryan'.[146] This culture historical model of archaeological interpretation was initially espoused by the German archaeologist Gustav Kossinna, described by Arnold as 'one of the chief architects of the political exploitation of archaeology under National Socialism'.[147] Like Kossinna, Childe hoped, in his own archaeological work, to discover the cradle of the Indo-Europeans. His original interest was in comparative philology and he had received his degree in Latin, Greek and Philosophy from Sydney University. A Eurocentric worldview was typical of archaeologists of this period and Childe himself tended to be Eurocentric in his work, which may reflect the archaeological tradition to which he was exposed as a student at Oxford.[148]

In Childe's discussion of a 'European cradle-land' for the Aryans he described 'the tall blonde stock, the European race *par excellence*', or tall Nordic dolichocephalic. He noted that 'all advocates of a cradle in Europe who have appealed to anthropological results at all, have conceived of the original Aryans as blondes'.[149] It was his opinion that 'much evidence could be adduced to show that in regions linguistically Indo-European, where blondes are now virtually extinct, such types had existed in antiquity'.[150] He also took the view that if the racial link was accepted as being identical with the linguistic then 'the theory of an Aryan cradle in Europe receives confirmation, since everyone agrees that such blondes were characterised somewhere in the European area'.[151] However, in *The Aryans*, Childe displayed an awareness of the dangerous political implications of these ideas and wrote that 'the word "Ayran" has become the watchword of dangerous factions and especially of the more brutal and blatant forms of anti-Semitism'. He disapproved of the 'extravagancies' of the British-born philosopher and racialist writer Houston Stewart Chamberlain, author of *Aryan Worldview*, published in 1905 and the American eugenicist Lothrop Stoddard, author of *Racial Realities in Europe*, published in 1924.

Childe was an admirer of Gustav Kossinna whom he described as a 'profound student' who had 'a complete mastery of the archaeological data' and agreed with his Scandinavian theory of Aryan origin. Childe and Kossinna shared the same methodology and Childe adopted and adapted Kossinna's recognition of an archaeological culture, famously defining it in his book *The Danube in Prehistory*, published in 1929, as 'certain types of remains – pots, implements, ornaments, burial rites, house forms – constantly recurring together'.[152] In *The Aryans* Childe expressed the view that 'today the Scandinavians preserve the type in a purity nowhere else to be equalled'.[153] The Aryans were described as 'promoters of true progress'.[154] Later, while Childe embraced the concept of archaeological cultures as espoused by Kossinna, he rejected the association of cultures with particular races and the equation of German cultural creativity in the past with ethnic purity.[155] Childe became highly suspicious of the nationalist ideology which underpinned the culture historical model of interpretation. Trigger explains that Childe had 'adopted an implicitly functional view of cultural items, even if he did not yet apply this concept to whole cultures'.[156] American anthropologists regarded Childe as being one of the founding fathers of 'Neo-evolutionism'.[157] Peter Gathercole referred to the 'American anthropological influences on Childe's view of culture, signalized by his three visits to the United States in the 1930s'.[158]

To Irish cultural nationalists of the nineteenth century the western isles of Aran were the utopia where purity of race and culture could be found. To Irish Americans in the 1930s it was rural Ireland which represented this utopian ideal of purity. The 'Hibernian hunt for shadowy Celtic ancestors',[159] driven by nationalist ideology combined with the racialist and eugenic agenda of the American anthropologists of the Harvard Mission continued in the 1930s. The quest now had been given the respectability of science. To borrow a phrase from Emile Durkheim: 'If today the stamp of science is usually sufficient to give them a kind of privileged credit, that is because we have faith in science'.[160]

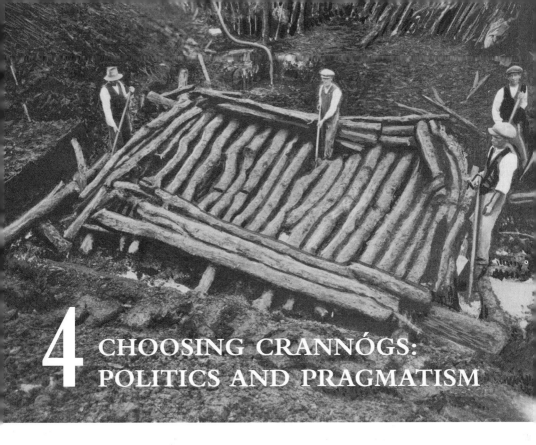

# 4 CHOOSING CRANNÓGS: POLITICS AND PRAGMATISM

If Ireland was invaded by the Celts at the end of the Bronze age, which, as we have already seen, is suggested by a considerable amount of archaeological evidence, did the newcomers drive the round-headed people of the Bronze Age to take refuge in the crannógs?[1]

– Cecil P. Martin, Chief Demonstrator of Anatomy, TCD (1935)

## Celts and Cultural Continuity

Adolf Mahr, described by Hooton as the Harvard Archaeological Expedition's 'chief adviser and sponsor',[2] was instrumental in the identification of sites for excavation. He was very keen that the Harvard archaeologists would focus on the excavations of crannógs. Most of the research work of the Harvard Mission was concentrated on the excavation of three crannóg sites – Lagore in County Meath, Ballinderry 1 in County Westmeath and Ballinderry 2 in

County Offaly. Erin Gibbons suggests that 'the emphasis placed by the Nazis on the continental lake dwellings may partly explain Adolf Mahr's particular interest in the Irish examples'. She notes that Adolf Mahr organised for Seán P. O Ríordáin to visit the excavations directed by Karl Keller-Tarnazzer on Lake Constance, which were 'of key importance to National Socialist theorists'.[3] Keller-Tarnazzer was an academic collaborator of Hans Reinerth, one of the leading archaeologists of Amt Rosenberg, an organisation established by the race theorist Alfred Rosenberg, which prioritised research aimed at scientifically proving the cultural and racial superiority of the Germans. In 1934 Reinerth was appointed by Rosenberg to the position of Reich Deputy of German Prehistory'.[4] Reinerth 'considered all the wetland habitats of Switzerland and central Europe as Germanic settlements built by Northern tribes of Indo-Aryan origin'.[5] Christina Fredegren also suspects that Mahr's Nazi connections 'may have influenced his interpretative framework and rationale for crannóg research' in Ireland'.[6]

The politics of race in Irish archaeology was important even before the arrival of Adolf Mahr to Ireland in 1927. The nineteenth-century antiquarian, W.G. Wood-Martin, was interested in the various races of man that inhabited Ireland in the remote past and was influenced in his studies of the crannógs by the writings of the archaeologist, biologist and politician, Sir John Lubbock, who published *Prehistoric Times* in 1865. In 1886 Wood-Martin published the first synthesis of crannóg research in Ireland entitled *The Lake Dwellings of Ireland or ancient Lacustrine Habitations of Erin, commonly called Crannógs*. He expounded the view that waves of newcomers had reached Ireland in the past and that this period 'was eminently characterized by the sway of brute force'.[7] He believed that the occupants of the crannógs were members of the native population and not newcomers: 'A race inferior in numbers, in arms, or in physical development, would avail themselves of artificial or natural bulwarks to ward off the attacks of dreaded enemies, and water and woods have from the earliest times formed important factors in the art of defence'.[8] Supplanting of natives with newcomers to correlate with cultural progress enabled archaeologists in the nineteenth century 'to play an important role in shaping influential views about the nature of man'.[9] Philosophers of the Enlightenment had viewed progress as desirable, and some, such as the eighteenth-century French economist, A.R.J. Turgot, viewed it as being an inevitable law of nature.[10] This reflects the Darwinian view that cultural change and adaptation to the environment is essential for human survival. The idea of cultural continuity in Irish archaeology paradoxically incorporated the notion of progress. Cultural continuity suggests homogeneity but also cultural stagnancy. Wood-Martin believed that 'to look back to antiquity is one thing; to go back to it is another. If we look back to antiquity it should be as those who are winning a race – to press forward the faster, and to leave the beaten still farther behind'.[11] A lack of cultural change was seen by nationalist archaeologists as a type of sustained cultural purity which was often identified with racial purity. However, a lack of cultural change could also suggest a lack of progress and inadaptability to a changing environment. The 'more Irish than the Irish themselves' motif in Irish history accommodates the idea of invasion with that of cultural continuity. The combination of elements of an invading Celtic culture intermingling with the native or Pre-Celtic culture ensured continuity of an enriched native culture. In terms of the invasion hypothesis in the case of Ireland, the duality between inferior versus superior culture was not borne out by the material evidence. The Iron Age culture was not materially superior to what went before. But the idea of a Celtic invasion persisted. It was a useful construct in which nationalist Ireland could revel.

Wood-Martin reflected his own bias and the times in which he lived, describing 'the Celt clinging to his watery home with as much pertinacity as in latter days he clings to his cottage on terra firma'.[12] His racial interpretations of cultural change were suffused with Darwinian ideas. He observed that 'on the principle of the survival of the fittest, it could only be the robust who lived through the hardships and climatic exposure incidental to a savage life'.[13] Survival of the fittest was also correlated with the survival of culture. Typological studies of artefacts and monuments were also influenced by Darwinian ideas: the more technologically advanced cultural objects and structures were believed to have derived from primitive forms. The idea of diffusion as an explanation for cultural change held that a cultural practice or artefact was invented only once and the idea then spread throughout the world. This idea didn't allow for independent invention even in widely dispersed geographical areas. In his study of the Irish sites, published in 1886, Wood-Martin argued that 'considerable ingenuity' was displayed by the builders of the crannógs and that their similar construction to the Scottish lake dwellings suggested that they were 'erected by the same race'.[14] In 1882, Robert Munro had published *Ancient Scottish Lake-Dwellings* in Edinburgh. Munro was a distinguished Scottish archaeologist whose work on the lake dwellings of Europe, according to Mahr, 'placed him in the front rank of the students of prehistory of the late nineteenth and early twentieth centuries'.[15] (Adolf Mahr himself was appointed the Robert Munro lecturer in anthropology and prehistoric archaeology for 1938–9.) Munro was of the opinion that a study of the distribution of the Scottish lake-dwellings indicated that they were 'peculiar to those districts formerly occupied by Celtic races'.[16] He also believed that they were constructed by 'semi-Romanized Celtic inhabitants', as a means of protecting themselves from the attacks of the Picts, Scots and Angles, after the withdrawal of the Roman legions from Britain.[17]

William Wilde claimed that he was the first to acknowledge crannógs as a monument type in Ireland. He described Dr Ferdinand Keller of Zurich, author of *The Lake-Dwellings of Switzerland and Other Parts of Europe* (London, 1866) as 'my learned friend and correspondent'.[18] Keller, the President of the Society of Antiquaries in Zurich, was 'the unchallenged authority on the subject [of lake dwellings] in Switzerland'.[19] He regarded the nationality of the builders of the lakeside settlements in that country to be significant and believed them to be 'a people whose distinguishing feature within the great Celtic nation had been their taste for living on water'.[20] In Wilde's assessment of crannógs in Ireland found in Counties Leitrim, Longford and Antrim he concluded that 'These vestiges of man's handiwork not only determine with greater precision the track and spread of this branch of the Indo-European family, but really afford us a tolerably good idea of their character and social condition'.[21] However, he acknowledged that he could not ascertain 'whether their makers and original occupiers spoke Sanscrit or Celtic'.[22]

In 1927, Macalister interpreted the crannógs as defensive in character. He believed that the Celts, despite the fact that their numbers were small, had conquered the natives quickly by means of superior weapons and 'reduced the aborigines to vassalage'.[23] He described the 'Celtic baron' who 'found in his estate a lake containing an island, on which he could sleep in peace untroubled by fears of his vassals, he established himself thereupon. When there was no island, he made one'.[24] This inferred that the crannóg type of site could not be invented independently in Ireland but was brought in by the culturally and racially superior Celtic invader. Macalister's view was that the prehistoric Celtic invaders arrived in Ireland during the Iron Age and that none of the crannógs predated that period.[25] The politics of race and the Celtic invasion hypothesis was still important in the 1930s and, therefore, important to crannóg research. Cecil P. Martin, Chief Demonstrator of Anatomy at Trinity College, Dublin, carried out examinations of many prehistoric skulls in Ireland under the auspices of Adolf Mahr and the National Museum. In his book, *Prehistoric Man in Ireland*, published in 1935, he attempted to construct an account of the various races which invaded Ireland. He was aware that there had been attempts to construct racial histories of Ireland, but that these were always founded on the accounts of early Irish historians and annalists and not on archaeological evidence and actual skeletal remains.[26] He deduced from his studies that many of the skulls from the crannógs were round-headed and that in the burials on the mainland, dating from the Iron Age, the round-headed people were conspicuously absent. Martin queried the idea that the Celts (represented by dolicocephalic skulls) invaded Ireland in the Late Bronze Age and drove the native people (represented by brachycephalic skulls) to live in the crannógs.[27]

He pointed out that there was no evidence that the crannóg type of structure gradually evolved from simple to more complex, which might be expected if they had been invented by the round-headed people as places of refuge from invaders.[28] He concurs instead with Macalister's view that they were constructed by the Celtic invader which would explain the 'sudden appearance of these structures as finished and complicated buildings'.[29] Martin explained the existence of the round-headed skulls as the descendants of these invading Celts. He suggested that they probably only consisted of a handful of people who had arrived without their women and went on to 'intermarry with the surrounding people'.[30] He argued that this resulted in the degree of round-headedness of the crannóg peoples being distinctly less than that of the Bronze-Age people; thus confirming Macalister's views.[31]

The civilisation of the 'pre-Celtic bronze-age folk' of the crannógs, Macalister believed, had been crushed by Celtic incomers, 'greedy for the store of gold which the country was understood to possess'.[32] He maintained that the lack of artefacts dating to the Iron Age in comparison with those found dating to the preceding Bronze Age and the succeeding Christian period could be explained by the fact that 'in the first centuries of the Celtic occupation the equilibrium of society must have been unstable'.[33] The term 'Pre-Celtic' used by Macalister to describe the immediate period before the Iron Age suggested a cultural continuity that did not fit with the hypothesis of a Celtic invasion. This apparent contradiction of identifying Ireland as a Celtic nation even before the so-called Celtic invasion simultaneously and paradoxically suggests and negates the idea of cultural continuity. As Macalister explains: 'There may have been occasional settlements of foreigners among them, but not enough to disturb the racial uniformity'.[34] This idea of racial and cultural uniformity and continuity was still in vogue in Ireland in the 1930s and was evident in the work of the Harvard Mission archaeologists.

Waddell wryly describes the idea of successive invasions in Irish archaeology: 'An almost incessant stream of immigrants appears to have tramped ashore from the Mesolithic period to the Iron Age'.[35] This story, perhaps, reflects the traditional history of the coming of the Gaels to Ireland, enunciated in the *Lebor Gabála* (Book of Invasions) compiled originally in the second half of the eleventh century.[36] But these various migrations made no real difference to the racial and cultural purity of the nation, according to nationalist archaeology, because despite successive invasions, the native culture remained dominant. Hencken postulated about Lagore that 'the cultural pattern was so firmly fixed that foreigners were absorbed into it without causing radical change'.[37] The new racial and cultural mix could somehow be blended with the existing one, allowing for a continuity.

## 'The Classical Crannóg Country'

Adolf Mahr wished to prove that the Celts invaded Ireland in the Late Bronze Age and that they brought the idea of the crannóg construction with them. He wrote in a report in 1934 that 'Dr Hencken and myself, like many other antiquarians, have by no means yet given up the hope of finding a crannóg belonging to the Bronze Age, and if that hope materialises, one of the most important problems of Irish archaeology will have been solved'.[38] It was in pursuit of a Bronze Age date that Mahr instigated the excavation of a crannóg at Cloonfinlough, Co. Roscommon under the Unemployment Schemes.[39] Cloonfinlough was located in an area from which the National Museum had recently obtained 'an astonishingly high percentage of very remarkable Bronze Age finds'.[40] Mahr was satisfied that the whole Strokestown district in which Cloonfinlough was situated was 'now teeming with friends and correspondents of the Museum'.[41] Bronze Age antiquities from this site were also held in the British Museum. Other crannóg sites excavated under the Unemployment Schemes included Lough Gur in County Limerick, Ardakillen in County Sligo and Knocknalappa in County Clare. Mahr was satisfied that he had found a crannóg dating to the Late Bronze Age with the excavation of Knocknalappa, described by him as 'the first definite Bronze Age crannóg in these islands which produced excellent bronze objects'.[42] It provided, in his view, evidence that 'crannógs are due to the continental influences which eventually brought also the Late Bronze Age culture to Britain and Ireland'.[43] Knocknalappa antedated the famous Lisnacrogher crannóg, from which artefacts dating to the La Tène Period had been recovered. One of Mahr's predecessors at the Museum, George Coffey, had interpreted the Lisnacrogher material as evidence of the coming of the Celts to Ireland from the continent.[44] This looking to the continent for explanation of cultural change reflects Coffey's own nationalist views rejecting British cultural influence in the past. Another National Museum archaeologist, E.C.R. Armstrong, had argued that 'the Irish crannógs were the strongholds of the Celtic invader'.[45] In a lecture on the topic of the origins of crannógs delivered at the First International Congress of Prehistoric and Protohistoric Sciences which was held in London from 1–6 August 1932, Mahr described Ireland as 'the classical crannóg country'.[46] In his paper, he considered the possibility that 'the lake dwelling type in Europe would actually have to be taken as one single phenomenon'.[47] This suggests his belief in a Celtic Europe with crannógs as an expression of a pan-European culture. The Knocknalappa evidence was considered by Mahr to be one of the 'four major results' of excavations and corresponding Museum work carried out during the 1930s in Ireland.[48]

Hencken interpreted skulls found beneath the crannóg site at Ballinderry 2 (published in 1942) as belonging to the 'Celts' who may have settled the site or who may have been killed by the settlers themselves. Hencken noted that after several centuries 'Early Christian settlers built a crannóg on the same spot'.[49] This idea expresses cultural continuity between race and religion – Celts and Christians. From the physical type of the skulls, Hencken concluded that 'the British Iron Age Celts existed in Central Ireland at the time of this Late Bronze Age settlement'.[50] The only reference used by Hencken to come to this conclusion in his paper was *Races of Europe* by Carleton S. Coon, published in New York in 1939. Hooton had provided Coon, his former student, with some of the early results from the Harvard physical anthropological and archaeological work in Ireland to incorporate into his book. Coon's work was later used by segregationists in the USA.[51] Coon concluded that 'the composite Irishman might well be considered a Nordic in the Iron Age sense, of the Hallstatt variety as represented by living inhabitants of eastern Norway, or even of the Celtic Iron Age variety as represented by abundant skeletal series from England'.[52]

In Hencken's report on Lagore, published in 1950, there is no emphasis on the subject of race. One female skeleton was described as dolichocephalic. There is no mention of the 'Celtic' race nor the Irish race. By the time this report was published racial studies as practised before the Second World War within archaeology were discredited. Hencken instead refers to 'the strange combination of Celtic, Roman, Christian and Germanic elements that characterized the fortress of these Irish kings of the early Middle Ages.'[53] This amounts to a recognition that there was a lack of cultural homogeneity at Lagore and presages Malcolm Chapman's assertion that 'Any individual in the British Isles, wherever he or she lives, and whatever language he or she speaks, is as likely to be descended from a Roman soldier, a German mercenary, or a Viking raider, as from any prototypical Celt.'[54] By the time Hooton, Dupertuis and Dawson published their results in their book *The Physical Anthropology of Ireland* in 1955 the word 'type' was used instead of 'race'.[55] It was explained that physical anthropologists were 'afraid to use the term *race* in any except the most generalized application, lest they be accused of *racial discrimination* or of being *racists*'.[56] They concluded that 'the strongest Irish type in the matter of survival is the long-headed, dark-haired, pure light-eyed Celtic type.'[57]

According to Earnest A. Hooton, the crannógs at Ballinderry 1 and Ballinderry 2 and Lagore were the richest sites investigated by the Harvard Archaeological Expeditions. He was of the opinion that 'this work has initiated a renaissance of Irish archaeological activity, and should lead to a complete reunion of the prehistoric past with the cultures of historical antiquity and the present.'[58] This crannóg research by the American archaeologists in the 1930s could, perhaps, be described as a continuation of 'the golden age of lake settlement research' which Aidan O'Sullivan ascribes to the flurry of research activity on crannógs at the end of the nineteenth century.[59] There were pragmatic as well as political reasons for choosing crannógs for excavation by the Harvard Mission. There was the guarantee of large quantities of artefacts because of the preservative qualities of crannógs. Mahr suggested Lagore for excavation because he believed it would 'yield many finds for comparatively little expenditure.'[60] Also, at that stage it was believed that crannógs were occupied from the Iron Age up to the seventeenth century[61] so they were likely to contain material evidence of cultural continuity over many centuries which was important to the Harvard excavators and to Irish archaeologists. The availability of documentary sources was also an advantage, as Irish archaeologists relied heavily on them for their interpretations of the history of Celtic Ireland within a traditional culture-historical paradigm and to aid in the dating of artefacts not found in stratified conditions. The project was directly controlled by Adolf Mahr which meant that it was essentially a museum project and the recovery of artefacts was prioritised. The archaeological reports produced reflected this and were descriptive rather than analytical. Hencken, in his own academic training and his archaeological work in Ireland, Britain, Europe and America personified the archaeological zeitgeist of the times.

## A Proposed American School of Celtic Studies at Ballinderry

In 1933, during the second Harvard Archaeological Mission, Alfred Marston Tozzer, Chairman of the Department of Anthropology at Harvard, visited the excavations at Ballinderry 2, to examine the possibility of establishing an American School of Celtic Studies in Ireland based at Ballinderry.[62] This decision was, perhaps, influenced by the rich assemblage of artefacts recovered from Ballinderry 1 crannóg in 1932. Ballinderry 1 had been suggested to the Harvard Mission by Mahr 'as a suitable site upon which to begin excavation'.[63] It was initially investigated in May 1928 when the Board of Works was cleaning the drain at Ballinderry bog. A man employed by them, Richard Greene, had found a Viking sword bearing the name of the blade maker, Ulfbehrt and the name of the sword cutler, Hiltipreht. Shortly afterwards Mahr visited the site and obtained the sword for the National Museum. He read a paper to the Royal Irish Academy on 25 June 1928 and observed that 'It is the first time that a Teutonic antiquity of this type has been found in a Celtic settlement'.[64] It was his view that the sword had been made in Upper Germany and that 'Obviously a Celt got the sword after a fight or by peaceful commerce and brought it to their crannóg'.[65] While he recognised the site as a crannóg he interpreted it, probably because of the sword as a 'military outpost'.[66] In his letter to Dr Alexander Scott of the British Museum Laboratory in London, Mahr described the sword as 'remarkable' because of its fine preservation, and the fact that it had the name of the maker inscribed on it and by 'its association with Celtic relics in a crannóg'.[67]

Approximately 650 artefacts were recovered from the Ballinderry 1 crannóg. Hencken was satisfied that 'Outside a classical country, say, Italy or Greece, it is seldom you find such an enormous quantity of material and of such a very high calibre as was found at Ballinderry'.[68] Two of the artefacts were to subsequently become synonymous with the Harvard Archaeological Mission to Ireland at home and abroad. They included a Viking gaming board, considered by Hencken to be a 'product of Celto-Norse art' and a bronze hanging bowl considered by him to be 'with the exception of the gaming board, the finest object found in 1932 in the crannóg'. He compared the lamp with similar versions made by 'Romanized and at least partly Christianized Celts' from Britain.[69] The importance of these items was predetermined by the state framework for Irish archaeology established after independence and the embeddedness of culture-historical concepts in the protective legislation and cultural policy documents. The production of archaeological knowledge was essential to the underpinning of national identity. These carefully selected artefacts symbolised the past golden ages of the independent nation-state. They also symbolised Ireland's cultural and political place in the world. While the Christian identity of the state was given priority, the importance of the gaming board perhaps reflects that a Northern European identity was also desirable in the 1930s and links with the Nordic countries of Scandinavia were sought. Hencken conceded that while a certain amount of Viking influence was evident in the material at Ballinderry 1 it was his view that 'this does not mean that the northern settlers ever lived there' and that 'there is no reason to suppose that the people of the crannóg were anything but Irish'.[70] Ruth Johnston, in her reassessment of the site, writes that 'Ballinderry 1 remains one of the most important excavated Viking Age sites in Ireland' but only allows for 'a slight possibility that the population at the site was a Viking or mixed Hiberno-Scandinavian group connected with Dublin, Limerick or one of the other Viking ports in the Irish Sea area'.[71] At Lagore crannóg Viking finds included a fragment of a silver bracelet, three long combs and a probable comb with a handle and a spear. Hencken commented that 'this insignificant degree of intercourse with Norse Dublin only 20 miles away emphasises the self-contained nature of Lagore as a social unit'.[72] But, equally couldn't this 'self-containment' have kept the inhabitants of Lagore separate from surrounding Christian establishments? This conjures up the idea of incomers becoming 'more Irish than the Irish themselves' and the idea of a cultural continuity which could incorporate diverse cultural traits without its essential character of Irishness being compromised. Eoin MacNeill pointed out that in the tenth century the Norse settlements in Ireland 'became part of the Irish body politic'.[73] Therefore it was not at all surprising to find evidence of Scandinavian culture on sites in Ireland. Hencken found a way of explaining the existence of awkward or non-homogenous cultural traits. Those artefacts, out of synch with the mosaic of material culture conjured up by nationalist archaeology, had to be explained away, incorporated or airbrushed out. This subjective element in interpretation, according to Childe, arises 'in deciding which idiosyncrasies should be ignored in defining a culture'.[74]

Ballinderry 2 Crannóg was excavated by the Harvard Mission in 1933.[75] Hencken regarded it to be very important because, in his opinion, virtually nothing was known of the archaeology of Ireland between the years 300

BC and AD 600.[76] He considered this period to be 'the greatest gap in our knowledge of the material culture of the country', as it was the time during which Ireland was in contact with the Roman Empire and the time during which she became Christian. It was also the era of the heroic sagas.[77] Up to the time of the Harvard work at Ballinderry, only one crannóg of this period, Lisnacrogher, County Antrim had been excavated in Ireland and this had been, in Hencken's view 'very disappointing'. E.C.R. Armstrong concurred with this view, writing in 1923, that 'With the exception of Lisnacroghera, Irish crannóg finds are disappointing, it being difficult to determine the approximate periods when they were inhabited'.[78] Hencken described Ballinderry 2 as 'the first glimpse afforded by science of what Irish life was really like in the days of the Irish Kings and heroes who were about contemporary with Christ, Nero, and the other earlier Roman emperors, and the destruction of Pompeii'.[79] It was discovered in 1845 when the lake had to be partially drained during the building of a railway. There were many objects of varying dates said to have come from Ballinderry 2 in the collections of the National Museum of Ireland. These ranged from a Neolithic antler axe-holder to a harp which Wood-Martin dated to the sixteenth century. However, in his abstract, included in Adolf Mahr's Presidential Address for 1937 to the Prehistoric Society, Hencken wrote that there was 'no trace of La Tène civilisation' at Ballinderry 2.[80] A number of small round wicker huts were found in an earlier stratum beneath the crannóg. It was postulated that these may have been erected as temporary shelters for accommodation for those who were building the bigger house, discovered in the same stratum. In a report to Hooton in 1933 Hencken explained that 'there are frequent references to wicker buildings in the earliest Celtic literature'.[81] However, in this report, he does concede that 'inasmuch as the Celts are clearly identified with the Iron Age elsewhere, this has been difficult to reconcile with the known character of the Irish population from the dawn of history'.[82] In his published report on Ballinderry 2 Hencken attributes a Late Bronze Age date to the wicker huts.[83]

Alfred Marston Tozzer, who visited the site in 1933, became chair of the Department of Anthropology at Harvard in 1921 and earmarked a substantial share of their Rockefeller grant for the work of the Harvard Mission to Ireland.[84] It seems hard to fathom why the curator of Middle American archaeology and ethnology at Harvard, described as 'the greatest all-time teacher of Maya archaeology'[85] would be interested in establishing an American Celtic School in Ireland in the 1930s when it was clearly outside his area of academic expertise. He may have been politically

motivated as Ireland was in a strategic geographical location in relation to
Britain and its topography was of interest to America in the 1930s. Tozzer,
a captain in the Signal Corps, served as director of the Honolulu office of
the Office of Strategic Services (OSS) from 1943 to 1945.[86] The OSS was a
wartime intelligence agency of the United States during the Second World
War and a predecessor of the CIA. Other Harvard academics in Ireland in
the 1930s also worked for military intelligence during the war. Hallam L.
Movius, for example, joined the US Army Air Force in 1942 and worked in
Italy as an intelligence officer.[87] Hencken was a prominent member of the
American Defense Harvard Group which collaborated with the OSS. This
group also prepared manuals on totalitarianism and Nazism and extensive
lists and manuals on art monuments for the American Commission for the
Protection and Salvage of Artistic and Historic Monuments in War Areas.[88]
Conrad Arensberg, from the Harvard Mission's social anthropology strand,
served in the US Army Military Intelligence Division (G-2).[89] Tozzer had
served as Director of the International School of American Archaeology
and Ethnology in Mexico City, a collaborative project involving Harvard,
Columbia, Pennsylvania, and the universities of Mexico, Berlin and Paris
in 1913–14.[90] A 'spy scandal' involving archaeologists working as military
intelligence officers during the First World War in Central America was
uncovered in 1919. 'Cooperation between academia and military agencies
continued during World War II'.[91] As already mentioned in Chapter 2, Adolf
Mahr was suspected of working as a Nazi spy in Ireland during the 1920s
and 1930s. He was head of the *Auslandsorganisation* in Ireland, regarded as
'useful for propaganda and espionage activities'.[92]

Professor F.N. Robinson, then Dean of the Faculty of English and Celtic
at Harvard University, also visited the Balinderry 2 excavations during the
Second Harvard Archaeological Mission in 1933. He spoke to the *Irish Times*
about the proposal to establish an American School of Celtic Studies:

> The Ballinderry investigators might form a nucleus of the school. They
> would help to promote co-operation between the American Universities
> and various institutions of learning here. At the present moment there
> would be difficulty in raising money in America for any project, but the
> opportunities for archaeological investigation in Ireland are greater than
> in most other countries.[93]

Robinson explained that while many American universities had been
affected significantly by the economic depression and their staffs and

salaries had been reduced Harvard 'was fortunate in that its stipends were maintained.'[94]

Other American academics also took an interest in the archaeological work being carried out by Harvard University. Professor Clark H. Slover of the University of Texas came to Dublin in 1933. In an interview with the *Irish Times* he expressed the desirability of establishing an American school of Irish Archaeology.[95] He had received a Guggenheim Fellowship in 1931 for the study of Irish history and literature[96] and was in Ireland to carry out research on the Celtic contribution to English culture. He told the *Irish Times* that the increasing interest of America in the Middle Ages was due 'not so much to mere luxuriating in the past as to an increasing tendency to recognise that it is in mediaeval Europe, rather than in classical Greece and Rome, that you find the vital constituents of modern civilisation.'[97]

As the study of Ireland was an important part of the study of the Middle Ages, American scholars were increasingly interested in Irish antiquities. It was Slover's view that the American School in Ireland should be similar to the American School at Rome and the various American establishments for the study of Oriental archaeology and should be under the protection of one of America's learned societies and the National Museum of Ireland.[98] There was no mention of Irish universities in his proposal. In a letter published in the *Irish Times*, James McGurrin, President-General of the AIHS of New York, also referred to the proposal 'to form an American School of Irish Studies in Dublin under the direction of the National Museum.'[99] In 1934, Adolf Mahr asserted that 'all work of an archaeological character carried on under the authority of the State should be centred in the National Museum.'[100] The archaeologist, Liam S. Gogan, was interviewed by the *Irish Times* about his views on the subject of an American School in Ireland:

> Other people fully realise today that Ireland offers many opportunities for archaeological investigation. The fact that we are archaeologically related to Italy and Egypt is in itself a justification for the establishment of such a school. During the past two years the great majority of foreign visitors to the National Museum have been Americans; much excellent work is being accomplished by the American groups throughout the world, and the Harvard Mission here, under the leadership of Dr. O'Neill Hencken, is an earnest of what yet might be done. A strong feeling of friendliness exists in the archaeological relationships of Ireland and America, and scientific workers in Chicago, Boston, and other American cities, as well

as Harvard, are co-operating with men engaged in the same subjects here.[101]

It was mentioned in this newspaper article that the idea of an American School was not new and that Professor Kingsley Porter, an expert in medieval art studies and a professor of Art at Harvard in the 1920s, had previously discussed the proposal with Gogan.[102] Gogan expressed the hope that Kingsley Porter's widow 'will use her influence in University circles in America to push the work'.[103] It was hoped that the establishment of an American School would not cost the Irish citizen any money and that an initial outlay of £10,000 would be funded by sources in America. This would cover the cost of a building in Dublin, its staffing and a special photographic and reference section.[104] However, this proposal did not materialise and, as discussed in Chapter 1, the Institute for Advanced Studies, modelled on a similar institute at Princeton was established by de Valera in 1940.

In 1935, Adolf Mahr wrote to Kathleen O'Connell, private secretary to de Valera, informing her that 'there was considerable opposition in some American circles against the Harvard people excavating in Ireland' and suggested that 'a few lines of appreciation might be a considerable backing to Dr Hencken in his attempts to link up the Harvard School of Archaeology with the National Museum and its activity over all Ireland'.[105] The desire to set up an American School reflected the growing interest in the archaeology of Old Europe in Harvard in the 1930s. It was also an expression of the rediscovered Celtic self-consciousness in Europe prevalent in academic discourse. At the Celtic Congress in Brittany in 1935, for example, Professor J.E. Daniels of Bangor University in Wales presented a paper in which he spoke about the restoration of the 'consciousness of their Celticism' by an Inter-University union of Wales, Scotland, Ireland and Brittany.[106] He said that the Celts must co-operate to restore the Celtic type of life 'to which Ireland remained faithfully – a life wedded to the soil'.[107] He observed that there was one independent Celtic nation – Ireland, and expressed the view that: 'We, who are fighting the battle of our Celtic civilisation against an imperial power greater than Rome, must now look for inspiration to Ireland'.[108] He lamented the fact that the Celtic peoples 'tended only to have a past' and observed that whatever Celtic consciousness we have is the direct result of political imperialism. He defined a Celt as 'one who always has his back to the wall; wherever acquiescence takes place, Celticism ceases to be, so my definition of Celt is psychological and based on this common need of defence against danger'.[109]

It was hoped that at the end of the Celtic Congress they would 'provide a programme which would knit Celtic nations more closely together for the purposes of national culture'.[110]

Crannóg research was deemed very important in terms of national and European cultural identity. Leone suggests that 'archaeological interpretation must be understood in a social, political and historical context and that archaeologists must pay attention to how societies, or groups within a society, shape the interpretation of the past for their own ends'[111] By the end of the nineteenth century nationalism and racism rendered ethnicity essential to archaeological interpretation.[112] Ethnicity was an important factor in the shaping of the interpretation of crannógs and their material culture in the 1930s, which was driven by Irish nationalism and underpinned by an international eugenic ideology. An emphasis on the history of the Celts, promoted in an official way after independence, meant that culture-historical archaeology was controlled for political purposes and embedded in the state framework for Irish archaeology. The Harvard Mission project, a culture-historical enterprise, attempted to directly connect the prehistoric culture of the Celts to the modern nation-state using archaeology, complemented by physical anthropology.

The work of the social anthropological strand of the Harvard Mission carried out by Arensberg and Kimball explored a population in County Clare which they considered to be in transition between a traditional society and a modern one.[113] Clare was also the county which had the highest number of people examined (1,114) by the Harvard physical anthropologists who measured approximately 12,000 people in thirty-two counties.[114] These results were originally intended to be correlated with the results from the social strand and the archaeological strand. Skulls from excavations deemed to belong to prehistoric 'Celts' or medieval 'Celtic' Christians represented interpretations implicit to the cultural and political understanding of the 1930s. The physical anthropological measuring enterprise was expected to confirm ideas about racial cultural continuity into the modern period. However, the Second World War overtook events and ideas about race, current in the 1930s, were no longer tenable or acceptable in the archaeological reports. Hooton and Dupertuis refer to Hencken's ideas about racial cultural continuity in their book, *The Physical Anthropology of Ireland,* published in 1955:

> Dr. Hencken feels that in such a small country as Ireland there is little chance of cultural isolation, and too great freedom of population

movement throughout the island to promise anything in the way of a correlation of archaeological sites with differences in the physical characteristics of ancient populations – much less with those of modern peoples who have moved about extensively in historical times.[115]

Adolf Mahr, a Celtic archaeologist and Nazi from Austria, was appointed Director of the National Museum by Éamon de Valera in 1934. This image is reproduced with the kind permission of the National Museum of Ireland.

Éamon de Valera, President of the Executive Council, instigated the Unemployment Schemes for Archaeological Research in 1934. AJ8OM6, The Print Collector, Alamy stock photo.

Dr. Hugh O'Neill Hencken, Director of the Harvard Archaeological Mission (centre) with unidentified American Anthropologists, in Ballyglass, Co. Mayo (1933). PM #998-27-40/14628.1.14, Peabody Museum of Archaeology and Ethnology, Harvard University.

Hallam L. Movius, Assistant Director of the Harvard Archaeological Mission. Courtesy of the State Library of South Australia.

## THE DUBLIN ANTHROPOMETRIC LABORATORY.

The Laboratory is in the Museum of Comparative Anatomy, Trinity College, Dublin. The Laboratory is open to the Public from 2 to 4 p.m., on Tuesdays, Thursdays, and Saturdays.

| Date of Measurement. | | | Initials. | Sex. | Birthday. | | | Eye Colour. | Hair Colour. | Page of Register. |
|---|---|---|---|---|---|---|---|---|---|---|
| Day. | Month. | Year. | | | Day. | Month. | Year. | | | |
| 11 | Feb | 1893 | JMcN. | M. | 15 | May | '67 | 1 | B. | 314 |

| HEAD MEASUREMENTS. | | | | | | | STATURE. | | | | | LIMB MEASUREMENTS. | | | |
|---|---|---|---|---|---|---|---|---|---|---|---|---|---|---|---|
| Cranial length. | Cranial breadth. | Cranial height. | Auriculo-alveolar length. | Auriculo-nasal length. | Face length. | Face breadth. | Height standing, less heels of boots. | Height sitting above seat of chair. | Tip of mid-finger to styloid. | Tip of mid-finger from centre of patella. | Styloid to Epicondyle. | Epicondyle to Acromion. | Acromion from ground, less heels of boots. | Span of arms. |
| 198 | 162 | 132 | 101 | 98 | .121 | 149 | 1748 | 922 | 189 | | 252 | 363 | 438 | 1836 |

| Weight in ordinary clothing (in lbs.) | Strength of grasp (in lbs.) | | Greatest speed of blow in feet per second. | Breathing capacity (in Cubic inches). | Colour sense. | Keenness of Eyesight. | | | Is the Sense of Hearing normal? | Highest audible note by whistle (Vibrations per second). | Reaction time, in hundredths of a second. | | Left Thumb. | Right Thumb. |
|---|---|---|---|---|---|---|---|---|---|---|---|---|---|---|
| | Right hand. | Left hand. | | | | Distance in mm. of reading standard numerals. | | | | | To sight. | To sound. | | |
| | | | | | | Right eye. | Left eye. | | | | | | | |
| 158 | 113 | 100 | ✓ | 238 | normal | 17 | 16½ | | yes | 19,000 | 26 | 18 | | |

One page of the Register is assigned to each person, in which his measurements at successive periods are entered in successive lines. A copy of these made at any specified date may be obtained on application by the person measured, or by his or her representative, on receipt of a stamped envelope.
N.B.—In the case of Students, it is very desirable that their measurements should be recorded every six months, so that they may thereby have an accurate means of estimating their physical as well as their mental development.

ACH. Initialled ACH (Prof. Haddon)

Eoin MacNeill's Anthropometric Chart. Reproduced by kind permission of UCD Archives.

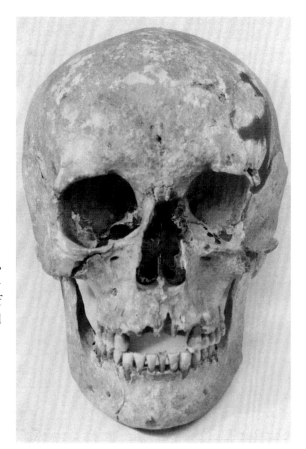

Bronze Age skull from Carrownacon, Ballyglass, Co. Mayo. PM#998-27-40/14628.1.20.1, Peabody Museum of Archaeology and Ethnology, Harvard University.

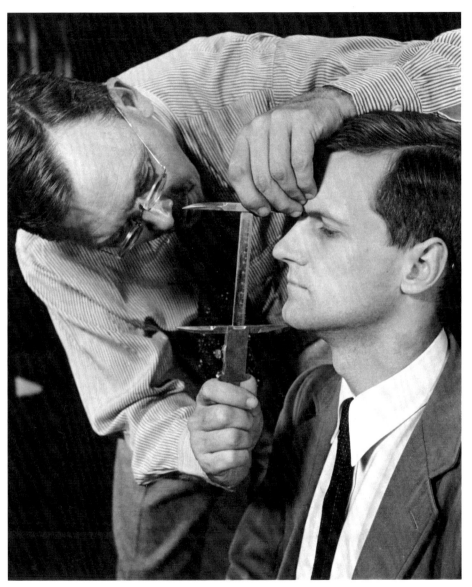

Earnest A. Hooton using a craniometer for measuring. Eric Schaal / Getty Images.

Ballinderry Crannóg No. 1., Co. Westmeath. PM #995-1-40/14629.1.3, Peabody Museum of Archaeology and Ethnology, Harvard University.

Hanging bowl from Ballinderry Crannóg No. 1, Co. Westmeath. This image is reproduced with the kind permission of the National Museum of Ireland.

Viking Gaming Board from Ballinderry Crannóg No. 1, Co. Westmeath. This image is reproduced with the kind permission of the National Museum of Ireland.

Dug-out Boat from Ballinderry No. 2 Crannóg, Co. Offaly. PM#995-1-40/14629.1.8, Peabody Museum of Archaeology and Ethnology, Harvard University.

Lagore Crannóg, Co. Meath. Courtesy of the National Monuments Service Photographic Unit.

# 5 LAGORE CRANNÓG: ARCHAEOLOGY IN THE SERVICE OF THE STATE?

Another element in the Lagore culture, Christianity, comes from the late Roman world, though there was next to no archaeological evidence of it at Lagore. Still it cannot be doubted that the inhabitants were Christian.[1]

– H. O'Neill Hencken

Lagore crannóg was considered by Hencken to be 'one of the classic sites of Irish archaeology as well as the most important of the many hundreds of existing crannógs'.[2]

It serves as a good case study from the Harvard Archaeological Mission to examine, as it demonstrates the influence of politics on the creation of archaeological knowledge. As previously discussed culture-historical archaeology in Ireland during the 1930s was managed by the state. Central to this framework was the Lithberg Report, 1927 and The National Monuments Act, 1930, which influenced the possibilities of the interpretation of the data.

The interpretative framework used compromised the evidence presented by the archaeological record at Lagore as there was an over-reliance on documentary sources for dating purposes and the site was used as a template for the interpretation of other archaeological sites considered to date to the same period. Lagore was included in the Irish Free State Unemployment Scheme for Archaeological Research even though this scheme was initially set up with the intention of investigating prehistoric sites. At that time it was believed that there was no need to excavate Early Christian sites as they were historic and information was already available from historical sources. H.G. Leask argued that 'there are periods, well within historic times – like that of Irish Romanesque architecture (say 1050–1200) and of the Norman invasion (the motte building era) which should not be excluded [from the Unemployment Schemes]'.[3] Leask noted that Mahr was in agreement that 'a site which yielded objects of the Christian period from its upper strata might well prove, on examination, to belong to the Bronze Age or an even earlier period. Such a site would be of the highest archaeological importance and to bar it because, superficially, it belonged to historic times would be indefensible'.[4] Lagore was to open the door to excavations of other historic sites under the Unemployment Schemes, such as the controversial excavation at Castleknock, County Dublin, discussed in Chapter 7.

Lagore was excavated between 1934 and 1936 but was not published until 1951 under the title 'Lagore Crannóg: An Irish Royal Residence of the 7th to 10th Centuries A.D.' in the *Proceedings of the Royal Irish Academy*.[5] The influence of a changing global political landscape on archaeological interpretation can be traced in the unpublished and published reports on Lagore. By the 1950s ideas about one race/ one nation in European archaeology were discredited. There was a retreat to the safety of empiricism and the eschewing of theoretical approaches. Culture-historical archaeology was on the wane and there was more emphasis on the context of the site in terms of the environment and the economy. While the desired fusion in the 1930s of Celtic biological heritage and religious heritage at Lagore was not in evidence, the political potential of ethnic archaeology combined with Early Christian archaeology in crannóg research was important in the underpinning of the identity of the state as Ireland's struggle for independence from Britain was deemed to be as much a religious struggle as an ethnic one.

## Interpreting Christianity in the Archaeological Record

Fowler argues that 'one of the primary symbolic resources controlled by nation-states is religious ideology and its supporting myths'.[6] Lagore was important to the government of the day and de Valera showed his support for the work of the Harvard Mission by visiting it on at least one occasion in October 1934.[7] The quest for a religious interpretation of Lagore began in the nineteenth century when it was first discovered in 1839. Dean R. Butler of Trim, Co. Meath wrote to the Reverend H.R. Dawson (owner of a large antiquities collection sold to the RIA), about the collection of Mr P. Barnewall of Grenanstown, on whose farm Lagore was situated. Butler observed that the things absent from Lagore were as important as those in it: 'There was no vestige of anything connected with Christianity – No Gold – No Celts – No Fibulae – No Coins'.[8] The following year Sir William Wilde wrote a paper about Lagore, explaining that 'there were no crosses, beads or *Christian* sacred ornaments found in the excavations'.[9] In 1848 and 1849 when the river was being cleaned and turf-cutting took place, the site again came to the attention of antiquarians. W.F. Wakeman visited it at the time but did not write about it until 1882, when he described it as 'our first crannóg noticed in modern times'.[10] He believed it to be 'a chief stronghold of the O'Melaghlins princes of Meath' and the antiquities to be of interest to those 'who would compare the habits and *ménage* of some crannóg dwellers with those of our Aryan forebears'.[11] He described the objects recovered, including artefacts of bronze, glass, iron, wood, clay and bone but did not describe the antiquities to be part of a Christian assemblage or the inhabitants of the site to be Christian.[12] In 1932, Adolf Mahr made a general comment about the crannóg type site as being: 'like the rath, essentially the inhabitation [sic] site of early Christian Ireland and of the country outside the later English Pale'.[13]

Religion was an important signifier of identity in the Irish Free State and archaeology was important in the provision of scientific evidence to legitimise that identity. In 1935, Hencken wrote that he considered Lagore to be 'the most important site in the country for the Early Christian period'.[14] Like Butler, Wilde and Wakeman before him, Hencken did not recover any 'sacred ornaments' at Lagore during his extensive excavations of the site in the 1930s. Despite this he contradicts his own archaeological evidence by claiming in his published report that 'it cannot be doubted that the inhabitants were Christian'.[15] This was stated as a fact, despite Hencken's own acknowledgement on the introduction of Christianity to Lagore, in his paper, that 'there was next to no archaeological evidence of it'.[16] This demonstrates that the desired national story was implied in the archaeological nomenclature employed at that time. It also reflected, in a broader sense, the influence and power of the Catholic Church in areas such as government, social life, education and medicine. When a classificatory period is given a religious name, such as the 'Early Christian Period', the implication is that the users or makers of the objects assigned to this classification were of a particular religious persuasion. While it may apply to an individual dating framework, objects are ascribed a reverence which they do not deserve. This kind of taxonomy results in the skewed perception and interpretation of the archaeological data. The problem with nomenclature is that it can concretise an idea so that it becomes an unassailable fact. Naming an artefact within a category imprisons it in a predetermined concept of reality, giving it meaning and context simultaneously. Hencken expresses his awareness of this problem in his paper. In a discussion on the dating of combs found at Lagore he admitted that 'combs and pins of Early Christian type do not imply any form of religion.'[17] The only object recovered which may have exhibited overt Christian symbolism was a ring made of a plain and thin band of bronze with a roughly incised cross on the bezel, which came from an unstratified position in the crannóg. Hencken's opinion was that 'This may be the Christian symbol, but in the case of so simple a representation it is hard to be sure.'[18]

Aidan O'Sullivan notes in his book, *The Archaeology of Lake Settlement in Ireland* that 'crannógs often produce high-quality ecclesiastical and monastic metalwork associated with the early church's liturgical rituals.'[19] However, despite the great preservative properties of Lagore there were no ecclesiastical objects recovered. Instead a whole secular assemblage survived to be interpreted as the material culture of Christians. In his section on the history of Lagore, included in Hencken's report, Liam Price does not explicitly state that the inhabitants were Christian nor that the kings of Lagore were Christian. He noted that the name MacGiollaseachloinn was that of the kings of Deisert Brega, who ruled Lagore. This was significant because, according to Price, 'it suggests a connection with Domnach Seachnaill, which was the name of the very ancient church foundation now called Dunshaughlin.'[20] The site of the monastery of Saint Sechnaill, dating to the fifth century, was situated at Dunshaughlin, one mile from Lagore. In 1936, a lintel with a pre-Romanesque sculpture of the crucifixion was found at the church site. That same year Hencken wrote that it 'might be as old as the latest occupation of the crannóg.'[21]

The treatment of the human remains at Lagore was problematic in terms of the interpretation of the site as a Christian settlement. There was no archaeological evidence from Lagore for the Christian burial rite of extended inhumation.[22] Instead, at the construction stage of the crannóg, a scattering of human bones, including fourteen occiputs were found. The people had been killed by having the backs of their heads partly cut off with a sword or axe. These included men, women and children. The skulls had been removed from the site and the dismembered remains had then been strewn around. As the bones were all found at the same location on the crannóg it would seem that the killings were as a result of a single event. This was interpreted by Hencken as probably a massacre of the workers at the site.[23] Hencken includes a drawing of a fragment of a skull in his published paper on Lagore 'cut with marks that suggest the light Early Christian sword'.[24]

At Ballinderry Crannógs 1 and 2 and at the stone fort at Cahercommaun, all excavated by the Harvard Archaeological Mission, human skulls were found buried in a context interpreted by Hencken as foundation burials.[25] The upper parts of three human skulls, which had been mutilated with a knife, were found under the layers of branches of the construction phase of Ballinderry 2. As no other body parts were found, Hencken initially deduced that they were 'the only surviving evidence of some pagan ceremonial intended to render the spot a fit place on which to dwell'.[26] Later, he reported that the position of the skulls in the stratigraphy at Ballinderry 2 and their condition suggested that they may have been a 'foundation sacrifice' or a 'ritual deposit'.[27] At Cahercommaun, excavated by the Harvard Mission in 1934, 'a ceremonial skull burial' with a ninth-century gold and silver brooch decorated with six silver animals and some amber studs were discovered in a souterrain.[28] Hencken was of the opinion that 'the skull was intentionally buried' and that 'the iron hook suggests that it may previously have been displayed'.[29] In her reassessment of the site Claire Cotter postulated that internment probably took place after the souterrain had been abandoned and that 'There are no known parallels for Hencken's 'foundation burial' theory'.[30] This type of funereal activity does not denote the actions of Christian inhabitants. Curiously, Hencken compared it to the practice of burying the skulls of horses and other animals beneath the hearth-stone of a new house or under the floor of a dance hall 'to give a good sound'.[31] In Hencken's abstract on Cahercommaun, included in Mahr's 1937 paper, the former observed that there were human remains scattered evenly around the site. Some had been chopped but none had been split for marrow. This led him to conclude that 'proof of cannibalism is lacking, and it is hard to interpret the presence of broken human bones lying mixed with kitchen debris'[32] clearly a non-Christian way of dealing with human remains.

The possibility that the inhabitants of Cahercommaun or Lagore were not Christian even though the sites dated to the Early Christian Period was not entertained at that time. 'Idiosyncratic' burial practices found on sites were not used to challenge the traditional narrative about Christian conversion then as the historical evidence was deemed to be superior than that afforded by material culture.[33] Hencken wrote about Cahercommaun in 1934 that 'It was inhabited by a community, no doubt of Christian Irish Celts'.[34] He inferred this social identity from the material culture at Cahercommaun which contained over 1,000 artefacts. The main dateable assemblage ranged between the fifth and ninth centuries AD. This preconceived idea of the religious habits of the inhabitants is reinforced in Hencken's published report on the site in 1938, in which he refers to the 'Christian population'[35] which lived there, despite the fact that no ecclesiastical objects were found and there was no evidence for Christian burial.

The terms 'Early Christian' and 'Celtic' were established concepts by the 1930s. Even Harvard archaeologists with their advanced scientific techniques could not penetrate the thickness of the walls of a well-established Irish antiquarian tradition. Nor could they work outside the confines of the culture-historical approach in vogue in academia at that time. The mixture of the terms *Christian*, *Irish* and *Celt* by Hencken in 1934, as if these terms were interchangeable, reflects his use of the terms as loose identity labels. His description likely reflects the deep-seated belief among Irish archaeologists and those of Irish-American extraction that the identity of the Irish was Celtic and Christian (perceived as Catholic following independence). Hencken asserted in the published report on Cahercommaun that 'The culture is purely Irish'.[36] An iron bell which was found unstratified at the site was described as being 'like St. Patrick's Bell and several other Irish ecclesiastical bells in the National Museum of Ireland'. He had earlier described it as being 'like those associated with the earliest Celtic saints'.[37] As archaeology as a discipline had obvious limitations when it came to the interpretation of non-tangible aspects of life such as religious practice in the past, historical documents were depended on to substitute for material evidence. The tendency was to fit the archaeological evidence to the already existing historical narrative and to use the archaeological material as both scientific evidence and a visual expression of the established origin-myths of the nation.

## Historic High Kings: the Archaeological Evidence

About one third of the site of Lagore was excavated in 1934. It was not completed that year because it had been late in the season when it commenced and because of the size of the project. The work on the crannóg continued between 4–19 July 1935. Hencken considered Lagore to be very important because of the richness of the material remains and the fact that it was 'the only excavatable one which can be definitely associated with a ruling dynasty and also dated (A.D. 768-980) by reference to the early Irish annals'.[38] With regard to interpretation and dating of Lagore, Hencken commented that 'a considerable part of the site had been dug over, but the final excavation produced some stratified areas as well as a large body of finds for which dates may be suggested from historical sources'.[39] Hencken found the documentary material in the National Museum useful and endeavoured to provenance all material that came from Lagore. To this end he consulted the two volumes by Sir William Wilde entitled *A Descriptive Catalogue of the Antiquities in the Museum of the Royal Irish Academy*, published in 1857; two manuscript copies of W.F. Wakeman's *Catalogue of the Collection of Dr. George Petrie*; two volumes of W.F. Wakeman's *Catalogue of the Collection of the Royal Irish Academy*, published in 1894; and W.G. Wood-Martin's *The Lake Dwellings of Ireland*, published in 1886. However, he excluded this as a reliable source because Wood-Martin included items which did not definitely come from Lagore. Hencken acknowledged that despite the help of documentary sources in the dating of the crannóg, 'to the question, when was the first artificial island made in the lake, history gives no answer'.[40]

As far as Hencken was concerned the first occupation layer of the crannóg at Lagore represented 'the fortress of the high king'.[41] This layer contained objects datable to the seventh century and later. Subsequent strata did not give satisfactory evidence of date which led Hencken inevitably to the documentary sources. The historical date for first use of the crannóg was AD 651, influencing Hencken's deduction that 'the crannóg was built not very long before 651, perhaps by the high-king Diarmait Ruanaid himself'.[42] The basis for Hencken's Lagore dates was information gleaned from references in the *Annals of Loch Gabor* which identified it as the residence of the Kings of Southern Brega. He had written excitedly to Hooton in 1935 that 'Most important of all this year's discoveries, however, is the finding of the "palace" itself'.[43] The 'palace' consisted of a series of overlapping wooden structures with floors and hearths at several levels. C.J. Lynn describes how 'the excavators of Lagore were over-optimistic in their expectations of the quality of buildings on the crannóg, perhaps being misled by the "royal" history of the site and the wealth of artefacts recovered, as a result of which some important aspects of the structural history of the crannóg may have been misinterpreted'.[44] The expectation of the existence of a palace resulted in an imaginative interpretation of brushwood as palatial. This reflects what Stephen

Jay Gould refers to as 'the social embeddedness of science' which results in 'the frequent grafting of expectation upon supposed objectivity'.[45] During the excavations, the idea that Lagore was a royal site led Hencken to describe the huge quantities of animal bones recovered as 'the remains of centuries of regal feasts'.[46] Wild geese and ducks accounted for more than 60 per cent of the bird bones and were interpreted as 'delicacies for the royal table'[47] Hencken was promoting Lagore as a royal site without the corroborating material evidence. Archaeologists at the OPW also accepted the royal status of Lagore. In a report written in 1938 the site was considered to present 'a remarkable picture of the activities of an Irish kinglet's establishment in the 8th -10th centuries'.[48] By the time of the publication of his report in 1951, Hencken had thought better of his discovery of the 'palace' at Lagore and noted that dwellings of some kind must have existed on the crannóg but that no structures could be traced apart from two very large posts in the central area which must have belonged to 'something substantial'.[49] However, the idea that crannógs such as Lagore 'could certainly be interpreted as the island residence of kings or nobles' is still current.[50]

Rich archaeological assemblages recovered from other crannóg sites excavated by the Harvard Mission were also correlated with royal status. Conor Newman, in his reassessment of Ballinderry no. 2, remarked that the large zoomorphic brooch found at the site would normally be regarded as 'a mark of royalty'. He also infers from the artefactual assemblage recovered that 'The sociological profile implicit in this evidence is further emphasised by the remaining three, or possible four, penannular brooches and the E ware, which was surely a preserve of the upper echelons of early medieval Irish society'.[51] Ruth Johnston also argues that 'the excavated finds indicate that Ballinderry 1 was a high-status site in the tenth and eleventh centuries'.[52] Warner warns that 'the evidence of wealth is not a sufficient indicator of kingship', even though it does not contradict such a status.[53] He argues that the weapons found at Lagore were 'consistent with the requirement for the king to have armed persons around him'. However, Warner finds it difficult to accept 'the notion of the social and functional necessities of kingship, as we have them described in detail by contemporary writers, taking place in the small wattle huts identified by the excavator', and that 'the case for a forty-metre house at Lagore remains unproved'.[54]

The Annals recorded that Lagore was burnt in AD 850 and destroyed again in AD 934 by Olaf, the Norse king of Dublin. The archaeological material, according to Hencken, suggested that the site was abandoned at the end of the tenth century or the beginning of the eleventh. The historical record ended in AD 969. Much later medieval material was found on the surface of the crannóg but was disregarded for dating purposes because they could not be connected with 'the regular occupation of the crannóg'.[55] Hencken wryly commented that 'the excavator of Early Christian Ireland learns to discount anachronisms'.[56] Discounting anachronisms was a useful tool when faced with the interpretation of a site such as Lagore which was fraught with difficulty as many of the layers were mixed up, the site had been dug previously, and the excavator was also dealing with many 'Old Finds', most of which had come from the Petrie collection. The amount of stratified information available was, therefore, limited. Also many types of artefacts, such as beads, changed little in form over long periods of time.[57] The stratified occupation deposits of Lagore consisted of 'isolated patches' which had escaped disturbance at the hands of previous explorers of the site. Hencken mentioned in his report the difficulties with regard to the correlation of strata in the different parts of the site in the absence of signifiers such as pottery. Another 'anachronism' described by H.G. Leask as 'most remarkable' was the well preserved large male figure of wood recovered from Lagore.[58] Hencken noted in his published paper that this figure, which came from a disturbed layer in the crannóg, 'showed no means of attachment to anything, and its purpose is unknown'.[59] It is possible that this wooden figure was some sort of prehistoric religious or magical icon. It was subsequently radiocarbon dated to the Early Bronze Age.[60] During his excavation of the site in 1934 Hencken found evidence for an earlier structure underneath part of the crannóg which he concluded was older than AD 500.[61]

## Problems with Dating

Surprisingly, despite the many difficulties encountered with the Lagore material outlined above, Hencken used it in part to date Cahercommaun Fort and Ballinderry Crannóg No. 2.[62] Cahercommaun was very important because Hencken was satisfied that 'no such stone fort had ever before been excavated'.[63] In his paper, 'Concerning Chronology', Joseph Raftery explored the problems inherent in the interpretation of chronology at Lagore and the subsequent use of this chronology to date other sites such as Ballinderry 2 and Cahercommaun.[64] He pointed to the 'conditions of uncertainty, doubt and even contradiction' concerning chronology, evident in the Hencken report. He lamented the fact that 'It should here be noted that in all the cases mentioned by Hencken opinions only are given; never once has factual proof as support for such opinions been forthcoming'.[65]

Richard Warner argues that 'Lagore is a key site in Irish Early Christian archaeology, and one whose chronological implications are of extreme importance'.[66] While agreeing with Hencken on the dating of the site, he referred to his use of historical sources for chronological purposes as 'Hencken's historical constraint'.[67] This resulted in the interpretation of the artefactual and stratigraphical chronology within predetermined historical dates. Artefacts which could not be accommodated within this framework became problematic and were largely ignored and their significance in terms of the obtaining of accurate information about the past was not fully realised. The collective views of archaeologists questioning the reliability of Hencken's dates, because of the chronology of some of the Lagore material, are dismissed by Warner as 'post-Hencken revisionism'.[68] The historian F.J. Byrne also questioned the reliability of the historical reference that provided the AD 651 date for the initial construction of Lagore.[69] Cahercommaun has also come under scrutiny with regard to the date of its construction. Barry Raftery asserted that the ninth century date ascribed to the site by Hencken was erroneous. He postulated that 'Cahercommaun and a number of Irish sites, hitherto dated to the second half of the first millennium AD, may well have to be back-dated by at least half a millennium'.[70] Seamus Caulfield argued that the construction and initial occupation of Cahercommaun 'could potentially have a BC rather than AD date'.[71] William Holmes Forsyth, curator at the Metropolitan Museum of Art in New York, in his review of Hencken's paper on Lagore, in the *American Journal of Archaeology* (1953) observed that 'Hencken with commendable honesty, points out the difficulties, which others have sometimes glibly ignored, of the chronological dating of Irish medieval objects'.[72]

At the close of the nineteenth century Wood-Martin had posed the question: 'Supposing we did not possess the fanciful Irish Annals, how would archaeology have been written?'[73] This question is one which has posed difficulties among generations of archaeologists. F.J. Byrne's assessment of the use that Irish archaeologists made of the historical sources in this period was, in John Waddell's opinion, 'perceptive'. Byrne wrote that 'Irish archaeology was then in its infancy, and under the direction of Macalister in MacNeill's lifetime it tended to borrow from and intrude into the realms of documentary history – not always to the benefit of either discipline – rather than to offer independent evidence of its own finding'.[74] But cherry-picking tendencies continued unabated among scientific archaeologists. In the context of excavations of the crannógs, for example, the scientific team from Harvard did not challenge the orthodox view of the Irish story even though there was scientific archaeological evidence to suggest that they should have. The published report included typological comparisons of many of the artefacts with similar objects contained in the collections of museums around Europe; also bone, wood, textiles, leather and plant analysis by a variety of experts; and a history of the site. Joseph Raftery's comments on the issue echo Byrne's: 'A chronological scheme for the material remains of the first millennium AD based on the Annals and other native records must be looked at with severe reservation if not, indeed, with downright suspicion. In other words, "text-aided" archaeology in Ireland is a very dubious commodity'.[75] It is likely that the problem was not only 'text-aided' archaeology because as Fowler explains: 'When archaeology (or history) is used for nationalist purposes, the resultant pictures of the past are severely distorted to reflect nationalist goals and ideals'.[76] Joseph Raftery believed that 'a sounder basis for our history' lay in the natural sciences, including pollen analysis, radiocarbon methods, dendrochronology, thermoluminescence, geology, technology, osteology, and statistics'.[77]

## Were there Romans at Lagore?

Hencken came to Ireland as part of a functionalist team of anthropologists. While they applied more stringent scientific techniques in the recovery of data from archaeological sites, interpretation was limited. While the interpretative process is open to political influence, the retrieval of information through the activity of excavation and the various sciences used to enhance information is essentially sterile if it is not interpreted. If the empirical data is descriptive only it remains within the antiquarian tradition of collection. The creation of knowledge about humans in the past is dependent on the interpretative process to understand material culture. During the 1930s in Ireland historical origin stories could not be easily challenged by archaeologists as nationalist ideology would not allow it. This implicit and unquestioning acceptance of the ideological tenets of nationalism was influenced by the broad Irish cultural milieu within which the practice of archaeology took place. This resulted in certain aspects of material culture, such as Roman assemblages, for example, not being given due significance or simply being explained away. Joseph Raftery explains:

> It is clear from all this and from other statements in the Lagore report that the historical evidence, such as it is, is taken to provide the initial

date for the site and that anything in the archaeological record likely to conflict with this tends to be explained away. The possibility that the first stages at Lagore could be as early, say as late Roman times is barely allowed birth.[78]

As already noted, the desire to connect prehistory seamlessly to the historic period was a tenet of the culture-historical approach to archaeological interpretation. This meant that equal recognition was not given to the place of Roman artefacts and sites in the historical narrative as it would challenge the perceived continuity of cultural and racial Celtic purity from prehistory into the present. RAS Macalister's view, expressed in 1928, that 'the Romans made no direct impression on the country' was still being reiterated in 1955 by the American anthropologists, Hooton and Dupertuis, who asserted that 'Ireland escaped Roman invasion and domination'.[79] As previously discussed the primary collections in the National Museum of Ireland were 'firmly based on Ireland's native culture' as recommended by the Lithberg Report and included artefacts from the Bronze Age, the pre-Roman Iron Age and the Early Christian Period.[80] Roman material, like Asian and Greek material was not 'native' and was used for comparative purposes only. Ireland desired to be part of 'Celtic' Europe, which was deemed to have supplanted Classical (i.e. Roman and Greek) cultural influence in Ireland.

A fragment of a sherd of Roman pottery, termed *terra sigillata* in the Lagore report, was, Hencken believed, probably brought in with the building materials from an earlier site. During the excavations he expressed the opinion that 'There was also a taste for curios which might almost be considered antiquarianism, for a few Roman trifles occurred, including fragments of Samian pottery, one of which had been used as a pendant'.[81] R.B. Warner later confirmed Hencken's view that the *terra sigillata* was brought into the country at a date considerably later than its date of manufacture and that the importation of these sherds was due to their 'value as relics'. He also claimed that 'their origin included Rome, or other Mediterranean cities with a strong Christian association' and that their deposition on a site had a 'certain sanctifying effect'.[82] Any attempt by archaeologists to establish an earlier date for Lagore, based on material recovered from the earliest layer, was dismissed as a 'Roman red-herring' by Warner.[83]

Two unstratified sherds of decorated pottery were deemed by Hencken to be Central Gaulish and of the type 'that was exported to Roman military sites and civil settlements in the Romanized provinces'.[84] These were dated to c. AD150 – 160 and c. AD140 – 150 respectively but came from an unstratified location. According to Hencken a number of artefacts found at Lagore could be attributed to 'purely Roman contacts'. These included weapons, tools, querns, sherds of coarse pottery, bone pins, toilet implements, bronze bowls, rings with sliding knots, barrel padlocks and keys, twisted iron bucket handles, beads and fragments of glass vessels, and a button-like disc with a small perforated tang. Making millefiori enamel at Lagore was also a technique which emanated from the western part of the Roman Empire. In a report dated 1933 on Roman material recovered from Ballinderry 2 Hencken commented that 'a study of Roman glass mosaics and Celto-Roman enamelling and their transference into Ireland would be very illuminating'.[85] He concluded that 'These Roman objects, however, make one wonder whether future excavation may not produce in Ireland a Roman Iron Age like that well known in Scandinavia'.[86] However, difficulties in interpretation of this assemblage arose because, in Hencken's opinion, 'it is not always easy to separate La Tène and Roman forms, for the same Mediterranean ideas often underlie both'.[87] He wondered if 'future excavation may reveal in at least parts of Ireland a phase of the Iron Age under Roman influence'.[88] However, in his published Lagore report, Hencken promoted the idea that the various cultural waves which reached Ireland were 'not in sufficient force to blot out what was there already'[89] implying that the native culture stayed intact and remained unthreatened by outside cultures. The native culture supposedly incorporated new cultural ideas, including Roman ones, without its essence being altered in a process of cultural change. A perceived lack of cultural homogeneity was still anathema to nationalist ideology in the 1950s. Hencken's solution to this problem was found in diffusion of ideas and cultural traits without supplanting the indigenous culture.

Roman pottery was found at other sites excavated under the Unemployment Schemes in the 1930s, including at the forts at Ballycatteen and Garannes in County Cork.[90] A sherd of Arretine ware, dating to the first half of the first century AD, was also found on Ballinderry 2 Crannóg in County Offaly.[91] Ó Ríordáin concluded that the amount of this type of pottery from any one of these Irish sites is not great but its occurrence on widely separated sites and on sites differing in date by several centuries was significant as it indicated 'the acceptance of a technique of Roman pottery making and its continuation over a long period'.[92] The chronological range of the sites and the minor variations in the pottery led Ó Ríordáin to suggest that 'after early examples had been imported the manufacture was carried on in the country'.[93] Roman material was often explained away by pointing out

the survival of the material into later centuries. For example, with reference
to an imitation Roman coin of Constantius II (Roman Emperor from AD
337–361), found at Lough Gur, Ó Ríordáin wrote 'We can only remark that
this is not the only example of long survival of material like this and on
sites of approximately the same period. The fragment of Samian ware from
Lagore is another example of the same phenomenon'.[94] Some writers have
suggested that Samian ware had been picked up from Roman sites in Britain
for use as relics and shrine pieces.[95] Bateson argued that 'there is no reason
to believe that they were not imported during the normal period of currency
of Samian ware'.[96]

In 1973 Bateson asserted that 'there is, as yet, no archaeological
evidence for a Roman invasion of Ireland'.[97] He acknowledged that 'Britain
would thus seem to be the source of most, if not all, of the Roman objects'.[98]
This reluctance by Irish archaeologists to consider the possibility of a
Roman invasion of Ireland is understandable as the invasion model for the
interpretation of Roman cultural material (like Celtic/La Tène material)
is clearly inadequate. It is a model much overused in archaeological
writing as a means of explaining cultural change, often when the amount
of material available is miniscule. This sensitivity over the interpretation
of Roman material can still be found embedded in Irish archaeological
interpretation. For example, the burials at Stoneyford and Bray, which
were clearly Roman in character, were interpreted as being carried out by
those 'familiar with Roman practices', and not by actual Romans.[99] The
possibility of archaeological evidence for a Roman presence in Ireland at
the site of Drumanagh, near Loughshinny, Co. Dublin became the subject
of intense controversy in 1996 when it was suggested that the Romans had
invaded Ireland and that there had been a Roman presence in Ireland in
the past.[100] The controversy was described as 'a tale of state secrecy and
scholarly sniping'.[101] It had less to do with historical reality and more to do
with the political context within which the academic and popular debate
took place. Anglo-Irish relations at that time were very tense and any hint
of compromising the identity of the Irish as pure Celtic by postulating a
Roman invasion in history was strongly rejected. In 2004 Waddell expressed
the opinion that 'the ludicrous cliché that the Irish are different because
the Romans never came here is an extreme instance of auto-exoticism and
deserves to be seriously questioned'.[102] The 'blatantly sectional interpretations
of the Irish past'[103] which the Drumanagh controversy represented reflects
the deeply political nature of archaeological interpretation since political
independence. Waddell is of the opinion that the putative Romanisation of

Ireland is a subject which 'demands serious assessment free of xenophobic and daft claims about the special nature of the Celt'.[104] It is possible, with the successful unfolding of the Peace Process in Northern Ireland and the accommodation of diverse identities that the Roman influence in Ireland will no longer seem quite so threatening as it did in the past. This process is beginning: Alexandra Guglielmi published her short paper 'My kingdom for a pot! A reassessment of the Iron Age and Roman material from Lagore Crannóg, Co. Meath' in 2014.[105] Jacqueline Cahill Wilson and her team carried out an innovative study, *Late Iron Age and Roman Ireland*, under the auspices of the Discovery Programme, publishing its results, also in 2014.[106] J.P. Mallory, in his book *The Origins of the Irish* points out that 'The real irony is that in some ways it seems easier to demonstrate a Roman presence in Ireland than it is to prove an Iron Age intrusion'.[107] While this may well be the case ideas about an Iron Age 'Celtic' invasion persist. For example, in an article published in *Archaeology Ireland* (Summer 2017) Paddy Boyle expressed confidence that future excavations at Drumanagh would 'bear out the presence of Belgian Celts'.[108]

## Post-War Interpretations

A shift in emphasis from culture-historical models of explanation in archaeology and their inherent racist and political undertones to economic models only began in earnest with the publication of J.G.D. Clark's *Prehistoric Europe: The Economic Basis* which was published in 1942. V. Gordon Childe had already begun to experiment with these new theories in his work distancing himself from Kossinna's culture-historical theories in the process.[109] It is clear that Hencken's published report on Lagore reflected this shift to economic and environmental concerns and an acceptance of the diversity of cultural influences reflected in the archaeology of the site. He interpreted Lagore as 'a large lay establishment which seems to have been almost wholly self-supporting'.[110] He observed that imports were very few. Farming, bronze-working, iron-working, wood-working, weaving, shoe-making, millefiori-enamel making, glass-making, quern-making and textiles production were some of the activities carried out on the site. The glass workshop at Lagore was the first one ever found in Ireland. Though evidence for bronze-working was found at the site there was no information about the possible sources of tin. There were very few fish bones and it seemed that crannóg dwellers were not fishermen. Hencken described the crannóg as the centre of an agricultural community. Old finds include a heavy iron coulter and share of a plough. No evidence for saddle querns was found but there were forty-one fragments of rotary querns recovered. It seemed, according to Hencken that 'the court of Lagore lived more on meat and dairy products than on grain'. Hencken's Lagore paper was moving in the direction of Clark's economic model and can be seen as a transitional paper between culture-historical archaeology in Ireland which still had a strong antiquarian component and new economic and environmental ideas reflected in corroborating scientific evidence from the natural sciences.

Hencken's paper was reviewed by the American anthropologist, William Duncan Strong, in 1953, in the *American Anthropologist*.[111] In his view 'The historical, legendary, and archaeological history of the site is somewhat conflicting;' Liam Price's detailed history of the site was 'not very conclusive;' and 'the work of earlier "Antiquarians" sometimes helps even less'. He concluded that:

> The paper under review had no outline of subject matter, no list of figures or plates, no index, nor general conclusions. However, it covers a fascinating subject and its content is rich. The reviewer would like to see it tied more closely to the 'Irish Countryman' and to the factual and theoretical work of many other British and North American anthropologists. It is time the continents got together on wider ethno-archaeological interpretation.[112]

## Heterogenous Cultural Continuity

Christina Fredengren lamented the lack of interpretation by Hencken of the crannóg sites and ascribed this to the fact that 'the rich excavations imposed such a burden of information that an understanding of the nature of the sites was nearly impossible to reach'.[113] In their book, *Rethinking Wetland Archaeology*, published in 2006, Van de Noort and O'Sullivan pointed out that it remained the case that 'in its theoretical approaches it could be argued that wetland archaeology retains a strong empirical, functionalist core'.[114] This 'problem' of rich assemblages may be partly the reason for the paucity of interpretative analysis by the Harvard Mission. Hencken may also have been anxious not to step too much outside the narrative framework with its embedded nationalist ideology already established in Irish tradition with regard to crannóg research. The explanation of the reasons why American archaeologists conducting a purely scientific excavation on a crannóg in Ireland would come to the conclusion that Christians inhabited the site when there was no direct material evidence to substantiate such an interpretation was probably because historical sources were valued more highly than archaeological evidence at that time. It was considered to be the scientific proof necessary for the authentication and validation of the historical narrative. As H.G. Leask, the Inspector of National Monuments, commented 'In effect archaeology ceases to exist only where well and fully documented history begins'.[115] If historical sources deemed Lagore to be a royal Christian site, then archaeological science did not challenge that assertion or put forward an alternate hypothesis even though the data recovered demanded it.

The social nature of archaeological science and the inclination to fit the data to prior expectations without realising the lack of objectivity this represents, also provides a partial answer to this conundrum. In the social strand of the Harvard Mission little attention was paid to religion. According to Gibbon and Curtin 'it was a reflection of the contemporary ideological power of one aspect of Fianna Fáil's republicanism [its pro-smallholder stance] and its clerical endorsement'.[116] In an intriguing letter dated 1 February 1940 to Dumas Malone of Harvard University Press, de Valera wrote that he had submitted the book *Family and Community Life in Ireland* by Conrad M. Arensberg and Solon T. Kimball to readers who 'unanimously report adversely'. He advised that 'publication, particularly of chapter 11, will cause considerable misunderstanding and resentment' and he strongly advised against it. A civil servant from the Department of the Taoiseach, in a note on the file, wrote that 'the most objectionable parts of chapter 11 did not appear in the book. I destroyed the page proof'.[117]

While nationalist ideology influences archaeology, nationalism itself is dependent on the discipline for interpretation of the past and the hard evidence underpinning the establishment of the nation and the provision of visual markers of identity. Archaeological data from crannógs provided important material evidence for the identity of Ireland as Celtic and Christian in the early decades of independence. The label 'Celtic' became synonymous with Irishness across the globe, with Europeanness and with whiteness. In 1920, de Valera had written an open letter to Woodrow Wilson, President of the United States, stating that:

> The people of Ireland undoubtedly constitute a nation – one of the oldest and most clearly defined in Europe. Their nation is not a nation merely in the sense of modern political science – it was a sovereign

independent state for over a thousand years, knowing no external master but moulding its own institutions to its own life in accordance with its own will.[118]

European and American archaeologists were influencing and controlling Irish archaeology in the 1930s, repositioning Ireland culturally in the past of a Celtic Europe and in the future within the Irish-American diaspora.

Fredegren viewed Hencken as 'almost repeating his predecessors' views on the unchanging nature of crannógs'.[119] This reflects a clinging to the notion of cultural continuity where it makes little difference whether the material culture varies or not as it will be interpreted as contributing to an already existing culture and enriching it. With regard to cultural homogeneity in Ireland, Simon James's opinion on the Celtic race and cultural purity could well be applied to the crannógs:

> Neither of the two major islands, then, was a distinctive monolithic cultural, political or ethnic entity at any time in the past, as they still are not today. There never was a pristine cultural or ethnic uniformity ('Celtic' or anything else) across the archipelago, but always multiple traditions, undergoing contest and change.[120]

The embeddedness and longevity of the idea of Celtic Ireland in the popular imagination is demonstrated in Hugh O'Neill's Hencken's obituary in the *New York Times* dated 4 September 1981, which contained the following statement: 'One of their early finds, recovered from a clay mound near Moate in County Westmeath, was a large wooden building that Dr. Hencken and the others believed was a lake house constructed by the Celts, who travelled to Ireland from the continent in the Bronze Age'.

Once identity is established, its roots run deep, and it tends to endure. At Lagore there was a mosaic of identities including Roman, Viking, Germanic and Celtic. What the excavators chose to give prominence to was influenced by their own academic training, the expectations of those who facilitated their work, and by political bias, even though this might have been unconscious. This multi-cultural site, containing archaeological material from different periods and cultures reflected heterogenous and colourful cultural continuity, and not the homogenous, uni-cultural development beloved of nationalists. C.J. Lynn paid tribute to Hencken and his team in the excavation of the crannógs, despite criticising the fact that the location of stratified finds in relation to plan, strata and contexts were not described in enough detail: 'It is a tribute to the Lagore and Ballinderry publications considered above that hopefully more plausible interpretations can be offered without encountering any logical impasse in the data.'[121]

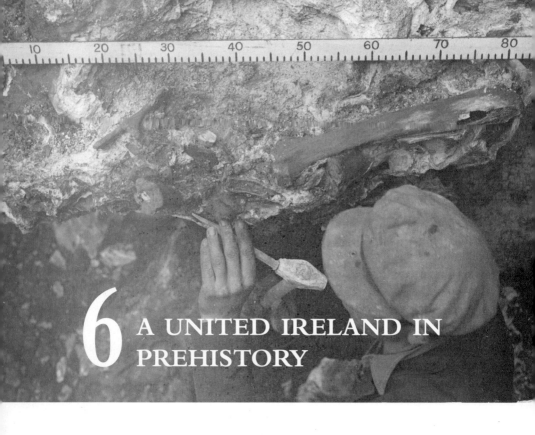

# 6 A UNITED IRELAND IN PREHISTORY

We anthropologists look upon it [politics] with nearly complete detachment as we know that the present national and racial boundaries are a thing of very late origin and that the boundaries which separated mankind in the Stone Age are probably more important than the make-shifts of our present politicians.[1]

– Adolf Mahr, 1932

## Border Politics: Modern and Prehistoric

Earnest A. Hooton believed that 'the Irish people are rooted in their prehistory'[2] which reflected the status of the subject in the 1930s. Prehistory became the focus of nationalist politics as identities in the past had implications for current and future political positions where different visions for the future are passionately fought out in the present.[3] In the case of Ireland the exploration of the Irish prehistoric past and its boundaries included the vision of Ulster nationalists, Irish Free State nationalists and Irish-American archaeologists from Harvard. Unfortunately, this struggle for control of the interpretation of the past can result in a tendency 'to create the past in our own image'.[4] Jones notes that 'the idea of a bounded, monolithic cultural cum ethnic unit is also a modern classificatory myth'.[5] Irish archaeology serviced this myth in the nineteenth century. With the consolidation of the political border in 1922 the discipline was hijacked by narrow ideological traditions on both sides for political ends. The prestigious status of science was used to bolster various theories. Prehistorians in the south sought to transcend the border. The pursuance of hominid fossils and associated artefacts resulted in an extension of the Harvard Mission Irish Free State Anthropological Survey to Northern Ireland. Academics in the north sought to reinforce the political border, citing geography and prehistory; the demand for continued political separation was bolstered by perceived past cultural differences. In the Irish Free State the demand for a dismantling of the political border was bolstered by perceived all-Ireland cultural homogeneity in the past.

The Harvard Mission archaeologists and Adolf Mahr did not acknowledge any borders in Irish prehistory but were aware of the political implications, tensions, and the contested nature of the political border. In 1938 Adolf Mahr considered that the Irish had 'their own Sudeten in Northern Ireland'.[6] The Sudetenland was a predominantly German-speaking area which was incorporated within the borders of Czechoslovakia after the First World War. Mahr, whose family was of Sudeten origin, was interested in the authenticity of prehistoric boundaries over current ones. His own politics obviously influenced his practice of archaeology in Ireland. He believed the prehistoric borders were more important than current political ones. This suggests the use of archaeology to establish the territorial claims of nations. Mahr's sentiments about prehistoric borders, as suggested in the quote at the beginning of this chapter implies a disapproval of the border between Northern Ireland and the Irish Free State. And it begs the question, why, in the opinion of Mahr were Stone Age borders more important or authentic than recently constructed ones? The answer to this conundrum probably lies in Mahr's own political and family background. Hencken held similar views on the Irish border to Mahr when it came to archaeological research, writing in 1933 that 'we, like the government in Dublin, regard Ireland as a unit and consider the northern boundary artificial'.[7]

The idea of the island of Ireland as one cultural unit was reflected in archaeological scholarship. As previously mentioned, articles for the *Proceedings of the Royal Irish Academy* and the *Journal of the Royal Society of Antiquaries of Ireland* covered artefacts and monuments from both jurisdictions. It was Mahr's view that 'the border between the two Irish States, as far as Prehistoric Science is concerned, is largely non-existent, and this is exactly as it should be'.[8] This all-Ireland approach to archaeological research was also the policy of the National Museum of Ireland. Mahr referred to the Belfast Municipal Museum and Art Gallery as 'the regional Museum for British Ulster' but he acknowledged the positive relationship between the two museums. For this he gave credit to the curator and assistant curator, A. Deane and J.A.S. Stendall, respectively. Stendall, who was editor of the *Irish Naturalists' Journal*, in Mahr's opinion 'has the interests of the whole country at heart'.[9]

## The Idea of Irish Prehistory

The idea of prehistory became popular through books such as Sir John Lubbock's *Prehistoric Times* published in 1865. By the 1920s it was established as an academic discipline and brought, according to Glyn Daniel, 'a new perspective of the human past'.[10] However, it took a long time to gain respectability in Ireland. As late as 1954, the Celtic scholar, Professor Daniel Binchy, referred to 'that curious science that calls itself prehistory'.[11] Binchy disliked prehistoric science because of its political and racist connotations. Prehistory got a bad name in Germany when the work of the nationalist prehistorian, Gustaf Kossinna, whose theories were also influential in Irish archaeology, was misused by the Nazis. The Kossinnian notion of using archaeology to establish a historical right to territory became a feature of Irish prehistoric archaeology. In Germany, if the artefacts found could be deemed to have belonged to ancient Germans then that territory, by definition, was deemed to be rightfully German.[12] According to Glyn Daniel they 'harnessed prehistory to their racial-mad chariot'.[13] When they came to power in 1933 the Nazis began to fund archaeological research and by 1939 courses in prehistoric archaeology were being offered in twenty-five German universities. The Nazi leader, Heinrich Himmler, one of the founders of the Ahnenerbe, an organisation established in 1935 to research the archaeological and cultural history of the Aryan race, was adamant that 'the thing these people are paid for by the state, is to have ideas of history that strengthen our people in their national pride'.[14]

It was thought that only prehistorians could provide the necessary evidence of the superiority, antiquity and racial purity of the ancient Germans. Kossinna, a Eurocentric prehistorian, believed that Germany was the centre of European civilisation and that its cultural influence spread outwards in antiquity. It was his view that the megalith builders spread from Germany throughout ancient Europe. Kossinna, initially trained as a philologist, was appointed Professor of German Prehistory in the University of Berlin in 1902. He published *Die Herkunft der Germanen* (The Origin of the Germans) in 1911. He became famous for correlating ethnic groups with assemblages of artefacts and for the application of a direct historical approach to the study of archaeology. Like other archaeologists of his time he believed that cultural continuity indicated ethnic durability. Because the Germans had stayed in their own homeland they were not mixed with foreign blood and therefore remained racially pure and culturally superior to other Indo-European peoples. Kossinna believed that each *Volk* had its own *Kultur* and that archaeological monuments and artefacts were ethnic markers. The prehistory of the German race could essentially be established by this equating of the *Kultur* with the *Volk*.[15] According to Trigger, Kossinna was 'inspired by a fanatical patriotism'. [16] In 1933, Liam S. Gogan of the National Museum of Ireland expressed similar sentiments in his opinion that Irish archaeology was 'a science that is essentially and fundamentally national'.[17]

Bruce Trigger insisted that, despite Kossinna's sometimes nonsensical and often amateurish ideas he should be 'recognized as an innovator whose work was of major importance for the development of archaeology'.[18] Glyn Daniel, in contrast, was of the view that Kossinna's ideas were a 'perversion of prehistory'.[19] Colin Renfrew described the reaction of most archaeologists to the misuse of the prehistoric studies of Kossinna by the German establishment as follows:

> Most archaeologists of the time were appalled to see what were not more than plausible theories about prehistoric languages and cultures converted into military propaganda about racial superiority and brought to a nightmarish *reductio ad absurdum* in the destruction of millions of people, supposedly belonging to other 'races', in the holocaust.[20]

During the 1920s archaeology was concerned with race, ethnicity and migration of peoples. There was little emphasis on the technologies used by prehistoric peoples, the ecology and economic basis of societies or on social organisation. After Kossinna's ideas were developed by Childe, who used the concept of the archaeological culture in his book *The Dawn of European Civilization* (1925), the concept became widespread in archaeological discourse.

Kossinna's work was ripe for political use by the emerging nation states of Europe, including Ireland. Unfortunately, because Kossinna's work was misused by the Nazis, it resulted in what Simon James referred to as 'the retrospective tainting of his reputation'.[21] However, unlike Kossinna, Childe did not seek in his early work to establish cultural continuity between the Palaeolithic and the Neolithic. Bruce Trigger explains that 'A diffusionist position had no vested interest in such cultural continuity, whereas Kossinna's theories required it for an Indo-European homeland'.[22] In 1926 Childe acknowledged the limitations of prehistory as a scientific discipline when he wrote that 'As a science based upon abstraction and comparison, prehistoric archaeology cannot aspire to the concreteness of history'.[23] In Ireland Macalister, like his British counterparts, was receptive to Montelius's ideas about the relationship between Prehistoric Europe and the Near East and the notion of Europe's cultural development being influenced from outside. In a *Textbook of European Archaeology*, published in 1921, he did not apply the concept of the archaeological culture. Eoin MacNeill admired Macalister's work, describing *A Text-Book of European Archaeology* as 'a masterly achievement of learning'.[24]

## The First Irishman

In Ireland, the question of the first arrival of prehistoric man was imbued with political significance. In 1931, Ó Ríordáin observed that the question 'is one which is even yet admittedly shrouded in darkness'.[25] The implications of the discovery of evidence for the earliest Irishman in the Irish Free State rather than in Northern Ireland were interesting. If the bones of Palaeolithic man were found in Northern Ireland it could be claimed that he arrived from Britain and spread to the rest of Ireland. The Harvard Mission attempted to find the earliest skeletal remains for the white Irishman in Kilgreany Cave in County Waterford and the earliest remains of his handiwork at a number of prehistoric sites in Northern Ireland. Kilgreany Cave was excavated under the Unemployment Schemes for Archaeological Research in 1934 by Hallam L. Movius with the assistance of Frederick T. Riley of TCD and Amory Goddard of Harvard. Progress reports on the site dated 8 September 1934 and 27 October 1934 respectively were sent to de Valera, who took a keen interest in the work.[26]

The earliest Irishman was believed at the time to date to the Palaeolithic period. Movius was well placed to carry out this research as he was 'a Palaeolithic archaeologist, a specialist in the interpretation of human behaviour and its environmental context during the latter part of the Old Stone Age'.[27] He came to Ireland as a graduate student of Hencken's, working on Mesolithic sites in Northern Ireland and gathering data for his PhD dissertation in the process. The previous year he had been on a study tour with the American School of Prehistoric Research where he had visited archaeological sites and museums in England, France, Germany, Switzerland, Austria, Czechoslovakia and Yugoslavia. He had remained on in Czechoslovakia to excavate with the Harvard-Penn expedition. In the spring of 1932 he had joined the excavations being carried out jointly by the American School of Prehistoric Research and the British School of Archaeology in Jerusalem at the site of Mugharet es-Skhul in the Mount Carmel range of Israel. He was involved in the discovery of a human fossil in the Skhul cave, dating to between 80,000 and 120,000 years ago. This represented one of the earliest groups of modern humans to be found outside Africa.[28]

In a letter dated 2 June 1937 to Hencken, Movius joked that Louis Leakey was 'in East Africa now studying his sociological brothers and sisters'.[29] Leakey had just published his book entitled *White African: an Early Autobiography*. He had graduated from Cambridge in 1926 in archaeology and anthropology and had set out to prove Darwin's theory that Africa was humankind's homeland. In 1931 Leakey discovered the earliest stone tools used by man at Olduvai Gorge in Tanzania. He later became famous for his recovery of human fossils and his contribution to the understanding of human origins. The joking between Hencken and Movius on this subject perhaps reflected the unease among archaeologists surrounding the evolutionary relationship between man and primates and their desire at that time to find the earliest evidence for white man in Europe. Harvard Mission archaeology in Ireland became part of this American/Old Europe cultural quest.

Canon Patrick Power, Professor of Archaeology at University College Cork, had written in 1925 that: 'The first appearance of man in Ireland was, almost certainly in Neolithic times. At any rate, we have no evidence of an Irish Palaeolithic man – a fact which does not preclude the possible existence of such a being'.[30] He believed that 'it is practically certain the Palaeolithic had no place in Irish prehistory'.[31] However, this belief did not deter Power from penning an imaginative description of Palaeolithic man:

> Palaeolithic man was a savage; his home, when he had a home at all, was a pit in the earth or a rock shelter; his weapons were splintered stones and tree branches; he was mainly a hunter, and had neither an agriculture, domesticated animals, nor industrial art. Notwithstanding all this, however, we now know that this man of the dawn had a high artistic sense, and he actually painted and carved wonderfully realistic figures which are the puzzle and admiration of modern archaeologists.[32]

The prehistorians J.P.T. Burchell and J. Reid Moir considered it 'probable that man did live in Ireland during the Palaeolithic epoch'.[33] They published a memoir *The Early Mousterian Implements of Sligo, Ireland*, in 1928, in which they asserted that it was well established that 'Palaeolithic Man inhabited Ireland'.[34] The Mousterian implements of the title belonged to a Middle Palaeolithic culture, a period characterised by the use of flint implements. Their 'discovery' resulted in what Peter Woodman has described as 'one of the most acrimonious disputes in Irish archaeology'.[35] Over forty contributions, including papers and letters, had been written on the subject.[36] J. Reid Moir, in an article dated 5 March 1929, published in the *Irish Times*, expressed the view that 'it is generally the case that new ideas relating to prehistoric man have to run the gauntlet of very determined opposition. There are, in fact, few subjects in science which have generated more dialectical heat'. The contention that the Sligo palaeoliths were made by early humans was supported by A.L. Armstrong, President of the Prehistoric Society of East Anglia; R.A. Smith, Keeper of the Department of British and Mediaeval Antiquities in the British Museum; M.C. Burkitt, Lecturer in Archaeology at Cambridge; and the Palaeolithic experts J. Reid Moir, Dorothy Garrod and H. Dewey.[37] That humans made the implements was challenged by other academics including Macalister and Mahr; the naturalist, botanist, archaeologist and geologist Robert Lloyd Praeger; the entomologist and conchologist Arthur Wilson Stelfox and the geologists J. Kaye Charlesworth and T. Hallissy. In a document dated 14 May 1928, Reid Moir and Burchell expressed disappointment that 'Professor Macalister should believe that we are so lacking in a knowledge of these matters as, under any circumstances, to regard chunks of rock such as he picked up, as having been flaked by man'.[38] In 1998, Peter Woodman published an article entitled 'Rosses Point [County Sligo] revisited', in which he discussed how personal biases influence interpretation of lithic assemblages. He suggested the Sligo Palaeolithic controversy has lessons for archaeologists and warned that 'this tendency to select the elements which help justify one's own perceptions of a particular assemblage is an inherent danger in all publications of lithics'.[39]

In the 1930s Hooton expressed his reservations about the limitations of typology as a technique for the extraction of relevant knowledge about the past. The idea of typological changes being in the eye of a hopeful beholder was described by him as a 'typological delusion' and as 'a sort of auth-hypnosis brought on by too concentrated and prolonged gazing upon a single class of archaeological objects, as into a crystal. The archaeologist begins to see things which are not there'.[40] Hooton also makes a more serious observation about assemblages of artefacts being correlated with particular races:

> Many so-called 'types' of stone implements are so crude, amorphous, and variable that no sensible observer can escape the conclusion that they are the results of the uncertain fumblings of unskilled workers rather than the products of purposeful techniques. When these dubious types are called upon to define whole cultures and are supposed to be exclusive products of single prehistoric races, typology becomes ridiculous and its implications nonsensical.[41]

## A Palaeolithic Irishman in Kilgreany Cave?

J. Reid Moir remained convinced of the authenticity of the Sligo Palaeoliths and wrote in 1929 that 'I entertain no more doubt that the specimens collected by Mr. Burchell are of human origin than I do that the pen with which I am writing this article was made by man'.[42] Liam S. Gogan of the National Museum gave an address to a meeting of the Dublin Rotary Club on 18 February 1929. He noted that the Mousterian, or middle Palaeolithic Period, was significant to Irish people because of the recent discoveries by Reid Moir. He regretted 'The heat and lack of good taste with which what may be called the Irish side of the case was presented'.[43] The *Irish Times* reported on Gogan's lecture, 'Tracing the First Irishman, Remains of the First Highbrow', and noted that 'it is possible that the first Irishman was a Neanderthal man, unless the remains which have been found at various places in Ireland were merely those of Palaeolithic tourists'.[44]

During the controversy, charges were levied at those who expressed the opinion that the 'palaeolithic' implements were inauthentic, that they were 'actuated by a desire to uphold at all costs a prejudice against the existence of any traces of Palaeolithic Man in Ireland'.[45] This would not seem to be the case as Charlesworth, Stelfox, Macalister and Praeger enthusisastically embraced the idea that Palaeolithic Man had been located in Kilgreany Cave in Waterford by the Bristol Spelaeological Society. They wrote, in a letter published in *Nature* dated 18 May 1929, that it was 'with very special pleasure that we welcome the news contained in the accompanying statement, that the discovery has at last been made'.[46]

The object of the Kilgreany excavation by the Harvard Mission, according to Adolf Mahr, was to continue excavations carried out previously by the Bristol University Spelaeological Society.[47] E.K. Tratman and the Bristol University Speleological Society undertook an excavation in 1928, acting on behalf of the Fauna and Flora Committee and the Archaeological Excavation Committee of the Royal Irish Academy. This was funded by the Percy Sladen Memorial Fund which had been founded for the 'encouragement of scientific research in its correlation to human history'.[48] Tratman gave a lecture on 'The finds made during the recent excavation at Kilgreany, County Waterford, in July 1928' to the Royal Irish Academy.[49] He told the meeting about the skeleton he had recovered: 'The opinion of eminent anthropologists to whom the skull was submitted is that it has several very ancient features, and is probably of late Palaeolithic date'.[50] The *Irish Times* reported that 'The extreme antiquity' of the human remains of Kilgreany was confirmed by the authority of Sir Arthur Keith, the Scottish anatomist and anthropologist, and claimed that 'one of the riddles of Irish antiquity is solved'.[51] The Palaeolithic date was supported by the presence of late Pleistocene animals including the brown bear, wild cat, wolf, an early form of ox, Irish elk, reindeer, stoat, hare, lemming, marine and land molluscs and 'the first vole recorded from Ireland'. Tratman told the audience that 'The individual is put down as a member of the Celto-Iberian race – that is, a Mediterranean type'.[52] Tratman concluded his lecture by congratulating the Royal Irish Academy on the important part it had played in bringing to light the first discovery of Palaeolithic Man in Ireland. The find was of great significance as it was 'a discovery of the utmost importance in the story of the prehistoric archaeology of Ireland and Europe as a whole'.[53] Tratman published his results in the *Proceedings of the University of Bristol Spelaeological Society* in 1928.[54]

Mahr considered Tratman's excavations to be a 'remarkable success', and that the caves 'would undoubtedly repay further examination'. [55] Other

Irish archaeologists were also excited by the discoveries of the University of Bristol Spelaeological Society. In 1931, Ó Ríordáin described how 'the latest discoveries have been epoch-making in succeeding in proving beyond doubt the fact that Ireland had a Palaeolithic population'.[56] The careful scientific approach of Movius in the excavation of Kilgreany Cave was in sharp contrast to that of E.K. Tratman earlier. Tratman's lack of expertise caused problems for Movius and on 24 September 1934 he sent a report on the first fortnight's work to Adolf Mahr, outlining his frustration with the site. According to Movius, Tratman and his team had published an 'inaccurate' plan, their sections were 'false' and Movius was unable to follow their stratigraphy. He described their excavation as 'a disturbance rather than a piece of archaeological work'.[57] Despite this, he considered the site to be 'amazingly rich' and wrote that he hoped to obtain bone material comparable to that yielded by crannógs and to find complete burials. He was also hoping to find a flint industry associated with the lower levels. However, he reiterated his frustration, stating 'I have never seen such a rotten piece of excavation in my life'. Movius, however, did not blame Tratman for this as he 'lacked experience'.[58] The lack of experience referred to was probably Tratman's complete lack of training as an archaeologist. He was a dentist.[59] He was described by A.M. ApSimon as someone who 'has interested himself in every branch of archaeology, not least in field work, and even, after some initial repugnance, in Romano-British archaeology'.[60] Hugo V. Flinn, Parliamentary Secretary to the Minister for Finance, wrote to de Valera on 5 October 1934 stating that 'further excavations by technically unqualified outsiders are to be seriously discouraged'.[61] This sentiment reflected the realisation at an official level that archaeology needed to be professionalised and restrictions placed on those who were unqualified in order to protect sites from destruction.

While the legislation was in place to protect monuments it took time for attitudes towards amateur archaeologists to change. S.P. Ó Ríordáin, in a note on the work of the University of Bristol Spelaeological Society at Kilgreany, published in *Antiquity* in 1931, was unconcerned about what Movius was later to describe as 'exceedingly confusing' stratigraphy. Ó Ríordáin wrote that 'It is not necessary to deal here in full with the stratification, since we are concerned only with the evidences afforded by it for the existence of the Irish Palaeolithic period'.[62] Neither was he concerned by the fact that no implements were found in association with the human remains and commented that 'this is unfortunate since it compels us to fall back on the evidence afforded by the fauna as a means of dating this occupation'.[63] He accepted that Tratman's 'important excavation', resulted in 'the first definite proof of the existence of Palaeolithic Man in Ireland.' In his view it was better than the collections of 'eoliths' reported from near Belfast, which he happily dismissed as 'freaks of nature'.[64] Movius sent a report, dated 6 October 1934, on the progress of the Kilgreany excavations, to Harold G. Leask.[65] He wrote of the extreme difficulty of removing the deposits from the cave because the excavation team were working at about twenty feet below the level of the dump. The following year he published the full results of the excavation in the *Journal of the Royal Society of Antiquaries of Ireland*.[66]

Movius compared the skull of the possible Palaeolithic Man (identified as 'Kilgreany B') to a skull found at Ringabella and one found in Stoneyisland bog, both of which were described as 'dolichocephalic'.[67] The skeleton was also examined by Sir Arthur Keith, who believed that there was nothing primitive in the morphology of 'Kilgreany B'.[68] Movius also sought corroborating evidence from various scientific experts. Charcoal samples were taken from a hearth associated with the 'Kilgreany B' skeleton. These were examined by J. Cecil Maby, who was advised by Professor Knud Jessen, then Director of the Botanical Gardens in Copenhagen and involved in work on bogs under the Irish Quaternary Research Scheme. The rocks from the site were examined by Professor L.B. Smyth, ScD of the Geology Department, Trinity College. The faunal remains were examined by Arthur Wilson Stelfox and Geraldine Roche M.Sc of the Natural History Division of the National Museum of Ireland. Movius considered the findings to be 'of extreme significance with regard to the problem of the antiquity of man in Ireland'.[69] Liam Price read a paper on his behalf to the Royal Society of Antiquaries of Ireland on 10 December 1935.[70] This was reported in an article in the *Irish Times* the following day and it was concluded that 'the skeleton found in 1928 could not be attributed to the late Palaeolithic period, but was more probably Neolithic in date'.[71] In 1962 the skeleton was radiocarbon dated to the Neolithic.[72]

In 1936, J.G.D. Clark noted in the *Proceedings of the Prehistoric Society* that 'most of us will agree with Mr Movius that it seems safe to conclude that, whereas abundant remains of an ancient fauna are present at Kilgreany, their association with the remains of man is no proof of contemporaneity'.[73] Clark expressed the opinion that 'The Kilgreany episode affords yet another example of the over-dating of a find corrected by a critical re-investigation'.[74] It was his view that this over-dating arose frequently in archaeology as a result of credit being attached to objects and sites according to their antiquity. This meant that 'a premium is set upon mere antiquity, which has no basis in reason'.[75] Another reason for over-dating of archaeological remains was because of patriotic sentiment. Communities desired to trace their pedigree as far back in time as possible. This was nationalism in action. The creation of nation-states after the Second World War had done much to intensify what Clark refers to as 'the international competition in antiquity'.[76] He was critical of the 'recrudescence of what one can only term "nationalist-racialism"' which encouraged this competition. The requirements of political propaganda had increased the prestige and financial resources in particular European countries for prehistoric archaeology, but in Clark's opinion 'they are hardly conducive to work of scientific value'.[77] He was also critical of the collections focus of many archaeologists: 'I was concerned to attack ... the kind of archaeology promoted by museum curators'.[78] Unfortunately, the Harvard Mission archaeologists were unduly influenced in their selection of archaeological sites and the acquisition of artefacts by Adolf Mahr. However, they were also diligent in the acquisition of expertise from a wide variety of scientists to aid in the interpretation of the archaeology.

In the 106th *Annual Report of the Commissioners of Public Works 1938* the Kilgreany excavations were described as 'disappointing'. The conclusion was reached that 'Up to the present no satisfactory evidence of Palaeolithic man in Ireland, north or south, is forthcoming, a negative fact which is, however, of importance in itself'.[89] Mahr viewed the Kilgreany excavation as having one result of value, in that it indicated how much care must be taken to excavate cave deposits completely and to avoid drawing inferences from incomplete data. It had, in his opinion, 'by reason of its very complexity', revealed the major difficulties to be met with in cave excavation and its results provided a most useful 'cautionary guide'.[80] However, the knowledge that the Bristol University Spelaeological Society may have contained 'technically unqualified outsiders' did not stop them conducting further excavations on behalf of the Royal Irish Academy at Munster cave sites in 1934. They obtained a licence to excavate at Killiwillin 'through the kindness of the Provost of Trinity College'.[81] This perhaps indicates that social connections were still more important in obtaining archaeological licences than the expertise of the potential excavators, despite the new legislation. Marion Dowd, in her reassessment of the excavations concluded that 'Kilgreany Cave has a biography of human activity spanning approximately 5,000 years' and was considered 'a sacred place on the landscape, outside the domain of profane life'.[82]

## Emyr Estyn Evans and Ulster Nationalism

Emyr Estyn Evans described the border in Ireland as 'sometimes a battleground, regarded by both sides as the last frontier of the British Empire'.[83] He wrote of the 'saints and sinners alike moving to and from across the turbulent seas between western Scotland and the north of Ireland'.[84] He later explained his interest in the cultural influences from Scotland:

> In Ireland we need to know what conditions prevailed in the various areas from which colonists were derived in the seventeenth century. This really means delving in a period for which little documentary evidence exists, and I use the word delving deliberately. Excavation of abandoned clachans in Ulster is producing promising results. May we hope that similar efforts will be made in Scotland.[85]

In Northern Ireland, prior to the arrival of the Harvard Mission archaeologists, Evans dominated the discipline of archaeology in Ulster. Born in Shrewsbury in England to Welsh-speaking parents, he studied at the University of Aberystwyth and came under the influence of H.G. Fleure, a distinguished geographer, anthropologist and authority on the question of race. After graduation in 1925 Evans began postgraduate studies in archaeology at New College, Oxford. He arrived at Queen's University Belfast (QUB) in 1928 to take up the position of lecturer in geography. Even though the subject of archaeology was not formally established at Queen's until 1948, Evans engaged in much archaeological research during the 1930s. In his paper sketching the history of prehistoric studies in Ulster, Evans recalled that when he came to Belfast in the late 1920s and proposed that he should investigate the Ulster megalithic tombs, he was told that 'everything that could be learnt about them had already been discovered, and that excavation would be fruitless'.[86] He believed that 'south-west Scotland must have been involved in the transmission of culture to and from north-eastern Ireland in Neolithic times'.[87] He carried out excavations on the megalithic monuments of Ulster with the archaeologist and publisher Oliver Davies.

A survey of types of megaliths and their distribution was undertaken as part of the general field-survey of antiquities organised by the Belfast Naturalists' Field Club. Twenty-four examples of 'horned cairns' were identified, with 500 megaliths identified in Northern Ireland. Evans claimed that 'horned cairns constitute a very significant and early element in the megalithic civilization of north-eastern Ireland'.[88] A series of excavations of this type of megalithic tomb began with the investigation of Goward Hill, Co. Down.[89] Evans's paper on 'Archaeological Investigations in Northern Ireland A Summary of Recent Work', was published in 1935. He acknowledged that 'Already much new light has been thrown on several outstanding problems in Northern Irish chronology, e.g. the age of the much-discussed Bann culture'.[90] This was a reference to Movius's excavation at Newferry, Co. Derry in which the excavator concluded that 'the Bann culture, with its blade implements, is basically an indigenous North Irish development', describing it as a Late Neolithic culture dating to the beginning of the second millennium BC.[91]

Evans was not invited to participate in the work of the Harvard Mission in Northern Ireland, which was mediated through the National Museum of Ireland. Mahr had sidelined the universities, in particular Macalister at UCD and he was then sidelining Evans at QUB. In Northern Ireland, Mahr dealt directly with the curator, A. Deane and assistant curator, J.A.S. Stendall of the Belfast Municipal Museum.[92] Being a pragmatist, however, he was not averse to using Evans's skills when it suited. Evans was allowed to participate in the excavations undertaken under the Unemployment Schemes in the Irish Free State and was approached by Mahr, in 1934, for example, to excavate the megalithic monument and cemetery-cairns at Aghnaskeagh, County Louth.[93] During 1933 and 1934 several excavations were carried out in Northern Ireland under the auspices of the Belfast Municipal Museum. It administered an annual grant of £50 from the Belfast Corporation for prehistoric research in Northern Ireland. Under this scheme Wilfrid Jackson carried out excavations at the raised-beach caves at Ballintoy, Co. Antrim in 1933 and 1934.[94]

Matthew Stout considers Evans to be an 'Ulster nationalist' who 'contributed to the creation of a national identity for Northern Ireland'.[95] This is not surprising because Evans arrived in 1928 when the border had already been established and his remit in terms of research and excavation was already delimited and defined. Evans acknowledged in his paper 'Archaeology in Ulster since 1920' that archaeological research in Northern Ireland and in the Republic was 'quickened by political self-consciousness'.[96] However, this insight did not stop him from clinging to his own geographical determinism with regard to Northern Ireland and dismissing the work of archaeologists in the Republic of Ireland decades later because of what he perceived to be an ultra-nationalist ideology influenced by Sinn Féin policies:

Southern Ireland has experienced a kind of Sinn Féin movement in prehistoric studies, and archaeologists, seeking the sources of new cultures, have looked for lines of diffusion coming from Iberia, untainted by English contacts. Northern Ireland has remained more British, and cultural change has been attributed to contacts with and successive invasions from the larger Island. These different attitudes, apparently reflecting differing political outlooks, may truly reflect the facts behind politics, geographical reality.[97]

While the Irish Free State (and later the Republic of Ireland) would claim the six counties as its territory, even did so under its constitution, the Northern Irish state was not making similar claims, culturally or politically, of territory south of the border. Therefore, it is to be expected that Evans, in what Stout refers to as his 'Ulster exceptionalism',[98] would cling to, what he perceived to be, the life raft of British archaeology. This cultural distancing between the archaeology north and south of the border was an expression of the political climate of the times. It influenced interpretation. For example, Evans believed that there were two entry points for megalithic tombs: 'The two main entrances used by the megalithic builders were the Boyne Valley [County Meath] and Carlingford Lough [on the border between Northern Ireland and the Republic of Ireland] and no doubt this contributed to the enduring distinction between north and south'.[99]

Stout accused Evans of having a 'preconceived notion' about the two entry points for megalith builders which influenced his research on the Ulster court cairns.[100] Ruaidhrí de Valera, in his paper on the court cairns, published in 1960, suggested an entry point for these megaliths on the north Mayo coast.[101] Evans responded to this idea by saying de Valera had 'preconceived notions'.[102]

In the 1930s, the Harvard archaeologists, Adolf Mahr, Macalister and Evans all had their own ideas about what constituted Celtic Ireland. As all were practising archaeologists the inherent political nature of the subject with which they were engaged could scarcely be avoided. All of these archaeologists were products of their time and various political situations. They were interpreting past cultural worlds and creating new ones simultaneously to reflect their current political realities. The establishment of the political border prepared the ground for cultural battle in the 1920s and 1930s. The Harvard Mission excavations were central to this process. With the onset of the Troubles in Northern Ireland in the late 1960s Evans's work became more entrenched and more provocative, his contemporaries in the Republic of Ireland more Anti-British, pro-European and pro-American. Evans complained that 'one detects a reluctance on the part of the Dublin school to admit that Ireland was ever civilized from Britain'.[103] He wrote that to those 'Irishmen whose eyes are glazed with the glory of Celtic Christiandom', Ireland was 'the centre of Atlantic Europe'.[104] In his view the reality was a physical and geographical one: 'It is in the north-east that Ireland's connections with Britain are oldest, closest and most enduring; and if we turn to geological history, whether to the remote pre-Cambrian and Primary or to the Tertiary and Quaternary periods, it is in Ulster that the physical relations between the two islands can be most clearly discerned'.[105]

Evans had a broad view of history and was multidisciplinary in his approach to the past. He wrote that 'It is part of my purpose to show how history can profitably co-operate with these sister subjects [geography, anthropology and archaeology] in regional research'.[106] He was also interested in the study of folklife, which he regarded as 'part of history in another sense, for it inspired nationalist revivals in many European countries'.[107] He believed in the cross-fertilisation of ideas and that the ideas about purity and uniformity of race and culture were false. He admired the work of Childe and Fleure, whose student he had been.[108] In his book *The Personality of Ireland* Evans quotes Fleure as stating that geography, history and anthropology are a 'trilogy to be broken only with severe loss of truth'.[109]

## The Importance of Collectors to Archaeology in Northern Ireland

In 1934, the quest for the earliest Irishman was shifted by the Harvard Mission to Northern Ireland and from a focus on the recovery of evidence for the existence of Palaeolithic to Mesolithic man. Excavations were carried out at Glenarm, Cushendun and Curran Point at Larne, all in Co. Antrim; Rough Island on Strangford Lough, Co. Down; and Newferry, Co. Derry. Evidence of the earliest human handiwork had already been found at the Mesolithic site of Cushendun, County Antrim. However, prior to the arrival of the Harvard Mission, and with the exception of work carried out by Evans and his team in the 1930s, little had been done in terms of scientific excavations. R.A.S. Macalister was not impressed by the archaeologists from Northern Ireland and wrote that only a few had 'made contributions of value to the science'. Macalister, like Earnest A. Hooton, disapproved of collectors and dismissed them as 'an unmitigated curse to archaeology'.[110] This was because of the commercial aspect which he considered to be to the detriment of the scientific subject of archaeology. He was of the opinion that the only legitimate place for important antiquities was in a public museum and took the rather harsh view that 'to make antiquities merely the sport of a collector is to degrade them'.[111] Prior to the arrival of the Harvard Mission attempts to trace the origin and development of the Irish Stone Age were based largely on typology and the study of collections. Movius, echoing Hooton, was of the opinion that 'the archaeologist must regard traits functionally and not fall into the pitfall of the typologist, who observes them as isolated abstractions'.[112] He believed that an attempt should be made to explain why tools evolved, what they were used for, how they were made and their function in assisting man to control his environment. In his opinion 'even more important than the typology of a culture is its chronological position and its relation to comparable developments in other regions'.[113]

But some collectors were diligent. W.J. Knowles, the famous antiquary and collector from Ballymena, was described by Evans as 'a serious student and a pioneer of scientific archaeology' whose material was generally well documented.[114] Knowles was famous for his discovery of the axe-factory site at Tievebulliagh, Co. Antrim in 1902. Despite the fact that he had no training as an archaeologist Knowles wrote about a diverse range of archaeological sites and artefacts including souterrains, crannógs, bronzes, amulets, beads, sepulchral pottery, spindle-whorls, leather and wood remains from bogs.[115] He published papers in the *Journal of the Royal Society of Antiquaries of Ireland*, the *Proceedings of the Royal Irish Academy* and in the *Ulster Journal of Archaeology*. Papers authored by him were read at the British Association for the Advancement of Science in Dublin, Belfast, Glasgow, Liverpool, Southport, Sheffield and York. He was a Fellow of the Royal Society of Antiquaries of Ireland and served as a Vice-President between 1897 and 1900. He was a member of the Royal Irish Academy and of the Belfast Naturalists' Field Club and a Fellow of the Royal Anthropological Institute, London. The Knowles collection, estimated at between 32,000 and 50,000 objects, was auctioned in 866 lots at Sothebys in 1924 and its contents widely dispersed. Mesolithic studies in Ireland owed much to collectors in the nineteenth and early twentieth century, before the advent of scientific excavation and the recognition of the Mesolithic as a period in Irish archaeology.[116] Peter Woodman, in his book *The Mesolithic in Ireland: Hunter-Gatherers in an Insular Environment*, acknowledged that 'the larger portion of the material which can be considered to be Mesolithic in date or tradition is that gathered by collectors'.[117] Waddell described Knowles's main contribution to archaeology as 'probably to Stone Age studies' but chided him as 'an assiduous if horrifyingly destructive explorer' of the sandhills at Whitepark Bay, Co. Antrim, and Portstewart, Co. Derry.[118] According to

Movius, Knowles was 'the first archaeologist to publish a clear statement regarding the relative antiquity of the two fundamental series of stone implements from Northern Ireland'.[119]

In 1909 Nina F. Layard of the Prehistoric Society of East Anglia, helped by Knowles and her friend, a Miss Outram, excavated at Larne and recovered 1,200 flints in 16 hours.[120] Curran Point at Larne contained particularly rich deposits. Layard included a drawing of the stratigraphy of the site and two of the implements. She described Larne as 'the battle-field of the Irish anthropologists'.[121] In 1921 Macalister argued that the flints from the site 'conform to a definite type comparable with the Campignian of the Continent, and they can be easily picked out from a pile of miscellaneous Irish flints'.[122] The Campignian culture was a survival of an older tradition of Mesolithic of Northern and Western Europe and continued as long as flint and stone were utilised as material for tools. Movius considered that the paper authored by George Coffey and Robert Lloyd Praeger in 1904 on the Antrim raised beaches to be 'the most important one that has ever appeared dealing with the Curran deposits [at Larne]'. Coffey and Praeger considered Larne to be a workshop or factory site and dated the implements to the Neolithic.[123] At the time of the publication of their paper the Mesolithic in Ireland was not widely recognised as a period. In Movius's view this meant that 'the true significance of the archaeological material in question was not appreciated'.[124]

In his use of a functionalist approach to the study of the Irish Mesolithic, Movius considered that 'Stone Age archaeology takes on a new and more comprehensive character, and falls in with the human sciences, disassociating itself from the more definitely subjective approach of the taxonomic disciplines'. [125] While the large collection of artefacts recovered at Larne had to be dealt with in as systematic a way as possible, Movius urged caution on what he termed 'categorical pronouncements' of the taxonomists. He quoted Rouse: 'Culture does not consist of artifacts. The latter are merely the results of culturally conditioned behaviour performed by the artisan'.[126] Typological categories, according to Movius were arbitrary, subjective and inexact and should not be overemphasised in the interpretation of cultures.[127] In his report he noted that new implements had been devised 'in response to the exigencies of the new environmental conditions'.[128] In a letter dated 3 December 1935 Hencken referred to Praeger's unhappiness with the geological work of Movius at Larne.[129] Movius was being criticised for digging a site dug twice before, once by Praeger and Coffey and a second time by the Belfast Naturalists' Field Club.[130] However, during the 1935 season alone the Harvard Mission recovered over 5,500 artefacts. In 1953 Movius published an article in the *Ulster Journal of Archaeology* on the history of previous research carried out at Larne, County Antrim in order to place the 1935 excavation in its proper historical context.[131]

## The Key to the Irish Stone Age

The Harvard Mission excavated at Cushendun in County Antrim in 1934. That same year it was reported to Hooton that 'the result of this excavation was the key to the Irish Stone Age'.[132] This conclusion was also reported in the *Irish Times* in an article entitled 'Hidden History', in which it stated that the Harvard Mission was 'doing nothing but good in its visits to Ireland, and its work for us deserves our very best thanks'.[133] Hencken explained that the cultural sequence of this period was for the first time found in a series of stratified deposits which 'illustrated with remarkable clarity the geological changes in the region since the Ice Age'. There were eight strata dating from late Pleistocene times to the present, and four of these contained flint tools. The earliest layer containing a tool assemblage dated to c. 6000 BC, and 'must be regarded as the earliest human handiwork in Ireland'. The discovery, for the first time in Ireland, of four previously known cultures in definite stratigraphic sequence made the site, in Hencken's view essential to the interpretation of the Irish Stone Age.[134] Knud Jessen, the Danish botanist and quaternary geologist, examined the site, declaring that it was 'one of the most important post-glacial sections in Western Europe'.[135]

The final report was published by Movius under the auspices of the Royal Irish Academy in 1941.[136] One of main results of the excavation was 'the recognition of a new Mesolithic culture in North-East Ireland – the Larnian'.[137] In Movius's view, this happened because the areas of North-East Ireland and South-West Scotland constituted a 'cultural pool' where the survival of Upper Palaeolithic tradition led to the development of a new Mesolithic culture.[138] He argued that in the late Mesolithic period there was divergence and the transgression of the Litorina Sea permanently separated the two areas, resulting in a distinct culture which could be described as 'an independent Mesolithic complex'.[139] He extrapolated that there was an ensuing 'natural growth of homogeneous native culture'.[140] This concept allowed for the native culture to be dominant while also being culturally enriched by foreign ideas.

Movius's examination of Larne was as 'a living, functioning organism, and not a conglomeration of isolated traits and techniques making stone tools'.[141] He believed that it was the flint resources at Larne which attracted settlers to the area during the Stone Age. However, he did not interpret the archaeology in a very narrow nationalist way and traced the British associations. Despite his view that the island of Ireland was one cultural area, he did not adopt an isolationist approach. He wrote about his own attitude as follows: 'The writer, trained as an archaeologist and approaching the problem from the purely objective viewpoint of an outsider, sees no valid reason for doubting an intimate relationship between Britain and Ireland on the one hand and Northern Europe on the other during Late-Glacial and Early Post-Glacial times'.[142] Movius had no problem in identifying the descendants of these original Early Post-Glacial settlers in 'certain sections of Ireland at the present day'.[143] He wisely did not mention which section of the population he was referring to. In 1935 Hencken had advised Movius that 'in differences of opinion about controversial matters in Ireland it is extremely foolish to make any definite statement'.[144] Movius was of the opinion that North-East Ireland and South-West Scotland, where Upper Palaeolithic stock survived after the retreat of the ice, could be interpreted as 'an outgrowth of the Creswellian of Southern Britain, under influence from the Azilian of the Continent, as well as environmental factors'.[145] The Creswellian was a British late Upper Palaeolithic industry. The Azilian industry was the final Palaeolithic or initial Mesolithic of southwestern Europe, first identified by Piette in 1887 at Le Mas D'Azil. Movius also believed that climate and geological features affected the diffusion of ideas as freedom of movement, settlement patterns, lifestyle and use of materials would be affected by them.

The excavations in Northern Ireland were attracting plenty of attention. In a letter to Hencken dated 19 August 1935, Movius expressed his panic at the prospect of a visit to the Larne site from local and international dignitaries and academics: 'My heart sank however, when I saw two Charabancs and a fleet of private cars come streaming out the Curran Point'.[146] A week later, Movius informed Hencken that Dr D.A. Chart from the Ancient Monuments Advisory Committee of Northern Ireland was coming to visit the site on Thursday and that Praeger was coming on Wednesday. Movius looked forward to 'going over the ground with him [Praeger] and getting a great deal which I am uncertain of, straightened out'.[147] On 16 August 1935 Henry Cairns Lawlor visited the site. Lawlor informed Movius that Blake Whelan 'gave a most valuable report and high endorsement of the work, and the way it was being carried out' at the Ancient Monuments Advisory Committee meeting. Lawlor was President of the Belfast Natural History and Philosophical Society in 1934 and 1935 and has been described as 'an amateur, but by no means dilettante, archaeologist during the transition from antiquarianism to scientific understanding of field monuments and their associated finds'.[148]

Movius's book *The Irish Stone Age: Its Chronology, Development and Relationships*, published by Cambridge University Press in 1942, was inspired by J.G.D. Clark's *The Mesolithic Settlement of Northern Europe* published also by Cambridge University Press in 1936.[149] Like Clark, Movius considered it very important for the archaeologist 'to strive for as detailed a reconstruction as possible of the geographical setting of prehistoric cultures'.[150] However, Movius acknowledged that it was Whelan who first suggested the term 'Northern Irish Mesolithic' to describe the assemblages from the raised beaches. Movius noted that Whelan was happy to place all his sites at the disposal of Harvard for consideration and that 'It has been largely Mr Whelan's unselfish attitude that has led to the successful results of many of the excavations'.[151] In 1935, Movius had expressed the opinion that Larne was 'a most important and impressive site'[152] and later, described it as 'one of the richest localities of its kind in Western Europe.'[153] Liam S. Gogan wrote to Movius on 19 June 1936, stating that 'your contribution to the Irish Stone Age is certainly of great importance.'[154]

In his book review published in the *Journal of the County Louth Archaeological Society* Estyn Evans expressed his opinion that 'It is inevitable, in a work embracing the methods and evidence of so many sciences – geology, glaciology, climatology, palaeobotany and archaeology – that specialists will find something to quarrel with in their own subjects'. However, he congratulated Movius on 'a work of synthesis which appears at a convenient resting-period in the quickening tempo of archaeological research.'[155] In a further article on Movius's book published in the *Geographical Review* Evans observed that 'the field work was confined to Northern Ireland, the bridgehead by which prehistoric cultures no less than historic found their way into the island from Great Britain'.[156] Evans also co-authored a review with Frank Mitchell, published in the *Ulster Journal of Archaeology*, in which it was suggested that the book should have been titled *The Stone Age of North-Eastern Ireland*.[157]

Joseph Raftery in his review, published in the *JRSAI*, complained about Movius's 'pre-occupation with the north-east of the country'. He queried the use of the term 'Larnian' 'to describe the Irish Mesolithic and regarded it 'to be somewhat forced'. However, he regarded Movius's book as 'a very fine work' of 'absolute importance'.[158] Macalister also expressed reservations about the term 'Larnian' in his review published in the *Journal of the Galway Archaeological and Historical Society*:

It is to be feared that in the long run this word – like most of the similar territorial designations – will be more of a nuisance than anything else. The tools on the one hand, are too diverse *inter se*, and on the other one too closely cognate with flints from sites outside of Ireland, to justify any one in setting them up as a self-contained and homogenous culture.[159]

Peter Woodman in his book, *The Mesolithic in Ireland*, published in 1978, also explored the problems with terminology inherent in Mesolithic studies. He noted that the distribution of material was a product of the history of the study of the Mesolithic. His research showed that the concept of an initial occupation in the extreme North-Eastern corner of Ireland was no longer tenable: 'The false equation of the Irish Mesolithic with the exploitation of Antrim chalk has totally biased the attitudes of workers outside the North East. It is possible that Mesolithic man may have been present to some extent in the whole of Ireland'.[160] Woodman, however, praised the results of the Harvard Mission excavations which made available 'a large quantity of material which could be placed in a stratigraphic succession.' In his view, the chronology devised by Movius for the Irish Mesolithic was 'one of the few independently derived chronologies in Europe.'[161] Woodman argued that there was no archaeological evidence for an 'early Ulster-Scots connection' as there was no dating evidence to prove that man was present in western Scotland earlier than in Ireland. Also, there was no evidence for an early industry from Scotland of a type similar to that found at Mount Sandel, Co. Derry. The samples of the occupation of Mount Sandel (Upper) may have begun as early as 7000 BC.[162] Woodman also points out that early man first arrived in Ireland in Early Post-Glacial times, that there was no land bridge and that he probably arrived in a skin boat.[163]

## 'New Aspects and Problems in Irish Prehistory'

The tensions between northern and southern archaeologists manifested in the 1930s can be seen in the reaction to Adolf Mahr's paper 'New Aspects and Problems in Irish Prehistory' which was his address to the Prehistoric Society in 1937.[164] This 'magesterial survey of Irish prehistory' was described officially in the Irish Free State in glowing terms: 'This is really the most authoritative statement available and covers the whole field of Irish

Archaeology to date and its connections with those of Britain and Europe'.[165] Not all archaeologists were in awe of Mahr's publication. Oliver Davies in a review of Mahr's paper in the *Ulster Journal of Archaeology* for 1939 considered that 'the time was not yet ripe for a general summary of Irish prehistory, considering that scientific excavation hardly started before recent years, and that the number of workers is still disappointingly small'.[166] While Davies acknowledged 'the great powers of research' which Mahr displayed in his paper he also regarded him as 'rather out of touch with the latest developments in the six Counties'. Davies considered his own criticisms of Mahr's paper to be 'additional scientific contributions'.[167] While seeing some merit in Mahr's theories about a proposed 'Riverford' culture, Davies was of the opinion that it 'made his [Mahr's] account of other phases of Mesolithic life disproportionately meagre'.[168] He referred to the fact that Mahr had little to say about the 'raised-beach peoples of north-east Ireland'.[169] He also complained that Mahr had neglected the important material from Island McHugh, some of which was on display in the Belfast Museum. He claimed that the evidence to prove that it was a Neolithic crannóg that was unearthed in 1937 and that this would require Mahr's own interpretations with regard to crannógs to be treated 'with caution'.[170] Davies considered Mahr's account of horned cairns to be out of date because the latter did not take into account recent excavations and publications undertaken in Ulster. Mahr was also considered to be erroneous in his statement that horned cairns contained many burials, as some of the tombs had only one or two. Other criticisms of Mahr's paper included his failure to comprehend the northward extension of wedge-shaped graves and his 'limited grasp of Ulster Neolithic pottery'. Davies also regarded Mahr's information on stone circles and alignments as 'meagre'.[171] With regard to Mahr's account of the Iron Age, Davies noted the omission of a probable urn-field near Glenshane County Derry, and some Hallstatt pottery at Goward. He also complained that Mahr had little to say about the interaction of Ireland with Roman Britain but acknowledges that 'there is not yet much evidence for Roman influences in Irish culture'.[172] Davies, however, accepted his own harshness in reviewing Mahr's paper in his statement 'In general, mud-slinging is a sport for those reviewers who have little to criticise'.[173]

Mud-slinging is perhaps an apt way of describing the warring factions in archaeological interpretation; Evans and his followers in Northern Ireland and the 'Dublin School'. This cultural confrontation in archaeological terms, expressed in academic sniping, was perhaps a microcosm of political realities, with ultra sensitivity and point-scoring on both sides. Of course, it must be realised that the cultural in Ireland is invariably political and often the precursor of political action. But the cultural also transcends the political. Indeed, this is the point made by Virginia Crossman and Dympna McLoughlin in their article 'A Peculiar Eclipse: E. Estyn Evans and Irish Studies', in which they defend the reputation of Estyn Evans and his work. They include a quote from D.W. Meinig who wrote about the geographer as artist and noted that 'all pedantic compartmentalisations of art and science dissolve within the creative individual'.[174] A transcendence of politics results in the acceptance of a culturally diverse past for Ireland.

The poet Paul Durcan, an admirer of Evans's work, recounted the time when he read the latter's book *The Personality of Ireland*, published in 1973, and how it enabled him 'to jettison much of my own cant and prejudice and to articulate suspicions I had been having for many years about the murderous mythologies of an Irish racial purity'.[175] As *The Personality of Ireland* brings many different themes which Evans had written about together in a readable narrative, it is pertinent to the study of his views which were being formed in the 1930s. In it Evans wrote about his desire for 'a broader and less political view of Irish history'.[176] He expressed concern that 'The patriotic Irishman's picture of the Irish past tends to be coloured by his hopes for the future, and by the dream of Irish unity'.[177] While Evans is correct in this assertion his statement could also be paraphrased and applied to patriotic Ulstermen dreaming of a past which involved Irish disunity and a continued union with Britain. He was particularly critical of Patrick Pearse's use of the heroic tales of Ulster to support his pleas for blood sacrifice and for the glorification of violence in the pursuit of political ends.[178] The concepts of cultural continuity and homogeneity were a feature of the nationalist school of Irish archaeology. Evans was a firm believer in cultural diversity, but perhaps had a blind spot with regard to the political nature of his own work.

## Ulster Journal of Archaeology

The Harvard Mission archaeologists took an interest in the revival of the *Ulster Journal of Archaeology*. Hencken wrote to Movius on 21 July 1937:

> It would probably please them if you offered them a paper. They are all the same old crowd, Carmody, Whelan, Deane and all the other people, that we know up there. I don't know whether you would want to risk a paper in their hands, but it would depend on whether you thought it was worth it to help us keep the flints.[179]

On 4 August 1937 Movius wrote to Hencken about the Rough Island, County Down report that he would tell Liam Price, editor of the *Journal of the Royal Society of Antiquaries of Ireland*, that 'they had asked for it in the Black North'.[180] In correspondence with Movius Adolf Mahr also refers to the 'archaeology of the black north'.[181] Movius considered the implications of submitting a paper to the *UJA*: 'I will leave it here on your desk, and you can send it out, whether to Price or the Ulster Journal, whichever seems the wiser move. As for myself, I think that it will be quite safe in the hands of the Ulsterites'.[182] On 14 September 1937 Hencken sent a radiogram from Stockholm to Movius noting that Stendall, the assistant curator of the Belfast Museum 'booed heavily upon the idea of the journal, said it was bound to fail'.[183] Evans promoted the idea that the *Ulster Journal of Archaeology* abided by the principle that 'archaeology should not be the handmaid of any political propaganda'.[184] He expressed strong disapproval of the stance taken by Grahame Clark on Irish archaeology in his book *Archaeology and Society*. Clark expressed the view that 'it is hardly possible to discuss any major problem of Irish archaeology without implicitly demonstrating the essential unity of the country and emphasising the artificiality of the partition'.[185] Evans found these and other remarks to be 'unworthy of a scientist' while acknowledging that 'official intervention in archaeology leads to concentration on those aspects which have immediate propaganda-value'.[186] While this is undoubtedly true, Matthew Stout attributes a political motivation to Evans's own work, also. In his view of the early editorials in the *Ulster Journal of Archaeology* he argued that Evans had established it as 'an organ of the British establishment in Ulster'.[187] In the editorial for 1939 it was announced that 'It is with much pleasure that we are able to announce the consent of Lord Charlemont to act as chairman of the Journal Committee'[188] Lord Charlemont, Chairman of the Ancient Monuments Advisory Council replaced Dean Carmody, on the latter's death. It is no surprise that in Northern Ireland a titled man was invited to become patron whereas in the Irish Free State the royal patronage was dispensed with by the Royal Society of Antiquaries of Ireland and General Eoin O'Duffy was invited to be patron.[189]

In his article written with Davies and Blake Whelan entitled 'The Celts in archaeology', published in the *Ulster Journal of Archaeology* in 1939, according to Stout, 'Evans set out to minimize the perceived Celtic influence in Ireland'.[190] Evans acknowledged that 'It is difficult to identify the various archaeological invasions with the Celtic groups which we know linguistically or by tradition.'[191] He believed that the Gaelic tongue was introduced to

Ulster between 700 and 900 BC. Native craftsmanship was 'refertilised', which resulted in new types of weapons, tools and pottery which were subsequently diffused throughout the rest of the country. He concluded that 'This is the first immigration attested by archaeology as on a sufficient scale to warrant its identification with the advent of the Celts'.[192] However, he also noted that artefacts of the developed Celtic style including brooches, spear-heads and massive iron swords were rare in Ireland. He reckoned that the ancient civilisation of Ireland survived and that 'Ireland maintained little, if any, contact with the centres of Celtic culture on the Continent'.[193] Evans believed that 'the enduring essentials of Irish civilisation and the basic element of the Irish population are pre-Celtic'.[194] Stout's view was that 'Evans refuted the "celticism" which is invoked as the foundation of Irish national identity: for Evans, Celtic Ireland became the non-enduring, non-essential aspect of the island's past'.[195] Earlier Stout referred to Evans's life-long preoccupation with a search for continuity'.[196] Refuting the Celticism of Ireland and searching for roots in Pre-Celtic times seem to be contradictory. A search for continuity between Pre-Celtic, Celtic and modern times was a feature of Irish nationalist archaeology in the South. By using Pre-Celtic as a synonym for Irish Prehistory before the La Tène-influenced period, Evans is infusing the idea of Celticism into any period in prehistory, prior to the Celtic Iron Age. The idea of Celtic Ireland is a cultural and political idea and not a scientific explanation. Stout's own view with regard to continuity is that 'this belief in continuity in the landscape has had a long and detrimental influence on the study of archaeology and historical geography in Ireland'.[197] Stout finished his paper on Evans by admitting 'This paper has not presented a balanced view of Evans' career in Irish Studies'.[198] However, the author conceded that Evans had become one of the few international figures of his day in Irish studies. Stout refers ominously to 'the darker side of his academic perspective',[199] apparently without realising that the same darkness adhered to archaeology as practised by those with an opposing political perspective to Evans.

It could be argued that Evans's stance on the question of the Celticness of the nation, is in certain respects, overemphasised. This is because, while corroborating archaeological (and therefore scientific) evidence would be welcome it was not the sole arbiter of Celtic identity. Barry Raftery's assertion that 'it is only archaeology which can ultimately shed light on the origins of celticity in Ireland'[200] is only true from an archaeological perspective. A multi-disciplinary approach to the subject is likely to be more productive. It is telling that the School of Celtic Studies in the Dublin Institute for

Advanced Studies, set up by de Valera in 1940, did not include archaeology as a discipline and does not do so to this day. This can be contrasted with the Institute of Irish Studies which was set up in Queen's University Belfast in 1968. Evans became its first director and according to Ann Hamlin 'there could have been no more distinguished or appropriate holder of that position'.[201]

## Dissolving the Border in Prehistory

Stuart Piggott, in his article 'The coming of the Celts: the archaeological argument' wrote of the misunderstandings which may arise 'from the projection of the irrelevant concepts of modern nation-states into prehistoric archaeology'.[202] Hencken, Movius and Mahr practised a prehistory which dissolved the border, whereas Evans practised one which reinforced it. The Harvard Mission, by their presence in the North, challenged Evans's view that a cultural frontier had existed from prehistoric times between North and South. They simply refused to acknowledge any cultural or political frontier. The Harvard Mission, by the extension of its mission into the north, was reclaiming culturally on behalf of the Irish Free State and for Catholic Irish Americans, what was seen as lost territory, and part of the Celtic homeland. While material evidence for the Iron Age Celts may not have been prolific, the establishment of pre-Celtic continuity in the archaeological record would suffice. Grahame Clark in a discussion on Irish archaeology in his book *Archaeology and Society*, commented that 'the free development of archaeological research is the finest imaginable propaganda for the liquidation of partition and the full achievement of Irish nationality'.[203] It is perhaps true that the cultural dissolution of the border would precede the political one. The use of the past to predict the future meant that a United Ireland in Prehistory would pave the way to legitimising one in the future. However, Movius's results did not show that the island of Ireland was one cultural pool in the Mesolithic Period because the Harvard archaeologists did not excavate comparable sites in the Irish Free State.

   In the 1930s, nationalist archaeologists believed that the archaeological evidence from the Neolithic Period onwards showed that Ulster was part of a United Ireland in prehistory and a homogenous cultural zone. Their desire to discover a United Ireland rooted in prehistory mirrored the regionalism of Estyn Evans, which reflected a desire to remain part of Britain. This process, played out through the medium of archaeological interpretations, reflects what Trigger describes in his discussion of Kossinna's work as an 'archaeological attempt to link material culture and identity'.[204] The battle to interpret Irish material culture was a similar undertaking. It was underpinned by rival nationalisms and the desire to create particular identities. While Evans considered the border to be 'culturally productive',[205] the border was seen as a threat and an imposition which could be dissolved at will in prehistory by the archaeologists of the Irish Free State. This imaginative dissolution of the border in prehistory was an aspiration for the political future of Ireland.

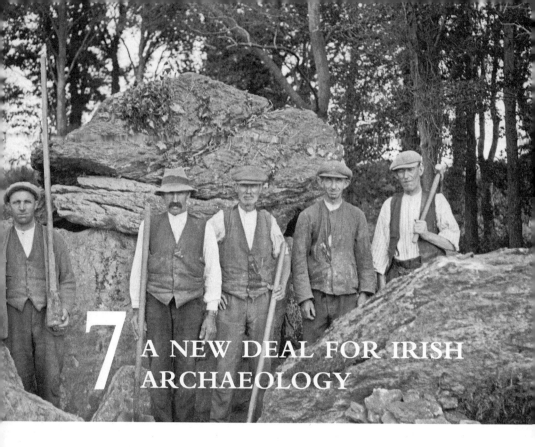

# 7 A NEW DEAL FOR IRISH ARCHAEOLOGY

When the matter of archaeological excavation first came up in June 1934, we asked for fuller information, in which 'archaeological' was defined as being 'prehistoric, proto-historic, etc' and we naturally assumed that the work would not relate to anything that belonged to a period definitely later than the dawn of history.[1]

– Arthur D. Codling, Dept of Finance to H.G. Leask, 6 September 1938

## A New Deal for Irish Archaeology

Labour costs for some of the Harvard Mission excavations were paid by the Irish Free State (Relief of Unemployment) Scheme for Archaeological Research,[2] administered by the Office of Public Works in collaboration with the National Museum. These included the important excavations of Lagore

Crannóg in Co. Meath, Knocknalappa Crannóg in Co. Clare, Kilgreany Cave in Co. Waterford and Gallen Priory, Co. Offaly – the results of which have been discussed in previous chapters.[3] Other sites were investigated as an extension of the Harvard Research programme and a snapshot and not a comprehensive account of the Unemployment Schemes for archaeological research will be given in this chapter. Adolf Mahr included a list of sites excavated between 1934 and 1937 in his 1937 address to the Prehistoric Society.[4] In Leask's opinion, the most productive sites excavated between 1934 and 1938 included Lagore Crannóg in Co. Meath, Lough Gur megaliths and Temair Érann/Cush in Co. Limerick, Castleknock and Drimnagh in Co. Dublin, Gallen Priory in Co. Offaly and Garranes in Co. Cork.[5]

The cemetery site at Castleknock is used in this chapter as a case study to demonstrate how sites were selected for the Unemployment Schemes and the administrative process involved. In the 1930s archaeology was becoming public property rather than exclusively an academic or scholarly pursuit. Public attitudes to archaeology were being formed through the medium of the press. The case of Castleknock gives an insight into Adolf Mahr's view of what constituted value, culturally and financially, with regard to archaeological excavation of sites that were not prehistoric or rich in artefacts. The tensions over the excavations at Castleknock reflect the tensions between the practitioners of archaeology and history in the 1930s with regard to sites dating to the historic period. Ó Riordáin's extensive programme of research excavations under the Unemployment Schemes, particularly those at Lough Gur, Cush and Garranes matched the work of the Harvard Mission in terms of scale of excavations, skill, technique, knowledge, innovation and attention to detail. The Lough Gur excavations were to continue in the following decades. Ultimately, Ó Ríordáin was to become 'one of the formative figures in twentieth-century Irish archaeology' and 'a major figure in European archaeology'.[6] Despite the fact that he had worked in the National Museum, the priority for Ó Ríordáin was not the acquisition of artefacts but the scientific recovery of data in order to interpret the past.

Labbacallee, the first wedge tomb ever excavated in Ireland, was funded under the Unemployment Schemes. In 1938 Howard Kilbride-Jones excavated the Neolithic burial site at Drimnagh, Co. Dublin also under the Unemployment Schemes. This was a state rescue excavation and the site was chosen in order 'to record for the sake of posterity an impressive monument which was daily in danger of destruction'.[7] Other sites such as Aghnaskeagh B, Co. Louth and Lissard, Co. Limerick were considered important to research on the Celts during the 1930s.[8] An Early Iron Age 'Hallstatt' urn was discovered at Aghnaskeagh B and interpreted as 'the earliest and purest indication of Iron Age intrusion into Ireland yet discovered'.[9] Hallam L. Movius believed that the results of trial excavations carried out on one of the very low mounds in Lissard, Co. Limerick in 1934 was 'of first-rate importance in establishing the existence of an Irish urn-field',[10] regarded as evidence for the spread of the Celts across Europe. However, subsequent detailed excavations on barrows in the area by Ó Ríordáin did not yield the hoped-for results.[11] Sites were only considered for funding if it was believed that the anticipated results would add some significant new information. Funding for the Unemployment Schemes was also allocated to Quaternary Research Committee projects such as Ballybetagh bog, investigated by the Danish Mission in 1934.[12]

In his broadcast message to the Irish diaspora in 1932, de Valera made the following comments about the social problem of unemployment:

> In the Irish Free State, as in America, there is an economic crisis. Whatever be the causes of such a crisis in this State it is going to call forth all the energies of both the Government and the people to provide adequate remedies. Our most urgent problem is that of unemployment and my colleagues and I intend to work without ceasing until that gravest of evils has been eliminated.[13]

The following year, in 1933, John Maynard Keynes, an active eugenicist[14] and one of the foremost economists of the era, came to Dublin to deliver the Finlay lecture on the topic of 'National Self-Sufficiency'. He said that 'If I was an Irishman, I should find much to attract me in the economic outlook of your present government towards greater self-sufficiency'.[15] He believed that 'private enterprise needs to be supplemented by public action if full employment is to be maintained'.[16] De Valera's public action included the setting up of the Unemployment Schemes for archaeological research in 1934. This initiative was modelled on Franklin D. Roosevelt's New Deal archaeology programme, to address the chronic rates of unemployment associated with the Great Depression (1929–1941). It was organised by the US Government who sent ordinary citizens who were unemployed and had no knowledge of archaeology to work on archaeological sites across the country.[17] The description of the status of American archaeologists at that time by Bernard K. Means is instructive and parallels the position of the profession in Ireland:

At the beginning of the Great Depression, archaeologists were few in number, had access to limited funding and were scattered across the U.S. in museums, institutions of higher learning, government agencies and local or state avocational archaeological or historical societies. Archaeology was slowly emerging from its antiquarian roots and many individuals were amateurs with a passion for the past but little formal training.[18]

Archaeology was very suited to the requirements of work relief programmes as large numbers of unskilled workers could be quickly employed for long periods as they were 'shovel ready'. Most of the funds could be spent on labour and equipment cost very little.[19] In Ireland the wage rate for labourers on archaeological sites was 'the county rate for agricultural labourers'.[20] In practice, an effort was made to keep the rate down below this figure. In a memo dated 6 March 1933 from the Department of Finance, it was recorded that 'in the majority of cases these efforts are successful'.[21] The sites selected represented great value for money and in Ó Ríordáin's opinion the results 'brilliantly justified the expenditure'.[22]

Macalister recognised that the excavations served a dual purpose – they 'not only resulted in valuable finds, but proved a considerable asset in absorbing the unemployed'.[23] The selection of sites was primarily defined by the tenets of culture-history and the political needs of the state. This was the first time that archaeological excavations were not just carried out for cultural reasons, but were used by the government in a broader social and economic context, becoming effectively an instrument of economic and cultural protectionism. The excavations initially took place with the backdrop of the Economic War between Britain and Ireland, waged between 1932 and 1938. Cultural protectionism involved state-controlled excavations to retrieve knowledge crucial as scientific evidence for the cultural identity of the state as Celtic and Christian. In the process, each site served as an important training ground for a new generation of scientific archaeologists.

## Archaeology on a Shoestring

During the period 1932 to 1937 a total of forty-three scientific excavations were undertaken in the Irish Free State.[24] Many of these had their labour expenses defrayed under the Unemployment Schemes. As a cost-cutting exercise, volunteers were encouraged to participate in the work. Information was gleaned by the accurate planning and retrieval of artefacts, the careful recording of data about the morphology of megalithic tombs and the use of the new technique of pollen-analysis for dating purposes. Irish archaeologists received on-site training in scientific methods and large-scale excavation techniques. T.D. Kendrick excavated Gallen and Ó Ríordáin undertook the important excavations of Lough Gur and Cush in Co. Limerick.

One reason why Mahr was elected as President of the Prehistoric Society in 1937 was that he had experience in Ireland of using unemployed labour on sites.[25] Between the years 1934 and 1938 twenty-nine scientific excavations were carried out specifically under the Unemployment Schemes. In 1938, the *Commissioners of Public Works* reported that:

> Almost every one of the excavations carried out under the Employment Schemes and the joint direction of the Office of Public Works and the National Museum since 1934 has yielded facts of value in the building up of a picture of the life and customs of Ireland in prehistoric and less remote times.[26]

Between the years 1934 to 1939 the total expenditure on Unemployment Scheme excavations was £6,490.[27] This archaeology on a shoestring was tightly controlled by Adolf Mahr and the archaeological conundrums which he wished to answer generally took precedence. However, there were exceptions as the OPW, represented by H.G. Leask, was also involved in the process.

De Valera, President of the Executive Council at the time, took a keen interest in the work. Notes were sent to him on the excavations in progress, together with directions for locating the sites and half-inch road maps showing the featured sites.[28] Civil servants queried the necessity of sending all the excavation reports to de Valera.[29] Information from them was also to be included in a statement that was being prepared for transmission to the National Monuments Advisory Council (NMAC).[30] Two reports on the progress and results of excavations, prepared by Mahr, were furnished to de Valera in September and October 1934.[31] Despite government support for archaeological endeavour, Mahr was still worried about the lack of resources within the National Museum to carry out archaeological fieldwork:

> It is impossible for the limited staff and with the limited travelling facilities at the disposal of the Museum to cover the whole country with field work activity unless there is definite reason for going to any

one individual spot: we simply had to wait until an opportunity offered itself.[32]

The Harvard Mission presented itself as the opportunity which the National Museum was waiting for. Mahr was satisfied that the Harvard archaeologists were 'anxious to fit in in our scheme as an enlargement of their scheme'.[33] Mahr was only interested in involving the Harvard Mission in the Unemployment Schemes provided it did not compromise their financial investment in Irish archaeology. His views were stated thus:

> I have made it perfectly plain to Dr. Hugh O'Neill Hencken, the leader of the Mission, and to Dr. Alexander Scott, the Director of the Peabody Museum, who visited us a month ago, that any such extension of the scheme cannot be contemplated in fairness to the Free State Government if it meant that in future seasons Harvard will not put up the same sum as it spent hitherto in the two previous seasons and in the present year.[34]

Harvard University had agreed to put up the same amount of money which had been spent in previous seasons; £770 in 1932, £1000 in 1933 and £1200 in 1934.[35] They had also agreed that the Unemployment Schemes would be additional to and not a substitute for their financial efforts. In Mahr's view this had the advantage 'that the money can be spent in a reasonable way whilst it entails very little expenditure other than the relief of unemployment'.[36]

Mahr harboured ambitions to make the Irish archaeological programme undertaken in the 1930s of international importance. He hoped, for example, to entice Dr Leonard Woolley, excavator of the Biblical city of Ur of the Chaldees, to participate. Describing Woolley as 'the most famous excavator in the world', Mahr wrote with evident pride that 'it reflects creditably upon the importance which is attached abroad to Irish archaeology that for a considerable time he was expecting to come himself'.[37] In any event, Woolley did not excavate in Ireland because of publication commitments. He had already visited Ballinderry 1 crannóg at the invitation of Adolf Mahr in 1932.[38] Mahr succeeded in coaxing T.D. Kendrick, Deputy Director of the British Museum, to come to Ireland at his own private expense to supervise an excavation 'as a kind gesture towards our Museum'.[39] Kendrick was described by Mahr as 'one of the leading archaeologists in Europe, a skilled excavator' who had 'always been extremely interested in the problems of Irish antiquities'.[40] One of Kendrick's interests was the contribution of Ireland to the creation of medieval art in the 'crucial centuries in which the

Hibernian style of the Early Christian Period came into being'. He was also described by Mahr as being 'particularly interested in the dark centuries at the transition from Pagan to Early Christian Ireland'.[41] Mahr was aware of how archaeological work in Ireland would be viewed internationally and Kendrick's participation in the excavations would show 'to what extent the work of our Museum is appreciated by our colleagues on the other side of the Irish Sea'.[42] Kendrick eventually undertook the excavation of Gallen Priory, Co. Offaly, during 1934 and 1935.[43]

Mahr arranged a meeting with Hugh O'Neill Hencken on 11 August 1934 to discuss archaeological sites that might be excavated by Harvard under the Unemployment Schemes. At that meeting it was agreed that Dr Hencken would investigate the Bruree, Co. Limerick, area 'to see if it was important enough to excavate, whether to do it that year and whether Harvard would do the work'.[44] De Valera expressed a personal wish to have the mounds at Bruree excavated, as he had been reared in Bruree by his grandmother, Elizabeth Coll.[45] Hugo V. Flinn of the Department of Finance informed de Valera that 'you will see that things are moving in the direction of an investigation of your favourite spot'.[46] Gold ornaments dating to the Late Bronze Age had been found in the vicinity of Bruree in 1929.[47] Mahr hoped that the excavation at Bruree would 'ultimately solve the problem of the coming into being of what is conventionally called the Hibernian style of the Early Christian Period, and the connection of which with the prehistoric Early Iron Age is still absolutely obscure'.[48]

He was not convinced that the Harvard archaeologists would take on Bruree for excavation as it 'may not be large enough for the American scheme'.[49] He contacted Flinn enclosing an abstract from Hencken who wrote that 'I should not especially want to dig any myself – indeed I should be rather adverse to the idea with crannóg possibilities offering themselves'.[50] Mahr expressed the desire 'to prevent a meaningless squandering of money on poorer sites in Bruree if better sites can be found'.[51] Despite the wishes of de Valera, Mahr diverted the Unemployment Scheme money in this instance to the excavation of Lagore crannóg, as requested by Hencken. De Valera ultimately supported this decision and visited the site in October 1934.

## Public Archaeology: the Case of Castleknock

Castleknock cemetery site is explored in this chapter in the context of the administration of archaeological excavation by the state under the Unemployment Schemes. This involved the control of the selection procedure, the recruitment of personnel, the interpretation of the data within the established state framework, and ultimately the creation of archaeological knowledge. The site was first reported to the Museum in 1937 and was investigated by Micheal Ó hÉanaigh, Assistant Keeper of Irish Antiquities. A report appeared in the *Sunday Independent* on 16 May 1937 describing the discovery of three skeletons and four skulls. Ó hÉanaigh told the reporter that 'It was likely that they were the victims of the plague or "black death."'[52] Mahr explained his disinterest in the site to Sergeant Patrick Kavanagh who reported the find to the museum:

> Human remains of that kind are of scientific interest only if they are associated with discoveries clearly indicating the age of the skeletons. In the absence of such associated finds, the skeletons may be of almost any age and in such cases, we do not as a rule take action.'[53]

Mahr told Kavanagh that the museum was interested in 'antiquarian finds', and 'principally prehistoric pottery as sometimes associated with the internments of a past age.'[54] The site was described in an OPW report as follows:

> At Castleknock, Co. Dublin, a Christian community cemetery probably of about 900 A.D. [was found.] Many skeletons were found which may yield to anthropological examination information of value to be correlated with what is known from other places including Gallen, Offaly a site which produced a great many memorial slabs belonging to the 7th–10th centuries.[55]

Mahr expressed no interest in Castleknock until he received a note from Hencken informing him that burials, a Danish coin and a jet bracelet had been found at the site.[56] Mahr responded by sending a letter to the landowner commending him for his 'laudable intention not to disturb anything which might be of importance to national archaeology' and assuring him that he would send somebody from the museum to examine the site.[57] He subsequently sent Joseph Raftery and Ó Ríordáin to investigate. As a result an excavation by Joseph Raftery was undertaken in June 1938. He was assisted by Gerard A. Hayes McCoy, a historian from Galway and by Eilis MacNéill, daughter of the Early Irish historian, Eoin MacNeill. The skeletal remains were transferred to University College Dublin for a report by Dr E.P. McLoughlin.[58]

Mahr wrote to Harold G. Leask, Inspector of National Monuments informing him that skeletons, an armlet of lignite, a coin, several bronze fragments and arrowheads had been found. He requested that Joseph Raftery be put on the pay roll with a daily payment of 10/-.[59] Leask recommended approval of the excavation of Castleknock cemetery under the Unemployment Schemes and estimated the cost to be approximately £156. This figure included payment to six labourers for one week and twelve labourers for five weeks at 33/- per week as well as wages for two supervisors from the National Museum – Joseph Raftery and Gerard A. Hayes McCoy. The Department of Finance approved the expenditure. Leask wrote to the Manager of the Employment Exchange, Department of Industry and Commerce, looking for lists of men resident in the surrounding rural areas who were in receipt of Unemployment Assistance.[60] Raftery was granted an excavation licence to carry out the work.[61] He employed Michael Masterson, a labourer, who had a cottage adjacent to the site, as a watchman, to protect the site. The excavations commenced on 30 June 1938.

Joseph Raftery's initial report was that eighty-six skeletons had been discovered. All the bones were in 'perfect condition'. The bodies were all extended lying approximately east to west, inhumation being the only rite practised. No coffins were used but in most cases the skulls were protected by small flat side stones and in one instance a small vault of primitive corbelling had protected the face of the corpse. It was Raftery's opinion that the bodies were those of people of a normal community – men, women and children and that there were no indications of a battle or plague. The skulls were large, and in three cases there was a frontal suture, 'a fact which must have condemned their owners to violent headaches in life'. The majority of the children were buried on the western edge of the area. Finds were 'rather meagre' and included bronze pins, amber beads, lignite rings, a bronze shoe buckle and a silver coin of the Anglo-Saxon King Edgar, dated to AD 967. Raftery based his dating of the site on this silver coin, concluding that 'the period from about 900-1,000 AD being the duration of the burial period of the cemetery'.[62]

A *Sunday Independent* headline on 10 July 1938 declared '30 Skeletons in Dublin Field: Only clues a ring and a coin: Public barred from scene: Experts baffled'. Adolf Mahr was interviewed about the 'amazing discovery'. He played down the significance of the site and contradicted the views of Joseph Raftery on dating:

> So far we have found nothing of importance. There has been nothing to establish date, period, or race, and nothing that we have found has thrown any light on the place. They may be skeletons of any period from 5,000 BC to 1938 AD.

The discoveries at Castleknock aroused a lot of interest from the public who contributed to the public debate on archaeology by writing letters to the papers expressing their own opinions on the skeletons. Some suggested plague or cholera as the cause of death of the people in the cemetery.[63] Mahr expressed his own frustration at the interest of the public and the media in the skeletons in an article in the *Irish Press*:

> There really is no significance in their being found and letters and stories in the papers tend to exaggerate the position. Undue publicity merely brings many people to the place who interfere with the workmen … All of the letters appearing in certain Dublin newspapers have been inaccurate. If there were anything historically remarkable about the skeletons the Museum would have published the fact.'[64]

The Department of Finance agreed with Mahr that from an archaeological point of view the site was 'unproductive'.[65] Eoin MacNeill visited the site in the company of Robert Lloyd Praeger on 22 July. He subsequently wrote to Hugo V. Flinn about it, expressing the view that the partial exploration of the cemetery 'would be a disaster'. MacNeill and Praeger believed that the discovery was 'unique not only in Ireland but anywhere in this side of Europe'.[66] Mahr's opinion was that 'from the purely archaeological viewpoint a continuation of the excavation does not appear to be worth while' and called for the filling in of the site so far excavated. However, as it was a Christian cemetery, he thought it should be preserved. He was concerned, however, that the compensation might be prohibitive 'as the land is very good and close to Dublin'.[67] Joseph Raftery did not regard the cemetery as a plague pit; the bodies were found in a single stratum simply because of the position of the underlying rock which would not allow for any other type of burial.[68] Raftery informed Leask that the 'anatomy experts' from the universities who visited the site were of the opinion that further examination 'will not yield anything new'.[69]

A meeting was held on 27 July 1938, attended by Eoin McNeill, Michael V. Duignan of the National Library of Ireland, Price, Raftery and Leask. Hencken was also in attendance even though the Harvard Mission had finished its work in 1936. Leask informed the meeting of the opinions of Mahr and Dr E.P. McLoughlin, an anatomist from UCD, who were unable to attend.[70] A number of decisions were made about the site; the skeletal remains of 266 people were to be treated with spirit and a solution of celluloid in acetone; they were to be put individually into cheap standard-size boxes and removed to the National Museum of Ireland for anthropometric survey; after the excavation the area of the site should be filled in; the cemetery was to be properly defined by trial excavation and control of it acquired by the state until a further excavation and survey was completed.[71] An alternative action, expressed by Leask, was to close the excavation and remove a sample of the skeletal material to UCD for study.[72] It was estimated that the work would take a month to complete. However, the Department of Finance was not prepared to meet the expenses of labour costs (including the employment of two supervisors), equipment and transport costs to the museum from the Employment Schemes Vote.[73] This was because of the paucity of artefacts which rendered the site 'unproductive'.[74] This attitude was still typical of some archaeologists at that time, particularly Mahr, who were prioritising the recovery of artefacts over other important scientific data. It was advised that the alternative option available was to take a supplementary estimate on Vote 49 Science and Arts as 'the scientific information obtained would be worth the money'.[75] Presumably, this refers to probable data gleaned from an examination of the skeletons by a physical anthropologist.

The excavation at Castleknock continued against Mahr's advice. He complained bitterly about the 'great amount of unwanted publicity and excitement about what was after all a not very important excavation'.[76] Mahr, who did not want to store the skeletons in the National Museum, suggested that an anthropologist should be invited to Dublin to examine the bones. Unfortunately, in his opinion there were only three men in Ireland that could be called 'with a stretching of imagination, anthropologists'. These included Dr E.P. McLoughlin in University College, Dublin; Professor Walmsley in Belfast; and Professor Stephen Shea of University College, Galway. If Shea was approached 'it would be an additional advantage that the whole material might perhaps be transported in a lorry to Galway'. According to Mahr:

> The remains would not teach us more than did the about 200 at Gallen, Offaly, of about the above dates already published: it is hardly likely that the population underwent any appreciable physical change in that short period (an 800 AD skull is probably worth as much, anthropologically speaking – as one of 1000 AD).[77]

In 1938, the Office of Public Works intended to have the whole site declared a National Monument.[78]

Eoin MacNeill visited the site again on 18 July 1938 with his brother Charles MacNeill. He subsequently wrote to Adolf Mahr about Castleknock cemetery, explaining that he believed the site to be a 'támhlacht' or 'plague-burial ground':

> I suggest an explanation in an event of AD 987 recorded in the Annals of Ulster under 986: A great sudden mortality which brought widespread death on men and domestic animals in [the countries of] the Saxons and Britons and Goedels. I hope to follow up the record in other chronicles.[79]

MacNeill advised Mahr to employ a competent geologist on the site. He was also very interested in the skeletal material, noting in his letter that 'From the anthropometrical standpoint, this discovery seems to give a unique opportunity. It must represent the population of a definite district at a probably definite time'.[80] The following week an article on Castleknock cemetery appeared in the *Irish Press* where it was claimed that archaeologists and historians were satisfied that the site was 'a momentous national discovery'.[81] It was reported that MacNeill considered it 'an event unique in the history of the world' and 'the only complete ancient plague cemetery ever explored'. He even invoked the spirit of Tutankhamun:

> Single burial-places, like the tomb of King Tutankhamun and 'skullerys' used continuously through the centuries, have been found from time to time, but the Castleknock discovery has never been approached in importance from a national, historical, or archaeological point of view.[82]

MacNeill added that 'public opinion of this country will have its sense of decency and propriety shocked if this remarkable Christian cemetery is allowed to become just a piece of land again'.[83] He believed that there was every probability that if the cemetery was thoroughly explored it would yield subsidiary data of special historical and anthropological value. He also considered that 'the workers in anthropological and ethnological science in every country will become interested in it, and it will certainly be a national reproach to us if we fail to realise an opportunity which is absolutely unique'.[84] Mahr did not agree with the views of MacNeill and explained his concerns in correspondence to Leask:

> Owing to the extreme scantiness of grave-goods we cannot say with certainty whether the corpses were buried within a very limited period (say in a year or two, whilst an epidemic may have ravaged), or whether

they are normal burials of a village of, say, between 800 and 1,000 AD. I, personally, favour the latter, though less sensationalistic view'.[85]

While Mahr believed that the graves were those of 'Christian Celts' he considered it 'quite impossible to be positive that Castleknock must have been a plague-pit. The orderly lay-out of the burials rather militates against this view'. In his opinion 'From an archaeological viewpoint it is hardly worthwhile to continue'.[86] However, despite Mahr's objections and his advice to fill in the site the excavations continued. Further skeletons were unearthed and Mahr complained to the Department of Finance that 'the continued excavation is [a] waste of money and of the time of Mr. Raftery (the excavator)'.[87]

A.J.E. Cave, Assistant Conservator, Royal College of Surgeons of England in London contacted Mahr by letter about the skeletons. He told Mahr that the office in London of the High Commissioner for Éire informed him of the 'recent extraordinary find of ancient human remains near Dublin':

> I am writing to you now therefore to urge the claims of this Museum
> – the home of the greatest and 'standard' collection of ancient human
> osteology from all parts of the British Isles – as a fitting resting place for
> any of this present material which may not be required for conservation
> in Irish Museums. [88]

In Mahr's opinion it was 'a bit disappointing that somebody from Britain should be expected to do the work'.[89] W.W. Howells, who examined the skeletal remains from Gallen Priory, Co. Offaly excavated in 1934 and 1935 under the auspices of the Harvard Mission also wrote to Mahr expressing an interest in examining the skulls, which he believed should be 'compared with the Gallen material'.[90] This proposal interested Mahr because of the possibility that the Museum of Natural History in New York would be willing to incur the expenses and have the boxes shipped to America.[91] However, this did not happen.

Arthur D. Codling, an official from the Department of Finance was concerned about the financial implications of acquiring the services of a physical anthropologist to examine the skeletons. In his opinion, the cost of engaging an expert in physical anthropology to examine the 266 skeletons should not be paid from the Vote for Employment Schemes as 'no one could maintain that the purpose of bringing over the expert would primarily be to provide employment; nor would the expert be an unemployed Irishman'.[92] Instead it should be paid for from the Science and Art Vote. He expressed his astonishment to Leask that a fair proportion of the archaeological excavation work was done on sites which were definitely historic and even Christian even though the expectation was that only prehistoric sites should have been excavated.[93] An archaeological report was not published on the Castleknock site but an account of the excavations was included in the National Museum's topographical file.[94] The area excavated was approximately 400 sq metres, and exposed a total of 383 skeletons laid in regular formation with their heads to the NW. The majority were at a depth of 90cm but there were a number in a layer 45cm deeper. Precise information regarding the extent of the burial ground could not be given as the burials continued beyond the limits of the excavated area. According to an estimate made at the time, however, only one third of the cemetery had been excavated.

The decision not to carry out further excavations at Castleknock throws light on the different approaches taken by the American and Irish archaeologists and Adolf Mahr. The Americans were influenced by cultural evolution and eugenic theories which meant that physical anthropology was a priority and considered to be very important to the discipline of archaeology. This was a culture-historical approach with an emphasis on physical anthropology. Irish archaeologists, in contrast, were less interested in physical anthropology and much more influenced by antiquarian tradition. Mahr was first and foremost a museum curator and his priority was the acquisition of artefacts despite his status as a scientific archaeologist. He advocated the excavation of sites dating to the historic period if they were, like Lagore Crannóg, rich in artefactual assemblages. This was despite the fact that the Unemployment Schemes for archaeological research were set up specifically to investigate prehistoric sites. Also, the 1930s was a time before the advent of radiocarbon dating which meant that archaeologists were more dependent on the recovery of artefacts in order to date and interpret a site. Mahr did not believe that much additional scientific information could be gleaned from the skeletal material. He was also constrained by financial considerations and there was a lack of finance to employ the services of a physical anthropologist. It is also possible that he wanted to undermine Eoin MacNeill who expressed an interest in the site and in the scientific possibilities of physical anthropology.

## Tara of the South? The Politics of Interpretation

Adolf Mahr suggested that Cush, Co. Limerick, should be excavated based on his belief that it 'must be the site, long sought for, of Temair Érann, an

assembling place and a sanctuary of the earliest period of Irish History'.[95]
The antiquarian, T.J. Westropp, had identified Cush as Temair Érann in an
article published in the *Journal of the North Munster Archaeological Society* in
1919. This was in the context of a general study, undertaken by Westropp, of
earthworks in Co. Limerick and surrounding areas, in which he attempted to
identify sites with those mentioned in early historical references.[96] However,
Ó Ríordáin avoided grappling with the question of Westropp's thesis in his
own paper because it had been claimed by T.F. O'Rahilly that the name
Temair Érann referred to Tara in Co. Meath.[97]

Ó Ríordáin began excavating Temair Érann, which had never been dug
before, on 7 August 1934. Arrangements were made with the Minister for
Defence to take aerial photographs.[98] The site became a training ground
for amateur and professional archaeologists alike. Ó Ríordáin explained the
modus operandi of the Cush excavations:

> Work was begun on Ring-Fort 1 and, because a technique of excavation
> had to be developed to suit the conditions of the site and also because
> the workmen had to be trained to the work, the excavation of this fort
> was carried out with particular care and more slowly than was necessary
> later when experience had been gained regarding the nature and
> appearance of the soil in a natural and disturbed condition.[99]

Ó Ríordáin complimented his foreman, Jock Kiely, who 'showed a never-
failing keenness and skill not only in his control of the workmen but also in
the technique of excavating in difficult soil'. The workmen, likewise, 'worked
loyally and carefully and in so many cases with great intelligence'.[100] This
example of training on the job was a feature of the Harvard Mission and
Unemployment Scheme excavations and resulted in the development of a
native school of Irish archaeology, the subject of the next chapter.

Mahr hoped to date several of the monuments on the site at Cush,
including standing stones, alignments of stones, earthbanks 'which may
indicate settlement sites' and several mounds and to find graves with
associated grave goods to clarify the 'chronological position' of monuments
in relation to each other. He worried that 'Mr. Ó Ríordáin's excavation is in
the line of an experiment and one must always be prepared for a washout'.[101]
The excavation, in 1935, of ring forts at Cush was deemed to reinforce
conclusions reached in 1934 that the site had been in use from the Middle
Bronze Age to well into the Christian Period. It was reported that ninth-
century brooches and articles of personal adornment and daily use were

found. Traces of iron-working were also discovered at the site. Evidence for timber houses and 'wattle and daub' houses were found, the latter considered by Leask to be 'new in Irish archaeology'.[102] A 'complex souterrain' was also discovered, which was dated by Ó Ríordáin to the Bronze Age.[103] At the time his excavation results and in particular his proposed dates were lauded by the OPW:

> That the ring fort and the underground chambers known as souterrains go as far back at least as the late Bronze Age has been proved by the Cush, Co. Limerick excavations. This is regarded as a spectacular result in Irish research; it could hardly have been obtained under any schemes less extensive than those aided by the State.[104]

The motivation to find a Bronze Age date for souterrains reflected the desire to find evidence for cultural and historical continuity between the two golden ages of the Bronze Age and the Early Christian Period and to bolster the thesis that the site was indeed Temair Érann.

Erin Gibbons claims that Ó Ríordáin's 'misinterpretation' of the souterrain as dating to the Bronze Age may have been influenced by Mahr's political perspective:

> Mahr's ideological approach must surely undermine claims about his prowess as a scientific archaeologist, for the evidence shows that he engaged in the same pseudo-science as that practiced by Gustav Kossinna, Hans Reinerth, Oswald Menghin and the other Nazi archaeologists.[105]

However, pseudo-science suggests the masquerading of the unscientific as scientific and the deliberate production of false results. It is true that all scientific data can be misused for ideological reasons. But all interpretation is influenced by the cultural and political context in which it takes place. In 1937, Ó Ríordáin wrote that 'I wish to excavate as much as possible because I regard it as the most important approach towards increasing our knowledge of Irish archaeology'.[106] While he was very conscientious in his meticulous recovery of archaeological data he was still influenced by his former mentor and boss at the National Museum, Adolf Mahr. While an employee at the museum Ó Ríordáin had applied for leave to study souterrains in France but the Department of Finance turned down his application.[107] In his published paper on Cush/Temair Érann it is clear that Ó Ríordáin was influenced by the idea, espoused by Mahr, that the souterrain was a 'sub-megalithic' feature and by comments made in favour of this idea by Oliver Davies in his review of Mahr's Presidential address for 1937.[108] Waddell explains that 'the broad framework for Mahr's prehistory was a familiar migrationary and culture-historical model' wherein he postulated that there were a number of distinct immigrations or invasions into Ireland in prehistory. Considering the short time-span in which these cultural movements supposedly took place 'it was not entirely unreasonable' to suppose that souterrains might reflect megalithic building practice.[109] Ó Ríordáin's work within this culture-historical framework was influenced by Irish nationalism and can be paralleled with both German and American archaeology during the interwar period.

Hallam L. Movius, considered by his contemporaries to be a very honest scientist, took Ó Ríordáin's results at face-value. He believed that the dates tallied with the idea that the site was the famous Temair Érann.[110] According to Movius, the discoveries made 'had been such as to add considerably to our knowledge not only of the site but of conditions of life in the period with which we deal'.[111] The discovery of prehistoric houses, according to him, were 'particularly gratifying' as archaeological evidence for these were lacking in Ireland. Movius regarded the obtaining of evidence for a prehistoric dating of ring forts to be also very important. Other significant discoveries, in his opinion, included a series of burials found in one of the ring forts which was used first as a habitation site and later for burial purposes; field systems, evidence for extensive tillage and numerous quern stones; and a Middle Bronze Age cist grave with cremated remains and two food vessels.[112] Certainly, Ó Ríordáin believed that the archaeological results justified Government expenditure on the Cush excavations.[113]

It was reported in the *Irish Times* that the work at Temair Érann was 'one of the major excavations under the new Government scheme'.[114] The site was also included in Leask's report on the more important results obtained in 1935.[115]

## Settlement Archaeology: Lough Gur

Seán P. Ó Ríordáin spent many seasons excavating a variety of sites at Lough Gur, Co. Limerick, beginning in 1936. He was adept at acquiring funding of excavations by the state under the Unemployment Schemes and managing the combination of scientific expertise with local labour on archaeological sites. This innovative process was community archaeology in action.

The Harvard Mission introduced the novel idea of large scale archaeological excavations to Ireland. This was initially to complement the work undertaken at Cahercommaun by the Harvard Mission, which Mahr described as 'a welcome rounding-off of the whole programme as far as settlement archaeology is concerned'.[116] Cahercommaun was considered important enough for Hencken to include it in the *List of Publications* sent to the Rockefeller Foundation.[117] Settlement archaeology in the 1930s 'did not signify the study of habitation sites but, rather, determining where particular ethnic groups had lived in earlier times'.[118] According to Grogan and Eogan, at Lough Gur 'Ó Ríordáin brilliantly perceived the potential of settlement archaeology and the relationship of settlement to its wider landscape and environmental context'.[119] Ó Ríordáin's archaeological research programme at Lough Gur involved the excavation of a large variety of sites,[120] beginning with the investigation of three stone circles and two forts in 1936. Lough Gur was a site of immense interest, not only to archaeologists but also to the general public because of the number of megaliths which it contained and the bronze and stone finds recovered. A small excavation had been carried out previously by Professor Harkness of University College Cork and published in the *Quarterly Journal of Science* in 1869.[121] The results of this were included with a description of the megaliths in a paper published by Sir Bertram Windle, President of University College Cork, in the *Proceedings of the Royal Irish Academy* 1912.[122]

The possibility of excavation at Lough Gur was contemplated as an extension of the work of the Harvard Mission. Adolf Mahr organised for Reverend L.M. Hewson, an antiquarian from Carbury, Co. Kildare, to meet Hencken on his way to Lough Gur and to show him around the site. Rev. Hewson was chosen because Mahr believed that 'he knows the site better than anybody else from an archaeological point of view'.[123] The approval for expenditure of £500 for the relief of unemployment to assist Harvard excavations on Lough Gur and Kilgreany Caves was given in a letter dated 3 August 1934 from Harold G. Leask to Adolf Mahr.[124] However, Mahr was disappointed to receive 'a wire from Dr. Hencken which leads me to believe that Lough Gur is off'.[125] Two years later, Ó Ríordáin wrote to Harold G. Leask outlining a proposal for the excavation of the site.[126] He suggested the appointment of Gabriel Hayes as an assistant as it was not his intention to spend the duration of the excavations at the site. Gabriel Hayes, who had excavated with him at Cush, Co. Limerick in 1935, was later to become Ó Ríordáin's wife.[127] She had a lot of experience in drawing finds for the Harvard Mission at the Museum and for Ó Ríordáin himself. He believed her to be competent to supervise staff and to survey monuments. He gave her authority to sign wages sheets while he was away at the Oslo Archaeological Congress in 1936.

Jock Kiely was suggested for the position of foreman. Kiely had worked with Ó Ríordáin at Cush in 1934 and 1935. He had, according to Ó Ríordáin, 'an excellent sense of soil conditions and changes'.[128] However, there was no mention of him being a qualified archaeologist. Kiely was to act as a night watchman and camp overnight at the site. Leask contacted the Employment Branch of the Department of Industry and Commerce in Kilmallock. He forwarded lists of workmen in receipt of Unemployment Assistance who would be available for work at the Lough Gur excavation.[129]

According to Ó Ríordáin, there had been no systematic excavation of the site prior to that carried out in 1936 when two stone circles were investigated. Ó Ríordáin claimed that these were the first stone circles in Ireland where the excavation had been carried out on a 'methodical basis'.[130] The excavation of one of the stone circles was carried out using the 'quadrant method', a technique employed by the Harvard Mission archaeologists. It was Leask's opinion that there was 'material for several seasons' excavation' at Lough Gur.[131] The following year, in July 1937, approval was granted for the continuation of excavations.[132] The employment of Michael J. O'Kelly as ganger on Lough Gur was approved at a payment rate of 10/- per day.[133] O'Kelly was later to become famous for his work on Newgrange. He became Professor of Celtic Archaeology at UCC in 1946.

On 22 September 1937 an extension of the excavations to the end of the month was approved by Leask.[134] The OPW, in a report, concluded that the excavation of stone circles at Lough Gur, Co. Limerick and Kealkill Co. Cork had 'not produced very definite results'. They were described as 'sepulchral but may have a ritual use' and probably 'part of the Bronze Age complexes in which they are found'.[135] Notes included in the *North Munster Antiquarian Journal*, 1936–1939, listed finds recovered from a fort at Lough Gur: 'combs and ornaments of bone, fine glass beads, querns, hones, spindle whorl, iron knives and pins, bronze pins and six stone axes'.[136]

The intensive archaeological research programme at Lough Gur was continued for seven seasons between 1939 and 1949 and was financed mainly under the Relief of Unemployment Schemes. Smaller amounts were received from UCD, UCC and the Murphy Bequest which was administered by the Department of Education.[137] These were important community initiatives in archaeology which provided work for the local people and gave them a sense of ownership and pride in monuments in their locality.

This engagement by the community in scientific endeavour, paid for by the state, was innovative. Ó Ríordáin praised the work of the local workmen employed on the sites 'whose loyalty and keenness it is a pleasure to acknowledge' and singled out a 'Mr. Tom Bourke, of Herbertstown, whose joy in the finding of, a potsherd, a bead, or a post-hole was an indication of his interest'.[138] A report on the Neolithic and Bronze Age houses of Lough Gur was published in the *Proceedings of the Royal Irish Academy* 1953–1954.[139] Also included in the proceedings was a paper by Frank Mitchell on a pollen-diagram from the site.[140] Scientific expertise included human bone analysis by Professor J. Keenan of the Department of Anatomy in University College, Dublin and Dr R.H. Inkster of the School of Anatomy, Trinity College Dublin. A dental report was provided by Dr L. McCaughey, Lecturer in Dental Anatomy in Trinity College, Dublin. Analysis of the animal bones was carried out by Arthur Wilson Stelfox of the National Museum of Ireland.

Ó Ríordáin's excavations of the habitation sites represented the only group of house-sites excavated in Ireland, dating from the Neolithic down to the Middle Bronze Age. Some of the sites were occupied continually and others periodically. Ó Ríordáin believed that he had discovered a village community. The sites provided 'a valuable accompaniment to the knowledge obtained from the study and excavation of contemporary ritual and burial places'.[141] His recognition and investigation of several habitation sites of Neolithic/Beaker was regarded by Grogan and Eogan as 'one of his most outstanding achievements'.[142] Ó Ríordáin discovered that the stone circles referred to by Windle in his paper as K and L were actually enclosed habitation sites defined by a concentric double kerbing.[143] Houses were round or curvilinear in plan and others were rectangular. Sizes of houses varied. Hearths were found in most of them and some had rubbish pits. The economy was based mainly on domestic animals, the bones of which were found in considerable quantities. Small scale tillage was practised. Ó Ríordain noted that some of the axes were made of porcellanite and came from the Tievebulliagh-Rathlin districts in Co. Antrim; glass beads were imported from Egypt or elsewhere in the Mediterranean; bronze objects were cast on Knockadoon, at Lough Gur, but copper and tin were obtained from outside sources.[144]

The most important item recovered, according to Ó Ríordáin, was the pottery. It occurred in greater quantities at Lough Gur than on any other site of early date excavated in Ireland. The variety suggested 'a population group which was constantly receiving new cultural impulses, and presumably, new immigrants'.[145] The occurrence of Beaker in considerable quantities provided 'a chronological datum which brings these sites into relation with those in Britain and on the Continent'.[146] In Ireland these were the first instances of habitation sites on which Beaker occurred prolifically. Ó Ríordáin concluded that 'the Beaker folk must have formed a significant ethnic element in the population of the Lough Gur area' but that they 'readily coalesced with the local population'.[147] Much of the ornament found on the Lough Gur Beakers could be paralleled in south-west Europe and lead the excavator to believe that successive bands of immigrants came into Ireland from Iberia from Neolithic times down to the early part of the Bronze Age. 'Lough Gur, on a miniature scale, reflects the larger incursions'.[148] According to Grogan and Eogan, Ó Ríordáin 'put Ireland on the Beaker map'.[149]

Ó Ríordáin excavated a total of fourteen habitation sites on Knockadoon at Lough Gur, dating to the Neolithic/Beaker times. He had been preparing for publication the remaining five sites[150] when he died prematurely on 11 April 1957. Eoin Grogan and George Eogan based their report on these five sites on Ó Ríordáin's preliminary reports, the field notebooks, some excavation drawings and a thorough examination of the finds, publishing it in *PRIA* 1987.[151] They regarded Ó Ríordáin's intensive study of the prehistoric settlement as demonstrating the excavator's 'innovative approach and commitment'.[152] The work of Ó Ríordáin at Lough Gur continues to be important in Irish archaeology and his work has been reassessed and further excavations carried out at Knockadoon.[153] Gabriel Cooney, in his retrospective piece on the work of Ó Ríordain at Knockadoon in 2007, wrote that 'Fifty years on, his research programme in this area still ranks as arguably the most intensive excavation-based investigation of a landscape anywhere in Ireland'.[154]

**Garranes**

In 1937 Ó Ríordáin applied to carry out the excavation at a 'very large earthen ring-fort with triple ramparts' at Garranes, Co. Cork because of its possible important historical significance:

> This is the site which has been identified as Rath Raithleann [...], the central site of the Ui Eachach a branch of the Eoghanacht. It is said to have been founded in the 5th century [....] and still in occupation at least as late as the 11th century because Cian Mac Maolmuadh who fought at Clontarf was ruler of Raithleann.[155]

Ó Ríordáin believed that 'the grounds on which the identification is based are good in this instance'. He wanted a grant of £165 and labour costs for 20 workmen, one foreman and two engineering students. He also requested permission to employ a non-local man, P.J. O'Sullivan of Annascaul, Co. Kerry, who had been recommended to him by Commander D.B. O'Connell of Killarney. O'Connell was engaged on a survey of the antiquities of Co. Kerry. O'Sullivan had worked for him and 'shown great keenness in his desire to help archaeology and to learn about it'.[156] O'Sullivan was approved as the foreman and Michael J. O'Kelly joined the excavation team as a charge hand. Ó Ríordáin regarded forts in general as representing 'one of the biggest problems in Irish archaeology' and the excavation of a number of examples as 'a matter of prime necessity that we might know something of the everyday background of life in early times in Ireland'.[157] H.G. Leask strongly recommended Ó Ríordáin's proposal as forts 'have not yet received the attention they deserve' and 'its excavation should prove of scientific value'.[158]

Funds for the excavation were approved and trial trenches were subsequently dug through the three concentric fosses and three banks revealing an entrance to the fort, protected by four wooden gates. It was evident that the posts had been cut out of the solid rock. According to Ó Ríordáin 'no other fort of quite the same type has yet been excavated'.[159] Ó Ríordáin was meticulous in the scientific recovery of archaeological features, including post-holes, and expressed caution about what he perceived as an overemphasis on the recovery of artefacts:

> They are not the only things of importance on an excavation and that the manner of their finding is as important as the objects found. I mean we must also note their position, their depth in the soil, relation to one another and to the structures found.[160]

The most important find from Garranes, according to Ó Ríordáin, was a little bronze button. The surface of it was silver and a triskele design was cut into the bronze of the flat face and filled with enamel, originally red in colour. In his opinion the design 'resembles in a simple form the ornament of the illuminated manuscripts as the book of Durrow'. He was so impressed by it that he wrote: 'I failed to find any very similar object on which the same balance, restraint and taste were exercised as on the Garranes button'.[161] He dated it to AD 600 and correlated it with historical evidence for St. Finnbarr's birth in the second half of the sixth century. According to tradition St.

Finbarr, the Patron Saint of Cork, was the son of Amergin a metal-worker in the employment of Tighernach the King of Raithleann.[162]

Ó Ríordáin informed the public of this in a broadcast about Garranes from the Royal Society of Antiquaries on 27 July 1937. He also explained that there was much evidence for metal-working at Garannes, mainly ornaments, some unfinished pieces, crucibles and several clay moulds and two stone moulds. One of these was intended for making a metal object shaped like a circular hand-mirror with a handle with a cross incised on the circular part. Ó Ríordáin suggested it might have 'to do with the making of breads from the sacrifice of the Mass'.[163] The recovery of Millefiori glass, used as insets in ornaments in brooches, was regarded as significant because it proved 'that the millefiori glass found on Irish ornaments was a native product'.[164] Other objects included iron implements including an iron shears, small knife-blades and a pincers which may have belonged to a blacksmith. Other finds considered important included fragments of pottery as prior to this there had been hardly any pottery from Early Iron Age or Early Christian sites in Ireland. Some of the pottery was described by Ó Ríordáin as 'obviously Roman while other pieces may have been copied from Roman types'.[165]

The main significance of the excavation was 'the evidence it provides of an intense metal-working tradition on a site datable to the early centuries of Christianity in Ireland'.[166] Ó Ríordáin published a full archaeological report on the site in the *PRIA* 1942.[167] He summed up the archaeological evidence as follows:

> The fort known as Lisnacaheragh at Garranes is an unusually large example of Irish ring-fort, which was well defended by its earth works and gates, and was occupied during the latter half of the 5th and the early part of the 6th centuries by a community of craftsmen who had trade relations and interchange of artistic motives with Gaul and Britain.[168]

Also included was a historical report by the historian Rev. John Ryan S.J. However, with regard to the history of the ruling family living at the site Ó Ríordáin conceded that 'there is no good archaeological evidence' and the interior 'yielded no clear indication of house types'.[169] He argued that the cumulative evidence pointed to AD 500 as the central date of occupation of Garranes even though he also entertained the idea that some of the finds were dated to an earlier period. These included a cooking pot, comparable to a similar artefact from Colchester, dating to the first century AD and a metal knob similar to those on Roman brooches dating to the first or second century AD.[170] He concluded that the correlation of the dating to that provided by historical sources strengthened the thesis that the site was indeed Rath Raithleann of the Ui Eachach and in this instance the excavation 'served history as well as archaeology'.[171]

## Labbacallee

In 1934 Mahr expressed the opinion that 'any excavation of a megalith is a useful and a justifiable undertaking especially so at the present limited state of our knowledge'.[172] Two megalithic tombs were excavated by the Harvard Mission: Poulawack, Co. Clare in 1934 and Creevykeel, Co. Sligo in 1936.[173] This work, according to Carleton Jones, 'played a key role in moving megalithic studies beyond the somewhat limited descriptions and comparisons of the antiquarians and into the more analytical realm of the modern discipline of archaeology'.[174] Under the Unemployment Scheme excavations, Mahr wanted to establish whether the cultural impetus for megaliths came directly from the continent and if it represented racial immigration. To this end, megaliths including Lough Gur and Ballycullane Upper in Co. Limerick; Moylisha and Baltinglass in Co. Wicklow and Aghnaskeagh, Cairn A in Co. Louth were investigated.[175]

One of the first archaeological sites to be excavated under the Unemployment Schemes was the wedge tomb at Labbacallee, Co. Cork.[176] It was taken into the guardianship of the Commissioners of Public Works in 1934 under the National Monuments Act.[177] Work began on 7 August 1934 and was under the supervision of Harold G. Leask. He was assisted in the excavation by Justice Liam Price who volunteered his services on a freelance basis. Price also worked as a volunteer assistant on Cahercommaun fort and had 'a deep interest in archaeology, place-names, folklore and history'.[178] Mahr described him as being 'devoted to the elucidation of the field monuments and of the known finds in Co. Wicklow'.[179] Price did not have academic qualifications in the discipline of archaeology but this did not stop him serving as editor of the *Journal of the Royal Society of Antiquaries of Ireland*. Hallam L. Movius and Laurence Mongey also assisted at the excavation. Mongey, a historian, Irish patriot and pharmacist was author of 'The Portal Dolmens of South-Eastern Ireland' published as volume 1 of the *Journal of the Waterford Spelaeological Society*.[180] Michael V. Duignan was to replace Price during the second half of the excavation. Mahr, ever mindful of his budget, and not averse to exploiting his young students, wrote that Duignan had been 'earmarked for scientific work in connection with archaeology, history and the study of folk culture in the country' and therefore, 'should bear a considerable part of his own expenses having regard to the unique opportunity of qualifying for field work under as able a guide as Mr. Leask'.[181]

According to Mahr the significance of the excavation at Labbacallee lay in the fact that it would be 'the first dolmen of considerable size ever scientifically excavated in this country'.[182] Leask, in his report considered that the word 'dolmen' was 'unsatisfactory as a generic term for the very varied sepulchral megalithic structures to which it is applied' and called for 'a classification of and nomenclature for the more complex structures'.[183] Mahr hoped that the excavation would shed light on the 'individual steps of its architectural development'. His views on the morphological features of this type of monument reflected theories about migration and diffusion common in archaeological literature at that time: 'The highly complicated monuments of the New Grange type are the original expression of the type, either in its inception or as an importation of the building idea, and that, as time passed on, simpler and smaller monuments took the place of the elaborate structures'.[184] The only way to settle this question, according to Mahr, was to conduct a search for the holes in which stones might have stood and later been removed: 'A little bit of experience in field work is enough to enable a man to read, as it were, in the book of the earth, and to trace such holes if the soil is at all favourable to such observations'.[185] Labbacallee was found to be composed of over 100 principal stones and to be constructed in a wedge-shaped plan. A large chamber was found and a smaller cist which was expected to contain the primary burial. Evidence for kerbing proved that a cairn originally covered the monument. Mahr had hoped that fragments of flint and pottery would be recovered from the soil which would help with dating.[186] However, the excavators of the tomb, Leask and Price, did not suggest a date for Labbacallee due to insufficient data.[187] They argued that it represented a cultural connection between Munster and Northern France and that because of its size it 'may be said to belong to a type hitherto unknown in Ireland or Great Britain'.[188]

A woman's skull was found in the main chamber. The rest of her skeleton was found in a crouched position, on her left side, in a small chamber filled to the roof with packing stones. Not all the bones of the skeleton were in the correct position which suggested that the woman may initially have been buried elsewhere. Radio carbon dates obtained decades later indicated a date for the burial of the headless woman c.2300 BC.[189] In an OPW report (1938), the importance of folklore to Irish archaeology was acknowledged in respect of Labaccallee and it was deemed to be 'a remarkable instance in the survival by tradition of a knowledge of the sex of the person buried there'.[190] All of the skeletal remains were examined by C.P. Martin. At least five people were represented. The shape and features of one female skull suggested to the archaeologists that it was 'exactly those of the brachycephalic skulls of the Middle Bronze Age people who were characterised by a round skull with a vertical forehead'.[191] Clay samples from the tomb were analyzed by Dr K.C. Bailey. Arthur Wilson Stelfox, of the Natural History Museum, examined and identified the bird and animal bones. Advice was sought from V. Gordon Childe and Christopher Hawkes about the pottery, who tentatively assigned dates in the Late Bronze Age or Early Iron Age to the sherds.[192] The report was published in *Proceedings of the Royal Irish Academy* (1935–1937).[193]

## Drimnagh: A State Rescue Excavation

Drimnagh, like the first phase at Poulawack excavated by the Harvard Mission in 1934, was an early example of what later was classified as a Linkardstown type burial (a typology not current during the 1930s).[194] The burial consisted of a polygonal cist containing an inhumation and a decorated pot. The cist was covered by a cairn and a sod mound. It was excavated by Howard Kilbride-Jones under the Unemployment Schemes as it was in danger of destruction from workmen digging a nearby gravel pit. It had remained intact up to that point because of traditional beliefs about the sacredness of the site. It was called the 'Grand Parlour' locally because stories circulated about the gentry holding balls in a room inside the mound. There were even rumours that it was the burial place of King John (Magna Carta fame) and his Queen.[195]

Ten men were employed under the Unemployment Scheme and Kilbride-Jones provides a physical description of one of them in *Archaeology Ireland*:

He was of medium build and height, of dark complexion, unshaved and undernourished. He was dressed in a badly worn and sometimes torn blue suit, mud-stained, and with trouser legs turned up above his ankles. About forty-five years of age, he walked seemingly with difficulty, his legs too weak to support the weight of his body. To the world he was of no importance, and he was unemployed. Yet he was the best excavator who ever worked for me.[196]

Four volunteer assistants also worked with Kilbride-Jones on the excavation, including Dubliner T.G.E. Powell, who was to become 'an outstanding scholar in the field of Celtic prehistory' and author of the classic text, *The Celts*.[197] The others included Gustav Mahr – the son of Adolf Mahr, Michael Hayes of the National Museum and Gwendoline Clare Stacpoole, an amateur archaeologist and a niece of the Irish antiquarian, Thomas Johnson Westropp. During their excavation they discovered that Early Bronze Age burials had been placed in the top of the mound and that it was enlarged and surrounded by a ditch. Kilbride-Jones described it as a 'mound within a mound'.[198] He regarded the primary sod-mound to be 'the most extraordinary feature 'of the site as it was made up entirely of burnt sods and prior to his excavation that type of tumulus was previously unknown.[199] He sent samples of soil and wood to Dr W. von Stokar, Institut fur Vor-und Fruhgeschichte der Universitat Koln, for scientific analysis but because of the outbreak of the Second World War the report was not forthcoming. Instead Dr P. O'Connor of the Natural History Division of the National Museum provided a brief report. Animal bones from the site were examined by Arthur Wilson Stelfox.[200]

Kilbride-Jones wrote an imaginative description of the man buried in the cist beneath the sod mound:

> [He] must have been a personage of extreme importance – a national hero, an ascetic, or holy man, who, by some magic means, had impressed the populace with his powers as a leader or prophet. As a consequence of this it seems that pilgrimages may have been the order of the times, as the primary mound was kept free of grass until the actual throwing-up of the secondary mantling-mound.[201]

Dr G.M. Morant, who provided the scientific report on the skeletal remains from Drimnagh, noted that this important personage probably had his legs tied as he found that the feet of the skeleton were found behind and close to the pelvis. The skull was badly preserved but the greater part of the skeleton was well preserved. This man died between his 30th and 40th birthday and was 5 feet 5 inches tall. No reliable measurements could be obtained from the incomplete brain-box but a cephalic index of about 78 was estimated. Morant concluded that 'no estimate of any value of the racial affinities of the population represented can be obtained from the single skeleton'.[202] He also examined the secondary cremation burial in the side of the primary mound found with a food vessel dating to the Middle Bronze Age. This was of a single individual, sex undetermined. The Cinerary Urn Burial, found at the apex of the primary sod-mound, dating to the Late Bronze Age, was that of a male aged between 20 and 40 years old.

## A Revolution in Irish Archaeology

The importance of the Unemployment Scheme sites was not always necessarily the results obtained, which were sometimes meagre. Apart from partially solving the dire unemployment problem, a new generation of scientific archaeologists received training. In America 'a nationwide professional community grew out of the shared experience of work relief archaeology'.[203] Haag explains that 'there has never been a greater revolution in American archaeology than that engendered by the New Deal period'.[204] During the New Deal, the American Irish started to be appointed and elected to important offices in the federal government. President Roosevelt included Irish Americans such as Joseph P. Kennedy (1888–1969) among his advisers.[205]

In Ireland, the Harvard Mission excavations, some of which were Unemployment Scheme sites, instigated a new and exciting period in Irish archaeology. Ordinary people were given an opportunity to participate in excavations and find interesting artefacts and features. Archaeology was popularised in the media and this further raised the awareness of Ireland's rich archaeological heritage. All of this was to shape the understanding of the nation's past and lead to the emergence of a Native School of Scientific Archaeology.

# 8 A NATIVE SCHOOL OF SCIENTIFIC ARCHAEOLOGY

Please don't put so much emphasis on the question of finding things. That is not the central idea of an excavation. It is rather the acquisition of knowledge and, while an excavator is human enough to be glad at the unearthing of nice finds such as we got at Garranes, as an archaeologist he regards them as the data which help him to build up the story of the site he is digging. This story is built up as much by the discovery of the remains or evidences of ancient structures as by the finding of objects, however more exciting these may be.

– Seán P. Ó Riordáin, 1937[1]

## From 'glorified stamp collectors' to scientific archaeologists

In 1932 Liam S. Gogan posed the question 'Where are our local archaeological schools or groups?'[2] He claimed to have made a proposal to Macalister in 1923 for collaboration between the National Museum and University

College Dublin so that 'it would have been only a matter of time till every student pursuing an archaeological course would have become practical archaeologists instead of mere cultivators of an interesting class of literature which led nowhere.[3] Macalister, apparently, declined his offer. Mahr believed that the presence of the Harvard Archaeological Mission in Ireland meant that an opportunity was created to build up a local school of excavation technique.[4] Paradoxically it was left to outsiders, such as Mahr himself, (involved in particular in the training of Seán P. Ó Riordáin) and the American archaeologists of the Harvard Mission to train native archaeologists in up-to-date scientific methodology. Perhaps this was because, from the perspective of nationalist archaeologists in independent Ireland, Macalister's pedigree was now considered suspect as he was considered to be of British origin. What was required, according to S. Gogan, was 'concentrated and specialised treatment of the archaeological material of Ireland in our universities' and the 'application to the science of the principles of Sinn Féin.[5] While Gogan appreciated the temporary and necessary collaboration of the members of the Harvard Mission in the scientific training of Irish archaeologists, he was very aware of the political potential of the discipline. His views echo that of Kossinna's who declared archaeology to be 'the most national of sciences and the ancient Germans the most noble subject for archaeological research.[6] Gogan believed that Irish archaeology was 'nationalistic' and that 'its final expression should come from our own nationals.[7]

Nicholas Allen argues that science was central to the Irish intellectual Revival from 1900 to 1930.[8] On 7 September 1907, an article entitled 'Wanted – A Scientific Revival' was published in the weekly Irish nationalist newspaper *Sinn Féin*, edited by Arthur Griffith. The author considered science to be a measure of national progress:

> The people have been enthusiastic in inaugurating an artistic and an industrial revival. Will they make one more grand effort, and create a recognised School of Science in Ireland? They must do so if our country is to take her proper place among the nations of the world, for it is only on the tripod of art, commerce, and scientific enlightenment that a country can stand firmly.[9]

Allen postulates that 'science offered objective sanction to subjective argument. It supplied the terms of enquiry and report for cultural projects.[10] This was certainly the case with the study of the Celtic race in Ireland by the Harvard Mission anthropologists and archaeologists with their use of specialist scientific expertise to interpret cultural sites and artefacts. Archaeology, as a discipline, became central to cultural and scientific progress. As Allen explains 'science and culture form a new language, constructed from the detritus of colonisation, continental modernism, and the intellectual revival in train for three decades previous'.[11] The respectability of scientific endeavour had implications for the interpretation of race, archaeology and history and the copperfastening of well-established beliefs about the Celtic race which had political implications for the Irish in America.

The Harvard Mission heralded the introduction of the improved scientific methods of American archaeology and anthropology into Ireland in order to recover the artefacts used by the noble Celts of prehistory and of their descendants in Early Christian Ireland. It was the view of the American anthropologists that Ireland had preserved intact an older culture which had been lost by England and many of the continental countries as a result of invasion and cultural diffusion. It was believed that the Irish still had an 'homogenous culture' and that this might render it possible to trace cultural continuity from the Stone Age to the present day as asserted by Hooton:

> Parts of Ireland present an almost unbroken history from the New Stone Age and Metal Ages through the earlier Christian period into late historical times and down to the present day. It is possible that a complete continuity could be traced in a detailed research in certain of the counties from pre-Celtic Neolithic Ireland to the modern culture, which would explain much of present-day Ireland.[12]

Hooton describes the Neolithic in Ireland as 'Pre-Celtic', which suggests a connection with a succeeding Celtic period, for which there is no archaeological evidence. This was common practice among Irish archaeologists, even though most believed that the Celts invaded Ireland during the Iron Age. It also suggests that the idea of the Celtic nation was already established as far as the Americans were concerned. John Collis, in his paper 'Celtic Myths' explores how classification and chronological concepts in archaeology can affect interpretation of data. He suggests that 'If we cannot change the nomenclature, we can at least be aware of how it directs our thinking'.[13]

The mechanics of archaeological recovery were important in obtaining an accurate picture of spatial and temporal cultural change. If artefacts were meticulously recovered and carefully planned, then information regarding their context and function could be obtained. Specialist scientific reports could recreate the environmental conditions which pertained to a particular cultural horizon. Previously unrecognised features added to this mosaic of knowledge. The transition from a collections and museum-led approach in the discipline of archaeology to a more scientific methodology reflected the desire to acquire knowledge about the past rather than exotic artefacts for display. This hard evidence was crucial in underpinning the identity of the state. Smith describes identity as 'a landscape of the mind' where 'the past may be selectively remembered'.[14] In archaeology, this is achieved by giving importance to particular material remains such as those deemed to be Celtic or Christian or both, and downplaying the significance of other assemblages such as Roman ones which are less politically useful. The Megaws noted in their article 'Ancient Celts and Modern Ethnicity' that 'all identity is to one degree or another 'invented' but that we must be 'on our guard against those who would totally deny a Celtic prehistory'.[15] While the Irish past can be mined for facts, they have to be interpreted by archaeologists and historians. The archaeological or historical imagination unwittingly has interpretational biases and corresponding political nuances. Stephen J. Gould sums up the problems of scientific preconceptions succinctly when he writes:

> Our ways of learning about the world are strongly influenced by the social preconceptions and biased modes of thinking that each scientist must apply to any problem. The stereotype of a fully rational and objective 'scientific method', with individual scientists as logical robots, is self-serving mythology.[16]

Hooton made many derogatory comments about archaeology despite the fact that it was his sole responsibility to ensure the success of the Harvard Mission including five archaeological expeditions. For example, he wrote that 'archaeology implies an interest in the obsolete paraphernalia of the past which to the multitude stigmatizes its students as unregardful of the necessities of the present – the senile playboys of science rooting in the rubbish heaps of antiquity'.[17] However, he did concede that archaeology was 'quite as legitimate an inquiry into the past as is history' sharing with the latter discipline 'the function of interpreting the present through knowledge of the past'. He lamented the 'magpie habit of collecting' as an alternative to a search for knowledge. This type of archaeology in his view was similar to looting or plundering the past. It did not represent the normal everyday activities of people from the past but 'the bizarre and exotic features of their culture which appeal to the pot-hunter'.[18]

The growth of archaeology as a science had diminished the number of curio-hunters but had not eradicated them entirely. Paradoxically, an interesting aspect of the Harvard expeditions was the desire shown by Adolf Mahr and others to dig sites which were likely to be rich in artefacts. There was much media attention given to the excavations and it was necessary to find artefacts which could be photographed and in which the public took an interest.[19] While Hooton regarded the digging up of the past in a quest for beautiful or unusual objects as a 'glamorous business' he insisted that 'the laborious task of dragging significant information from these inanimate objects requires more persistence, more imagination, and more downright hard-thinking than most archaeologists are able to command.[20] Hooton was adamant that 'Archaeology in general is still open to the charge that it is carried on primarily for the recovery of objects which seem desirable to the excavators and to museums rather than for the purpose of increasing knowledge.[21]

As mentioned earlier, Hooton was also highly suspicious of the archaeological technique of typology. This study and classification of artefacts according to type, particularly as a way of defining prehistoric cultures was 'too often a figment of imagination invested with a semblance of reality by elaborate nomenclature'. Hooton was not enamoured of the study of ceramics either and commented that 'races interbreed, but pots do not'.[22] Macalister disagreed with Hooton about the correlation of cultural products with the movement of people. He expressed the view that 'the distribution of types of pottery almost necessarily implies a similar distribution of types of pottery-makers'.[23] As a physical anthropologist, Hooton's priority was the recovery of skeletal material and, in particular, skulls.

Brian Fagan criticises American archaeology in this period, describing it as 'often a mindless collecting and ordering of artifacts without any theoretical or even historical context'.[24] The fact that it was the National Museum and not the universities who were central to the Harvard Archaeological Expeditions resulted in this prioritising of the accumulation of artefacts over interpretation and the creation of knowledge. While the careful and scientific recovery of data was obviously extremely important to future research and archaeological technique, the overall interpretation and analysis was lacking. Between 1927 and 1937 enough archaeological material was acquired by the museum, according to Mahr, 'to fill almost 800 drawers of its storage accommodation'. This was despite the fact that it was 'quite impossible, owing to the congested state of the exhibition galleries, to display even a small fraction of this new material'.[25] Between 1927 and 1939 Adolf

Mahr and the National Museum of Ireland had a profound effect on the shaping of modern archaeology. However, Mahr himself acknowledged the dangers inherent in the accumulation of large quantities of artefacts without corresponding research and understanding: 'Most curators of large museums are constantly facing the danger of becoming nothing else but glorified stamp-collectors'.[26]

Macalister's views on Irish archaeology, expressed in his paper on Kiltera, a cemetery site in County Waterford excavated under the Unemployment Scheme between 12 and 25 September 1934, were prescient:

> It must be confessed that the principal lesson which we may learn from this excavation is, that so little is certainly known about the archaeology of Ireland that even a very minor site may present a whole catechism of problems which we can hardly yet presume to try to solve. We are still, and are likely to remain for some time to come, in the fact collecting stage, and it is merely as a contribution to the collection that this paper is to be regarded.[27]

Macalister himself perhaps straddled the collections phase of Irish archaeology and the new scientific phase of the discipline represented by the Harvard Mission and the Unemployment Schemes. This growing awareness of a scientific approach to excavation was evident among volunteers and amateur archaeologists alike participating in the work. Jock Kiely, the foreman from Lough Gur, in a radio broadcast from Cork in September 1937, explained that the workers 'have first to learn that they are not digging for buried treasure and that a post-hole is as important as a portable find and that they must exercise care at every stage'.[28] The significance of features on sites was explained and it was emphasised that archaeologists were not synonymous with treasure-hunters. Kiely also explained the procedures followed on excavations:

> When the site has been surveyed and photographed in its undisturbed condition selected areas are marked out by pegs and lines and these areas are excavated. The sod (or turf) is first removed and piled neatly where it will not be in the way and will be handy for replacing at the conclusion of the excavation as we restore all sites as nearly as possible to their original state. The underlying soil is then removed and every change noted.

He also explained that the present excavations proved 'very difficult' but because the men received good training 'they got all the information possible from these remains'.[29]

Evans also praised the workmen involved in the excavation of Cairn A, Aghnaskeagh under the Unemployment Schemes 'who soon came to realise the difference between excavating a megalith and opening a quarry'.[30] In a press release from the Government Information Bureau, dated 20 August 1935, the new and improved scientific excavation techniques were emphasised. It was explained that 'the workmen who helped in unravelling this intricate problem of the past were all keenly interested in the methods of excavation and were quick to notice differences of soil colour and the many minute traces of human occupation which means so much to the archaeologist'.[31]

Evans acknowledged a variety of sources of scientific expertise in his paper which included the geologist Professor J. K. Charlesworth of Queen's University Belfast, Stuart Piggott, Seán P. Ó Ríordáin, Adolf Mahr and Harold G. Leask.

## From Scientific Antiquarianism to Modern Archaeology

R.A.S. Macalister could see the value of the new excavation techniques employed by the Harvard Mission and he praised Hencken's work at Knockast, which was excavated by the Harvard Mission in 1933. He described the excavation as 'one of the most impressive of his [Hencken's] works' in an *Irish Press* article on 11 June 1937: 'It was not much to look at; an ordinary tomb-plunderer would have found bits of burnt and unburnt bone, a few bits of pottery, and some odds and ends. Under the magic wand of Dr. Hencken a whole new history revealed itself'.[32] The interesting questions here are how did the 'ordinary tomb-plunderer' described by Macalister refer to himself and other archaeologists of this period and what archaeological material exactly had previously been dismissed as 'odds and ends'?

It is worth having a brief look at the excavation of Carrowkeel, a passage-tomb cemetery in County Sligo, in 1911, in order to examine the contrast between the archaeological methods used at that time and those employed by the Harvard archaeologists between 1932 and 1936.

Carrowkeel is a useful case study for this as it was excavated by three very distinguished men in Irish academic circles at the time – R.A.S. Macalister, Robert Lloyd Praeger and E.C.R. Armstrong. At the time

Macalister was Professor of Celtic Archaeology at UCD. The multi-talented Praeger had discovered the site in 1896 while he was engaged on field-work for *Irish Topographical Botany*.[33] E.C.R. Armstrong was an assistant at the National Museum of Ireland where he was later to become Keeper of Irish Antiquities in 1914. The excavation report produced by this well-educated triumvirate serves to illustrate the type of archaeology engaged in by those who occupied elite positions in the academic sphere of archaeology at that time.[34] It also reflects the gradual change from a burgeoning scientific antiquarianism with an emphasis on collection of artefacts to more developed scientific techniques which occurred in Irish archaeology in the early decades of the twentieth century. In 1937, Mahr described the archaeological investigation at Carrowkeel as 'Almost the only really very successful and important (also from the international viewpoint) excavation undertaken for many years'.[35] This excavation throws light on the 'treasure-trove' mentality still lingering in the discipline. The monuments themselves were not seen as the primary focus for research and the attainment of knowledge, but their imagined contents were. Praeger described the expectation of what the tombs at Carrowkeel might contain in his book *The Way that I Went*: 'Their contents tended to explode the popular idea that at least the more elaborate of the Irish cairns contained along with the human remains, golden torcs or lunulae, or other contemporary treasure belonging to those who were buried in these imposing mausoleums'.[36] The whole megalithic cemetery took a total of 16 days to 'excavate', a term which perhaps should not be used considering its modern definition. Three separate expeditions were made. The first consisted of Praeger, Macalister, Alexander Macalister (R.A.S Macalister's father, and professor of Anatomy at Cambridge) and Armstrong, along with two workmen. The second expedition consisted of Praeger, Macalister and Armstrong and a man called W.A. Green. On the third visit they were joined by four workmen. In contrast, Harvard had adequate financial resources, manpower and the timeframe in which to carry out their numerous scientific excavations. For example, fifteen workmen participated in the Harvard Mission excavation of Poulawack cairn, Co. Clare. It was undertaken by Movius and Hencken between 22 June and 10 July, 1934. They were joined by two scholars from Harvard including Amory Goddard and F.L.W. Richardson. Gerard Brett from Oxford and Joseph Raftery from the National Museum of Ireland also participated.[37]

The use of language in archaeological reports both directs and reflects the thinking of archaeologists. The language used in the Carrowkeel report, for example, reflects the mindset of the time. The excavators described their activities at the site as 'pitching out the ragged lumps of limestone', from one carn, 'attacking' other carns and 'clearing out' the chambers.[38] While appreciation for the construction skills of the builders and the organisational ability of the community was expressed and evidence for 'architectural forethought and design',[39] noted, the excavators proceeded to break up some of the stones used in the construction of the monument.[40] The procedure for the examination of Carn P of this megalithic cemetery was as follows: 'Carn P, situated on the spur overlooking Carn O, was then attacked. It occupied us almost the whole afternoon [20th April] and the entire upper part of it was removed without anything being discovered; we continued work till it became clear that no chamber was present'.[41] The fact that 'nothing' was discovered suggests that no gold or other treasures, anticipated by the archaeologists, were recovered. The assumption was that Celtic treasure would be found in the burial chamber. Carn A was not examined as it was considered not to be worth opening, as it seemed to the investigators to be too small to contain a burial chamber. The excavators were of the opinion that no metal was found in the carns because it 'may have been too valuable to be placed with the dead'.[42] In stark contrast to the blatant disregard for damage caused to an archaeological monument, displayed by Macalister, Praeger and Armstrong, the Harvard excavators attempted to restore monuments as carefully as possible to their original structures. For example, the complete mound of Knockast was removed, and the last three days of the project were devoted to attempting to restore the mound to its original appearance. Hencken explained in his report on Creevykeel Court Tomb, County Sligo, that it was necessary to replace the lintel on its original supports in order to excavate a chamber of the tomb. He admitted that such 'restorations' were often 'deplorable' but acknowledged that it was the only way that the excavation could be completed.[43]

Archaeological techniques used by Harvard Mission archaeologists included stratigraphy, the use of a theodolite for planning, employing the quadrant method of excavation, the recognition of features, photography, experimental archaeology, and the use of scientific expertise, such as pollen analysis and charcoal analysis. While all of these techniques had their various limitations, the cross-referencing of the information obtained resulted in a more accurate and scientific picture of the Irish past. The location of artefacts on archaeological sites was meticulously recorded by the Harvard Mission. The technique of stratigraphy, though known in geology since the time of Charles Lyell, was not mentioned in the Carrowkeel report of 1911.[44] However, stratigraphy also had its limitations as observed at Cahercommaun fort by Hencken where 'only a very small part of the material found in the fort was stratified. Since the bulk of the fill was composed largely of loose stones and had been infested with burrowing animals, the position of most objects had no significance'.[45]

The Harvard archaeologists used a theodolite to carefully divide the mound of Knockast cemetery-cairn into quarters and painstakingly excavated each one separately. The quandrant method was also used at Cahercommaun fort and at Poulawack cairn. The technique used at Poulawack combined the quadrant technique with a method invented by R.E.M. Wheeler of the London Museum.[46] Wheeler had divided a mound into parallel strips which he excavated in turn. This gave a series of faces at close intervals through the mound. This technique had to be adapted to suit the structure of the cairn at Poulawack. However, Hencken noted that 'the numerous parallel sections were also drawn and proved very useful in illustrating its rather complex interior'.[47]

Archaeological features such as post-holes, pits and burnt areas were carefully examined, planned, excavated and recorded by the Harvard team. For example, a row of stake holes, found at Creevykeel, were described and a possible interpretation offered.[48] Burnt areas and pits below the cairn were examined for activity prior to its construction. A shallow pit in the middle of the Creevykeel court was examined under the original flooring.[49] At Knockast, pits in the undisturbed ground below the mound were examined. Three pits were found to contain bones of domestic animals. The pits and animal bones and evidence of very hot fires were interpreted as traces of some ceremonial that had taken place before the cairn was erected. However, the excavators believed that the fires were not extensive enough to have been pyres for cremating the people subsequently buried in the mound. Burnt areas and pits would not have been examined in any great detail prior to the Harvard Mission as they would not have been expected to yield any useful information.

The painstaking recovery of artefacts was important to the Harvard Mission. For example, in one of the cists at Knockast the remains of a bowl, believed to have been a food vessel, was in such a bad state that all attempts to dry and harden it failed, so the excavators preserved the shape of its interior by encasing it in plaster of Paris before removing it.[50] Another cremation burial was found in what was described as the largest and most elaborately ornamented pot from the cairn at Knockast. It had been placed mouth downward and had been crushed by the large stones which had been piled around it. The excavators wound pieces of cloth tightly around the pot which enabled them to lift it out with the bones and put it into a box for transportation to the National Museum.[51] In contrast, an attempt to retrieve pottery for examination at the Carrowkeel site was unsuccessful.[52] In another instance, the Harvard Mission archaeologists were unable to remove a bronze knife from its position in Knockast. It was only possible to make a drawing of it in situ.[53] Photography was a technique employed by the Harvard Mission to record precise information about the stratigraphy, location of artefacts in situ, and the presence of features. It was used in the Gallen excavations in 1934 and 1935. A grant was provided by Oxford University specifically for this purpose.[54] Photographs had also been taken during the course of the Carowkeel excavations in 1911.

The excavations at Carrowkeel were described by E. Estyn Evans as 'hurried, crude and inadequate'.[55] Certainly, Macalister, Praeger and Armstrong practised a crude version of scientific archaeology in their excavation of Carrowkeel, but at the time the emphasis was still on the collection of artefacts rather than the careful planning of their spatial and temporal context in relation to the monument. However, it would have been considered a scientific excavation in 1911 and Mahr was still reporting on it favourably in 1937. Techniques employed by the excavators included 'pacing' to measure the approximate diameter of the monument and the use of a 'plane-table' to make a plan of it. A 'fine riddle' was used to find small items such as pierced stone pendants, bone fragments and beads and small fragments of pottery. The bone implements at Carrowkeel were examined by Dr R.F. Scharff, Keeper of the Natural History Collections in the National Museum. Mr T. Hallissy, of the Geological Survey of Ireland, examined the beads, pendants, and stone balls found. The anatomist Alexander Macalister examined the bones.

The services of a variety of specialists were also used to examine the thousands of artefacts recovered during the five Harvard Archaeological Expeditions. For example, the stone objects found at Creevykeel were examined and identified by Anthony Farrington, M.R.I.A., an engineer who published papers on glacial geology and geomorphology. A small bronze knife which was found in one of the burials at Knockast was straightened out to its original form by Dr Plenderleith of the British Museum.[56] Two species of shell were found associated with the cremation burials at Knockast. These were examined by W.J. Clench, Curator of Mollusks at the Museum of Comparative Zoology of Harvard University who identified them as *Pyramidula rotundata*, and *Lauria cylindrica*.[57] Joseph Cecil Maby examined fifty-two samples of slag from Creevykeel. He suggested that some of them 'were part of the siliceous lining of a furnace' and other pieces were 'laminated, as if by successive smeltings.'[58] Maby also examined some tiny pieces of charcoal found under a cist at Poulawack.[59] Charcoal from the burials at Knockast was examined by the anthropologist and archaeologist Emil W. Haury[60] who obtained his PhD from Harvard in 1934 and became director of the Arizona State Museum from 1938 to 1964. Haury concluded that the pyres were built as a rule of oak.[61]

In 1929, Liam S. Gogan had criticised 'the failure of the archaeological chairs in Dublin and Cork to put additional personnel into the field'. He remarked that their 'paper' contribution to the various phases involved during the past twenty years was of 'singularly little value'.[62] This was to change in the 1930s when a native school of scientific archaeology emerged in the context of a state framework for the discipline. The Harvard Mission excavations provided opportunities for scientific training on site. The development of state-funded unemployment schemes further developed this process and a new generation of scientific archaeologists were trained. Other important scientific initiatives complementing the archaeology included the work of the Committee for Quaternary Research.

Despite Macalister's involvement in the excavation at Carrowkeel the description of him as an 'antiquary' used in a derogatory way by Hencken was not only unfair but inaccurate. Macalister used the scientific techniques available to him at the time and was always ready to embrace any new science which helped to reveal the archaeological past. In 1927 the Cambridge archaeologist O.G.S. Crawford published a definition of *archaeology* in the first edition of the journal *Antiquity*: 'Archaeology is a branch of science which achieves its results by means of excavation, fieldwork and comparative studies: it is founded upon the observation of facts'.[63]

At that stage new scientific methods were being used in Britain and Europe but had yet to be introduced to the practice of Irish archaeology. The development of Irish archaeology from the 'scientific antiquarianism' of Macalister to the more stringent scientific methods of the Harvard Mission archaeologists was a continuum, as no clear break with the previous model was obvious. Both models relied heavily on literary and historical sources for interpretation of the 'Celtic' Iron Age period onwards. In Ireland, the culture-historical paradigm in vogue in the 1930s incorporated the antiquarian tradition with developed scientific techniques within a racial and political framework. Macalister's antiquarianism benefitted from techniques influenced by nineteenth-century science. According to Tim Murray 'it is ill-informed to interpret antiquarianism as a wrong-turning on the pathway to archaeological enlightenment'.[64] In Irish archaeology antiquarianism was the multi-disciplinary approach of its day and the forerunner of scientific archaeology.

This supposed paradigmatic change to more refined scientific archaeological techniques, like the changes in science in general over time, as discussed by Stephen Jay Gould in his book *The Mismeasure of Man*, 'does not record a closer approach to absolute truth, but the alteration of cultural contexts that influence it so strongly'.[65] This is why the Harvard team began with conclusions about Irish identity and finished their work with their preconceived ideas scientised and consolidated. Thomas Kuhn, in his book *The Structure of Scientific Revolutions* describes 'paradigm shifts' in terms of the replacements of the core theories which reflect the scientists' world-view.[66] It would seem that Irish archaeology did not undergo a paradigmatic shift in perspective with the coming of the Harvard Mission but a development of nascent scientific leanings in the context of large scale excavations.

## Hugh O'Neill Hencken

Joseph Raftery praised the work of Hugh O'Neill Hencken, the Director of the Harvard Archaeological Expedition, whose excavations of a wide variety of sites in the 1930s 'initiated for us the scientific approach to fieldwork'.[67] Many types of prehistoric and protohistoric sites were excavated including crannógs, burial mounds, middens, settlements and a cliff fort, during five consecutive archaeological expeditions. The construction of knowledge in this process involved an interpretative process taking place within an already established intellectual framework. This included the selection of sites; the methodologies employed to recover data; the use of historical sources as primary evidence; the nomenclature to define time periods into which assemblages of artefacts were fitted; the classificatory systems used for artefacts, features and sites; the idea of progress embedded in the typological studies of artefacts; the use of evidence from the natural sciences to provide additional information about context and environment in which sites were situated; and the inference of specific ethnic and social identities from material culture. These were the facets of the complex discipline that was Irish archaeology in the twentieth century. While much archaeological data was retrieved, the use of such a variety of information from other disciplines on a selective basis, in order to interpret the archaeological record, meant that interpretation could be open to manipulation.

Hencken, Curator of European Archaeology at the Peabody Museum in Harvard, was described by Gogan as having 'sound scholarship, keen archaeological conscience, amiable personality and American directness'.[68] In order to interpret his findings Hencken sought to fuse the historical and scientific approaches to archaeology. While he came to Ireland as part of a team of functionalist anthropologists[69] his influences were literary and firmly in the culture-historical model of archaeological interpretation.[70] He melded these two approaches effectively in his scientific archaeological reports. This reflected his academic training in America and England. He had received interdisciplinary training at Cambridge, England, where he was awarded a BA degree in 1926. Among his teachers were J.M. de Navarro and Hector Munro Chadwick. De Navarro was a lecturer in the Faculty of Archaeology and Anthropology at Cambridge. He gave the Sir John Rhys Memorial Lecture in 1936 entitled 'A Survey of Research on an Early Phase of Celtic Culture'.[71] It was De Navarro who initially introduced Hencken to Mahr.[72] Chadwick was Elrington and Bosworth Professor of Anglo-Saxon in the University of Cambridge from 1912 to 1941.[73] Hencken studied under Chadwick and de Navarro, a course described as 'that wonderful amalgam of proto-historic, archaeological, linguistic and historical studies created by H.M. Chadwick the study of the Classics of the North'.[74] The combination of these subjects was described by Kenneth Jackson as the 'essence of Chadwickianism'.[75] Chadwick himself was a historian, student of literature and a philologist. This Chadwickian training is probably one of the reasons why Hencken was not anti-historical, which was one of the signifiers of adherents of the functionalist school. As it happened this also turned out to be advantageous when responding to the political sensibilities of the day in Ireland.

Hencken's PhD thesis title was 'The Bronze and Early Iron Ages in Cornwall and Devon'. This was the basis of his book *Archaeology of Cornwall and Scilly*, which was published in 1932 and was deemed to have given 'a new impetus to the notion of regional archaeology'.[76] Hencken credited the British archaeologist O.G.S. Crawford for suggesting the subject to him and for providing assistance and advice to him throughout the project.[77] The chapters on megaliths and the prehistoric tin trade were regarded as remarkable for their time.[78] V. Gordon Childe, in a contemporary review of the book commended Hencken for his approach.[79] Hencken's book has since been described by Paul Ashbee as a 'landmark' because 'it brought together material from methodical personal fieldwork, as well as from periodicals, dusty museums and unusual private collections.[80]

Hencken wrote that the purpose of his work with the Harvard Mission was:

> not only to reveal the successive waves of culture that have been reaching Ireland from Europe ever since the arrival of the first Irishman, but to find out the origin of the physical types that comprise the population both ancient and modern, as well as to discover the kind of social organization that these people have evolved for themselves up to the present day.[81]

With regard to choosing sites for excavation Hencken observed that this presented a difficulty because 'probably no country in Europe is so rich in archaeological sites as Ireland'.[82]

Using a Chadwickian approach in his Harvard Mission work in Ireland in the 1930s, Hencken applied techniques learned in Cornwall to the large-scale excavations in Ireland which included the Ballinderry and Lagore Crannógs, the Cahercommaun Stone Fort and the Creevykeel Court Cairn. He also employed new scientific techniques in his excavations of Bronze Age sites at Knockast, Poulawack and Carrowlisdoouan. However, Brian Fagan criticises American archaeology in this period because almost all interpretations in American archaeology were largely descriptive with little effort made to explain the meaning of the archaeological record.[83] Indeed, the period 1914–40 is described by the historians of American archaeology Gordon R. Willey and Jeremy A. Sabloff as the 'Classificatory-Historical Period', characterised by continued improvements of field methods and excavations and the careful recovery of artefacts and features.[84] However, this over reliance on the establishment of chronological sequences and artefact recovery, while intrinsically worthwhile to the discipline, meant that already embedded notions about Celtic or Christian identity were neither explored nor challenged. The focus on techniques such as stratigraphy and chronology suited the nationalist agenda as it authenticated the nation's right to exist by obtaining scientific evidence from each archaeological stratum for its cultural continuity and development. Anthony D. Smith points out that the idea of authenticity of the nation is a multi-faceted one:

It includes a sense of the distinctiveness of a people and its folk culture; the proximate claim to originality, of unique authorship of that culture; the cognate feeling of cultural possession; of what is 'our very own' and nobody else's; and finally the romantic idea of cultural purity and diversity, popularised by Herder and his followers, the desire for what is unmixed and uncontaminated by alien elements.[85]

Hencken availed of a variety of scientific expertise to help interpret his excavations. Arthur Wilson Stelfox, together with his assistants, undertook a study of the huge quantities of animal bones at the site of Lagore, to establish what kind of animal husbandry or hunting took place at the site. Frank Mitchell of the Quaternary Research Committee undertook a geological survey of the lake bed to find out its history and former extent, and a palaeobotanical study by pollen analyses to ascertain the age of some 'apparently prehistoric remains' discovered underneath the artificial island.[86] Movius undertook the study of the human remains. The Royal Irish Academy published the archaeological report and included corroborating scientific studies as appendices.

The Harvard Archaeological Expedition is credited with the introduction of 'the methods of Pitt-Rivers' to the excavation of Ballinderry Crannóg 1, famous as the first scientifically excavated crannóg in the country.[87] This was accomplished, despite the fact that Hencken admitted 'I had little idea of how to dig a crannóg but I learned by doing it'.[88] The early decades of the twentieth century, Brian Fagan notes, was 'an era when one learned digging by doing'.[89] In the previous century, according to Briggs, 'crannóg enquiry seems to have been dominated more by a motive to acquire artefacts rather than by the recognition of the need for scientific investigation, systematic record or publication. The vigorous trade in Irish crannóg artefacts involved Ireland's most distinguished academicians'.[90] E.C.R. Armstrong had written in 1923 about previous research on crannógs that 'For the most part they have been excavated in a careless manner, no stratification levels being recorded, the objects found being considered to belong to the same date'.[91] Hencken, in an article in *The Irish Review* in 1934, noted that the crannógs which had so far been excavated by the Harvard Archaeological Expeditions had provided 'a large amount of new information about Ireland in the remote days before the English invasion'.[92] Before Harvard arrived much of the site at Lagore had been disturbed because of turf-cutting, draining and digging for bones and antiquities. Harvard attempted 'to rescue what remained'.[93] Hencken became a pioneer of Irish crannóg methodology in the process.

There were many practical difficulties associated with the excavation of crannóg sites in Ireland. At Lagore the prevention of flooding at the site was an onerous task. Dumps of earth had to be placed a good distance away because their weight would crack the boggy ground. These cracks would allow water in. This meant that the workers had to excavate 'as rapidly as was consistent with due care' before the site became flooded. By the end of the third season after a wet summer it was found that it was impossible to excavate the crannóg fully because of the difficulties in the prevention of the site from flooding even when pumping took place day and night. There was also a problem with post-holes. If a perfectly preserved wooden post was removed from the boggy ground then the hole would quickly close over leaving no post-hole. At Ballinderry 2, there was a problem with the plan of the Late Bronze Age stratum as it was impossible for the most part to be sure which of the wooden posts on the site belonged to the Late Bronze Age stratum and which to the Early Christian stratum.[94] Other problems included the fact that the site had been looted from time to time from its initial discovery in the mid nineteenth century. Quite a range of material of varying dates was found. Unfortunately, all the strata of the site had been penetrated by the makers of a drain with the result that the uppermost levels contained objects of all periods from the Viking Age down to modern times.[95] Objects may have also worked their way down through the layers.

The first attempt to use tree-ring dating techniques in Ireland was on wood samples from the crannóg at Ballinderry 1. These samples were brought from the crannóg to Harvard for analysis. The system of tree-ring dating used was that which had been developed by Professor A.E. Douglass of the University of Arizona and had been used successfully in the dating of prehistoric wood in the American Southwest. However, there were problems with the wood from Ballinderry 1 as it did not give good ring records. The reason for this was that rain, fog, long growing seasons and the moisture retaining marshy ground near the lake made most of the trees examined into 'complacent recorders' which meant that they were of little or no value. Some of the wood was also inclined to warp as it dried, making the rings unreadable.[96] There was also a problem with the pollen analysis at Ballinderry 2. The excavation had been conducted a year before Professor Knud Jessen's first visit to Ireland in 1934. When Frank Mitchell visited the site three years after the excavation the fixed points were no longer visible. There were discrepancies in the terms applied to the layers of the lake-bed.[97] Indeed, the American anthropologist and archaeologist, William Duncan Strong, makes the salient point about the methodology of archaeological drawings of a waterlogged site such as Lagore: 'The maps and diagrams are well presented – this despite the fact that water, human detritus, and clear delineations do not go well together'.[98]

Adolf Mahr's influence on the discipline, while positive initially from a scientific perspective, subsequently became very restrictive in interpretative and ideological terms and prevented the discipline from expanding from a narrow data collection and recording exercise to the extraction of more useful knowledge about people in the past, using broader interpretative techniques. The scientific pigeon-holing of Irish archaeology in this period meant that broader questions about society and ideological concerns about archaeological data were not debated. It could be argued that what Mahr had conducted, through the auspices of the Harvard Mission, was a massive state treasure hunt.

Mahr's influence on the crannóg research conducted by the Harvard archaeologists can be seen by the many references to his advice contained in the reports on Ballinderry 1 and 2 and Lagore. It is possible that the subsequent over-emphasis on cataloguing and minimal interpretation in Irish archaeology was as a result of Mahr's commandeering of the Harvard project. But as Pat Wallace explains there had been no scientific excavations before the Harvard Mission came to Ireland and Mahr was 'trying to do something new, something big, of world importance'.[99]

However, the archaeologist Flinders Petrie made the following observation on archaeological interpretation in general which is apt in the light of the inherent difficulties of crannóg research: 'The old saying that a man finds what he is looking for in a subject is too true; or, if he has not enough insight to ensure finding what he looks for, it is at least sadly true that he does not find anything he does not look for'.[100]

## Hallam L. Movius

The programme of excavations in Northern Ireland was described as 'an excellent example of how palaeontology, palaeobotany and geology can supplement archaeology'.[101] Specialist scientific reports were sought from these and other disciplines to complement the archaeological data recovered. Movius was assisted in his interpretation of these Mesolithic sites by the contribution of the Committee for Quaternary Research. This was set up in

1934 and resulted in Professor Knud Jessen coming to Ireland to conduct research on Irish bogs. Jessen and Dr H. Jonassen, his assistant, visited Movius's sites and examined the pollen deposits. Their reports are among the various detailed scientific reports included in all of Movius's papers on the Northern Irish sites published by the RIA and RSAI. Jessen, who had been a member of the Danish Geological Survey, had a background in the study of Early Post-Glacial deposits in the Baltic and 'made the geological interpretation of the sites far clearer'.[102] Movius visited Denmark in 1934 and was shown similar sites by Jessen. There, he took the opportunity to study the connection between the Irish and Baltic Stone cultures.[103] He visited the National Museum of Copenhagen where he was shown collections from the Mesolithic sites of Denmark.

Movius explained that the stratigraphy of the County Antrim sites including Island Magee, Curran Point (Larne), Glenarm, and Cushendun and Rough Island in County Down 'furnishes the key to the Mesolithic sequence of North-East Ireland'.[104] He was satisfied that the specialist scientific studies including palaeobotanical, palaeontological and geological reports complemented the important archaeological results obtained. He sought advice from the pioneering prehistorian and first woman to hold an Oxbridge Chair in archaeology, Dorothy Garrod, and from the eminent Cambridge prehistorian, Miles Burkitt. Various scientific reports were included as appendices to Movius's final archaeological report on 'the type site of the Mesolithic', Curran Point, Larne, Co. Antrim, published in 1953.[105] These included a palaeontological report by Knud Jessen on the estuarine clay at Island Magee in Co. Antrim which featured a discussion of the pollen-diagrams, the molluscs and a discussion on the palaeobotanical age of the maximum of the post-glacial marine transgression in North-Eastern Ireland. William S. Benninghoff, a graduate of Harvard and later Professor of Botany at the University of Michigan (1957–88) contributed an appendix in which he analysed the sediments. Nora Fisher McMillan, the self-taught and prolific conchologist (expert on the study of mollusc shells) and naturalist from Belfast contributed a report on the fauna of the site. She also co-authored a report with the civil servant and gentleman scientist, Arthur Earland, on the foraminifera (a group of microscopic marine animals that protect themselves with tiny shells). A report on the calcareous algae was contributed by Paul Lemoine, the French geologist who was appointed in 1920 to the chair of geology at Muséum National d'Histoire Naturell in Paris. Movius himself wrote the specialised report on the remains of vertebrates from the Curran deposits.

Movius also appended specialist reports on Glenarm, County Antrim. Knud Jessen made a palaeo-botanical examination of the strata to glean useful information about pollen-analysis and dates. This was the first time that such an examination was undertaken in Ireland in an archaeological context. Professor Glover M. Allen, Curator of Mammals at the Museum of Comparative Zoology in Harvard University contributed an appendix on the animal remains. Nora Fisher contributed a report on the molluscan remains and Frederick L.W. Richardson of Harvard University contributed one on the physiography. Richardson was interested in the geological and geographical influences that shaped ancient cultures. Later he became an industrial consultant focusing on human interaction and an anthropology teacher in business schools.

Movius's work on the human remains involved innovative experimental archaeology. When he examined the remains of the inhumed individuals at the cemetery-cairn at Knockast and compared them to the cremated remains from the site he concluded that the cremated people were generally smaller and of a different type. He did not believe that this was due to shrinkage in the funeral pyres and carried out an experiment to prove his hypothesis.[106] As oak was the wood used in the Knockast cremations it was also used in the experiment. Fresh skeletal material was acquired, a pit was dug, a fire was lit and burned down to a bed of hot coals. The bones were placed on it. More oak was added. When the bones turned an ashy white and began to crack the cremation was deemed to be complete. The bones were removed and measured. There was little difference between the measurements of the burnt and unburnt bones. It was concluded, therefore, that the bones of the cremated burials were not smaller as a result of their exposure to intense heat. Therefore, Movius concluded that they were a different type to that found in inhumations at the site. This is the first time that experimental archaeology was used as an interpretative tool in Irish archaeology.

While the Harvard Mission took an interdisciplinary scientific approach and included many specialist reports with their excavations they were not, however, as interested as the National Museum was in animal bones, as their focus was on human remains. They were interested in animal remains only in terms of their use by humans. The primary concern of the Harvard Mission was in its own racial and eugenic survey and the scientific heritage of the Celtic race. This tied in with Irish nationalist archaeology which was essential to establishing the cultural and racial purity of the 'citizens' of the nation through the latest scientific techniques. The Harvard Mission scientists had to be sensitive about the importance of animal bones. After the excavation of Ballinderry 1 crannóg Hencken suggested that the badly broken animal bones at the site should be discarded. The Natural History Division of the National Museum was displeased with this, and with the fact that many bones were broken en route to the museum.[107] With Ballinderry 2 the Harvard team adopted a new system for dealing with the bones 'in order to avoid criticism from governmental quarters'.[108] They were more careful not to break them, and as soon as they were recovered they were soaked in a preservative provided by the National Museum. While Hencken acknowledged the value of studying the bone material for dating purposes and for studying the ratio of one domestic animal to another, as well as the ratio of domestic animal to wild animal in each separate stratum, he thought it unnecessary to transport all the scrap bone to Dublin.

Twelve tons of animal bones, including both domestic and wild varieties, were found at Cahercommaun. All of these were dispatched to Arthur Wilson Stelfox, a specialist on cave-bones, and Deputy Keeper of Natural History at the National Museum. A total of thirteen truckloads of bones were sent to the National Museum in 1933 at a cost of £65, which Hencken considered a waste of money and 'an expenditure quite out of proportion to the rest of the excavation.[109] Being politically astute, Hencken decided against his better judgement to spend the money in order 'to disarm criticism' and to prepare the museum for accepting another time only the 'really useful material'.[110] 'Really useful material' referred to human bones, especially skulls. Adolf Mahr ensured that museum staff were very accommodating to the Harvard Team and this was acknowledged by Hencken, who commented that 'although the buildings, which adjoin the Dáil (Parliament), are closely guarded by Military Police and Civic Guards, we were accorded the remarkable privilege of using the Museum at all hours'.[111]

The contribution to the development of the discipline of scientific archaeology in Ireland by the Harvard team and their productive use of associated scientific findings was appreciated by J.D.G. Clark, even if he was critical of the delays in the introduction of these improvements. In a note on the Bann River Culture of Northern Ireland, published in the *Proceedings of the Prehistoric Society* for 1936, he made the comment that despite the fact that it was nearly seventy years since Sir John Evans had published a description of the flint blades and tanged flakes found in the valley of the Bann River, near Lough Neagh, it had been left to 'an expedition from across the Atlantic in co-operation with scientists from

Denmark to determine the antiquity of the industry on a scientific basis'.[112] Clark acknowledged that the Bann River flints had been a common type in Irish collections. Before the First World War W.J. Knowles and Wilfrid Jackson had already established that the flints occurred in association with a deposit of diatomite.[113] In 1927 Dr G. Erdtman of Stockholm took samples for pollen analysis at the site, suggesting a possible date for the diatomite in Late Atlantic and Sub-Boreal times,[114] climatic periods dating to c. 7,500–5000 BP and c. 5000–3500 BP. In 1930 Blake Whelan established the main horizon of the industry at the base of the deposit.[115] The Harvard Mission archaeologists acknowledged that they were 'heavily obligated' to him.[116] In 1936, Clark stated that the excavations which had been carried out at Newferry, 'have only served to confirm what had already to some extent been established by previous work'. But, he suggested that 'this does not in any way diminish the importance of the excavations, which, at one blow, have determined beyond cavil, the age of the Bann River industry both in relation to local forest development and to other cultural phenomena'.[117] In Clark's view, 'the Newferry excavation only serves to illustrate once again what can be accomplished by systematic excavations even on a small scale (the area examined was only 30 feet square), when carried out with precision and backed up by the intelligent co-operation of scientific specialists'.[118] Movius himself acknowledged the work carried out by Evans, Jackson, Knowles and Whelan, noting in his paper that: 'The classic Bann industry is too well known to be described in detail in the present paper'.[119] Clark also acknowledged that Jessen's important pollen analysis at the site had established definitely that the industry associated with the ash stratum at the base of the diatomite deposit and the hearths belonged to the Late Atlantic and Early Sub-Boreal time.[120]

Movius, while acknowledging the prior contribution of antiquarians in prehistoric research, was not unduly influenced by history in his interpretation of prehistoric archaeological data. As a Palaeolithic archaeologist he was more interested in the corroborating findings of the natural sciences. In correspondence with Adolf Mahr, for example, Movius questioned the validity of the 'Riverford Culture' suggested by Mahr in his 1937 paper, in which the latter devoted a substantial part (48 of 175 pages). Mahr associated the Riverford people with the Picts. He acknowledged that he was influenced by the publication of Eoin MacNeill's paper on 'The Pretanic Background in Britain and Ireland' in which the author included a map of Pictish tribes in Ireland.[121] MacNeill wrote 'that the Celts of Pre-Roman Gaul regarded Britain and Ireland as Pictish Islands' and that the ancient description of Ireland as a Pretanic Island is justified.[122] Mahr compared his own distribution map of 'Riverford' material with MacNeill's map and came to the conclusion that 'it will be agreed upon even by the most inveterate sceptic that they tally to an extent which I feel justified in calling identity'.[123]

However, he was aware of the problems inherent in his conclusion: 'It may seem very daring, almost lunacy, to try to identify the Riverford people ethnographically, let alone to connect this early element with a historical ethnic name. Yet there appear to be valid reasons for doing so'.[124]

In a letter dated 26 July 1938, Movius congratulated Mahr on the honour of a professorship conferred on him by Hitler. In this letter Movius also commented that 'I haven't found out yet who the Riverford people are' and 'I do not see how the complete absence of occupation sites can let one invoke a new people coming into Ireland, especially on the basis of rather scattered finds'.[125] Movius concluded his letter by suggesting that the material was a survival of Neolithic materials in the Bronze Age, noting that he believed that 'one can expect almost anything to have survived in such an area of peripheral insularity'.[126] Mahr replied that he expected that many of the ringforts near rivers would, after excavation, 'yield finds belonging to the same culture'. He expressed the wish that 'the Harvard Mission started only now so that we could put the spade to some of the Riverford sites'.[127] In a letter dated 14 October 1938 Movius agreed that 'the essential thing is for someone to have the moral courage to break away from the school of thought in Ireland dominated by our friend "leetle Mac," [R.A.S. Macalister] but I am afraid I do not agree with you concerning the Riverford People'.[128] Mahr's riposte was blunt: 'I do not care a damn whether I did or did not convince you of the Riverford people, and all I could do was to speak my mind'.[129] In a letter dated 8 December 1938 Mahr refers again to his 'great discovery of the Riverford culture'.[130] This misinterpretation by Mahr of this assemblage demonstrates the problems inherent in the interpretation of archaeological material based on documentary sources alone without the corroborating hard evidence which excavation yields.[131]

## A Native School of Archaeology: Irish and International

Adolf Mahr's view was that 'the technique of crannóg excavation, as seen against the international background, obtained a 'tremendous fillip' from the work of the Harvard Archaeological Expeditions in Ireland.[132] A native school of Irish archaeology was also an international one. People participating from Ireland, America and Britain included archaeologists, anthropologists, illustrators and art historians. Most were volunteers but in some cases, expenses were paid. Volunteers brought their own expertise to bear, got an opportunity to hone their own skills and learn new techniques. The Harvard Mission sites in Ireland during the 1930s were international training sites for emerging scientific archaeologists. Mahr expressed the view that it was 'desirable that freelances join the excavation, preferably people who are already in touch with the Museum and belong, as it were, to its wider circle, and people who are likely to remain interested in an active way in the problems of Irish archaeology'.[133] On the Second Harvard Archaeological Expedition three Harvard students and about forty local men were employed.[134] Elizabeth Bigelow of the Fogg Art Museum of Harvard University spent some time on excavations and she was deemed to have 'rendered a great deal of most valuable service'.[135] What her service was is not elaborated upon in the reports but it may be that there was an expectation that gold objects would be recovered from Celtic sites. This may also account for the participation in the Second Harvard Archaeological Expedition of Waldo Forbes from Harvard. He was a grandson of the poet Ralph Waldo Emerson and became director of the Fogg Art Museum in 1909. He went to Abyssinia after his trip to Ireland to take part in a Harvard anthropological expedition. In 1935 he was appointed the Martin A. Lawrence Ryerson Professor in the Fine Arts at Harvard.[136] Others who were involved in the Second Harvard Archaeological Expedition included Amory Goddard from Harvard, who had excavated in Egypt in 1923.

Volunteer assistants for the Third Harvard Archaeological Expedition in 1934 travelled from Britain and America to take part and came from the London Museum and the Universities of Harvard, Oxford, Cambridge and London. There were also volunteer assistants from the National University of Ireland, the National Museum, Dublin University (TCD) and the NMAC. The staff for this expedition included four Harvard men including John Otis Brew, Hencken, Movius and Goddard who received full or partial expenses. Goddard and F.T. Riley of Trinity College, Dublin, both worked for Movius at Kilgreany Cave, Co. Waterford. Movius described Riley as 'an able assistant', who was entered as a charge hand on the pay sheet and paid under the Unemployment Schemes for archaeological research.[137] In 1931, John Otis Brew had been director of the Peabody Museum Southeastern Utah Expedition to Alkahi Ridge. He was described as 'remarkably skilled at keeping track of the daily minutiae of field research without losing sight of the major goals of the work'.[138] He became curator of southwestern archaeology at the Peabody Museum in 1941 and was appointed Director of the Peabody Museum in 1948.

At Poulawack the assistants included Movius, Goddard and Frederick L.W. Richardson all from Harvard, Gerard Brett of Corpus Christi College, Oxford and Joseph Raftery (a future director of the National Museum). Raftery was also involved in the excavation of Cahercommaun fort in County Clare for which six assistants were employed. The other Irish assistants included Mary Eily de Putron of the National Museum of Ireland and Liam Price. Raftery, de Putron, Brew and Richardson joined the excavation at Lagore under the Third Harvard Archaeological Expedition in 1934. Eleanor Hardy of Girton College, Cambridge and Norah Jolliffe of the Royal Halloway College, University of London, assisted on the site. Thalassa Cruso (later to become Hencken's wife) travelled to Lagore from the London Museum to join the excavation team.[139] In 1935, a total of ten assistants were employed at Lagore, including people from Ireland, England and America. These included Dr Gordon Macgregor, an assistant in Anthropology at Harvard University and six volunteers who received no remuneration for their work.[140] At Lagore in 1936, staff included Thalassa Cruso Hencken, and Dorothy Newton of the Peabody Museum alongside de Putron and Raftery of the National Museum of Ireland.[141] Macgregor also worked alongside seven other assistants and twenty-three workmen employed at Creevykeel, Co. Sligo. These included Price and Raftery from Ireland, Agnes J.W. Newbigin and G.F. Wilmot of Oxford; W.W. Howells, Research Associate in Physical Anthropology at the American Museum of Natural History; Antelo Devereux of the Board of Managers, the University Museum, University of Pennsylvania; and Lauriston Ward, Curator of Asiatic Archaeology at the Peabody Museum. Ward later became founder and President of the Council for World Archaeology from 1953 to 1960 and Chairman of the American School of Prehistoric Research between 1954 to 1960. He was described as 'very involved in archaeology, not as a dirt archaeologist per se, but as a creative organising force'.[142] Ward also joined Dorothy Newton of the Peabody Museum and Gordon Palmer of Harvard to assist Movius on Curran Point Larne, Co. Antrim. An archaeological illustrator from Australia, Nancy de Crespigny (who later became Movius's wife) also worked at the site.

In 1937 the NUI awarded Hencken a doctorate for his archaeological work in Ireland. Hencken wrote in a letter to Movius about it: 'It was damn decent of them to recognize what we have done. The only trouble that it should really have gone to E.A.H. [Earnest A. Hooton]'.[143] On 17 June 1937, James Bryant Conant, President of Harvard University, wrote to de Valera that he believed that 'the Harvard Anthropological Survey of Ireland, in addition to its eventual contribution to knowledge of the history and prehistory of the nation, has served to strengthen and to renew the bonds of friendship and understanding which unite the Irish and the American peoples'.[144]

# 9 THE PAGEANT OF THE CELT: IRISH ARCHAEOLOGY, MEDIA AND THE DIASPORA

Among the general public, familiar enough with Tutankhamen's tomb, the thrilling archaeological discoveries that are constantly being made in the strongholds and cemeteries of early Europe go largely unnoticed. But the developing civilizations and the remarkable achievements in the world of art of the real ancestors of the American people, thousands of years ago in their ancient homes on the other side of the Atlantic, are as full of importance to us as the better known cultures which contributed little or nothing to modern America.[1]

– Hugh O'Neill Hencken, 1934

## The Celtic Image

Prior to the work of the Harvard Mission in Ireland the physical image of the Celt was not a positive one. Victorian caricaturists in popular presses in

Britain and America in the nineteenth and early twentieth century depicted the Celt as barbarous and as a 'White Negro'.[2] Magazines such as *Punch* often featured the Irishman as an ape-like creature.

By the 1930s the political and economic position of the Irish in America was changing for the better. However, attitudes towards the immigrant Irish were slow to change. In 1932, the following description of the work of the Harvard Mission in Ireland and, in particular, the recovery of the Viking gaming board from Ballinderry 1, was included in an article which appeared in the *Herald Examiner*, Chicago:

> They have already dug up truck loads of animal bones, axes, bronze combs and iron shillelahs. One of the finds was a carved backgammon board which was used a thousand years before St Patrick came along. A couple of smashed skulls were unearthed alongside. This would seem to point at some ancient debate over rules.[3]

Malcolm Chapman expressed the opinion that the term 'Celtic' was initially one of racist abuse, writing that

> It is probably no exaggeration to say that we had by far better translate *keltoi* with some generalised term of modern vernacular racist abuse than by a prim and sanitised term from the lexicon of Indo-European linguistics. The Celts, for ancient Greece, were, so the speak, the wogs in the north.[4]

Chapman does not present any evidence to back up this assertion but, in fact illustrates, Neil MacGregor's contention that 'Celtic' is a cultural construct that has changed its meaning many times and can be considered a label 'continually redefined to echo contemporary concerns over politics, religion and identity'.[5] In the case of Chapman's book the author's challenge to the construction of Celtic identity reflected concerns about the prospect of Scottish devolution in the 1990s. The term 'Celtic', however, was a term of racist abuse for the Irish in the English and American media in the nineteenth and early twentieth century but gained traction in a positive way from the 1930s onwards. With the gradual change in the fortunes of the Irish in America, 'Celtic' became associated with Irish and diaspora nationalism. The Harvard Mission, it was hoped, would show that the Irish were descended from a noble Celtic stock. It was hoped to rehabilitate the Celt for successful twentieth-century Irish-Americans, many of whom donated generously to the research.[6]

Ireland was considered, by the Harvard archaeologists, to be 'one of the mainsprings of American culture and a major source of our racial inheritance' and therefore to be 'of world importance as a political entity'.[7] It was certainly part of the global eugenic project being undertaken across Europe in the 1920s and 1930s. Harsh new immigration laws had been enacted in 1924 in the United States as a result of vigorous lobbying by eugenicists, in an effort to restrict the immigration of those deemed 'defective'. The Harvard Mission was about to discover if Ireland was a 'eugenically fit' nation. Defining it as a Celtic white European nation of great antiquity would not only satisfy the Irish-American lobby and those who contributed financially to the project but would enhance Ireland's cultural profile globally. This would have implications for her economy and tourism prospects in the future.

In the early decades of independent Ireland Celtic Art became an expression of Catholicism, nationalism and ethnicity and was considered to be one of the signifiers of the glories of a great Celtic nation in the past. Irish-American identity could also be expressed by the appropriation of selected artefacts that could be ascribed a Celtic provenance or decorative style. In an article published in the *Irish Review* in 1934, Hencken praised 'the splendour' of the collection of Bronze Age gold objects and 'the remarkable works of art' of the Early Christian Period in the National Museum of Ireland.[8] In the 1930s, R.E.M. Wheeler described how 'an artistic impulse, like life itself, defies ultimate analysis. We can no more really explain the genesis of a thing like Celtic Art than we can really explain the genesis of a bumble-bee'.[9] The genesis of Celtic Art continued to be debated many decades later. In 1997, John Collis expressed the opinion that 'the links between La Tène art/La Tène culture and the ancient Celts are dubious in the extreme'.[10] He explained in his paper 'Celtic Myths' that the correlation of La Tène with the Celts only really began with Joseph Déchelette when he published his *Manuel D'Archéologie Préhistorique Celtique et Gallo-Romaine* in 1913 and 1914. Ruth and Vincent Megaw described a sense of ethnic or national identity, defined by Celtic Art, as 'a state of mind'.[11] It had been hoped that Celtic objects with La Tène art might be recovered from the Harvard Mission and Unemployment Scheme excavations. This was because, since the nineteenth century, the existence of La Tène material in Ireland has been interpreted as evidence for an Iron Age 'Celtic' people. However, there were many problems with the study of the Iron

Age in Ireland, which paradoxically included a wealth of written material. This was because in some instances it was detrimental to the development of objective archaeology. Barry Raftery explained that 'this is so not only because the written sources have been misused but also because the complete and vivid picture of society in Iron Age Ireland apparently presented by the literature is at variance with, and obscures, the very real darkness which so often confronts the archaeologist in his study of the material remains of the period'.[12] Unfortunately, cherry-picking of philological and literary sources and the discarding of unwanted information in the study of the Celts was a feature of Irish state archaeology after independence. This reflected the culture-historical academic framework within which archaeologists interpreted their material; the emphasis on ethnicity which this entailed; and the status which historical sources enjoyed over archaeological evidence.

Joseph Raftery, in his abstract on the Irish Early Iron Age material, included by Mahr in his 1937 address, observed that terms such as 'Hallstatt' and 'La Tène' did not apply to Ireland. These terms are generally regarded as applying to the culture of Celtic Europe from about 1200 to about the middle of the first millennium BC for the Hallstatt Period, followed by the La Tène Period which lasted to the Roman conquests. Joseph Raftery noted that Hallstatt material was largely unrepresented in Ireland. The so-called La Tène material was 'purely native' even though at different stages it had adopted and adapted foreign decorative motifs. Raftery came to the conclusion that 'the more one studies the material, the more difficult is it to decide what is *not* native'.[13] The absence of typical pottery had to be taken into account and Iron Age burials were extremely rare. This was despite the fact that, in Joseph Raftery's opinion, 'the country must have been rather thickly populated and teeming with energy enough to give rise to the great missionary and artistic outburst which followed almost immediately upon the end of the Irish Early Iron Age'.[14] His view was that the La Tène culture was a native one, with 'adapted decorative motifs of Gallo-British affinities'.[15] Simon James's views, considered radical sixty years later in the nineties, echo what Joseph Raftery was writing in the 1930s about regional variation and native influence being the explanation for the material culture of Iron Age peoples in Ireland:

The model envisages the Iron Age isles not as a peripheral backwater of continental Celticity but as areas with their own manifold regional traditions which, to varying degrees at different times, looked across the waters of the Irish Sea, the Channel and the North Sea to neighbouring lands, engaging in two-way traffic in ideas, goods and some people who, intermittently and in an ad hoc manner, were added to the map of the isles...[16]

As the metalwork was obviously different from what went before, representing 'a complete and radical break with earlier traditions',[17] some writers interpreted this cultural change as evidence of an 'invasion'. Walther Bremer, who served briefly as Director of the National Museum of Ireland described 'a ruling caste, numerically very small, which imposed itself upon the aborigines, and forced upon them their type of civilisation and language'.[18] The La Tène invasion, which was dated to about 400 BC was considered by some archaeologists to be the solution to the problem but by Mahr as a 'stop-gap solution'.[19] This was because, in his view, the La Tène invasion should have been dated 200 years earlier as well as the fact that the La Tène finds discovered in Ireland were concentrated in the north-eastern part of the island, suggesting a British route of immigration.

## Archaeology and the Media: Irish and International

In 1939, a Department of Education official acknowledged the importance of the 'Harvard University Social and Economic Survey' and the 'Harvard University Racial Survey' but pointed out that 'the archaeological missions to Ireland very probably outshone them all, principally from the viewpoint of the appeal archaeological excavations and discoveries make to the public mind'.[20] This appealing quality was obvious in the media in Ireland and in America. The excavations undertaken under the Unemployment Schemes were also of great interest to the general public and broadcasts were made, interviews given and articles written for the press. In this way it became part of popular culture and was not just confined to dilletantes from wealthy backgrounds or professional archaeologists. The popularisation of Irish archaeology served a social function as it instilled a pride in the past of the Irish nation among the public. Its function was similar to that of a display or exhibition in the National Museum. It was being carefully selected, sanitised and packaged for a specific audience. Members of the public were now being informed and could have an opinion on Irish archaeology. In 1934 a Government Information Bureau was set up. Leask described its function for archaeology to H.L. Movius:

This Bureau is under expert journalistic control and is freely at your disposal for publicity regarding the works which you have been so good as to supervise for the State. It will be much appreciated if you will make full use of the facilities which are provided by the Bureau, sending the statements for publication to me or to Dr. Mahr. Arrangements will be made by us with the Bureau for publication in the principal papers and, if it is specially desirable, more detailed statements in the journals published in the areas near the excavation.[21]

By the 1930s the idea of Celtic Ireland was immovably fixed in the national imagination and by extension in the Irish-American imagination. The global media reinforced this idea by printing pictures from the Harvard expeditions such as the iconic images, including the Viking gaming board, and the hanging bowl from Ballinderry No. 1. The arrival of the Harvard Mission to Ireland in 1932 was greeted by the *Irish Independent* with the headline 'Ireland's Buried Antiquities. Excavation Expedition from U.S.A. Ancient Celtic Glory'.[22] Hugh O'Neill Hencken was described as the grandson of a Dublin man who emigrated to the US who had 'devoted his life to Celtic archaeology'. Hencken reinforced this idea and had the following to say about his work in Cornwall: 'I found very interesting remnants of a great Celtic civilisation, and many of the relics point to a close connection with Ireland. I found a town at least 2,000 years old and a quantity of pottery of Celtic type'.[23]

Adolf Mahr regarded the excavation of three crannógs by the Harvard Mission as 'the most imposing achievement of the Harvard excavators'.[24] This was because of the richness of the finds and the media potential of selected artefacts. P.A. O'Connell, President of the Charitable Irish Society, in an article published in the *Boston Evening Transcript*, understood the reasons for choosing Ireland by Harvard to be as follows:

Ireland was chosen because it offers so pure a racial development, having practically no other races except the pre-Celt and the Celt; because, compared with the rest of Europe, its archaeological treasures are almost untouched; and because it is particularly interested now in beginning archaeological work.[25]

Another example of coverage of the Harvard Mission work in Ireland included the headlines: 'Study of the Irish qualities of character making an Irishman will be brought out in a unique Anthropological Survey of

Ireland'[26] and 'Anthropologists Plan Survey of Essential Characteristics of Race'.[27] This association of physical attributes with behaviour was one of the tenets of eugenic ideology pervading the social sciences in the United States and reflected the biological determinism of Hooton.

Seán P. Ó Ríordáin was very involved in the writing of scripts on the subject of archaeology for broadcast on radio and television and publication in local, national and international newspapers. For example, on 22 August 1937 he broadcast a talk about Garranes, County Cork, which he had finished excavating. This was arranged by the Royal Society of Antiquaries of Ireland. The Parliamentary Secretary of the OPW sanctioned a report to be sent to the Government Information Bureau with information on the excavations. This was to be issued to 'the papers circulating in West Cork, to the *London Times*, and to the *Manchester Guardian* in addition to the usual papers'.[28] The report appeared in the *Irish Press* and the *Irish Independent* on 11 October, the *Irish Times* on 12 October, the *Cork Examiner* on 14 October 1937 and in the *Southern Star* on 16 October 1937.

In September 1937, Ó Ríordáin made a broadcast about Lough Gur from Cork.[29] Initially it was thought that the broadcast could be made from the actual site of the excavation using a portable microphone as had been done by Macalister at Tara in April of the same year,[30] but technical difficulties prevented this course of action. Ó Ríordáin got over the technical hitch by creating a word-picture of the landscape in which Lough Gur was situated and asking the listener to imagine 'that our microphone is really stationed on the top of a hill near Lough Gur'. Ó Ríordáin showed a good awareness of the medium of radio and presented the material in a light, easy to understand and direct way. He was later, in the 1950s, to become a television personality and contributed to the BBC series entitled *Animal, Vegetable, Mineral?* For the BBC programme *Buried Treasure*, broadcast in 1954, he was involved in experimental archaeology which included the reconstruction of one of the houses on Lough Gur.[31]

Ó Ríordáin explained to the listener that Lough Gur was selected for excavation because of the number of prehistoric monuments situated within a small radius and the number of prehistoric finds recovered from the area. Two were described, which included a bronze spear-head with delicate gold inlay which was in the Pitt Rivers Museum at Oxford and a bronze shield in the National Museum of Ireland. He listed the monuments in the area – stone circles, standing stones, megalithic graves, stone forts, burial mounds, lake dwellings and modern castles. A description of the excavations of two stone circles was given. The post-hole found in the dead centre of the smaller stone circle was explained as 'the centre from which the prehistoric workmen described the circle where they erected the stones surrounding the mound'. To the side of this post-hole were found two burials of urns containing cremated bone. The urns belonged to the Late Bronze Age or Early Iron Age and were important in providing dating evidence for the Lough Gur circles. One of the interesting features of the larger stone circle was the fact that it had a fosse placed inside the concentric bank. As a fosse intended for defensive purposes is normally outside the bank this feature, Ó Ríordáin claimed, was 'proof of the ritualistic purpose of this circle'.[32] He went on to describe the excavations carried out in 1937 at a stone fort. The entrance to the fort was on the east side. The strength of the walls suggested that it was built for 'military purposes'. It was dated to the seventh or probably eighth century. Evidence for stone-walled houses was found within the enclosure. Finds included bone ornaments and combs, fine glass beads, domestic utensils and querns for the grinding of corn, spindle whorls, hones, iron knives, bronze, iron pins and six stone axes. Bones included those of ox, sheep, goat, horse, fish, fowl, and dogs.

Claude Blake Whelan broadcast a talk from the Belfast Station on 14 February 1935 on the subject of 'The First Ulstermen'.[33] In it he mentioned the sites at Rathlin, New Ferry, Cushendun and Glenarm, all of which had been excavated by the Harvard Mission. With reference to Glenarm he described its variety of flint tools which reflected clearly 'the manifold purpose of an adaptable and progressive community'. He also described ancient craftsmen, with their tool-kits of rude stone implements, who were 'able to build boats capable of sustaining sea passages of one mean order'.[34] V. Gordon Childe was later to express reservations about the popularising of archaeology through the media. He was of the opinion that the serious study of archaeology would earn it 'a more secure position than can be earned by sensational finds and even witty wireless programmes'.[35]

Occasionally problems arose with archaeological discoveries and the media. In one instance, Hencken was displeased when he found a dug-out boat in Ballinderry 2, the discovery of which he regarded to be 'a distinct embarrassment'. This was because, in his opinion, it was 'of very little scientific value'.[36] The National Museum did not want it and refused to pay the expenses of its removal to Dublin as it had similar boats and didn't want any more. Hencken noted that 'we feared hostile criticism if we left it behind, for all visitors to the site and especially the press gave it a great deal of attention. It served some use in the latter connection, however, for the photograph of the boat in situ was one of the very few excavation scenes that could be used for press purposes'.[37] He described in an article in the *Irish Review* in 1934 how the boat had to be sent to the National Museum, sixty-five miles away. It took twenty men to haul it with ropes across the bog on a plank track and it took three days to get it to the museum.[38] Adolf Mahr gave the Harvard Mission some unspecified archaeological material in compensation for the expense involved, which Hencken purchased for the Peabody Museum from the grant allocated to him for the acquisition of European material.[39] In December 1932, it was mentioned in the *Boston Herald* that a report on their work was given to seventy-five members of the American Irish Historical Society at the Harvard Club by members of the Harvard Mission.[40]

## Artefacts and the Politics of Ethnicity

The excavations undertaken as part of the Unemployment Schemes and the Harvard Mission did not produce any items of La Tène material for use in the media. Ballinderry 1 crannóg became the most important and celebrated of the Harvard sites because of its feted artefacts. The bronze hanging bowl and an elaborately carved wooden Viking gaming board became synonymous with the Harvard Archaeological Expeditions and were featured in newspapers in Ireland, England and America.[41] Mahr lost no time in exploiting this success and organised to have the Governor-General of Ireland, James MacNeill (Eoin MacNeill's brother) give a luncheon at the Vice Regal Lodge, inviting a contingent of people who were interested in archaeology.[42] In the *Boston Evening Transcript* it was reported that 'The bronze lamp undoubtedly was made in Ireland and Dr. Hencken considers it second in value only to the board'.[43] A photograph of the gaming board, the bronze hanging bowl, and Hencken, Movius and Mahr at Ballinderry 1 were used to illustrate an article by Movius, also in the *Boston Evening Transcript* of 12 November 1932.[44] Movius described the artefacts as 'two of our most valuable finds'. He claimed that the bowl was 'the only hanging bronze lamp ever found in Ireland' and that the gaming board was 'the finest object of the Viking period ever found in Ireland'. The *Irish Times* reported that 'Hundreds of crannógs exist in Ireland and many have been trenched and plundered but no complete excavation has revealed their structure until the present year'.[45] In Hencken's view the most important objects recovered from crannógs included these objects and a Viking sword, all recovered from the Ballinderry 1 crannóg.[46]

Adolf Mahr was involved in the preparation of press releases on behalf of the Harvard Mission. It seems that his 'cabinet of curiosities' did not stop at the National Museum. It extended as a virtual exhibition in the pages of the Irish and international media. In his press release in 1932 he described the hanging bowl as 'the first of its type to be found in Ireland' and described its ornamentation as 'Celtic style with three bronze animal heads which closely resemble that of the famous Tara brooch'.[47] An article on the excavation of Ballinderry 1 published in the *Irish Times* suggested that the comparisons made with the Tara brooch meant that the find was 'of supreme importance'.[48] The author of the article extrapolated that 'The original inhabitants, however were undoubtedly Celts, perhaps with an Iberian or Aryan strain'.[49] Hencken agreed that the Ballinderry bowl's 'Irish origin is certain'.[50] He wrote that 'If the surmise that the lamp is ecclesiastical is correct, it might have been stolen at any date, if stolen it was, from the church where it hung'.[51] Another newspaper report described how 'It now has been scientifically cleaned and handling it with quite tender care, bordering on veneration, Dr. Hencken showed the lamp to the *Irish Independent* representative'.[52] There was much controversy about the provenance of bronze hanging bowls prior to the 1930s. In 1898, J. Romilly Allen described hanging bowls as being of Celtic origin.[53] He produced the first book on 'Celtic Art' in 1904, entitled *Celtic Art in Pagan and Christian Times*. Reginald Smith described the hanging bowls as Anglo-Saxon in an article published in the *Proceedings of the Society of Antiquaries* (1907–9).[54] This conundrum was still not settled by the 1930s. T.D. Kendrick believed that the enamelled hanging bowls were the work of the Romano-British population.[55] R.E.M. Wheeler argued that decorative Celtic escutcheons belonged to the Pagan Saxon period and to the Saxon areas of England.[56] This was disputed by Francoise Henry, the French art historian, who asserted that the decorative features were Irish in style but derived from Celtic motifs.[57] She believed that hanging bowls were church-lamps, the earliest example of which dates back to the La Tène Period and that they were introduced into Ireland during the fifth century.[58] The fact that the majority of them had been found in Anglo-Saxon graves was explained by the fact that 'the Irish being Christian, did not bury precious objects with their dead'.[59] Henry was also involved in disputes about the Irish or Anglo-Saxon origins of beautifully illuminated gospel books.[60] Henry's vigorous defence of Irish art against British appropriation and influence earned her the title 'the Jeanne d'Arc of Irish art'.[61] Waddell aptly described 'those tedious arguments of years gone by' concerning whether certain pieces of metalwork were of Irish or British manufacture. He believed that those debates 'created more heat than light and it became evident a long time ago that it was time to move on and to recognize the enduring complexity of the relationships between two islands sharing an inland sea'.[62]

'The Gaming Board of the Viking Age' in Mahr's opinion, was 'the finest object found by the Mission'.[63] It was published in *Acta Archaeologia* in 1933 which was included in a list of publications sent to the Rockefeller Foundation by Hooton.[64] Much attention was devoted to it also in the pages of Hencken's report on the site. Examination of the ornament on the object led Hencken to believe that it was manufactured in the Isle of Man in about the third quarter of the tenth century.[65] He regarded it as a product of 'Celto-Norse art', its most obviously Celtic feature being the fret ornament.[66] He believed that, like the Vikings and their predecessors, the insular Celts also had board games, ultimately derived from Roman ones.[67] Gaming pieces were also found on other crannógs such as the bone discs recovered from Cloonfinlough, County Roscommon, a site excavated by Hencken under the Unemployment Schemes.[68] The editions of the *Evening Telegraph* and *Evening Press*, published on 13 August 1932, reported that a delegation of archaeologists had spent the morning with Adolf Mahr at the National Museum of Ireland, inspecting the Viking gaming board. The archaeologists had attended the International Conference of Prehistorians which had just finished in London. They included Rev. Professor Dr Hugo O. Cermaier, Madrid University; Professor Dr A.E. van Giffen, Director of the Archaeological Service, Netherlands; Dr Willems, Prehistoric Service Dutch East Indies; Professor Gustav Schwantes, Director of the Kiel Museum and Professor at Hamburg University; Professor Dr Broensted, Copenhagen Museum and Professor at Copenhagen University; and Professor Dr E. Wahle, Heidelberg University. It was reported that Hencken commented: 'Without exaggeration, one may safely say that this find is one of the most valuable that has ever been made in an Irish bog. It is of extreme importance'.[69]

Macalister was dubious about the level of attention paid to the gaming board, hanging bowl and sword from Ballinderry 1. In an article entitled 'A Five Year Plan for Research' included in 'The New Ireland Five Years of Progress', a supplement issued with the *Irish Press* dated 11 June 1937, he referred humorously to the site and the objects recovered:

> The last occupant of Ballinderry, we fear, was a common pirate. He had brought together, into his house some Norseman's sword, carried by its

original owner from South Germany; a hanging lamp stolen from some church; and a wooden draughtboard from the Isle of Man. These three incongruous objects now live together in a case in the museum, and could exchange many queer reminiscences if the necessary organs of speech and of hearing could be provided for them.[70]

The desire to establish artistic continuity between the prehistoric period and the Early Christian Period expressed by Harvard Mission archaeologists would fulfil the Irish political agenda and its cultural identity requirements. For Irish people, this would mean a strengthening of their status as citizens of a deservedly independent nation through the celebration of the creative artistry of their ancestors. The more beautiful and well-crafted the ancient artefact the more pride could be taken in its creation. If it could be deemed to be the creative work of a particular ethnic group, then cultural purity could be associated with physical purity of bloodlines, which in turn could be identified with a particular territory. These icons of memory and symbols of cultural and ethnic purity were essential to the forging of Irish Celtic and Christian identity, especially abroad. For example, a report on the work of the Harvard Mission in Ireland in the *Boston Evening Transcript* contained the headline 'Golden Age of Ireland's History is Brought to Light by Cambridge Scientists Excavating in Lake Country', with its sub-heading 'Modern Celts One of Purest Races; Crannógs Trace Development of People'.[71]

The selection of artefacts became an act of rejection of imposed identity and the embracing of a desired identity, whether by visual presentation of artefacts by exhibition in the National Museum of Ireland or as photographs in the pages of national and international newspapers in which Adolf Mahr and the Harvard team engaged. This is the process by which the political identity of the nation was expressed culturally and in a non-threatening way in the 1930s. Therefore, the recovery of artefacts which were suitable for use in the media to laud the culture of the race which produced them and to illustrate the already established Irish origin-myths became an important focus of the Harvard Expeditions and the state-run Unemployment Schemes. To this end, any homogeneity of artistic motifs was seized upon to construct an artistic continuum within which Irish cultural identity could be secured and expressed. The Early Christian Period was rich in material culture and art objects which enhanced and consolidated the idea of an island of saints and scholars. Macalister, in an address delivered to the RSAI in 1925, noted that a friend had quipped that 'the Irish base their claim to Home Rule on the beauty of the Book of Kells.[72] Adolf Mahr referred to the art styles of the Bronze Age and the Early Christian Period as 'Celtic'. Mahr's use of the word 'Celtic' reflects the actual dearth of material culture for the Iron Age in Ireland and the lack of evidence to substantiate the theory of an invasion of Celtic peoples during that time period. Art was being used in this instance to fill the gap in the Iron Age artefact assemblage. In 1937, Mahr expressed the hope that 'sooner or later also the hiatus will be bridged over which still separates the end of the prehistoric developments in the Celtic regions, notably in Ireland, and the blossoming-forth of the Early Christian Celtic Art'.[73]

Mahr's desire to see the hiatus of Celtic Art bridged by the recovery of suitable objects d'art by the Harvard Mission was largely unfulfilled, despite the recovery of thousands of artefacts from the crannógs. Tom Condit humorously refers to the 'more popular image of blue-eyed, fair-haired, spear-wielding warriors who inhabited these parts before Patrick converted them and diverted their intertwining spirals onto artefacts of a more ecclesiastical nature'.[74]

The desire to fill Mahr's artistic hiatus resulted in some bizarre comparisons of Irish art across the ages. For example, a stone bead found at Creevykeel, County Sligo, which Hencken noted was common in the Early Bronze Age of Scotland and northern England was described by him as 'the prototypes of the Irish gold lunulae'.[75] While this notion may emphasise the idea of cultural continuity it is very difficult to understand the connection between stone beads and gold lunulae apart from the fact that they could both be loosely described as jewellery. Examples of jewellery found on the sites excavated in the 1930s included a small 'Early Christian brooch' also from Creevykeel. It had zoomorphic terminals with circular settings intended for millefiori enamel.[76] A Viking bronze penannular brooch, dated by Hencken to the tenth century was found at Knockast cemetery-cairn. A ninth-century brooch with silver head and bronze pin, decorated with enamel and depicting six fantastic animals was found in a souterrain at Cahercommaun.[77] This brooch was described by Hencken as 'by far the best single find from the site'.[78] While Henken considered it to be 'utterly different from the Tara brooch', he wrote that 'it need not cause surprise that they are considered here side by side'.[79] In a press release issued from the Government Information Bureau, dated 1 August 1935, Lagore Crannóg was described as 'among the most important sites in the country for the study of ancient Ireland in the Early Christian period'.[80] One of the more important artefacts recovered was an ornamented belt buckle with 'complex spirals' and a conventionalised animal 'in somewhat the same style as the Book of Kells'. There was evidence for the manufacture of coloured glass beads and bracelets and a fragment of a mould for casting large bronze rings, indicating bronze-working on the site. It was stated in the press release that:

> Very little is as yet known of the development of art and craftsmanship in Early Christian Ireland, and the large number of objects retrieved from this site, throw a flood of light on the country at the time when its indigenous art had reached its maximum of development – in the 8th century AD and during the succeeding Danish period.[81]

The artistic ability and craftsmanship of occupants of Ballinderry 2 was also attested to by the large collection of coloured glass beads, bracelets of bronze and lignite, bronze pins and amber beads recovered. One of the bronze pins had a head inset with a blue stone and red enamel, imitated from a Roman seal box. A beautifully decorated seventh-century penannular brooch with a pin nearly eight inches long also came to light. It was ornamented with millefiori glass mosaic of a sub-Roman type, animal heads, and red enamel. Hencken described it in *The Irish Review*, in 1934, as the 'finest of its class ever found in Ireland'.[82] Movius dated the main occupation at Kilgreany Cave, County Waterford, to early Christian times on the evidence of an object described as 'possibly part of a shrine'.[83] An arc-shaped bronze object, it was plated with silver and ornamented with two animal heads and snakes which terminated in crossed bird heads. Movius considered that 'the bird heads on the Kilgreany object are comparable also to similar heads on the Tara brooch'.[84] He described the object as 'The most outstanding single specimen found at the site'.[85]

## National Monuments Pamphlet for Propaganda Purposes

The Harvard Mission included excavations in Northern Ireland in their research programme as they considered the whole of Ireland to be one cultural area. However, this idea presented difficulties when it came to choosing archaeological monuments and artefacts for inclusion in Irish Free State official publications. The selections reflected the political use of archaeology to reinforce the identity of the state. A booklet, *Séadcomartaí Náisiúnta Saorstáit Éireann: The National Monuments of the Irish Free State*, was published in 1936. Its original working title was *National Monuments*

*Pamphlet for Propaganda Purposes,* which suggests that the publication was not just an exercise in informing the public about archaeological monuments and encouraging them to help in their preservation, but it was also an exercise in the use of archaeological monuments for political propaganda. Collective pride in these 'national' monuments was encouraged for nationalistic reasons. In a letter from the Department of Finance to the Secretary of the Board of Works in 1936, it was suggested that the booklet in question 'might more appropriately be entitled "The National Monuments of the Irish Free State".[86] Harold G. Leask, Inspector of National Monuments, was also concerned about the title of the publication. The booklet's original official title was *The National Monuments of Ireland.* Leask wrote that 'The suggested change of title to *The National Monuments of the Irish Free State* is perhaps desirable but not absolutely necessary since the Northern Irish monuments are known only as "ancient" monuments'.[87] This is significant in the context of the legislation for the protection of archaeological remains, in Northern Ireland and in the Irish Free State, enacted in 1926 and 1930 respectively, as it suggests that the word 'national' only applied in the Irish Free State. This agonising about the title of the booklet reflects the political implications of it. In the introduction to *Séadcomartaí Náisiúnta Saorstáit Éireann: The National Monuments of the Irish Free State,* the author expressed the view that:

> Everyone who feels the beauty and the strangeness of antiquity – everyone who possesses what is called the historic sense – will wish to preserve intact the visible remains of ancient times: and many who do not feel this sentiment about antiquity in general will be moved by love of their country to help in preserving those remains which are perhaps its most distinguishing adornment and which are, in part, a witness to the period of its greatest glory.[88]

The fact that the reader is exhorted to help preserve archaeological remains out of 'love of their country' is telling. The writer is obviously appealing to nationalist sentiment here. In Irish nationalist archaeology, artefacts and monuments reflecting the 'greatest glory' of Ireland were perceived to be pre-Celtic, Celtic and Early Christian.

The preservation or otherwise of 'National Monuments' also depended on the funds available. It was stated in the booklet that: 'As public funds must be carefully conserved, it is not possible for the Commissioners to become owners or guardians of every monument that is worthy of preservation; they must restrict themselves to the most important.[89] It would seem from this statement that the term 'monument' was arbitrary. Even if the monument was deemed 'worthy' of the appellation 'national' it still did not mean that it would automatically be preserved. That was a matter of finance. It was noted that 'only very well-preserved buildings of special interest can be accepted by the Commissioners for preservation out of the great choice available'.[90] Pride in a shared national heritage was part of the construct of an Irish national identity. As an instrument of political propaganda published under a de Valera-led government, it is puzzling that the booklet did not include monuments north of the border. In de Valera's transatlantic address on 12 December 1933 he made a comment about Northern Ireland: 'Ireland never can abandon the hope of regaining a territory hallowed by so many memories, the scene of so many of the most heroic incidents of her history'. He went on to say that 'The area that Ireland has lost contains many of her holiest and most famous places'.[91]

The booklet was reviewed in newspapers throughout Ireland including the *Irish Press*, the *Irish Independent*, the *Irish Times*, the *Irish Builder and Engineer*, the *Dundalk Democrat*, the *Tipperary Star*, the *Connacht Tribune*, the *Tuam Herald* and the *Derry Journal*. Most reviews were favourable and all agreed that the preservation of antiquities was an important aspect of national identity.[92] An article in the *Irish Press* reported that the Board of Works had performed a useful service: 'These prehistoric survivals, in fact, constitute almost our sole claim to a distinctive architecture, for the endless succession of destructive wars which the struggle for nationhood imposed upon us rendered impossible that continuity in art without which a cultural tradition cannot grow and develop'.[93] The role of archaeology in the education of people in the cultural ideology of the state was also acknowledged in the *Irish Builder and Engineer*, recommending that 'if it be possible, that a copy could be placed in the hands of every pupil attending our primary and secondary schools'.[94] The *National Monuments Pamphlet for Propaganda* purposes and the discussions around it illustrates the problems inherent in the classification of archaeological monuments as 'national' and how they can be used to justify and advertise a particular political ideology by their employment in the official literature of the state.[95] In the process archaeological artefacts and monuments are transformed into national symbols. Peter Alter poses an interesting question about national symbols and asks were they 'manipulated from above as calculated creations for influencing the masses?' He believes that fascist movements had consciously created a 'symbol cult' for this very purpose.[96] To use Alter's term, the 'symbol cult' of Irish nationalism involved the appropriation of Celtic and Early Christian artefacts as symbols of the nation. These included artefacts such as the Tara Brooch, the Ardagh Chalice, various book shrines, the Book of Kells and beautiful gold objects dating to the Bronze Age. They became shorthand for the Irish nation and were instantly recognisable both at home and abroad. They could be used symbolically to illustrate nationalist myths. They acted as powerful symbols as they were a tangible connection to people in the past who used them. Early Christian Ireland has been described as 'a period which can only be seen as the zenith of achievement in the country's long cultural history'.[97] This 'zenith of achievement' was reached during a time when Ireland was independent, before colonisation. It was referred to in a Government press release in 1935 as 'Art of Irish Independence Period'.[98] The implication was that the possibility existed that a similar level of cultural achievement could be reached now that Ireland governed herself. The marshalling of artefacts as cultural emblems of the political state asserted the Irish Free State's right to independence in 1922 and her nationalist aspirations for a United Ireland in the future.

With the arrival of the Harvard Mission the archaeological landscape in its entirety became a focus of study. In the process archaeological monuments became not just cultural markings but also territorial markers. Brian Graham, writing on the concept of heritage, has argued that the importance of a heritage icon does not depend on the monument or artefact itself but on its interpretation and suggested that heritage is regarded as an essential component of the foundation of the myth of the nation-state.[99] The past becomes a symbol of identity formation as Crooke argues: 'The past is not static, but continually replayed according to the needs of the contemporary age'.[100]

### *Saorstát Eireann Irish Free State Official Handbook*

Art O'Murnaghan, the manuscript illuminator, designed the cover of the *Saorstát Eireann Irish Free State Official Handbook*, commissioned by the Cosgrave government in 1932. In de Valera's opinion this book was 'a splendid specimen of Irish printing and Irish production'.[101] It 'offered a window into the philosophy underlying the Irish Free State, the philosophy of an Irish Ireland uncontaminated by its colonial past'.[102] The handbook contained many illustrations of archaeological monuments and artefacts associated with the first and second 'golden age' in Ireland which Adolf Mahr identified as the Early Bronze Age and the Early Christian

Period respectively.[103] As Smith noted in his discussion of nationalism and golden ages: 'Without a golden age, it would be difficult, if not impossible, to discover the "true self" of the people'.[104] This Celtic/Christian 'self' was expressed archaeologically in the *Handbook* by pictures of Scellig Michael, the Rock of Cashel, the Shrine of St. Patrick's Bell, the Tara Brooch, a capital letter from the Book of Kells and gold lunulae from the Early Bronze Age. These illustrations in an official handbook gave credence and dignity to the indigenous culture of the Irish people, suggesting in visual terms, a possible blueprint for the future nation. This official publication presented Ireland as a rural society with strong links to a glorious Celtic and Christianised past. Unsurprisingly, there were no depictions of Big Houses. In this handbook archaeology was being transformed into a symbolic visual language used to express the political ideals of the state. Their use reinforced the idea of a collective, homogenous, indigenous and long-established culture in Ireland, linking past and present strongly, as a platform to launch a future for an Irish-Ireland, devoid of British influences. Beautiful objects of the Early Christian Period such as brooches and book shrines were commandeered, in Whelan's phrase as 'icons of identity'.[105] In this context they become material expressions of a collective 'memory'. The deliberate remembering and the deliberate forgetting[106] of certain aspects of the Irish past enabled the construction of a palatable national identity, which in turn, legitimised the position of those in power at that time.

## The Pageant of the Celt: Race, Religion and Identity

Hencken's article on 'Harvard and Irish archaeology' was reprinted from the *Irish Review* in the catalogue of *The Pageant of the Celt*, a re-enactment of episodes from Irish history at the Chicago World Fair in 1934, which 'extolled the glories of the ancient Celtic civilization'. The pageant was designed to dramatise the racial inheritance of 'Americans of Irish blood' and to reveal to them 'the Celtic chapter in world achievement' and so 'awaken in them a just pride of race and a faith in racial destiny'.[107] Artefacts, described as Celtic or Christian or both were interpreted in a culture-historical frame of reference in racial terms. In the 1930s they were also used to market Ireland abroad and were construed as markers of ethnic identity across the globe.[108] This reflected what Mahr believed to be 'the worldwide appeal possessed by Irish archaeology'.[109] In his pamphlet, *A Century of Progress in Irish Archaeology Exhibits collected by The National Museum of Ireland* for the World Fair,

Mahr used the term 'Celtic' to describe the gold artefacts of the Early Bronze Age and the manuscripts of the Early Christian Period: 'The Museum which is annually frequented by some 400,000 visitors is one of the centres where research in Celtic archaeology naturally focuses and its gold collection shares with the famous "Book of Kells" in Trinity College Dublin, the claim to be of the greatest interest in the domain of Celtic Art'.[110] The Celtic and Christian identity of the nation, after independence became associated exclusively with Catholicism. Ruth and Vincent Megaw, in their paper 'Ancient Celts and Modern Ethnicity', noted that 'religion, too, is a factor which can map ethnic identity'.[111]

Mahr, who regarded the Irish Antiquities Division of the National Museum as 'one of the great treasure houses of international art', was instrumental in the selection of objects for the Chicago World Fair exhibit.[112] He included the bronze hanging bowl and the Viking gaming board from Ballinderry 1 which he described as 'absolutely unique' and forming 'a very welcome addition to our knowledge of ecclesiastical art'.[113] Other antiquities which expressed 'the genius of the old Celtic race'[114] included replicas of Bronze Age gold jewellery, the bell of St. Patrick, the Tara Brooch and the Ardagh Chalice. Liam S. Gógan's book *The Ardagh Chalice: A description of the minstral chalice found at Ardagh in County Limerick in the year 1868; with a note on its traditional conformity to the Holy Grail of legend and story*, published in 1932, was also part of the exhibit.

In the 1930s, despite the dearth of appropriate archaeological evidence, the assumption was made that there had been a Celtic invasion in Ireland's history. In 2006, Barry Raftery stated bluntly that 'there is simply no evidence of invading Celts'.[115] In any event, archaeology was just one of the constituent strands of study employed by scholars for over a century to boost their thesis of Celtic exceptionalism. The Celtic identity of Ireland was never based solely on the archaeological evidence and relied mainly on literary and linguistic evidence. In the nineties, it became fashionable to critique archaeological evidence for the Celts in Britain and Ireland. Simon James, who referred to himself as a 'post-Celticist', wrote about the 'insular Celts': 'It has absolutely no ancient pedigree: it is a modern interpretation not unambiguous historical truth'.[116] He also posed the question about the idea of Ancient Celts in the British Isles 'If it is a fiction, does this mean that modern Celtic identity is a fraud as well?'[117] The question could also be asked if this means that the creation of an Irish-American identity for the diaspora in the 1930s with its roots in Celtic Christian Irishness is also fraudulent? The answer to this conundrum presumably depends on what the essence of cultural identity actually is and was and if it is dependent on material culture for its definition and/or sustainability. With regard to cultural identities James reflects that: 'It is important to maintain these identities, but equally vital to recognize them for what they are: evolving cultural constructs, not primordial immutable truths about ourselves, our origins and our historical antagonists'.[118]

But can an abstract concept such as identity be considered somehow untrue? Defining identity is a subjective exercise. John Collis suggests that 'the way in which groups define and name themselves, is grounded more on emotion than logic'.[119] In the 1930s, with the increasing prestige attached to science in society it was considered desirable to underpin any claim to a Celtic identity with corroborating scientific evidence. However, within the culture-historical framework within which the Irish, Austrian and American archaeologists worked in Ireland at that time, the purpose of material culture was to scientifically prove and illustrate national origin-myths, to provide iconic Celtic symbols of the nation and generally slot into an already agreed national narrative. Therefore, the dearth of material evidence for the Celtic race did not pose a problem. The selective use of a small assemblage of cultural items sufficed to define Irish and Irish-American Celticness.

Colin Renfrew defined the Celts in terms of language, noting that he used the term to mean 'people who spoke a Celtic dialect' and 'not people who buried their dead in urn-fields or had leaf-shaped swords or any particular kind of pottery'.[120] James views this as unacceptable as '"Celt" was originally a group name applied to one or more peoples, not a linguistic description, and it is still understood as an ethnonym by most people today'.[121] However, Celtic identity is not necessarily dependent on speaking a Celtic language today any more than Celtic identity is exclusively dependent on the recovery of Celtic artefacts. The Manx language, for example, did not survive in the Isle of Man but its modern identity is a Celtic one. An impressionistic cultural backdrop consisting of a smattering of similar language groups and a selective array of material cultural objects suffices. Cultural elements such as artefacts and monuments were considered to be accoutrements which defined a particular race. With regard to the origins of the Celts, the spread and survival of languages was also considered to be indicative of the spread and survival of specific ethnic groups. According to Malcolm Chapman 'Language, culture, people, race and nation were, in important senses, the *same thing*'.[122] Debates about Celtic evidence and origins reflects the continuing political nature of archaeological discourse.

In the 1930s, a new white nationalism resulted in Celts becoming associated with mythical white Aryans, also conjured up in archaeological terms in the early decades of the twentieth century by nationalist archaeologists such as Gustav Kossinna. Nationalist archaeology positioned Ireland culturally within a network of European nation-states. Celticness served the dual purpose of Irish nationhood and Europeanness. This continental Europeanness conveniently excluded the 'non-Celtic' part of Britain. A global American culturalism incorporated Ireland in a global white world. This was a eugenic ideal in the 1930s but had roots much earlier in Ireland from about the mid nineteenth century. The myth of the Celt may have been a parallel strand or offshoot of the Aryan myth but without its shadowy or sinister connotations which the latter accrued by its appropriation by the Nazis. It was essentially a more palatable type of nationalist myth which, it was thought, could be proven by scientific archaeology. This chimed easily with eugenic ideology and its over-reliance on scientific solutions to solve social and political problems.

In the 1930s the discourse on the Celts was primarily around the issue of race, which was the predominant ideology of the times. The pursuit of the Celts by the Harvard Mission was through the study of material culture and physical anthropology. The new scientific archaeologists of the 1930s sought to provide absolute authenticity and legitimation by recovering scientific proof that Irish ethno-histories were valid. Grave-Brown, Jones and Gamble make the point that this authentication process of the past is what 'cultural groups desire and require in their claims for self-determination and/or secession'.[123] However, the nature of cultural identity was not necessarily predicated on scientific evidence being available. For example, if there was a paucity of Iron Age settlement sites in the country, then proof for the existence of the Celts can be looked for in the Bronze Age as was attempted by Adolf Mahr. The label *Celtic* could be ascribed to anything loosely deemed Irish, like Hencken's 'communities of Irish Celtic Christians' or Mahr's Celtic Art of the Bronze Age and Early Christian Period. The confusion surrounding nomenclature including the words *Celtic*, *Christian* and *Irish* arose because there was an inclination to use them subjectively and/or politically. Material culture was and still is used to bolster cultural labelling for political reasons. Cultural engineering was a factor in the definition of Ireland as Celtic and Christian after independence. Nineteenth-century archaeology had been characterised by theories of racial superiority, and used to legitimise imperialism.[124] The concept of race itself, according to the British anthropologist, Ashley Montagu, was a 'social construct and a product of perceptions'.[125] In the 1930s the concept of Celtic Ireland had been transformed from a cultural idea into a marketable brand name. Cultural identity was being consumed by corporate identity. A newspaper image of an artefact or site or a punchy headline in the international media captured the essence of the Celtic idea and implanted it firmly in the minds of Irish people at home and abroad.

In the 1930s nationalist ideology offered a narrow prism through which artefacts and monuments could be interpreted. There was an imagining of a homogenous culture to fit an imagined nation.[126] Inconvenient artefacts in the archaeological record could be metaphorically discarded along with archaeological objectivity. Their importance may or may not have been recognised and only became relevant when the political landscape changed. The Kossinian desire to link material culture and ethnicity was evident in the scientific work carried out under the auspices of the Harvard Mission and the Free State Unemployment Schemes. The idea that Ireland was internally homogeneous and historically continuous and defined by its cultural, linguistic and racial distinctiveness was current. According to Jones and Gamble identity is 'dynamic and historically contingent' and any territorial claims made on the basis of cultural identity should be open to scrutiny.[127] Hall describes identity as a fluid and contextual process, 'an always open, complex and unfinished game – always under construction which 'moves into the future by a symbolic detour through the past'.[128]

In Ireland in the 1930s Celtic cultural engineering was driven by nationalism, validated by science and focused on archaeology. Adolf Mahr wrote in 1934 that 'archaeology is a great force in the shaping of a sound self-consciousness in a nation'. This was the backdrop and broader cultural context of the work of the Harvard Mission in Ireland from 1932 to 1936, one of the most important cultural undertakings in the state during that period. The excavations carried out under the Unemployment Schemes paralleled and complemented the work of the Harvard Mission. During the 1930s, unfortunately, nationalism and racialism distorted a rich cultural heritage, politicising it and damaging the perception of it in the process. This means that the full importance of expressions of native culture, and in particular archaeology, in an independent democratic Irish Free State, have not been fully understood or appreciated. This study of the Harvard Mission, exploring the concepts and identities of the racial Celt in the context of Irish and diaspora nationalism, attempts to address this issue. The Harvard Mission can be seen as part of the Celtic cultural revitalisation programme undertaken by the first two nationalist governments in the

Irish Free State which involved initiatives in archaeology, Irish language, folklore and medieval history; the embedding of a Celtic identity in institutes, legislation, cultural policy documents and administrative processes; and the dissemination of information through national and international media. This cultural programme, of which the Harvard Mission was a component, was 'a modernist one in an internationalist context' which 'consolidated the identity of the state and established its unique position in world culture'.[129]

# APPENDIX 1

# Harvard Archaeological Mission Sites

| Name of Site | Type of Site[1] | Date of excavation |
|---|---|---|
| Knockast, Co. Westmeath | Late Bronze Age multiple cairn | 1932 |
| Ballinderry I, Co. Westmeath | Crannóg, Early Christian | 1932–3 |
| Ballinderry II, Co. Offaly | Crannóg, Early Christian | 1933 |
| Carrownacon, Co. Mayo | Indeterminate Bronze Age graves | 1933 |
| Cahercommaun, Co. Clare | Early Christian settlement | 1934 |
| Carrowlisdooaun, Co. Mayo | Late Bronze Age flat grave | 1934 |
| Kilgreany, Co. Waterford | Lithic site (cave) | 1934 |
| | Late Bronze Age and Early Christian Settlement | |
| Poulawack, Co. Clare | Indeterminate Bronze Age cairn (multiple) | 1934 |
| Gallen, Co. Offaly | Early Christian settlement and cemetery | 1934–5 |
| Lagore, Co. Meath | Crannóg, Early Christian | 1934–6 |
| Creevykeel, Co. Sligo | Early Bronze Age megalith | |
| | Early Christian settlement traces | 1936 |
| Cushendun, Co. Antrim | Mesolithic site | 1934 |
| Glenarm, Co. Antrim | Mesolithic site | 1934 |
| Newferry, Co. Derry | Riverford site | 1934 |
| Curran Point, Larne, Co. Antrim | Mesolithic site | 1935 |
| Island Magee, Co. Antrim | Mesolithic site [examined by the Quaternary Research Committee] | 1934 |
| Rough Island, Co. Down | Mesolithic site | 1936 |
| Ballynagard, Rathlin Island | [Neolithic] lithic site | 1934 |

[1] Descriptions of sites by Adolf Mahr from *Gazzeteer A and B*, 'New aspects and problems in Irish prehistory, Presidential address for 1937', *PPS* no. 11 (July–Dec.), pp. 422–3.

# APPENDIX 2

# Unemployment Scheme Sites, 1934–7

| Name of Site | Type of Site[1] | Date of excavation |
|---|---|---|
| Collierstown, Co. Meath | Early Christian settlement and cemetery | 1934 |
| Ballybetagh bog, Co. Dublin | [Quaternary Research Scheme] | 1934 |
| Lissard, Co. Limerick | Indeterminate Bronze Age tumuli | 1934 |
| Kilgreany, Co. Waterford | Lithic site (cave) Late Bronze Age and Early Christian settlements | 1934 |
| Labbacallee, Co. Cork | Early to Middle Bronze Age megalith | 1934 |
| Ballymacmoy, Co. Cork | Quaternary (cave) site | 1934 |
| Burren, Co. Mayo | Indeterminate Bronze Age tumulus | 1934 |
| Dromore, Co. Waterford | Nondescript site[2] | 1934 |
| Cush, Co. Limerick | Late Bronze Age settlement (conjoined ring-forts with souterrains, etc.) graves, and tumuli; Early Iron Age settlement | 1934–5 |
| Aghnaskeagh, Co. Louth | Two Early Bronze Age megaliths | 1934–5 |
| Gallen, Co. Offaly | Early Christian settlement (ecclesiastical) and cemetery | 1934–5 |
| Baltinglass, Co. Wicklow | Early to Middle Bronze Age megalith | 1934–6 |
| Lagore, Co. Meath | Crannóg, Early Christian | 1934–6 |
| Ballycullane Upper, Co. Limerick | Early Bronze Age megalith | 1935 |
| Leigh, Co. Tipperary | Early Christian settlement (ecclesiastical) | 1935 |
| Lug, Co. Offaly | Late Bronze Age multiple tumulus | 1935 |
| Pollacorragune, Co. Galway | Late Bronze Age tumuli | 1935 |
| Shanaclogh East, Co. Limerick | Early Christian settlement ('rath') | 1935 |

[1] Descriptions of sites by Adolf Mahr from Gazzeteer A 'New aspects and problems in Irish prehistory, Presidential address for 1937,' *PPS* no. 11 (July – Dec), pp. 422-423.

[2] This site was excavated by R.A.S. Macalister. See R.A.S. Macalister, 'The Excavation of Kiltera, Co. Waterford,' *PRIA* vol. xliii (1936-7), pp. 1-16.

| | | |
|---|---|---|
| Carrowjames, Co. Mayo | Late Bronze Age and Early Iron Age tumuli | 1935–6 |
| Carbury, Co. Kildare | Early Iron Age tumuli | 1936 |
| Lough Gur, Co. Limerick | Two Late Bronze Age megaliths | 1936–7 |
| Garranes, Co. Cork | Early Christian settlement ('rath') | 1937 |
| Moylisha, Co. Wicklow | Early Bronze Age megalith | 1937 |
| Knocknalappa, Co. Clare | Late Bronze Age crannóg | 1937 |
| Carrowbeg North, Co. Galway | Late Bronze Age tumuli | 1937 |
| Carrigalla, Co. Limerick | Early Christian settlement ('cashel') | 1937 |

# APPENDIX 3

# Contributors to Irish Archaeological Expedition[1]

| Name | Address | Year | Amount US$ |
|------|---------|------|------------|
| Baldwin, James H. | Boston, Mass | 1936 | 10.00 |
| Barbour, Mrs Thomas | Boston | 1933 | 100.00 |
| Barry, William J. | Boston | 1936 | 10.00 |
| Bird, Charles Sumner, Jr. | Boston | 1935–6 | 125.00 |
| Blake, Harry J. | Boston | 1936 | 25.00 |
| Brickley, B.A. | Boston | 1936 | 10.00 |
| Brennan, James P. | Boston | 1936 | 10.00 |
| Briggs, L.Vernon | Broadway, N.Y.C. | 1932 | 1000.00 |
| Burke, Edmund | Boston | 1936 | 10.00 |
| Burr, I. Tucker, Jr. | Boston | 1935 | 20.00 |
| Byrne, James | New York | 1936 | 500.00 |
| Campbell, Patrick T. | Boston | 1936 | 10.00 |
| Carney, Francis J. | Boston | 1936 | 10.00 |
| Carney, James H. | Boston | 1936 | 10.00 |
| Clark, James N. | Boston | 1936 | 10.00 |
| Clarkin, Harold E. | Fall River | 1936 | 10.00 |
| Collins, George H. | Boston | 1936 | 10.00 |
| Collins, Hon. Thomas J. | Springfield, Mass. | 1936 | 10.00 |

[1] E.A. Hooton Papers, #995-1, Box 21.10. Peabody Museum of Archaeology and Ethnology, Harvard University. Full postal addresses of contributors are contained in the file.

Male figure of wood, Lagore Crannóg, Co. Meath. PM# 995-1-40/14629.1.5. Peabody Museum of Archaeology and Ethnology, Harvard University.

Workmen at Knockast Bronze Age cemetery-cairn, Co. Westmeath, in 1932. Courtesy of the National Monuments Service Photographic Unit.

Creevykeel Court Tomb, Co. Sligo. PM# 995-1-40/14629.1.9, Peabody Museum of Archaeology and Ethnology, Harvard University.

Bronze Age burial site at Carrownacon, Ballyglass, Co. Mayo. PM# 998-27-0/14628.1.15, Peabody Museum of Archaeology and Ethnology, Harvard University.

Bronze Age Cairn at Poulawack, Co. Clare. PM #995-1-40/14629.1.4, Peabody Museum of Archaeology and Ethnology, Harvard University.

Kilgreany Cave: workman removing bones of giant deer from the lower stalagmite near the cave entrance in 1934. PM #998-27-40/14628.1.8, Peabody Museum of Archaeology and Ethnology, Harvard University.

Workmen at Kilgreany Cave, Co. Waterford. PM # 995-1-40/14629.1.1, Peabody Museum of Archaeology and Ethnology, Harvard University.

Workmen excavating Labaccallee Wedge Tomb, Co. Cork. Courtesy of the National Monuments Service Photographic Unit.

Moylisha Megalith, Co. Wicklow. Courtesy of the National Monuments Service Photographic Unit.

Workman at Glenarm, Co. Antrim. PM #998-27-40/14628.1.9, Peabody Museum of Archaeology and Ethnology, Harvard University.

Mesolithic site at Cushendun Co. Antrim. PM #998-27-40/14628.1.11, Peabody Museum of Archaeology and Ethnology, Harvard University.

Workman at Mesolithic site of Newferry, Co. Derry. PM #998-27-40/14628.1.13, Museum of Archaeology and Ethnology, Harvard University.

The Celticist and early Irish historian, Professor Eoin MacNeill (second from left) receiving an honorary doctorate from the Catholic University of America, Washington DC, 1930. Copyright unknown.

Hugh O'Neill Hencken was awarded an honorary D.Litt from NUI in 1937 for his archaeological work. He is standing third from the left with Éamon de Valera on his immediate left and R.A.S. Macalister on his immediate right. Rev. John Hynes of University College Galway is on the far right. Courtesy of John Waddell.

Earnest A. Hooton (right) and Conrad Arensberg with map of Ireland. The caption under the photograph, published in *Life* magazine, 7 August 1939, was 'No long upper-lipped, baboon-faced Irishmen common in political cartoons were found'. Eric Schaal / Getty Images.

| | | | |
|---|---|---|---|
| Collins, Hon. Walter L. | Boston | 1936 | 10.00 |
| Connolly, James T. | Boston | 1936 | 10.00 |
| Connor, Roy E. | Boston | 1936 | 10.00 |
| Cotter, Richard J. | Boston | 1936 | 25.00 |
| Cronin, John W. | Boston | 1936 | 10.00 |
| Crosby, Frederic J. | Roxbury | 1936 | 10.00 |
| Crosby, Justice John C. | Boston | 1936 | 10.00 |
| Cummings, John B. | Fall River | 1936 | 10.00 |
| Cummings, Matthew | Boston | 1936 | 10.00 |
| Curran, Maurice J. | Boston | 1936 | 10.00 |
| Curtis, Mrs John S. | Boston | 1933 | 300.00 |
| Dodge, Robert G. | Boston | 1936 | 10.00 |
| Donahue, Hon. Charles H. | Newton | 1936 | 10.00 |
| Donoghue, Dr Francis D. | Boston | 1936 | 10.00 |
| Downes, J. Edward | Roxbury | 1936 | 10.00 |
| Doyle, William | Boston | 1936 | 10.00 |
| Dunn, Charles J. | Boston | 1936 | 10.00 |
| Everett, James R. | Boston | 1936 | 10.00 |
| Fahey, Michael L. | Boston | 1936 | 10.00 |
| Falvey, T.J. | Boston | 1936 | 10.00 |
| Fenton, Hon. John E. | Boston | 1936 | 10.00 |
| Fish, Maj. Gen. Erland F. | Boston | 1936 | 10.00 |
| Fitzgerald, Cornelius G. | Brookline | 1936 | 10.00 |
| Fitzgerald, William F. | Brookline | 1936 | 50.00 |
| Foley, Henry E. | Boston | 1936 | 10.00 |
| Ford, Francis J.W. | Boston | 1936 | 10.00 |
| Fraher, Philip | Boston | 10.00 | |
| Garvan, Francis P. | New York City | 1934–6 | 825.00 |
| Good, Dr Frederick L. | Boston | 1936 | 10.00 |
| Graham, Richard G. | E. Cambridge | 1936 | 10.00 |
| Halloran, Hon. James A. | Boston | 1936 | 10.00 |
| Hathaway, Harold F., Esq | Taunton, Mass. | 1936 | 10.00 |
| Hanify, Hon. Edward F. | Boston | 1936 | 10.00 |
| Hencken, Albert C. | New York City | 1934 | 1200.00 |

| | | | |
|---|---|---|---|
| Hencken, Mrs William F. | Greenwich, Conn. | 1934 | 100.00 |
| Hendrick, Philip A. | Boston | 1936 | 10.00 |
| Houlihan, F.D. | Cambridge, Mass. | 1936 | 10.00 |
| Hoy, James M. | Milton | 1936 | 10.00 |
| Hughes, John T. | Boston | 1936 | 40.00 |
| Hughes, Thomas | Brookline | 1936 | 10.00 |
| Innes, Charles, H. Esq. | Boston | 1936 | 10.00 |
| Kelleher, Michael C. | Boston | 1936 | 10.00 |
| Kelley, Dr Vincent | Boston | 1936 | 10.00 |
| Kerwin, James J. | Lowell | 1936 | 10.00 |
| Kidder, Mrs Alfred, II | Cambridge | 1933 | 5.00 |
| Kiernan, Louis R. | Chelsea | 1936 | 10.00 |
| Killion, Bernard J. | Boston | 1936 | 10.00 |
| Lavelle, Thomas D. | Boston | 1936 | 10.00 |
| Leahy, Francis T. | Boston | 1936 | 10.00 |
| Logan, Hon. Edward L. | Boston | 1936 | 10.00 |
| Lyne, Daniel J. | Boston | 1936 | 10.00 |
| Madden, M.L. | Boston | 1936 | 10.00 |
| Maguire, James, E. | E. Boston | 1936 | 10.00 |
| Maguire, William C. | Boston | 1936 | 10.00 |
| Maher, John B., Atty. | Rockland, Mass. | 1936 | 10.00 |
| Manning, Joseph P. | Boston | 1936 | 10.00 |
| Mason, Charles E. | Boston | 1936 | 10.00 |
| Maynard, Joseph A. | Boston | 1936 | 10.00 |
| James F. McDermott | Boston | 1936 | 10.00 |
| McSweeney, Morgan J. | Salem | 1936 | 5.00 |
| McSweeney, William H. | Salem | 1936 | 5.00 |
| Meagher, James F. | Boston | 1936 | 10.00 |
| Moran, John H. | Boston | 1936 | 10.00 |
| Mulcahy, Charles W. | Boston | 1936 | 10.00 |
| Murphy, Rev. Francis V. | Cambridge | 1936 | 10.00 |
| Murray, Thomas W. | Boston | 1936 | 10.00 |
| McGrath, James F. | Boston | 1936 | 10.00 |

| | | | |
|---|---|---|---|
| O'Brien, J.J. | Chicago, Ill. | 1934 | 75.00 |
| O'Connell, Judge Daniel T. | Boston | 1936 | 10.00 |
| O'Connell, Joseph E. | Boston | 1936 | 10.00 |
| O'Connell, Joseph F. | Boston | 1936 | 10.00 |
| O'Connell, P.A. | Boston | 1936 | 10.00 |
| O'Connor, Thomas D. | Cambridge | 1936 | 10.00 |
| O'Malley, Charles J. | Boston | 1936 | 50.00 |
| Prindiville, John J. | Framingham, Mass. | 1936 | 10.00 |
| Quinn, Fred A. | Boston | 1936 | 10.00 |
| Reardon, Dr Daniel B. | Quincy | 1936 | 10.00 |
| Ryan, John | Boston | 1936 | 10.00 |
| Rothwell, Bernard J. | Boston | 1936 | 10.00 |
| Saltonstall, Leverett | Brookline | 1933–6 | 220.00 |
| Saltonstall, Mrs Richard M. | Brookline | 1933–6 | 600.00 |
| Scannell, Dr David D. | Boston | 1936 | 10.00 |
| Scott, Donald | Peabody Museum | 1934 | 65.00 |
| Scullin, Matthew P. | Somerville | 1936 | 25.00 |
| Sears, Miss Clara E. | Boston | 1933–6 | 300.00 |
| Shallow, Samuel J. | Boston | 1936 | 10.00 |
| Sisk, Richard L. | Lynn | 1936 | 10.00 |
| Spillane, Maurice P. | Boston | 1936 | 10.00 |
| Stanton, Dr Joseph | Boston | 1936 | 10.00 |
| Stone, Edward C. | Boston | 1936 | 10.00 |
| Sullivan, Edward J. | Boston | 1936 | 10.00 |
| Sullivan, Col. Thomas F. | Boston | 1936 | 10.00 |
| Traher, Philip J. | Boston | 1936 | 10.00 |
| Walsh, Judge Richard M. | Boston | 1936 | 10.00 |

# Endnotes

## Introduction

1  Anne Byrne, Ricca Edmondson and Tony Varley, 'Arensberg and Kimball and Anthropological Research in Ireland: Introduction to the Third Edition (2001)', in Conrad M. Arensberg and Solon T. Kimball, *Family and Community in Ireland* (Clare, 3rd edition, 2001), pp. xvii–xxx.
2  R.A.S. Macalister, 'A Five Year Plan for Research', in 'The New Ireland Five Years of Progress', a supplement issued with the *Irish Press*, 11 June 1937.

## Chapter 1

1  Adolf Mahr, 'Our Splendid Celtic Collection', *Irish Times*, 15 October 1927.
2  It is also called the Harvard Anthropological Survey of Ireland, the Archaeological Survey, the Harvard Archaeological Survey of Ireland, the Harvard Project, the Harvard Irish Mission and the Irish Survey 1932–1936.
3  A grant of $7,874.28 was received from the Rockefeller Foundation and $9,600 from the American Council of Learned Societies. Money was also made available through the Milton Fund, the Sheldon Travelling Fellowship and the Wenner-Gren Foundation. See Appendix 3 for list of private donations. E.A. Hooton papers #995-1, Box 21.11.
4  See Chapter 7 for further information on this topic.
5  Detailed research has been carried out on the social strand but there is no full-length published study of the archaeological or the physical anthropology strands to date. See Byrne, Edmondson and Varley, 'Arensberg and Kimball and Anthropological Research in Ireland,' pp. xvii–xxx.
6  George W. Stocking Jr. (ed.) *American Anthropology 1921—1945 Papers from the American Anthropologist* (Nebraska and London, 1976), p. 13.
7  Aresnsberg and Kimball *Family and Community in Ireland*, p. xviii.
8  Mairéad Carew, 'Eoin MacNeill: Revolutionary Cultural Ideologue' *1916 Birth Pangs of a Nation? Studies* (Spring 2016), vol. cv, no. 417, pp. 67–75.
9  'On Two Visits to Ireland by H. O'Neill Hencken to Investigate the possibilities of Archaeological Research', in E.A. Hooton Papers #995-1, Box 21.9.
10 'Matthew Stout, Emyr Estyn Evans and Northern Ireland: The archaeology and geography of a new state', in John A. Atkinson, Iain Banks & Jerry O'Sullivan, *Nationalism and Archaeology Scottish Archaeological Forum* (Glasgow, 1996).

11 See discussion of this idea in Yannis Hamilakis, 'Lives in Ruins: Antiquities and National Imagination in Modern Greece', in Susan Kane (ed.), *The Politics of Archaeology and Identity in a Global Context* (Boston, 2003), p. 54.

12 Benedict Anderson, *Imagined Communities. Reflections on the Origin and Spread of Nationalism* (London, 1983).

13 Mairéad Carew, 'Eoin MacNeill and the Promotion of Celtic Studies in America', *History Hub* special 2013 – series on 'Eoin MacNeill: Revolutionary and Scholar', School of History and Archives, UCD, www.historyhub.ie.

14 See Appendix 3 for list of private donations. E.A. Hooton papers #995-1, Box 21.11. See also Earnest A. Hooton and C. Wesley Dupertuis, *The Physical Anthropology of Ireland with a Section on the West Coast Irish Females by Helen Dawson* (Harvard, 1955), p. ix.

15 Thalassa Scholl (Hugh O'Neill Hencken's daughter) to author 17 June 2009; see also 'Death of Hugh O'Neill. Well known merchant passed away in his city home. Came from Ireland when a boy and built up his great dry-goods business after the Civil War', *The New York Times*, 17 June 1902.

16 Eoin MacNeill quoted in the *Irish Times*, 21 June 1934.

17 Carew, 'Eoin MacNeill and the promotion of Celtic Studies in the United States'.

18 Carew, 'Eoin MacNeill, Revolutionary Cultural Ideologue', pp. 67–75.

19 Bulmer Hobson (ed.), *Saorstát Eireann Irish Free State Official Handbook* (Dublin, 1932).

20 R.A.S Macalister, *The Archaeology of Ireland* (Third Edition), (London, 1949), pp. xii, x, & xiii.

21 Bruce Trigger 'Alternative Archaeologies: Nationalist, Colonialist, Imperialist', in Robert Preucel and Ian Hodder (eds), *Contemporary Archaeology in Theory* (Oxford, 1996), p. 628.

22 John Hutchinson, 'Archaeology and the Irish Rediscovery of the Celtic Past', in *Nations and Nationalism* vol. vii, no. 4 (2001), p. 506.

23 Grahame Clark, *Archaeology and Society*, (Suffolk, 1957), p. 257.

24 Ibid. p. 257.

25 John Waddell, *Foundation Myths: The Beginnings of Irish Archaeology* (Dublin, 2005), p. 219.

26 The *Irish Times*, 26 August 1933; see Chapter 4 for further information.

27 Michael Tierney, *Eoin MacNeill: Scholar and Man of Action*, edited by F.X. Martin (Oxford, 1980), p. 363.

28 Douglas Hyde 'The Necessity for de-Anglicising Ireland', in Charles Gavan Duffy, George Sigerson and Douglas Hyde (eds), *The Revival of Irish Literature* (London 1894), pp. 117–61.

29 Hyde 'The Necessity for de-Anglicising Ireland', p. 121; Brian Murphy, *Douglas Hyde and the foundation of the Irish Presidency* (Dublin, 2016).

30 Hyde 'The Necessity for de-Anglicising Ireland', p. 125.

31 See Chapter 5, 'Lagore Crannóg: Archaeology in Service of the State?'

32 Hyde 'The Necessity for de-Anglicising Ireland', p. 126.

33 Tom Garvin, *Nationalist Revolutionaries in Ireland* (Oxford, 1987), p. 78.

34   Eoin MacNeill, 'Irish Education Policy', *Irish Statesman*, 17 October 1925, p. 168.

35   Gregory Castle, *Modernism and the Celtic Revival* (Cambridge, 2001), p. 105.

36   Quoted in W.J. McCormack, *Dublin 1916: The French Connection* (Dublin 2012), p. 35: Eugen Weber, *Peasants Into Frenchmen, the modernization of rural France, 1880–1914* (Stanford, 1976).

37   See text of speech in Richard Aldous, *Great Irish Speeches* (London, 2009), p. 93.

38   Gregory Castle, *Modernism and the Celtic Revival*, p. 29.

39   Ibid. p. 1.

40   Ibid. p. 99.

41   Ibid. p. 35.

42   Ibid. p. 27.

43   John Brannigan, *Race in Modern Irish Literature and Culture* (Edinburgh, 2009), p. 84.

44   Nicholas Allen, 'States of Mind: Science, Culture and the Irish Intellectual Revival, 1900–30', *Irish University Review*, vol. xxxiii, no. 1, Special Issue: New perspectives on the Irish Literary Revival (Spring – Summer 2003), p. 158.

45   George W. Stocking Jr. (ed.) *American Anthropology 1921–1945*, p. 27.

46   Stanley M. Garn and Eugene Giles, 'Earnest Albert Hooton November 20, 1887– May 3, 1954', *Biographical Memoir of the National Academy of Sciences of the United States of America*, in http:www.nasonline.org, pp. 167–79.

47   'Importance of the Irish Free State: The Reasons for Choosing it', in 'The Harvard Study of the Irish Free State', Hooton papers, #995-1, Box 21.9.

48   Hugh O'Neill Hencken, *Indo-European Languages and Archaeology: American Anthropologist*, vol. lvii, no. 6, Part 3, Memoir 84 (December, 1955).

49   G.R. Isaac, 'The origins of the Celtic languages: language spread from east to west', in Barry Cunliffe and John T. Koch (eds) *Celtic from the West: Alternative perspectives from archaeology, genetics, language and literature* (Oxford, 2010), p. 165.

50   Janet Egleson Dunleavy and Gareth W. Dunleavy, *Douglas Hyde, A Maker of Modern Ireland* (Oxford, 1991), pp. 306 and 311.

51   Seán Ó Tuama, *The Gaelic League Idea* (Dublin, 1972), p. 26; Between 1900 and 1925 the Gaelic League published 400 works in Irish. The Minister for Finance at the time was Ernest Blythe. In 1929, the Department of Finance allocated £6,400 to the translation of novels into Irish. *Irish Times* 30 June 2014.

52   Dunleavy and Dunleavy, p. 361.

53   Declan Kiberd and P. J. Mathews (eds), *Handbook of the Irish Revival: An Anthology of Irish Cultural and Political Writings 1891–1922* (Dublin, 2015), p. 129.

54   Patrick Pearse, 'About Literature', *An Claidheamh Soluis*, 26 May 1906.

55   Castle, *Modernism and the Celtic Revival*, p. 255.

56   Paul Delaney, *Seán O'Faoláin, Literature, Inheritance and the 1930s* (Dublin, 2014), p. 22.

57   His antipathy to the Irish language revival and Irish-Ireland ideology might, possibly, owe more to his own personal disappointment when his application for the Chair of English litereature at UCC was turned down in 1931. The successful applicant was Daniel Corkery, the 'genuinely cultivated and widely read' Irish-Irelander, Gaelic League activist and former mentor of Seán O'Faoláin, Patrick

Maume, *The Rise and Fall of Irish Ireland: D.P. Moran and Daniel Corkery* (Coleraine 1996), p. 4 and p. 9.

58  Patrick Maume, *D.P. Moran, Life and Times* (Dundalgan Press, W. Tempest Ltd., October, 1995).

59  Hooton, Dupertuis and Dawson *The Physical Anthropology of Ireland*, p. 8.

60  'Douglas Hyde 1905', in Brendan Ó Conaire, *Douglas Hyde, Language Lore and Lyrics* (Dublin, Irish Academic Press, 1986), p. 184.

61  Smith defines the nation as 'a named human population sharing an historic territory, common myths and historical memories, a mass, public culture, a common economy and common legal rights and duties for all members'. A.D. Smith, *National Identity* (Nevada 1991), p. 14. Gellner considers that 'nations as a natural God-given way of classifying men, as an inherent though long-delayed political destiny, are a myth'. Gellner, *Nations and Nationalism* (London, 1983), pp. 48–9.

62  *Report of the Department of Agriculture and Technical Instruction* vol. xxii (1908), p. 14.

63  Garvin, *Nationalist Revolutionaries in Ireland*, p. 81.

64  Gearóid Ó Tuathaigh, Cultural Visions and the New State: Embedding and Embalming', in Gabriel Doherty and Dermot Keogh, *De Valera's Irelands* (Cork 2003), p. 176.

65  Mairéad Carew, *Tara and the Ark of the Covenant* (Dublin, 2003).

66  Ken Neill, 'The Broighter Hoard: or how Carson caught the boat', *Archaeology Ireland* vol. vii, no. 2 (Summer 1993), pp. 24–6.

67  Letter dated 24 March 1927 from Seosamh Ó Néill, secretary of Department of Education to Secretary of the Executive Council, NAI D/TAOIS S5392.

68  Barbro Klein, 'Cultural heritage, the Swedish folklife sphere and the others' in *Cultural Analysis* v (2006), p. 61.

69  Bruce Trigger, *A History of Archaeological Thought* (Cambridge, 1996, second edition), p. 211.

70  Mairéad Carew, 'The Glamour of Ancient Greatness': The importance of the 1927 Lithberg Report to Irish Archaeology', *Archaeology Ireland* vol. xxii, no. 1 issue no. 83 (Spring 2008), pp. 20–2.

71  'Dr Lithberg's Report', NAI D/TAOIS S5392, p. 18 and p. 22.

72  Elizabeth Crooke, *Politics, Archaeology and the Creation of a National Museum of Ireland: An Expression of National Life* (Dublin, 2000), p. 153.

73  Gellner, *Nations and Nationalism*.

74  Sir Thomas Bodkin, *Report to the Government of Ireland on various institutions and activities concerned with the Arts in Ireland*, Section II, 'The National Museum', p. 11, NAI D/TAOIS S14 559A.

75  R.A.S. Macalister, 'Some Unsolved Problems in Irish Archaeology: An Address delivered to the Academy', in *PRIA* vol. xxxvii, section C., no. 12 (June, 1927).

76  http://www.irishstatutebook.ie/1930/en/act/pub/0002/index.html. For further information on the protection of national monuments see Christiaan Corlett, 'The Royal Society of Antiquaries of Ireland and the protection of monuments (part 1), *JRSAI* vol. cxxxix (2009), pp. 80–100; 'The Royal Society of Antiquaries of Ireland and the protection of monuments (part II)' *JRSAI* vol. cxli (2011), pp. 167–89 and

'The Royal Society of Antiquaries of Ireland and the protection of monuments (part III)', *JRSAI* vol. cxlii-cxliii (2012–2013), pp. 166–83.

77   Mairéad Carew, 'Politics and the definition of National Monuments: the 'Big House problem', *The Journal of Irish Archaeology*, vol. xviii (2009), pp. 129–39.

78   Don D. Fowler, 'Uses of the Past: Archaeology in the Service of the State', in *American Antiquity* vol. lii, no. 2 (1987), pp. 229–48.

79   Terence Dooley, *The Decline of the Big House in Ireland: A Study of Irish Landed Families* (Dublin, 2001), p. 143.

80   Harold G. Leask, in an internal memorandum dated 16 October 1943, NAI OPW F94/574/1.

81   Carew, 'Politics and the definition of National Monuments', p. 129.

82   NAI OPW F94/574/1, memo by Chairman of Board of Works dated 1 Jan 1946.

83   NAI D/TAOIS S5935.

84   RSAI/MSS/IDV/26.

85   *Irish Press*, 28 May 1932.

86   H.O'Neill Hencken and Hallam L. Movius, 'The Cemetery-Cairn of Knockast', in *PRIA* vol. xli, Section C, No. 11 (1934), p. 232.

87   In a letter dated 17 February 1937 Movius informed Mahr that 'When the time comes, we shall make negotiations with the Belfast Museum in your interests to try and secure as much material for you as we feel justified in stealing.' H.L. Movius to Adolf Mahr , letter dated 17 February 1937, Hallam Movius Papers #998-27, 28.1. Movius collected a 'quite full type series representing the sites of Glenarm, Cushendun, Whitepark Bay, Bann Valley and Lough Neagh for the Peabody Museum'. 'Report [b] of the Second Harvard Archaeological Expedition to Ireland, 1933', E.A. Hooton Papers, #995-1, Box 21.9., p. 13. In a letter to Dean Carmody dated 26 July 1935 Movius wrote that he had 'arranged at the Museum to pack the material here at the dig [at Larne] for shipment directly to America'. H.L. Movius to Dean Carmody, letter dated 26 July 1935, H.L. Movius Papers #998-27, 127.3.

88   Sighle Bhreathnach-Lynch, 'Commemorating the Hero in newly Independent Ireland; Expressions of Nationhood in Bronze and Stone', in Laurence W. McBride, *Images Icons and the Irish Nationalist Imagination* (Dublin, 1999), pp. 148–65.

89   See, for example, H. O'Neill Hencken, 'A Long Cairn at Creevykeel, Co. Sligo', in *JRSAI* vol. lxix, part ii (1939), pp. 96–7. Hencken noted that Mr Connelly, a local who lived near Creevykeel, considered the monument not as a grave but as a dwelling inhabited in the present. In this way 'it takes its place with forts, raths and ruins of all ages, which are the regular abode of 'the other people'. Joseph Raftery collected information on the Irish names of the site at Creevykeel. See also Conrad M. Arensberg *The Irish Countryman An Anthropological Study* (Gloucester, Mass. [1937] Reprinted 1959), p. 181.

90   'Dr. Lithberg's report', NAI D/TAOIS S5392.

91   Séamas Ó Catháin, *Formation of a Folklorist The Visit of James Hamilton Delargy (Séamus Ó Duilearga) to Scandinavia, Finland, Estonia and Germany 1 April - 29 September 1928* (Dublin, 2008).

92   Micheál Briody, *The Irish Folklore Commission 1935–1970 History, Ideology, Methodology, Studia Fennica Folkloristica* 17 (Helsinki, 2008), p. 23.

93   Department of External Affairs to Maurice Moynihan, letter dated 2 November 1938, NAI D/TAOIS S9215A.
94   *Irish Times*, 11 March 1936.
95   Briody, *The Irish Folklore Commission*, p. 54.
96   Patricia Lysaght, 'Swedish Ethnological Surveys in Ireland 1934–5 and their aftermath', in H. Cheape (ed.), *Tools and Traditions, Studies in European Ethnology presented to Alexander* Fenton (Edinburgh, 1993), pp. 22–32.
97   Adolf Mahr, 'Quaternary Research in Ireland. 1934, from the Archaeological Viewpoint', in *INJ* vol. v (Jan 1934–Nov 1935), pp. 137–44. Adolf Mahr, 'Gazetteer D: Sites examined through the Committee for Quaternary Research in Ireland', in 'New Aspects and Problems in Irish Prehistory, Presidential Address for 1937', *PPS* paper no. 11 (1937), pp. 424–5.
98   Lithberg Report, p. 12.
99   Ibid. p. 1.
100  Malcolm Chapman, *The Celts The Construction of a Myth* (London, 1992), p. 117.
101  Joep Leerssen, *Remembrance and Imagination Patterns in the Historical and Literary Representation of Ireland in the Nineteenth Century* (Cork, 1996), p. 2.
102  Seán Ó Súilleabháin, 'Folk-Museums in Scandinavia', in *JRSAI* vol. lxxv (945), p. 67. Ó Suilleabháin lamented that fact that the folklife section 'can hardly be said to be representative or worthy of the country'. p. 69. The National Folklife collection was not properly housed until 2001 at the Museum of Country Life, Turlough Park, County Mayo.
103  Arensberg, *The Irish Countryman*, p. 17.
104  R.A.S. Macalister, *Ireland in Pre-Celtic Times* (Dublin and London, 1921), p. 17.
105  L.P. Murray, 'The Cemetery-Cairn at Knockast', in *JCLAS*, vol. viii, No. 1 (1933), p. 65.
106  Murray, 'The Cemetery-Cairn at Knockast', pp. 65–8.
107  Terence Brown, *Ireland A Social and Cultural History 1922–2002* (London, Third Edition, 2004), p. 4.
108  In a comment on the essay by Elizabeth Russell on the reading habits of ordinary people Augusteijn observes that her study 'clearly reveals that the state has been wrongly described as culturally barren and dreary'. Joost Augusteijn, *Ireland in the 1930s* (Dublin, 1999), p. 8.
109  Augusteijn, *Ireland in the 1930s*, p. 7.
110  Brown, *Ireland A Social and Cultural History*, p. 57.
111  Brian Fallon, *An Age of Innocence Irish Culture 1930–1960* (Dublin, 1998), p. 159.
112  Ian Morris, *Archaeology as Cultural History Words and Things in Iron Age Greece* (Oxford, 2000), p. 3.
113  Delaney, *Seán O'Faoláin*, p. 31.
114  Carew, 'Eoin MacNeill: Revolutionary Cultural Ideologue', pp. 67–75. Seán O'Faoláin wrote that "'Ireland-free' is ignorant of both the culture of Ireland and of the world, having bartered both for the sham-Irish traditions of a semi-illiterate Gaoltacht," in 'The Gaoltacht Tradition', *The Irish Statesman* 24 April 1926.

115 This Irish-Ireland ideology underpinned his academic work which encompassed Patrician studies, Irish language, ogham studies, early Irish history and law. See Carew, 'Eoin MacNeill: Revolutionary Cultural Ideologue, pp. 67–75.

116 Carew, 'Eoin MacNeill. Revolutionary Cultural Ideologue', p. 70, For further information on the Irish Manuscripts Commssion see Michael Kennedy and Deirdre McMahon, *Reconstructing Ireland's Past: A History of the Irish Manuscripts Commission* (Irish Manuscripts Commission 2009).

117 Censorship was described in 1930 as 'the process of restricting the public expression of ideas, opinions, conceptions and impulses which have or are believed to have the capacity to undermine the governing authority or the social or moral code which that authority considers itself bound to protect', See Harold Laswell, 'Censorship' in ERA Seligman (ed.), *Encyclopaedia of the Social Sciences* (New York, Macmillan, 1930). See also Peter Martin, *Censorship in the Two Irelands* (Dublin, 2006), p. 12.

118 Martin, *Censorship in the Two Irelands*, p. xiii. James Joyce's *Ulysses*, 'literary contraband' first published in 1922 and described by Kevin Bermingham as 'a snapshot of a cultural revolution' was banned in Britain and America but not in the Irish Free State. See Kevin Bermingham, *The Most Dangerous Book: The Battle for James Joyce's* Ulysses (London, 2014), pp, 3 and 15.

119 Meking, Muhlhausen, Brase, Reinhard, Stumpf, Herkner, Weckler were all members of the Nazi party in Ireland. Muller Dubrow was the deputy Leader of the *Auslandsorganisation* and a neighbour of de Valera's in Blackrock. O'Donoghue asserts that members of the Nazi party formed 'an important fascist nucleus in Ireland. See David O'Donoghue, *Hitler's Irish Voices The Story of German Radio's Wartime Irish Service* (Belfast 1998), p. 4. O'Halpin considers that 'the Axis émigré communities posed a threat, because of the Irish branches of the Fascist parties'. Eunan O'Halpin *Defending Ireland:The Irish State and its Enemies* since 1922 (Oxford, 1999), p. 235. Adolf Mahr described the Nazi party in Ireland as 'very small and quite harmless'. See letter from Adolf Mahr to John A. Costello dated 10 May 1948 in NAI D/FIN 2 E103/29/39.

120 M. Manning and M. MacDowell, *Electricity Supply in Ireland:The History of the ESB* (Dublin: Gill and Macmillan, 1984).

121 J.J. Lee points out that it was a massive sum when one considers that the government expenditure for the year 1926 to 1927 was only £24 million. See J.J. Lee, *Ireland 1912–1985* (Cambridge; Cambridge University Press, 1985), p. 109.

122 Allen, 'States of Mind', p. 158; see also McKayla Sutton, 'Harnessed in the Service of the Nation: Party Politics and the Promotion of the Shannon Hydroelectric Scheme, 1924–32', in Mel Farrell, Jason Knirck and Ciara Meehan (eds), *A Formative Decade Ireland in the 1920s* (Kildare, 2015), pp. 87–107.

123 'Notes and Comments', *Irish Statesman*, 21 March 1925, pp. 38–9.

124 Andy Bielenberg, 'Keating, Siemens and the Shannon Scheme', *History Ireland* vol. v, issue no. 3 (Autumn 1997).

125 Carew, 'The Pageant of the Celt', pp. 9–12.

126 M.G. Palmer, 'The Shannon stirs new hope in Ireland', *New York Times Magazine*, 12 January 1930.

127 Niamh Nic Ghabhann. 'Medieval Ireland and the Shannon Hydro-Electric Scheme: reconstructing the past in independent Ireland' *Irish Studies Review,* vol. xxv, issue 4 (2017), pp. 425–43.

128 David G. Holmes, 'The Eucharistic Congress of 1932 and Irish Identity', in *New Hibernia Review* vol. iv, no. 1 (Spring, 2000), p. 60.

129 Rory O'Dwyer, *The Eucharistic Congress, Dublin 1932 An Illustrated History* (Dublin, 2009), p. 35 and p. 90.

130 Chesterton quoted in O'Dwyer, *The Eucharistic Congress*, p. 96.

131 Anon., *Dublin The Book of the Congress* (Wexford, 1934), p. 55.

132 Holmes, 'The Eucharistic Congress, p. 55: See also Rory O'Dwyer, 'On Show to the World: the Eucharistic Congress, 1932', in *History Ireland* (Nov/Dec. 2007), pp. 42–7.

133 Anon., *Dublin The Book of the Congress*, 'Official visit of the Cardinal Legate at Government Buildings', p. 73.

134 Cyril Fox, Review Article, 'Christian Art in Ancient Ireland, vol. 1 Edited by Dr. Adolf Mahr, Keeper of Irish Antiquities, National Museum, Dublin, Dublin 1932', in *Man* vol xxxii (Sept. 1932), p. 219.

135 Brian P. Kennedy, 'The Failure of the Cultural Republic: Ireland 1922–39', *Studies: An Irish Quarterly Review,* vol. lxxxi, No. 321 (Spring, 1992), pp. 14–22.

136 'Academy of Christian Art', article iv, George Noble Count Plunkett's Papers, UCDA P79/88.

137 Fr Stephen Brown, SJ, 'The Central Catholic Library: the First Ten Years of an Irish Enterprise' (Dublin, 1932).

138 Maurice Moynihan (ed.), *Speeches and Statements by Éamon de Valera 1917–73* (Dublin 1980), p. 233.

139 M.J. Harford, Foreword, *The Pageant of the Celt*, p. 3, RIA MSS, AP 1934. See also Carew, 'The Pageant of the Celt', pp. 9–12.

140 'The Pageant of the Celt', p. 3, RIA MSS, AP 1934; *Chicago Daily Tribune*, 27 August 1934.

141 Quoted in Joan Fitzpatrick Dean, *All Dressed Up Modern Irish Historical Pageantry* (Syracuse University Press, 2014), p. 151. 'It was while reading the manuscript and notes of his father's book, *Ireland's Crown of Thorns and Roses* that he became impressed with the dramatic possibilities of Ireland's stirring story. *The Pageant of the Celt* is the result of two years of historical research and preparation by him'. *The Pageant of the Celt*, p. 18, RIA MSS, AP 1934.

142 John V. Ryan, *The Pageant of the Celt*, p. 2, RIA MSS, AP 1934.

143 Carew, 'The Pageant of the Celt', pp. 9–12.

144 Charles Fanning, 'Duelling Cultures: Ireland and Irish America at the Chicago World's Fairs of 1933 and 1934', *New Hibernia Review* vol. xv, no. 3 (Autumn 2011).

145 Adolf Mahr, *A Century of Progress in Irish Archaeology Exhibits Collected by the National Museum of Ireland*, RIA AP 1933/19, p. 3.

146 Carew, 'The Pageant of the Celt', pp. 9–12.

147 Eoin MacNeill Papers, UCDA, LA1/G/362.

148 Dunleavy & Dunleavy, *Douglas Author Hyde*, p. 362. Eoin MacNeill claimed in his memoir that a lecture given by Douglas Hyde in New York was the impetus for

setting up the Gaelic League in 1893; UCDA LA1/G/372: Eoin MacNeill Papers, Memoir, Bureau of Military History, 1913–21, p. 27.

149 Dunleavy & Dunleavy, *Douglas Hyde*, p. 362.
150 Eoin MacNeill Papers, UCDA, LA1/G/362: 'Stay at Home, Professor Eoin MacNeill gives advice to would-be emigrants to America, Tour of States', newspaper clipping, title unknown, n.d.
151 Ibid.
152 Roland Blennerhassett, 'A Brief History of Celtic Studies in North America', in *PMLA* vol. lxix (September, 1954), no. 4, part 2, p. 8.
153 *New York Herald Tribune*, 3 April 1930 and *New York City Journal*, 2 April 1930.
154 Michael Doorley, '"The Judge' versus 'The Chief' – Daniel Cohalan and the 1920 split within Irish America," *History Ireland* vol. xxiii, no. 2, p. 45.
155 Ibid.
156 Eoin MacNeill Papers, UCDA, LA1/G/362: newspaper clipping but name of newspaper or date not included.
157 The *New York Herald Tribune*, 23 March 1931.
158 Blennerhassett, 'A Brief History of Celtic Studies in North America', p. 14.
159 'Society of Friends of the Universities of Ireland, Letters exchanged between Professor J.L. Gerig, Columbia University, New York and Provost S.J. Gwynn, Trinity College Dublin, 'Irish are Neglecting their language, Culture and Ideals', newspaper clipping, title unknown, n.d., Eoin MacNeill Papers, UCDA, LA1/G/362.
160 The *Gaelic American*, 27 June 1931, Eoin MacNeill Papers, UCDA, LA1/G/362.
161 Ibid.
162 *Irish Independent*, 6 June 1931.
163 Eoin MacNeill Papers, UCDA, LA1/G/362.
164 *Irish Times*, 21 June 1934.
165 Eoin MacNeill, 'Promotion of Irish Cultural Publications', n.d., NAI D/TAOIS S9215A.
166 J.P. Walshe to de Valera, Letter dated 5 October 1937, NAI D/TAOIS S9215A.
167 Note dictated by the President to Miss O'Connell following his interview with Professor McNeill on 30.12.36, NAI D/TAOIS S9215A. An American-Irish Foundation was established 1962.
168 PDDE, vol. lxxix, 10 April 1940, col. 1078.
169 Ibid. col. 1109.
170 Ibid. col. 1109 and col. 1102.
171 Briody, *The Irish Folklore Commission*, p. 62.
172 Daniel A. Binchy, 'Adolf Hitler', in *Studies: An Irish Quarterly Review* vol. xxii, no. 85 (Mar. 1933), pp. 29–47, and 'Heirig Brunig', in *Studies* vol. xxi (Sept. 1932), pp. 385–403. See also Tom Garvin, *The lives of Daniel Binchy: Irish Scholar, Diplomat, Public Intellectual* (Dublin, 2016).
173 Bettina Arnold and Henning Hassmann, 'Archaeology in Nazi Germany: The Legacy of the Faustian Bargain', in Philip L. Kohl and Clare Fawcett (eds), *Nationalism, Politics and the Practice of Archaeology* (Cambridge, 1995).
174 S.P. Ó Ríordáin, 'Prehistory in Ireland, 1937–1946', PPS paper no. 6 (1946), p. 143.

## Chapter 2

1 R.A.S. Macalister's foreword in Walther Bremer, *Ireland's Place in Prehistoric and Early Historic Europe* (a translation, Dublin, 1928), p. 2.

2 Hutchinson, 'Archaeology and the Irish rediscovery of the Celtic past', p. 506.

3 'The Harvard Study of the Irish Free State', E.A. Hooton papers, #995-1, Box 21.9, pp. 8–9.

4 Hugh O'Neill Hencken, *Memories of Work and Travel Hugh O'Neill Hencken 1903–1981* (1981), p. 21. Mahr's 'reservations' were about the restrictions on excavation in place since the introduction of the National Monuments Act in 1930 and the necessity to acquire licences to dig archaeological sites.

5 Quotes from Mahr's letter to Bender 21 August 1932, from Gerry Mullins, *Dublin Nazi No. 1: The Life of Adolf Mahr* (Dublin, 2007), p. 42.

6 'The Harvard Study of the Irish Free State', E.A. Hooton papers, #995-1, Box 21.9, p. 9.

7 Adam Stout, *Druids, Ley Hunters and Archaeologists in Pre-war Britain* (Oxford, 2008); Philippa Levine, *The Amateur and the Professional. Antiquarians, Historians and Archaeologists in Victorian England, 1838–1886.* (Cambridge, 1986).

8 S.P. Ó Ríordáin, 'Palaeolithic Man in Ireland', *Antiquity*, vol. v (1931), p. 362.

9 Rev. P. Power, *Prehistoric Ireland A Manual of Irish Pre-Christian Archaeology* (Dublin, 1925), p. v.

10 Eoin MacNeill papers, UCDA LA1/D/5.

11 Adolf Mahr, 'Labbacallee Dolmen, Co. Cork', report dated 10 August 1934, NAI D/TAOIS S10940.

12 Trigger, *A history of archaeological thought*, p. 48.

13 Stuart Piggott, *Ruins in a Landscape* (Edinburgh, 1976), pp. 6–8.

14 Lisnacrogher, Co. Antrim, for example, had been 'totally obliterated without any archaeological supervision', during the latter half of the nineteenth century. See Barry Raftery, *La Tène in Ireland Problems of Origin and Chronology* (Marburg, 1984), p. 314.

15 Brian Fagan, *A Brief History of Archaeology Classical Times to the Twenty-First Century* (New Jersey, 2005), p. 140.

16 H.E. Kilbride Jones, 'Macalister, Leask and Ó Ríordáin', in *Archaeology Ireland*, vol. vi, no. 4 (Winter, 1992), p. 14.

17 Waddell, *Foundation Myths*, p. 216.

18 R.A.S. Macalister, *Archaeology of Ireland* (London [1927] Third Edition, 1949), p. 356.

19 Muiris O'Sullivan, 'The Life and Legacy of R.A.S. Macalister: a Century of Archaeology at UCD', in Gabriel Cooney, Katharina Becker, John Coles, Michael Ryan and Susanne Sievers (eds) *Relics of Old Decency: Archaeological Studies in Later Prehistory Festschrift for Barry Raftery* (Dublin, 2009), p. 521.

20 T. Ó Raifeartaigh (ed.), *The Royal Irish Academy a Bicentennial History 1785–1985* (Dublin, 1985), p. 155; See also Michael Ryan, 'A Long 1923', in *Relics of Old Decency*, pp. 543–8. Macalister had also been a candidate for the position of Superintendent of Irish Antiquities in 1897, a post awarded to George Coffey.

21    Macalister's foreword in Bremer, *Ireland's Place in Prehistoric and Early Historic Europe*.

22    Ibid.

23    'On Two Visits to Ireland by H. O'Neill Hencken to Investigate the Possibilities of Archaeological Research', Hooton Papers #995-1, Box 21. 9.

24    Annika Stephan and Paul Gosling, 'Adolf Mahr (1887–1951): His Contribution to Archaeological Research and Practice in Austria and Ireland', in Gisela Holfter, Marieke Krajenbrink & Edward Moxon-Browne (eds.), *Connections and Identities: Austria, Ireland and Switzerland* (Bern, 2004).

25    Ibid. pp. 108–9.

26    NAI D/TAOIS S6631.

27    NAI D/FIN 2 E109/20/34.

28    NAI D/FIN E103/29/39.

29    E. Estyn Evans, *Ireland and the Atlantic Heritage* (Dublin, 1996) p. 217.

30    Ibid.

31    Seósamh Ó Néill, Secretary at the Department of Education to the Secretary of the Department of Finance, letter dated 6 March 1933, NAI D/FIN E53/3/33.

32    John P. Duggan, *Neutral Ireland and the Third Reich* (Dublin 1989), p. 63; See also David O'Donoghue, *Hitler's Irish Voices The Story of German Radio's Wartime Irish Service* (Belfast 1998), pp. 20–1; Mark Hull, *Irish Secrets: German Espionage in Ireland, 1939–45* (Portland, Oregan and Dublin, 2003), pp. 29–30; C.W. Phillips, *My Life in Archaeology* (Gloucester, 1987), pp. 65–6; Eunan O'Halpin, *Defending Ireland: The Irish State and its Enemies Since 1922* (Oxford, 1999), p. 145. Robert Fisk, *In Time of War: Ireland, Ulster and the Price of Neutrality* (London, 1983), pp. 76 and 289.

33    NAI D/FIN 2 E103/29/39.

34    Adolf Mahr to Seosamh O Neill, Secretary of the Department of Education, letter dated 23 July 1938, NAI, D/TAOIS S6631A.

35    See Correspondence between Movius and Mahr contained in Box 28.21, Hallam L. Movius Papers #998-27.

36    Dermot Keogh, *Jews in Twentieth-Century Ireland Refugees, Anti-Semitism and the Holocaust* (Cork 1998), p. 106.

37    O'Donoghue, *Hitler's Irish Voices*, p. 7.

38    Arnold and Hassmann, 'Archaeology in Nazi Germany', p. 76.

39    The Celtic philologist, Professor Rudolf Thurneysen of Bonn, was chosen as first honorary president of the society. Other founder members included Professor Mühlhausen of Hamburg and Berlin; Dr Bauersfeld of Munich; Dr Weisweiler of Frankfurt-on-Main; Dr Wagner of Berlin; Dr von Tevenar of Berlin; and Herr Clissmann of Dublin. See *Irish Times*, 25 January 1937.

40    *Irish Times*, 25 January 1937.

41    For a summary of the political ideas underpinning the work of the Harvard Mission see Mairéad Carew, 'The Harvard Mission, Eugenics and the Celts', *Archaeology Ireland* vol. xxvi, no. 4, issue no. 102 (Winter 2012), pp. 38–40.

42    For biographies see www.dib.cambridge.org.

43    Obituary, Professor Seán P. Ó Ríordáin, *Irish Times*, 12 April 1957. For further information on Canon Power see Lawrence William White and Aideen Foley, 'Power, Patrick', in www.dib.cambridge.org.

44 Joseph Raftery, 'A Backward Look', in *Archaeology Ireland*, vol. ii, no. 1 (Spring, 1988), p. 24.

45 Patrick F. Wallace, 'Adolf Mahr and the making of Seán P. Ó Ríordáin', in Helen Roche, Eoin Grogan, John Bradley, John Coles and Barry Raftery (eds) *From Megaliths to Metal Essays in Honour of George Eogan* (Oxford, 2004), pp. 254–63.

46 Kilbride Jones, 'Macalister, Leask and Ó Ríordáin', p. 15.

47 'Professor Michael V. Duignan, 1907–1988', *Archaeology Ireland*, vol. ii, No. 2 (Summer, 1988), p. 45: See also CV of Michael V. Duignan, Eoin MacNeill Papers, UCDA LA1/D20.

48 Waddell, *Foundation Myths*, p. 216.

49 Joseph Raftery, 'A backward look', p. 24.

50 Fagan, Chapter 9 'Archaeology Coming of Age, 1920 to 1940', pp. 140–55. in *A Brief History of Archaeology*. See also Waddell, Chapter 7, 'The 1930s; growth and change', *Foundation Myths*, pp. 201–20.

51 R.A.S. Macalister 'Some Unsolved Problems in Irish Archaeology: an Address delivered to the Academy', in *PRIA* vol. xxxvii, section C., no. 12 (June, 1927), p. 245.

52 Mahr to Bender, letter dated 10 December 1936, in *Mullins, Dublin Nazi No. 1*, p. 70.

53 'On Two Visits to Ireland by H. O'Neill Hencken.

54 Ibid.

55 O'Sullivan, 'The Life and Legacy of R.A.S Macalister', pp. 521–30.

56 Ó Raifeartaigh, *The Royal Irish Academy*, p. 152.

57 Ibid. p. 152. General Augustus Pitt-Rivers is generally considered to be the 'father of modern excavation technique'. The Pitt Rivers Museum was founded in 1884 when he donated his collection of archaeological and anthropological artefacts to Oxford University. Heinrich Schliemann, famous for the discovery of Troy, was also known for his lack of interest in archaeological techniques and for illegally exporting antiquities.

58 Macalister, 'Some Unsolved Problems in Irish Archaeology', p. 258.

59 Éamon de Valera, 'Open letter to President Wilson, 27 October 1920', in Moynihan, *Speeches and Statements by Éamon de Valera*, p. 37.

60 Adolf Mahr, 'New Aspects and Problems in Irish Prehistory', Presidential Address for 1937, *PPS* no. 11 (July–December 1937), p. 400.

61 Ibid, p. 402.

62 Sir John Rhys, *Celtic Britain* (1882).

63 George Coffey, 'Some Monuments of the La Tène period', in *PRIA* vol. xxiv (1904), p. 257; George Coffey, 'Archaeological Evidence for the intercourse of Gaul with Ireland before the first Century', in *PRIA* vol. xxviii (1910), p. 103.

64 O.G.S. Crawford, 'A Prehistoric Invasion of England', *Antiquaries Journal* vol. ii (1922), p. 34. Henri Hubert, *The Rise of the Celts* (London, 1899).

65 Mahr, 'New Aspects and Problems in Irish Prehistory' p. 399.

66 Eoin MacNeill, *Phases of Irish History* ([New York & London 1919], reissued New York & London 1970), p. 48.

67 John Waddell, 'The Question of the Celticization of Ireland', in *Emania* no. 9 (1991), p. 5; for theories on the coming of the Celts to Ireland see J. Waddell, 'The

Celticization of the West', in C. Chevillot and A. Coffyn (eds), *L'Age du Bronze Atlantique* (1991). For discussion on the uses and abuses of the word 'Celt' see Patrick Sims-Williams, 'Celtomania and Celtoscepticism' in *CMCS* vol. xxx (Winter 1998), pp. 1–35.

68   'New Aspects and Problems in Irish Prehistory', p. 342.

69   Gordon V. Childe, 'Scottish Megalithic Tombs and their Affinities', *TGAS* (1931–3), pp. 120–37.

70   Gordon V. Childe, *The Prehistory of Scotland* (London, 1935), p. 33.

71   Christopher Hawkes, 'British Hill Forts A Retrospect', in *Antiquity* vol. v. no. 17 (1931), pp. 60–97; Christopher Hawkes, 'The ABC of the British Iron Age', *Antiquity* vol. xxxiii (1959), pp. 170–82.

72   Mahr, 'New Aspects and Problems in Irish Prehistory', p. 342.

73   Ibid. p. 403.

74   H. O'Neill Hencken and Hallam L. Movius, 'The Cemetery-Cairn of Knockast', in *PRIA* vol. xli, Section C, No. 11 (1934), p. 283.

75   Trigger 'Alternative Archaeologies: Nationalist, Colonialist, Imperialist', p. 616.

76   David Boswell and Jessica Evans (eds), *Representing the Nation: A Reader, Histories, Heritage and Museums* (London & New York, 2005), p. 236.

77   Bruce Trigger 'Alternative Archaeologies: Nationalist, Colonialist, Imperialist', p. 617.

78   Ibid. p. 616.

79   Gellner, *Nations and Nationalism*, pp. 48–9.

80   Carew, 'The Glamour of Ancient Greatness', pp. 20–2.

81   Robert Macalister, *The Present and Future of Archaeology in Ireland* (Dublin, 1925), pp. 11–12.

82   Robert Preucel and Ian Hodder, *Communicating Present Pasts Contemporary Archaeology in Theory* (Oxford, 1996), p. 4.

83   Smith, *National Identity* (Nevada, 1991), p. 11.

84   Bruce Trigger, 'Alternative Archaeologies: Nationalist, Colonialist, Imperialist', p. 620.

85   See Paul Ricoeur, *Memory, History, Forgetting* (Chicago & London, 2004).

86   It has been suggested by some scholars that Irish archaeology should be linked specifically with cultural rather than political nationalism. For example, Gabriel Cooney wrote that 'It is important to draw a distinction between cultural and political nationalism and to link archaeology specifically with cultural nationalism', quoted in Gabriel Cooney, 'Building the Future on the Past: Archaeology and the Construction of National Identity in Ireland', in Margarita Díaz-Andreu and Timothy Champion (eds) *Nationalism and Archaeology in Europe* (London, 1997), p. 148.

87   'The Harvard Study of the Irish Free State', p. 7.

88   Ibid.

89   'On Two Visits to Ireland by H. O'Neill Hencken': Mahr, 'New Aspects and Problems in Irish Prehistory', p. 268. Hencken and Movius also provide an account of the early communication with Mahr, See Hencken and Movius, 'The Cemetery-Cairn of Knockast', p. 232.

90   'On Two Visits to Ireland by H. O'Neill Hencken'.

91   Adolf Mahr, *Christian Art in Ancient Ireland* (1932); Mullins, *Dublin Nazi No. 1*, p. 34.

92   'On Two Visits to Ireland by H. O'Neill Hencken'.

93   Ibid.

94   'The Harvard Study of the Irish Free State', p. 7.

95   Ibid.

96   'On Two Visits to Ireland by H. O'Neill Hencken'.

97   Ibid.

98   Ibid.

99   E. Morris, 'A Northern Scholar in Co. Sligo', in M. Timoney (ed.) *A Celebration of Sligo* (2002), p. 251.

100  'On Two Visits to Ireland by H. O'Neill Hencken'.

101  See list of papers by J.N.A. Wallace in *North Munster Antiquarian Journal: Index of Authors Volumes i (1936) – xxx (1988)*.

102  'Report of the Excavations of the Third Harvard Archaeological Expedition in Ireland [b]', E.A. Hooton Papers #995-1, Box 21.9, p. 10.

103  Hallam L. Movius, Jr., 'Bronze Age burials from Carrownacon, near Ballyglass, Co. Mayo', *JRSAI* vol. iv, no. 1 (1934), pp. 72–85.

104  'Asturian' can be defined as an industry of the Mesolithic period, known almost exclusively from shell mounds. See 'On Two Visits to Ireland by H. O'Neill Hencken'.

105  Ibid.

106  'Report [b] of the Second Harvard Archaeological Expedition to Ireland, 1933', E.A. Hooton Papers, #995-1, Box 21.9, p. 12.

107  H. O'Neill Hencken, 'Harvard and Irish Archaeology' in *The Irish Review*, vol. i, no. 1 (April 1934), p. 27.

108  'Report of the Excavations of the Third Harvard Archaeological Expedition in Ireland [b]', p. 2.

109  'Second Harvard Archaeological Expedition in Ireland', E.A. Hooton papers, # 995-1, Box 21.9, p. 17.

110  Ibid. p. 17.

111  'Report of the Excavations of the Third Harvard Archaeological Expedition in Ireland [b]', p. 2.

112  'Report [b] of the Second Harvard Archaeological Expedition to Ireland, 1933', pp. 12–13.

113  C. Blake Whelan, 'Further excavations at Ballynagard, Rathlin Island, Co. Antrim', *PBNHPS* (1933-4), pp. 107-11.

114  Editorial, *The Irish Naturalists' Journal*, vol. iv, no. 4 (July, 1932), p. 65.

115  Hencken, 'Harvard and Irish Archaeology', p. 27; see also 'Second Harvard Archaeological Expedition in Ireland', p. 13.

116  'Report of the Excavations of the Third Harvard Archaeological Expedition in Ireland', p. 2.

117  Hallam L. Movius Jr., 'A Stone Age Site at Glenarm, Co. Antrim', in *JRSAI* vol. lxvii (1937), p. 183.

118  'On Two Visits to Ireland by H. O'Neill Hencken'.

119   Ibid.
120   Ibid.
121   Ibid.
122   'Report of the Excavations of the Third Harvard Archaeological Expedition in Ireland [b]', p. 12.
123   H. O'Neill Hencken, 'A Cairn at Poulawack, County Clare', *JRSAI* vol. lxv (1935), pp. 191–21; H. O'Neill Hencken, 'A Stone Fort in County Clare', *JRSAI* extra vol. (1938), pp. 1–82.
124   'Report 'On Two Visits to Ireland by H. O'Neill Hencken'.
125   Ibid.
126   'Report [b] of the Second Harvard Archaeological Expedition to Ireland, 1933', pp. 11–12.
127   'Report of the Excavations of the Third Harvard Archaeological Expedition in Ireland', p. 4. Hallam L. Movius, Jr., 'Bronze Age burials from Carrownacon, near Ballyglass, Co. Mayo', JRSAI vol iv, no. 1 (1934), pp. 72–85.
128   'Report 'On Two Visits to Ireland by H. O'Neill Hencken'.
129   'Ibid.
130   Ibid. p. 8.
131   See Chapters 4 and 5 for discussion of crannóg excavations by Harvard Mission.
132   NAI D/TAOIS 97/9/95.
133   Ibid.
134   Éamon de Valera to L. Loyd Warner, letter dated 19 August 1932, NAI D/TAOIS 97/9/95.
135   Dermot Keogh, *The Vatican, the Bishops and Irish Politics 1919–1939* (Cambridge, 1986), p. 87.
136   Correspondence Box 21.6, E.A. Hooton Papers, #995-1.
137   Arensberg and Kimball, *Family and Community in Ireland*, p. iv.
138   Press Release 'Harvard University Irish Expedition 1932', in E.A. Hooton Papers #995-1, Box 21.7.
139   Arensberg and Kimball, *Family and Community in Ireland*, p. lii.
140   Arensberg, *The Irish Countryman* and Arensberg and Kimball *Family and Community in Ireland*.
141   Earnest Hooton, 'The Harvard Anthropological Survey of Ireland', unpublished manuscript, n.d., in E.A. Hooton Papers #995-1, Manuscripts Box 1.54.

### Chapter 3

1   'The Harvard Study of the Irish Free State', p. 9.
2   R.A.S. Macalister, 'A Five Year Plan for Research', in 'The New Ireland Five Years of Progress', a supplement issued with the *Irish Press*, 11 June 1937.
3   Carew, 'The Harvard Mission, Eugenics and the Celts', pp. 38–40.
4   Macalister, 'A Five Year Plan for Research'.
5   Castle, *Modernism and the Celtic Revival*, p. 29.
6   Philip Phillips, 'Alfred Marston Tozzer, 1877–1954', *American Antiquity*, vol. xxi, no. 1 (Jul 1955), pp. 72–80; Herbert Joseph Spinden, 'Alfred Marston Tozzer,

1877–1954', *Biographical Memoir of the National Academy of Sciences of the United States of America* (1957), www.nasonline.org, pp. 384–97. David L. Browman and Stephen Williams, *Anthropology at Harvard A Biographical History, 1790–1940* (Harvard, 2013), pp. 302–5.

7  Browman and Williams, *Anthropology at Harvard*, p. 211.

8  Ibid. pp. 211–16; 'Roland B. Dixon', in *Encyclopaedia Britannica Online*; http://www.britannica.com.

9  Browman and Williams, *Anthropology at Harvard*, p. 301.

10  'The Harvard Study of the Irish Free State'.

11  'Importance of the Irish Free State: The Reasons for Choosing it', in 'The Harvard Study of the Irish Free State'.

12  Edwin Black, *War against the Weak Eugenics and America's Campaign to Create a Master Race* (New York, 2004), p. 137.

13  Ibid. pp. 137–8.

14  George W. Stocking Jr. (ed.) *American Anthropology 1921–1945 Papers from the American Anthropologist* (Nebraska and London, 1976), p. 16.

15  Black, *War against the Weak*, pp. 185 and 205.

16  Hooton, 'The Harvard Anthropological Survey of Ireland'.

17  Black, *War against the Weak*, p. 313.

18  In his book *Twilight of Man*, published in 1939, he devoted a chapter on the subject of the distinctiveness of the Jews. He referred to them as 'a gifted and successful minority people', which had been set up by the Nazis as 'a sort of national scapegoat to suffer for the sins of all', in Earnest A. Hooton, *Twilight of Man* (New York, 1939), pp. 232 and 247. See also E.A. Hooton, 'The relation of Physical Anthropology to Cultural Anthropology', E.A. Hooton Papers, #995-1, Box 1.67.

19  E.A. Hooton, 'The Relation of Physical Anthropology to Cultural Anthropology'.

20  Hooton, *Twilight of Man*, p. 248.

21  Christopher Hale, *Himmler's Crusade The Nazi Expedition to Find the Origins of the Aryan Race* (New Jersey, 2006), p. 44.

22  *Time* Magazine, 10 May 1954.

23  David H. Price, *Anthropological Intelligence: The deployment and neglect of American anthropology in the Second World War* (Duke University Press, 2008), p. 293, note 11.

24  Black, *War against the Weak*, p. 30.

25  From 1936 to early 1939 Nazi Germany was considered a threat to the other countries of Europe. See Black, *War Against the Weak*, p. 188.

26  Susan Currell and Christina Cogdell (eds), *Popular Eugenics, National Efficiency and American Mass Culture in the 1930s* (Athens, Ohio, 2006), p. 361.

27  Scott Ashley, 'The Poetics of Race in 1890s Ireland: An Ethnography of the Aran Islands', in *Patterns of Prejudice* vol. xxxv, no. 2 (2001), p. 9.

28  Ibid. p. 8.

29  William Stokes, *The Life and Labours in Art and Archaeology of George Petrie* (London, 1868), p. 49.

30  Ashley, 'The Poetics of Race in 1890s Ireland', p. 9.

31  J.T. O'Flaherty, 'A Sketch of the History and Antiquities of the Southern Islands of Aran, lying off the West Coast of Ireland; with Observations on the Religion of the

Celtic Nations, Pagan Monuments of the early Irish, Druidic Rites, & Co', in *TRIA* vol. xiv (1825), p. 139.

32  Ibid. p. 81.

33  MacNeill Papers, UCDA LA1/G/395.

34  H.J. Fleure, 'Alfred Cort Haddon 1855–1940', Obituary Notice Fellow of the Royal Society vol. iii, no. 9 (Jan 1941), http://rsbm.royalsocietypublishing.org., pp. 450 and 454.

35  Ashley, 'The Poetics of Race in 1890s Ireland', p. 7.

36  Ibid.

37  For further information on the Belfast Eugenics Society see Greta Jones, 'Eugenics in Ireland: the Belfast Eugenics Society, 1911–15', *IHS* vol. xxviii (1992–3), p. 82.

38  A.C. Haddon and C.R. Browne, 'The Ethnography of the Aran Islands, County Galway', in *PRIA* vol. xxxix (1892), p. 776; C.R. Browne, 'Some New Anthropometrical Instruments', *PRIA* vol. xxiv (1891), p. 397.

39  John Messenger, 'Literary vs Scientific Interpretations of Cultural Reality in the Aran Islands of Eire', in *Ethnohistory*, vol. xi, no. 1 (Winter 1964), p. 45.

40  Hyde, 'The Necessity for de-Anglicising Ireland', p. 159.

41  Eoin MacNeill, *Celtic Ireland* (Dublin 1921, reprinted 1981), p. xi.

42  Quoted in Bruce Nelson, *Irish Nationalists and the Making of the Irish Race* (Princeton, 2012), p. 234.

43  Macalister, 'Some Unsolved Problems in Irish Archaeology', p. 257.

44  MacNeill, *Celtic Ireland*, p. xiii.

45  Eoin MacNeill Papers, UCDA, LA1/D/62, n.d.

46  Ibid. UCDA LA1/D/5.

47  Macalister 'Some Unsolved Problems in Irish Archaeology', p. 254.

48  Christopher Evans, 'Archaeology in modern times: Bersu's Woodbury 1938 & 1939', in *Antiquity* 63 (1989), p. 436.

49  Macalister, 'Some Unsolved Problems in Irish Archaeology', p. 255.

50  Macalister, *Ireland in Pre-Celtic Times*, p. 49.

51  Greta Jones, 'Eugenics in Ireland: the Belfast Eugenics Society, 1911–15', *IHS* vol. xxviii (1992–3), p. 82.

52  Ibid.

53  Macalister, *Ireland in Pre-Celtic Times*, p. 49.

54  Ibid. p. 30.

55  Ibid.

56  Macalister 'Some Unsolved Problems in Irish Archaeology', p. 254.

57  Ibid. p. 37.

58  Ibid. p. 32.

59  Ibid. p. 37.

60  W.W. Howells, 'Carleton Stevens Coon 1904–1981', *Biographical Memoirs of the National Academy of Sciences of the United States of America*, http: www.nasaonline. org., p. 10

61  Ibid. p. 12.

62  Macalister, *Ireland in Pre-Celtic Times*, p. 33.

63  W. Frazer, 'A Contribution to Irish Anthroppology', in *JRSAI* vol. 1, no. 5 (1891), pp. 395–8.

64  Macalister, *Ireland in Pre-Celtic Times*, p. 34.

65  Ibid. p. 40.

66  Ibid.

67  Ibid. p. 32.

68  Liam S. Gogan, speech about Conrad Arensberg's address at the National University Graduates' Dining Club dinner, 22 February 1933, in L.S. Gogan Papers, UCDA LA27/345.

69  Hugh O'Neill Hencken, *Memories of Work and Travel Hugh O'Neill Hencken 1903–1981* (1981), p. 21.

70  See Appendix 3.

71  Stanley M. Garn and Eugene Giles, 'Earnest Albert Hooton, November 20, 1887 – May 3, 1954', Biographical Memoir of the National Academy of Sciences of the United States of America, http:www.nasonline.org. See also 'Inventory of the Papers of Earnest A Hooton', http://www.peabody.harvard.edu/archives/hooton2.html.

72  E.A. Hooton, 'The relation of Physical Anthropology to Cultural Anthropology'.

73  Ibid.

74  Garn and Giles, 'Earnest Albert Hooton', p. 168.

75  Walter Stockley, 'Hooton of Harvard', *Life* Magazine (7 August 1939), p. 63.

76  'The Harvard Study of the Irish Free State', p. 10.

77  Garn and Giles, 'Earnest Albert Hooton', p. 170.

78  Ibid. p. 174.

79  E.A. Hooton, 'The relation of Physical Anthropology to Cultural Anthropology'.

80  Stocking, *American Anthropology 1921–1945*, p. 16. For further information on Warner see Browman and Williams, *Anthropology at Harvard*, pp. 444–5.

81  George W. Stocking, *After Tylor: British Social Anthropology 1888–1951*. (London, 1996) pp. 289 and 291.

82  A.R. Radcliffe-Brown, 'The Present Position of Anthropological Studies', in *Report of the British Association for the Advancement of Science* (1931), pp. 167–8.

83  E.A. Hooton, 'The relation of Physical Anthropology to Cultural Anthropology'.

84  Ibid. p. xxxi.

85  'The Harvard Study of the Irish Free State', p. 10 and 'Hooton-Dupertuis Ireland MSS', E.A. Hooton Papers #995-1, Mansuscripts Box 2, p. 1.

86  'The Harvard Study of the Irish Free State', p. 10.

87  Stephen Lukes, *Emile Durkheim His Life and Work A Historical and Critical Study* (Stanford, 1986).

88  Hooton, 'The Relation of Physical Anthropology to Cultural Anthropology'.

89  Stocking, *American Anthropology 1921–1945*, p. 27.

90  W.H. Holmes, 'Biographical Memoir of Lewis Henry Morgan, 1818–1881, read before the National Academy of Sciences 20 November 1907', in *Biographical Memoirs of the National Academy of Sciences of the United States of America*, http:www.nasonline.org., p. 223.

91  *Irish Times*, 27 February 1935.

92  'Hooton-Dupertuis Ireland MSS', p. 3.

93  Ibid. p. 7.

94  Ibid. pp. 7–8.

95  Ibid. p. 8.

96 Stephen Jay Gould, *The Mismeasure of Man* (London, 1996), p. 85.

97 L. Perry Curtis Jr., *Apes and Angels The Irishman in Victorian Caricature* (Revised edition, Washington and London, 1997); Bruce Nelson, 'Celts, Hottentots and 'white chimpanzees.' the racialization of the Irish in the nineteenth century' in Bruce Nelson, *Irish Nationalists and the Making of the Irish Race* (Princeton, 2012), pp. 30–54.

98 Hencken and Movius, 'The Cemetery-Cairn of Knockast', p. 271. For information on Hrdlička see Adolf H. Schultz, 'Aleš Hrdlička 1869-1943', in *Biographical Memoirs*, National Academy of Sciences, vol. xxiii, pp. 305–338.

99 Hencken and Movius, 'The Cemetery-Cairn of Knockast', p. 260.

100 Ibid. pp. 259–60.

101 S. Shea, 'Description of Human Remains found in the Cist at Annaghkeen', in *JGAHS* vol. xii (1925), pp. 13–25.

102 Hencken and Movius, 'The Cemetery-Cairn of Knockast', p. 283.

103 Ibid.

104 Ibid. p. 243.

105 Ibid. p. 283.

106 Ibid. p. 268.

107 Ibid. p. 275.

108 Rupert Bruce-Mitford, 'Thomas Downing Kendrick, 1895–1979', *PBA* vol. lxxvi, pp. 445–71.

109 CV of Michael V. Duignan, UCDA, LA1/D20.

110 W.W. Howells, 'The Early Christian Irish The Skeletons at Gallen Priory', in *PRIA* vol. xlvi (1940–1941), pp. 103–219.

111 H.G. Leask, 'Archaeological Excavations, 1935. Synopsis of the more Important Results', in NAI D/TAOIS S10940.

112 Jonathan Friedlaender et al, 'William W. Howells 1908-2005' in Biographical Memoirs of the National Academy of Sciences of the United States of America, http:www.nasonline.org., pp. 3–18.

113 Howells, 'The Early Christian Irish: The Skeletons at Gallen Priory', p. 147.

114 Gould, *The Mismeasure of Man*, p. 57.

115 Howells, 'The Early Christian Irish: The Skeletons at Gallen Priory', p. 118.

116 'Hooton-Dupertuis Ireland MSS'.

117 Howells, 'The Early Christian Irish: The Skeletons at Gallen Priory', p. 214.

118 Ibid. pp. 103–219.

119 'Hooton-Dupertuis Ireland MSS', p. 6.

120 Mahr, 'New Aspects and Problems in Irish Prehistory', p. 404.

121 Howells, 'The Early Christian Irish The Skeletons at Gallen Priory', p. 139.

122 Aleš Hrdlička, 'The Principal Dimensions, absolute and relative, of the Humerus in the White Race', *AJPA* vol. xvi (1932), pp. 431–50.

123 B.G.E. Hooke, and G.M. Morant, 'The present State of our Knowledge of British Craniology in late Prehistoric and Historic Times', *Biometrika* vol. xviii (1926), pp. 99–104; G.M. Morant, 'A first Study of the Craniology of England and Scotland from Neolithic to Early Historic Times, with special Reference to the Anglo-Saxon Skulls in London Museums', in *Biometrika* vol. xviii (London, 1926), pp. 56–98;

G.M. Morant, 'The Craniology of Ireland', in *JRAI* vol. lxvi (London, 1936), pp. 43–55.

124 Howells, 'The Early Christian Irish The Skeletons at Gallen Priory', p. 194.

125 Ibid. p. 197.

126 Ibid.

127 Ibid. p. 202.

128 Ibid.

129 Cecil P. Martin, *Prehistoric Man in Ireland* (London, 1935), p. 133.

130 Howells, 'The Early Christian Irish The Skeletons at Gallen Priory', p. 212.

131 Martin, *Prehistoric Man in Ireland*, p. 140.

132 Howells, 'The Early Christian Irish The Skeletons at Gallen Priory', p. 214.

133 Ibid. p. 215.

134 Ibid.

135 E.A. Hooton, 'Stature, Head Form and Pigmentation of Adult Male Irish', *AJPA* vol xxvi (1940), pp. 229–49.

136 Eoin MacNeill Papers, UCDA, LA1/D/2/b, n.d.

137 Sally Green, *Prehistorian A Biography of V. Gordon Childe* (Wiltshire, 1981), p. xix.

138 V. Gordon Childe, *The Aryans: A Study of Indo-European Origins* (New York, 1993), p. xi.

139 Ibid. p. 4.

140 Bruce Trigger, *Revolutions in Archaeology* (London, 1980), p. 17.

141 Childe, *The Aryans: A Study of Indo-European Origins*, p. 5.

142 V. Gordon Childe, 'Retrospect', in *Antiquity* vol. xxxii (1958), pp. 69-74.

143 Childe, *The Aryans: A Study of Indo-European Origins*, p. 212.

144 R.A.S. Macalister *Ancient Ireland, a Study in the Lessons of Archaeology and History* (London, 1935), p. 75.

145 Andrew P. Fitzpatrick, '"Celtic" Iron Age Europe The theoretical basis', in Paul Graves-Brown, Sian Jones, Clive Gamble (eds), *Cultural Identity and Archaeology The Construction of European Communities* (London & New York, 1996), pp. 250–1.

146 Childe, *The Aryans: A Study of Indo-European Origins*, p. 12.

147 Bettina Arnold, '"Arierdammerung": Race and Archaeology in Nazi Germany', in *World Archaeology* vol. xxxviii, no. 1 (2006), p. 12.

148 Trigger, *Revolutions in Archaeology*, p. 17.

149 Childe, *The Aryans: A Study of Indo-European Origins*, p. 159.

150 Ibid. p. 159.

151 Ibid. pp. 160–1.

152 V.Gordon Childe, *The Danube in Prehistory* (Oxford, 1929), preface.

153 Childe, *The Aryans: A Study of Indo-European Origins*, p. 166.

154 Ibid. p. 211.

155 Trigger, *Revolutions in Archaeology*, p. 20.

156 Ibid. p. 18.

157 Ibid. p. 11.

158 Peter Gathercole, 'Gordon Childe: Man or Myth?' in *Antiquity*, vol. lvi (1982), p. 195.

159    Hutchinson, 'Archaeology and the Irish Rediscovery of the Celtic Past', p. 506. For
       an interesting study of archaeology, genetics, geology, linguistics and mythology on
       the origins of the Irish including 'the vexed question of the Celts', see J.P. Mallory,
       *The Origins of the Irish* (London, 2013)
160    Emile Durkheim, *The Elementary Forms of Religious Life* (Oxford University Press,
       2009), p. 334.

## Chapter 4

1    Martin, *Prehistoric Man in Ireland* (1935), pp. 129–30.
 2    'The Harvard Anthropological Survey of Ireland'.
 3    Erin Gibbons, 'The Hunt Controversy' (Centre Simon Wiesenthal, 2006), p. 162, n.
      220.
 4    Ibid. pp. 113–14; See also Francesco Menotti, *Living on the Lake in Prehistoric
      Europe 150 Years of Lake-Dwelling Research* (London & New York, 2004), p. 24.
 5    Francesco Menotti and Aidan O'Sullivan, *The Oxford Handbook of Wetland
      Archaeology* (Oxford, 2012), p. 834.
 6    Christina Fredengren, *Crannógs: A study of People's Relationship with Lakes, with
      Particular Reference to Lough Gara in the North-West of Ireland* (Dublin, 2002), p.
      46.
 7    W.G. Wood-Martin, *The Lake Dwellings of Ireland Or Ancient Lacustrine Habitations
      of Erin, Commonly called Crannógs* (Dublin and London, 1886), p. 3.
 8    Ibid. p. 9.
 9    Bruce Trigger, 'Archaeology and the Idea of Progress', in *Time and Traditions Essays
      in Archaeological Interpretation* (Edinburgh, 1978), p. 54.
10    Ibid. pp. 59–60. The first complete statement of the Idea of Progress was made in an
      essay by A.R.J. Turgot entitled 'A Philosophical Review of the Successive Advances
      of the Human Mind.' (1750). See *Turgot on Progress, Sociology and Economics
      Three Major Texts translated, edited and with an introduction by Ronald M. Meek*
      (Cambridge, 2010).
11    Wood-Martin, *The Lake Dwellings of Ireland*, p. 1.
12    Ibid. p. 35.
13    Ibid. p. 53.
14    Ibid. p. 31.
15    'Dr Adolf Mahr', *Nature* vol. 141 (2 April 1938), pp. 588–9.
16    R. Munro quoted in Wood-Martin, *The Lake Dwellings of Ireland*, p. 16.
17    Wood-Martin, *The Lake Dwellings of Ireland*, p. 18.
18    William Wilde, *PRIA* (1862), vol. vii, pp. 150–1.
19    Marc-Antoine Kaeser, *The Lake-Dwellers Archaeology and Historical Myth* (Zurich),
      p. 14.
20    Ibid. p. 17.
21    *PRIA* (1862), vol. vii, p. 151.
22    Ibid.
23    Macalister, *Archaeology of Ireland*, p. 183.
24    Ibid. p. 183.

25  Ibid. pp. 182–3.

26  Martin, *Prehistoric Man in Ireland*, p. 1.

27  Ibid. pp. 129–30.

28  Ibid. p. 130.

29  Ibid.

30  Ibid.

31  Ibid.

32  Macalister, *Archaeology of Ireland*, p. 132.

33  Ibid. p. 132.

34  Ibid. pp. 133–4.

35  John Waddell, 'The invasion hypothesis in Irish Prehistory', *Antiquity* vol. lii (1978), p. 121.

36  John Carey, *The Irish National Origin-Legend: Synthetic Pseudohistory*. Quiggin Pamphlets on the Sources of Mediaeval Gaelic History i (Cambridge, 1994).

37  Hugh O'Neill Hencken, with sections by Liam Price and Laura E. Start, 'Lagore Crannóg: an Irish Royal Residence of the 7th to 10th Centuries AD', *PRIA* vol. liii (1950–1951)', p. 17.

38  Adolf Mahr, 'Cloonfinlough, Co. Roscommon', report dated 13 August 1934, NAI D/TAOIS S10940.

39  See Chapter 7, 'A New Deal for Irish Archaeology' for further information on this topic.

40  Adolf Mahr, 'Cloonfinlough, Co. Roscommon', report dated 13 August 1934, NAI D/TAOIS S10940.

41  Ibid.

42  Joseph Raftery, 'Knocknalappa, Co. Clare', *NMAJ* vol. i (1936-9), p. 83.

43  *One Hundred and Sixth Annual Report Commissioners of Public Works* (31 March 1938), p. 49.

44  George Coffey, 'Archaeological Evidence for the Intercourse of Gaul with Ireland before the first Century', in *PRIA* vol. xxviii (1910), p. 103.

45  E.C.R. Armstrong, 'The La Tène Period in Ireland', in *JRSAI* vol. liii (1923), p. 10.

46  Adolf Mahr, 'The Origin of the Crannóg Type of Settlement', in *Proceedings of the First International Congress of Prehistoric and Protohistoric Sciences* (London, 1–6 August 1932), pp. 1–2.

47  Ibid.

48  Mahr, 'New aspects and problems in Irish prehistory', p. 280.

49  Hugh O'Neill Hencken, 'Ballinderry Crannóg No. 2' in *PRIA* vol. xlvii (1942), p. 2.

50  Ibid. p. 2.

51  C.S. Coon, *Races of Europe* (New York, 1939), p. 186.

52  Ibid. p. 378.

53  Hencken, 'Lagore Crannóg', p. 17.

54  Malcolm Chapman, *The Celts: The Construction of a Myth* (London, 1992), p. 81.

55  Hooton and Dupertuis, *The Physical Anthropology of Ireland*.

56  Ibid. p. 121.

57  Ibid. p. 201.

58  'The Harvard Anthropological Survey of Ireland'.

59    Aidan O'Sullivan, *The Archaeology of Lake Settlement in Ireland* Discovery Programme, Monograph 4 (1998), p. 7.

60    'On Two Visits to Ireland by H. O'Neill Hencken.'

61    Armstrong, 'The La Tène Period in Ireland', p 8

62    *Irish Times,* 26 August 1933.

63    H. O'Neill Hencken, 'Ballinderry Crannóg no. 1', *PRIA* xliii (1935–37), p. 105.

64    *Irish Times,* 26 June 1928.

65    Ibid.

66    Ibid.

67    Adolf Mahr to Dr Alexander Scott, letter dated 26 Feb 1929, NMI Topographical file 1928:382.

68    Hencken quoted in article 'American Scientists Striking finds' in *Irish Independent,* 29 September 1932.

69    Hencken, 'Ballinderry Crannóg no. 1', p. 191, p. 185 and p. 200.

70    Ibid. p. 226.

71    Ruth Johnston, 'Ballinderry Crannóg No. 1: a reinterpretation', *PRIA* vol. xcix (1999), pp. 24 and 65.

72    Hencken, 'Lagore Crannóg', p. 12.

73    Eoin MacNeill, *Phases of Irish History* (New York and London, 1919, reissued 1970), p. 265.

74    V. Gordon Childe, *Social Evolution* (London, 1951), p. 40.

75    Hencken, 'Ballinderry Crannóg No. 2', pp. 1–76.

76    'First Quarterly Report of H. O'Neill Hencken, Research Fellow of the American Council of Learned Societies, 1 June – 1 September [1933]' in Hooton Papers, #995-1, Box 21.9, p. 3.

77    Ibid.

78    Armstrong, 'The La Tène Period in Ireland', p. 8.

79    Hencken, 'Harvard and Irish Archaeology', p. 8.

80    Mahr, 'New aspects and problems in Irish prehistory', pp. 404–5.

81    'Report [b] of the Second Harvard Archaeological Expedition to Ireland, 1933', p. 3.

82    Ibid. p. 4.

83    Hencken, 'Ballinderry Crannóg No. 2', p. 7.

84    'Hooton-Dupertuis Ireland MSS'.

85    Browman and Williams, *Anthropology at Harvard,* p. 305.

86    Ibid.

87    Bricker, 'Hallam Leonard Movius Jr., 1907–1987', p. 9.

88    HUD 3139, 'American Defense Harvard Group', Records of American Defense Harvard Group: an Inventory. http://oasis.lib.harvard.edu, accessed 27 April 2017.

89    Price, *Anthropological Intelligence,* p. 30.

90    Browman and Williams, *Anthropology at Harvard,* p. 304.

91    Ibid. pp. 342–3.

92    Mervyn O'Driscoll, *Ireland, Germany and the Nazis, Politics and diplomacy, 1919–1939* (Dublin, 2017), p. 251.

93    *Irish Times,* 26 August 1933.

94    Ibid.

95   *Irish Times*, 24 August 1933.

96   *Scroll Phi Delta Theta* vol. lvi (October 1931), no. 1, p. 19.

97   *Irish Times*, 24 August 1933.

98   Ibid.

99   *Irish Times*, 21 June 1934,

100   Eoin MacNeill Papers, UCDA, LA1/D/16.

101   *Irish Times*, 1 September 1933.

102   Anon., 'Obituary Notices' [Professor Kingsley Porter], in *JRSAI* vol. lxvi (1936), p. 60.

103   *Irish* Times, 1 September 1933.

104   Ibid.

105   Adolf Mahr to K. O'Connell, letter dated 13 Feb 1935, NAI D/TAOIS 97/9/95.

106   *Irish Times*, 13 September 1935.

107   Ibid.

108   Ibid.

109   *Irish Times*, 13 September 1935. Modern claims to an American-Celtic identity such as the Wise Use activists in New Mexico in the 1990s defined Celt as 'everything that modern Western industrial capitalist society is not.' See James McCarthy and Euan Hague, 'Race, Nation and Nature: The Cultural Politics of 'Celtic' Identification in the American West', in *Annals of the Association of American Geographers*, vol. lxxxxiv, no. 2 (June, 2004), p. 391.

110   *Irish Times*, 13 September 1935.

111   Leone, 'Symbolic, Structural and Critical Archaeology', in David J. Meltzer, Don D. Fowler and Jeremy Sabloff (eds), *American Archaeology Past and Future: A Celebration of the Society of American Archaeology 1935–1985* (Smithsonian Institution Press, 1986), p. 432.

112   Trigger, *A History of Archaeological Thought*, p. 211.

113   Byrne, Edmondson and Varley, 'Arensberg and Kimball and anthropological research in Ireland.'

114   Ibid. pp. 21 and 23.

115   Hooton and Dupertuis, *The physical anthropology of Ireland*, p. 198.

## Chapter 5

1   Hencken, 'Lagore Crannóg, p. 16.

2   'Report of the Excavations of the Third Harvard Archaeological Expedition in Ireland'.

3   H.G. Leask, memo on 'Applicability of term 'archaeological', to Mr. MacLaughlin, Special Works Division, OPW, 9 September 1938, NMI Topographical file E29:1-260.

4   Ibid.

5   Hencken, 'Lagore Crannóg', pp. 1–247.

6   Don D. Fowler, 'Uses of the past: archaeology in the service of the state', *American Antiquity*, vol. 52, no. 2 (Apr. 1987), p. 230.

7   Hugh O'Neill Hencken to Éamon de Valera, letter dated 19 October 1934, NAI D/TAOIS 97/9/95.

8    R. Butler to Dean H.R. Dawson, 2 Oct 1839, in G.F. Mitchell, 'Voices from the Past; Three Antiquarian Letters', *JRSAI* vol. cxiii (1983), p. 47.

9    W. R. Wilde, 'On the Animal Remains and Antiquities recently found at Dunshaughlin', *PRIA* vol. i (1840), pp 420–6

10   W. F. Wakeman, 'On certain recent Discoveries of Ancient Crannóg Structures, chiefly in the County of Fermanagh', in *JRSAI* (1879–82), p. 325.

11   Ibid.

12   Ibid.

13   Mahr, 'Archaeology', in *Saorstát Éireann Irish Free State Official Handbook* (Dublin, 1932). p. 214.

14   'Fourth Harvard Archaeological Expedition in Ireland. 1935 Final Report', E.A. Hooton Papers #995-1, Box 21.9, p. 2.

15   Hencken, 'Lagore Crannóg', p. 16.

16   Ibid.

17   Ibid. p. 184.

18   Ibid. p. 78.

19   O'Sullivan, *The Archaeology of Lake Settlement in Ireland*, p. 139.

20   Ibid. p. 25.

21   'Report of the Fifth Archaeological Expedition in Ireland, 1936', in E.A. Hooton Papers #995-1, Box 21.9, pp. 2–6.

22   For a discussion of burial in the early medieval period in Ireland see Elizabeth O'Brien, 'Pagan or Christian? Burial in Ireland during the 5th to 8th Centuries AD', in Nancy Edwards (ed.), *The Archaeology of the Early Medieval Celtic Churches* (2006), p. 4.

23   Hencken, 'Lagore Crannóg', p. 203.

24   Ibid.

25   Ibid. p. 203; Hencken, 'Ballinderry Crannóg No. 1', p. 227; Hugh O'Neill Hencken, 'Cahercommaun: A Stone Fort in County Clare', in *JRSAI* extra vol. (1938), p. 23; Hencken, Ballinderry Crannóg No. 2', p. 17.

26   'Report of the Excavations of the Third Harvard Archaeological Expedition in Ireland', p. 7.

27   Hencken, 'Ballinderry Crannóg No. 2', p. 17; See also Seán Ó Súilleabháin, 'Foundation Sacrifices', in *JRSAI* vol. lxxv, no. 1 (1945), pp. 45–52.

28   'Report of the Excavations of the Third Harvard Archaeological Expedition in Ireland', p. 4. It is referred to as a 'foundation deposit' in the published report: Hencken, 'Cahercommaun, A Stone Fort in County Clare', p. 2.

29   Hencken, 'Cahercommaun: A Stone Fort in County Clare', p. 23.

30   Claire Cotter, 'Cahercommaun Fort, Co. Clare A reassessment of its cultural context', *Discovery Programme Reports* vol. v (RIA, 1999), p. 69.

31   Hencken, 'Cahercommaun: A Stone Fort in County Clare', p. 23.

32   Ibid. p. 67.

33   A growing body of archaeological data means that traditional concepts about Christian conversion have been gradually changing. See Aidan O'Sullivan, Finbar McCormick, Thomas R. Kerr and Lorcan Harney, *Early Medieval Ireland AD400–1100, The evidence from Archaeological Excavations* (Dublin, 2013), pp. 42, 43 and 285.

34  'Report of the Excavations of the Third Harvard Archaeological Expedition in Ireland [b]', p. 14.

35  Hencken, 'Cahercommaun: A Stone Fort in County Clare', p. 55.

36  Ibid. p. 2.

37  'Report of the Excavations of the Third Harvard Archaeological Expedition in Ireland [b]', p. 14.

38  'Fourth Harvard Archaeological Expedition in Ireland. 1935 Final Report', p. 2.

39  Hencken, 'Lagore Crannóg', p. 3.

40  Ibid. p. 34.

41  Ibid. p. 234.

42  Ibid. p. 6.

43  'Fourth Harvard Archaeological Expedition in Ireland 1935 Final Report', pp. 3–4.

44  C.J. Lynn, 'Lagore, County Meath and Ballinderry No. 1, County Westmeath Crannógs: Some Possible Structural Reinterpretations', in *JIA* vol. iii (1985–1986), p. 69.

45  Gould, *The Mismeasure of Man*, p. 98.

46  'Lagore Crannóg', from 'Report of the Excavations of the Third Harvard Archaeological Expedition in Ireland', p. 3. In the nineteenth century, Talbot, because of the level of bone recovered at Lagore, interpreted the site as a tomb. See J. Talbot, 'Memoir on some Ancient Arms and Implements found at Lagore, near Dunshaughlin, County of Meath: with a view on the Classification of Northern Antiquities', *AJ* vol. vi (1849), pp. 101–9.

47  Hencken, 'Lagore Crannóg', p. 229.

48  *106th Annual Report Commissioners of Public Works* (31 March 1938), p. 49.

49  Hencken, 'Lagore Crannóg', p. 54.

50  O'Sullivan et al, *Early Medieval Ireland AD400–1100*, p. 61.

51  Conor Newman, 'Ballinderry Crannóg no. 2, Co. Offaly: Pre-Crannóg Early Medieval Horizon', in *JIA* vol xi (2002), p. 114.

52  Ruth Johnston, 'Ballinderry Crannóg No. 1: a reinterpretation', *PRIA* vol. 99C (1999), p. 68.

53  R.B. Warner, 'On Crannógs and Kings (Part 1)', in *JIA* vol. lvii (1994), p. 65.

54  Ibid. p. 66.

55  Hencken, 'Lagore Crannóg', p. 7, n. 1.

56  Hencken, 'Ballinderry Crannóg No. 2', p. 76.

57  For example blue segmented beads found at Lagore could be found in Northern Europe in all periods from the Roman Iron Age to the Viking Period.

58  'Relief Schemes Archaeological Excavations 1934 Short Report on Progress and Results, 27 October 1934', in NAI OPW 19734/34.

59  Hencken, 'Lagore Crannóg', p. 168.

60  Bryony Coles, 'Anthropomorphic Wooden Figures from Britain and Ireland', *PPS* vol. lvi (1990), p. 327.

61  'Report of the Excavations of the Third Harvard Archaeological Expedition in Ireland'.

62  Hencken, 'Lagore Crannóg', p. 17.

63  Hencken, 'Cahercommaun: A Stone Fort in County Clare', p. 15.

64   Joseph Raftery, 'Concerning Chronology', in Donnchadh Ó Corráin (ed.) *Irish Antiquity Essays and Studies Presented to Professor M.J. O'Kelly* (Cork, 1981), p. 83.

65   Ibid, p. 84

66   R.B. Warner, 'The Date of the Start of Lagore', in *JIA* vol. iii (1985–6), p. 77.

67   Ibid. p. 75. Other archaeologists who agree with the Hencken dating include B.G. Scott, 'Iron "Slave-Collars", from Lagore Crannóg, Co. Meath', *PRIA* vol. lxxvii (1978), p. 228 and C.J. Lynn, 'Some 'early' Ring-forts and Crannógs', *JIA* vol. i (1983), pp. 52–3.

68   Warner, 'The Date of the Start of Lagore', p. 75. T. Fanning, 'Some aspects of the Bronze Ringed Pin in Scotland' in A. O' Connor and D. Clarke (eds), *From the Stone Age to the 'Forty Five'* (Edinburgh, 1983), p. 325 and p. 330; Barry Raftery, 'Irish Hill-forts', in C. Thomas (ed.) *The Iron Age in the Irish Sea Province* (London, 1972), p. 53. Joseph Raftery, 'Concerning chronology', p. 83. Seamus Caulfield has also demonstrated the central and possibly unsound, role of the Lagore excavation and the documentary references to the site in the dating of this group of Harvard excavations and of subsequent Early Christian excavations in general: Seamus Caulfield, 'Some Celtic Problems in the Irish Iron Age', in D. Ó Corráin (ed.) *Irish Antiquity* (1981). C.J. Lynn, 'Lagore, County Meath and Ballinderry No. 1, County Westmeath Crannógs: Some Possible Structural Reinterpretations', in *JIA* vol. iii (1985–1986), p. 69.

69   F.J. Byrne, 'Historical note on Cnogba (Knowth)', in *PRIA* vol. lxvi (1968), p. 397

70   Barry Raftery, 'Irish Hill-forts', p. 53.

71   Caulfield, 'Some Celtic Problems in the Irish Iron Age', p. 210.

72   William H. Forsyth, 'An Irish Royal Residence of the Seventh to Tenth Centuries A.D. by Hugh Hencken', in *American Journal of Archaeology* vol. lvii, no. 2 (April 953), p. 156.

73   W.G. Wood-Martin, *Pagan Ireland* (1895), pp. vi, 61, 64, 395, 418, 585.

74   F.J. Byrne, 'Ireland before the Norman Invasion', in T.W. Moody (ed), *Irish Historiography 1936–70* (1971), p. 2.

75   Joseph Raftery, 'Concerning Chronology', p. 89.

76   Fowler, 'Uses of the Past', p. 241.

77   Joseph Raftery, 'Concerning Chronology', p. 89.

78   Ibid. p. 84.

79   R.A.S. Macalister, *The Archaeology of Ireland* (London 1928), pp. 19–20. Hooton, Dupertuis and Dawson, *The Physical Anthropology of Ireland*, p. 216.

80   'Dr. Lithberg's Report', p. 17.

81   'Report of the Fifth Archaeological Expedition in Ireland, 1936', pp. 2–6.

82   R.B. Warner, 'Some Observations on the Context and Importation of Exotic Material in Ireland, from the First Century B.C. to the Second Century A.D.', in *PRIA* vol. lxxvi (1976), pp. 285–6.

83   R.B. Warner, 'The Date of the Start of Lagore', p. 76.

84   Hencken, 'Lagore Crannóg', p. 124.

85   'Report [b] of the Second Harvard Archaeological Expedition to Ireland, 1933', p. 8.

86   Ibid. p. 6.

87  Ibid. p. 16.

88  Ibid.

89  Ibid. p. 17.

90  Seán P. Ó Ríordáin, 'The excavation of a large earthen ring-fort at Garranes, Co. Cork', *PRIA* vol. xlvii, pp. 77–150; Seán P. Ó Ríordáin and P. J. Hartnett, 'The Excavation of Ballycatteen Fort, Co. Cork', *PRIA* vol. xlix (1943–1944), pp. 1–43. vol. xlix.

91  Hencken, 'Ballinderry Crannóg No. 2', p. 49.

92  S.P. Ó Ríordáin, 'Roman Material in Ireland', in *PRIA* vol. li (1945–8), p. 73.

93  Ibid.

94  Ibid. p. 76.

95  A.E.P. Collins, Excavations in Lough Faughan Crannóg, County Down', in *UJA* vol. xviii (1955), p. 59 and 'Further Investigations in the Dundrum Sandhills', in *UJA* vol. xxii (1959), p. 12; G.D. Liversage, 'Excavations at Dalkey Island, County Dublin, 1956–1959', in *PRIA* vol. lxvi (1967–1968), p. 167.

96  J.D. Bateson, 'Roman Material from Ireland: a Re-consideration', in *PRIA* vol. lxxiii (1973), p. 27.

97  Ibid. p. 30.

98  Ibid. p. 36.

99  Elizabeth O'Brien, 'Pagan or Christian?' p. 3, 'Iron Age Burial Practices in Leinster: Continuity and Change', in *Emania* vol. vi (Spring 1989), p. 39 and 'Pagan and Christian Burial in Ireland during the First Millennium AD: Continuity and Change', in N. Edwards and A. Lane (eds), *The Early Church in Wales and the West* (Oxford, 1992), p. 132; Bateson, 'Roman Material from Ireland', p. 30. Bourke interprets the Roman burial at Stoneyford as 'Roman merchants living with their Irish hosts' and notes that 'there was a market for Roman goods among the Irish aristocracy'. See Edward Bourke, 'Stoneyford: a First-Century Roman Burial from Ireland', in *Archaeology Ireland* vol. iii, no. 2 (Summer, 1989), p. 57.

100  Richard Warner, 'De Bello Hibernico A less than Edifying Debate', in *Archaeology Ireland* vol. x no. 3 (Autumn, 1996): Barry Raftery, 'Drumanagh and Roman Ireland', in *Archaeology Ireland* vol. x, no. 1 (1996); Richard Warner, 'Tuathal Techtmar: Myth or Ancient Literary Evidence for a Roman Invasion', in *Emania*, vol. xiii (1995), pp. 23–32; John Maas, 'Letter to the Romans John Maas Replies', in *Archaeology Ireland* vol. x, no. 2 (Summer, 1996), p. 38; Gabriel Cooney, Editorial, *Archaeology Ireland*, vol. x, no. 35 (Spring, 1996), p. 3; Richard Warner, 'Yes, the Romans did invade Ireland', in *British Archaeology* no. 14 (1996), www.britarch. ac.uk; Michael Herity, 'Roman invaders were more likely native Irish traders', *Irish Times*, 24 January 1996.

101  Shawn Pogatchnik, 'Experts claim Romans may have established Colonies in Ireland', in *Los Angeles Times,* 17 November 1996.

102  John Waddell, review article, 'Vittorio De Martino, Roman Ireland', in *JGAHS* vol. lvi (2004).

103  Richard Warner, 'Celtic Ireland and other Fables: Politics and Prehistory', based on a talk given to the Annual Conference of the Irish Association, Carrickfergus, 12–14 November, 1999; www.irish-association.org.

104   Waddell, 'Vittorio De Martino, Roman Ireland'.

105   Alexandra Guglielmi, 'My kingdom for a pot! A reassessment of the Iron Age and Roman material from Lagore crannóg, Co. Meath', in Graeme JR Erskine, Piotr Jacobsson, Paul Miller and Scott Stetkiewicz, *Proceedings of the 17th Iron Age Research Student Symposium* (Edinburgh 2014), pp. 12–19.

106   Jacqueline Cahill Wilson, *Late Iron Age and Roman Ireland* (Discovery Programme, 2014).

107   J.P. Mallory, *The Origins of the Irish* (London, 2013), p. 190.

108   Paddy Boyle, 'Drumanagh – An exciting prospect', *Archaeology Ireland* vol. xxxi, no. 2, issue no. 120 (Summer 2017), p. 14.

109   Trigger, *A History of Archaeological Thought*, pp. 250–4 and 268–70.

110   Hencken, 'Lagore Crannóg', p. 12.

111   William Duncan Strong, 'Lagore Crannóg: An Irish Royal Residence of the 7th to 10th Centuries A.D. by Hugh Hencken', Review Article, in *American Anthropologist*, vol. lv, issue 5 (December, 1953), pp. 732–3.

112   Ibid. p. 733.

113   Fredengren, *Crannógs: a Study of People's Interaction with Lakes'*, p. 50.

114   Robert Van der Noort and Aidan O'Sullivan, *Rethinking Wetland Archaeology* (London 2006), p. 10.

115   Leask, 'Applicability of term 'archaeological'.

116   Peter Gibbon and Chris Curtin, 'The stem family in Ireland', *ComparativeStudies in Society and History* vol. xxx, no. 3 (1978), p. 446.

117   NAI D/TAOIS 97/9/95.

118   Éamon de Valera, 'Open letter to President Wilson, 27 October 1920', in Moynihan, *Speeches and Statements by Éamon de Valera 1917–73*, p. 38.

119   Fredengren, *Crannógs: a study of People's Interaction with Lakes*, p. 50.

120   Simon James, *The Atlantic Celts Ancient People or Modern Invention?* (University of Wisconsin Press, 1999), p. 87.

121   Lynn, 'Lagore, County Meath and Ballinderry No. 1, County Westmeath Crannógs', p. 73.

## Chapter 6

1   Letter from Adolf Mahr to Albert Bender in 1932, in Gerry Mullins, 'Letters from our No. One Nazi', *Irish Times* 19 September 2000. See also Mullins, *Dublin Nazi No. 1*, p. 35.

2   'The Harvard Study of the Irish Free State', p. 9.

3   Adam Stout, *Creating Prehistory Druids, Ley Hunters and Archaeologists in Pre-War Britain* (Oxford, 2008), p. 1.

4   Shennan quoted in Paul Graves-Brown, Sian Jones & Clive Gamble, *Cultural Identity and Archaeology: The Construction of European Communities* (London and New York, 1996), p. 41.

5   S. Jones, *The Archaeology of Ethnicity: Constructing Identities in the Past and Present* (London & New York, 1997), p. 104.

6  Mullins, *Dublin Nazi No. 1*, p. 42 and Fisk, *In Time of War*, p. 71.

7  Hugh O'Neill Hencken, 'Report of the Second Harvard Archaeological Expedition to Ireland, 1933.'

8  Mahr, 'New Aspects and Problems in Irish Prehistory', p. 267.

9  Ibid.

10  Glyn Daniel, *The Idea of Prehistory in the Study of Language and Race, and in Politics* (London, 1962), p. 102.

11  D.A. Binchy, 'Secular Institutions', in M. Dillon (ed.), *Early Irish Society* (Dublin 1954), p. 52.

12  Trigger, *A History of Archaeological Thought*, p. 164.

13  Daniel, *The Idea of Prehistory*, p. 115.

14  Ibid. p. 115.

15  Ian Morris, *Archaeology as Cultural History: Words and Things in Iron Age Greece* (Oxford, 2000).

16  Trigger, *A History of Archaeological Thought*, p. 163.

17  Liam S. Gogan, speech about Conrad Arensberg's address at the National University Graduates' Dining Club dinner, 22 Febraury 1933, Liam S. Gogan Papers, UCDA, LA27/345.

18  Trigger, *A History of Archaeological Thought*, p. 167.

19  Daniel, *The Idea of Prehistory*, p. 118.

20  Colin Renfrew, *Archaeology and Language: The Puzzle of Indo-European Origins* (London 1987), pp. 3–4.

21  Simon James, *The Atlantic Celts Ancient People or Modern Invention?* (University of Wisconsin Press, 1999), p. 61.

22  Trigger, *Revolutions in Archaeology*, p. 22.

23  Childe, *The Aryan:s A Study of Indo-European Origins*, p. xii.

24  MacNeill Papers, UCDA LA1/D/5.

25  S.P. Ó Ríordáin, 'Palaeolithic Man in Ireland', *Antiquity* vol. v (1931), p. 360.

26  Adolf Mahr, 'Relief Schemes, Archaeological Excavations 1934, Short Report on Progress and Results, 8 September 1934' and 'Relief Schemes, Archaeological Excavations 1934, Short Report on Progress and Results, 27 October 1934', in NAI OPW 19734/34.

27  Bricker, 'Hallam Leonard Movius Jr., November 28, 1907 – May 30, 1987', p. 243.

28  Ibid. pp. 244–5.

29  H.L. Movius to Hugh O'Neill Hencken, letter dated 2 June 1937, H.L. Movius Papers #998-27, 127.3.

30  Rev. Patrick Power, *Prehistoric Ireland: A Manual of Irish Pre-Christian Archaeology* (Dublin, 1925), p. 12.

31  Ibid. p. 15.

32  Ibid. p. 16.

33  J.P. T. Burchell and J. Reid Moir, *The Early Mousterian Implements of Sligo, Ireland* (Suffolk, 1928), p. 9.

34  Ibid. p. 19.

35  Peter C. Woodman, 'Rosses Point revisited', *Antiquity* vol. lxxii (1998), p. 562.

36  Contributions had been published in the following journals: *Nature, Man, The Catholic Bulletin, Irish Naturalists' Journal* and *Scientific American*. See J.K. Charlesworth and R.A.S. Macalister, 'The Alleged Palaeolithic Implements of Sligo', in *PRIA* vol. xxxix (1929–1931), pp. 18–19; Peter C. Woodman, 'Rosses Point revisited', *Antiquity* vol. lxxii (1998), pp. 562–70; Burchell and Reid Moir, *The Early Mousterian Implements of Sligo* (1928); See also memoirs, correspondence and newspaper reports about the Palaeolithic controversy in RIA file no. SR 23/0/50.

37  Editor's note, 'The Sligo Archaeological Discovery', in *The Catholic Bulletin* (1928), p. 369.

38  J.Reid Moir and J.P. T. Burchell, document dated 14 May 1928, RIA file no. SR 23/0/50.

39  Woodman, 'Rosses Point revisited', p. 568.

40  Hooton, 'The relation of Physical Anthropology to Cultural Anthropology'.

41  Ibid.

42  J. Reid Moir, 'Palaeolithic Man, Traces in Ireland, Discoveries at Rosses Point', *Irish Times*, 5 March 1929.

43  'Tracing the First Irishman, Remains of the First Highbrow', in *Irish Times*, 19 February 1929.

44  *Irish Times*, 19 February 1929.

45  Charlesworth and Macalister, 'The Alleged Palaeolithic Implements of Sligo', p. 30, n. 7.

46  J. Kaye Charlesworth, A.W. Stelfox, R.A.S. Macalister and R.Lloyd Praeger, Letters to the Editor, *Nature*, 18 May 1929; from RIA file no. SR 23/0/50.

47  Adolf Mahr, 'Kilgreany Caves, Country Waterford', Report dated 13 August 1934, NAI D/TAOIS S10940.

48  Ibid.

49  Anon., 'Palaeolithic man in Ireland, Important Discoveries', *Irish Times*, 23 April 1929.

50  Ibid.

51  Anon., 'Irish Excavations', *Irish Times*, 23 April 1929.

52  Anon., 'Palaeolithic man in Ireland, Important Discoveries', *Irish Times*, 23 April 1929.

53  Ibid.

54  E.K. Tratman, 'Excavations at Kilgreany Cave, County Waterford', in *PUBSS* vol. iii (1928), pp. 109–53.

55  Adolf Mahr, 'Kilgreany Caves, Country Waterford', Report dated 13 August 1934, NAI D/TAOIS S10940.

56  Ó Ríordáin, 'Palaeolithic Man in Ireland', p. 360.

57  Hallam L. Movius Jr., Report dated 24 September 1934, NAI D/TAOIS S10940.

58  Ibid.

59  R.J.G.S., 'E.K. Tratman, O.B.E., D.Sc., M.D., F.D.S.R.C.S., F.S.A.', in *PUBSS* vol. xv, pp. 3–5, www.ubss.org.uk

60  A.M. ApSimon, '1919–1969: Fifty Years of Archaeological Research The Spelaeological Society's Contribution to Archaeology', Jubilee Contribution University of Bristol Spelaeological Society, in *PUBSS* (1969), vol. xii, no. 1 (1969), p. 52.

61  Hugo Flinn to Éamon de Valera, letter dated 5 October 1934, NAI D/TAOIS S10940.

62  Ó Ríordáin, 'Palaeolithic Man in Ireland', p. 361.

63  Ibid, p. 362.

64  Ibid. p. 362.

65  Hallam L. Movius, 'Kilgreany excavations', Report dated 6 October 1934, NAI D/TAOIS S10940.

66  Hallam L. Movius, Jr., 'Kilgreany Cave, County Waterford', in *JRSAI* vol. v (1935), pp. 254–96.

67  Movius, 'Kilgreany Cave, County Waterford', p. 282: S.P. Ó Ríordáin and C.P. Martin, 'A Prehistoric Burial at Ringabella, Co. Cork', in *JRSAI* vol lxiv (1934), p. 86; S. Shea, 'Report on the Human Skeleton found in Stoneyisland Bog, Portumna', in *JGAHS* vol. xv (1931), p. 73.

68  Sir Arthur Keith, *New Discoveries Relating to the Antiquity of Man* (New York), p. 429.

69  Movius, 'Kilgreany Cave, County Waterford', p. 254.

70  'Kilgreany Cave Excavations, The Skeleton Found in 1928', *Irish Times*, 11 December 1935.

71  Ibid.

72  A.L. Brindley and J.N. Lanting, 'Radiocarbon dates for Neolithic single burials', *Journal of Irish Archaeology* vol.v (1989–1990), p. 2.

73  J.D.G. Clark, 'Upper Palaeolithic Man in Ireland?' in *PPS* vol. ii, parts 1 and 2 (1936), p. 242.

74  J.D.G. Clark, 'A Premium on Antiquity' in *PPS* vol. ii, parts 1 and 2 (1936), p. 242.

75  Ibid.

76  Ibid. p. 243.

77  Ibid.

78  Grahame Clark, Prehistory at Cambridge and Beyond (Cambridge, 1989), p. 35.

79  *106th Annual Report Commissioners of Public Works* (31 March 1938), p. 47.

80  Adolf Mahr, 'Relief Schemes, Archaeological Excavations 1934, Short Report on Progress and Results, 27 October 1934', NAI OPW 19734/34.

81  Adolf Mahr, 'Cave near the town of Killawillin', Report dated 13 August 1934, NAI D/TAOIS S10940.

82  Marion Dowd, 'Kilgreany Co. Waterford: Biography of a Cave', *JIA* vol. xi (2002), p. 91.

83  E. Estyn Evans, *The Personality of Ireland Habitat, Heritage and History* (Dublin, 1992), pp. 30–1.

84  Ibid. p. 32.

85  E. Estyn Evans, 'The Cultural Landscape of Celtic Countries a Review', in *The Scottish Geographical Journal* vol. lxxiv, no. 3 (December, 1958), p. 190.

86  E. E. Evans, 'Archaeology in Ulster since 1920', in *UJA* vol. xxxi (1968), p. 3.

87  Ibid. p. 6.

88  E. Estyn Evans, 'Archaeological Investigations in Northern Ireland A Summary of Recent Work', in *AJ* vol. xv (1935), p. 166.

89    Oliver Davies and Estyn Evans, 'Excavations at Goward, near Hilltown, Co. Down',
      *PBNHPS* (1932–1933), pp. 1–16.
90    Evans, 'Archaeological Investigations in Northern Ireland', p. 166.
91    Hallam L Movius, Jr., Knud Jessen, V, Gordon Childe and C. Blake Whelan, 'A
      Neolithic Site on the River Bann', *PRIA* vol. xliii (1935–1937), pp. 29–30.
92    A Municipal Museum was built on a site in Stranmillis in 1929. This became the
      Ulster Museum, under the Museum Act enacted in 1961.
93    Adolf Mahr, 'Megalithic Monument at Aghnaskeagh, County Louth', Report
      dated 10 August 1934, NAI D/TAOIS S10940; E. Estyn Evans, 'Excavations at
      Aghnaskeagh, Co. Louth', Cairn A', *JCLAS* vol. viii, no. 3 (1935), pp. 234–55 and
      'Excavations at Aghnaskeagh, Co. Louth, Cairn B', *JCLAS* vol. ix (1937), pp. 1-18.
94    J. Wilfrid Jackson, 'Preliminary Report on Excavations at the Caves of Ballintoy,
      Co. Antrim', *INJ* vol. iv, no. 12 (1933), pp. 230–5 and 'Excavations at Ballintoy
      Caves, Co. Antrim, third report', *INJ* vol. vi, no. 2 (1936), pp. 31–42.
95    Matthew Stout', Emyr Estyn Evans and Northern Ireland: the archaeology and
      geography of a new state', in John A. Atkinson, Iain Banks & Jerry O'Sullivan,
      *Nationalism and Archaeology Scottish Archaeological Forum* (Glasgow, 1996), pp.
      11 and 18.
96    Evans, 'Archaeology in Ulster since 1920'.
97    Ibid. p. 5.
98    Matthew Stout, 'Emyr Estyn Evans and Northern Ireland', pp. 15 and 19–21.
99    E.E. Evans, *Irish Heritage: the Landscape, the People and Their Work* (Dundalk,
      1942), p. 31.
100   Matthew Stout, 'Emyr Estyn Evans and Northern Ireland', p. 19.
101   R. de Valera, 'The Court Cairns of Ireland', *PRIA* vol. lx, section C (1960), pp. 40–8.
102   E.E. Evans and O. Davies, 'Irish Court Cairns', *UJA* vol. xxiv–xxv (1962), p. 5.
103   Evans, *The Personality of Ireland*, p. 112.
104   Ibid. p. 20.
105   Ibid. p. 20
106   Ibid.
107   Ibid. p. 3.
108   Ibid. p. 9.
109   Ibid. p. 4.
110   Macalister, *Ireland in Pre-Celtic Times*, pp. 15–16.
111   Ibid.
112   Movius, *The Irish Stone Age*, p. 257.
113   Ibid. p. xxi.
114   Evans, 'Archaeology in Ulster since 1920', p. 3.
115   Peter Wilson, 'The Father of Ulster Antiquaries', in *Archaeology Ireland*, vol. xiv, no.
      1, issue no. 51 (Spring 2000), p. 20.
116   It was only after 1895 that the term 'Mesolithic' was recognised. This was when
      Piette first published the results of his excavations at the famous site of Mas d'Azil
      in the French Pyrenees.
117   Peter Woodman, *The Mesolithic in Ireland Hunter-Gatherers in an Insular
      Environment* (Oxford, 1978), p. 2.

118  Waddell, *Foundation Myths*, pp. 147 and 149.

119  Hallam L. Movius, Jr., 'Archaeological Research in Northern Ireland: An Historical account of the Investigations at Larne', in *UJA* vol. xvi (1953), p. 12.

120  Nina F. Layard, 'The Older Series of Irish Flint Implements', *Man* vol. ix (1909), pp. 81–5.

121  Ibid. p. 81.

122  Macalister, *Ireland in Pre-Celtic Times*, p. 374.

123  Movius, 'Archaeological Research in Northern Ireland,' p. 15: G. Coffey and R. Ll. Praeger, 'The Antrim Raised Beach: A Contribution to the Neolithic History of the North of Ireland', in *PRIA* 25C (1904), pp. 139–40.

124  Movius, 'Archaeological Research in Northern Ireland', p. 20.

125  Ibid. p. 257.

126  Irving Rouse, 'Prehistory in Haiti: A Study in Method', in *Anthropological Publication* No. 21 (Yale University, 1939), p. 15; Hallam L. Movius, Jr. 'Curran Point, Larne, County Antrim: The type site of the Irish Mesolithic', in *PRIA* vol lvi, section c. no. 1 (1953), p. 36.

127  Movius, 'Curran Point, Larne, County Antrim', p. 37.

128  Ibid. p. 4.

129  H. O'Neill Hencken to H.L. Movius, letter dated 3 December 1935, Hallam L. Movius Papers #998-27, 127.2.

130  H. O'Neill Hencken to H.L. Movius, letter dated 7 October 1935, Hallam L. Movius Papers #998-27, 127.2.

131  Movius, 'Archaeological Research in Northern Ireland', p. 7.

132  'Report of the Excavations of the Third Harvard Archaeological Expedition in Ireland', Box 21.9, p. 3.

133  *Irish Times* of 13 November 1934.

134  'Report of the Excavations of the Third Harvard Archaeological Expedition in Ireland', p. 3.

135  Ibid.

136  Hallam L. Movius Jr., 'An Early Post-Glacial Archaeological Site at Cushendun, County Antrim', in *PRIA* vol. xlvi (1940–1941), pp. 2–84.

137  Ibid. p. 6.

138  Ibid.

139  Ibid. pp. 70 and 73.

140  ibid. p. 74.

141  Movius, *The Irish Stone Age*, p. xxiv.

142  Ibid. p. xxi–xxii.

143  Ibid. p. xxiv.

144  H. O'Neill Hencken to H.L. Movius, letter dated 3 Dec 1935, Hallam L. Movius Papers #998-27, 127.2.

145  Movius, *The Irish Stone Age*, p. xxiv.

146  H.L. Movius to Dr Hugh O'Neill Hencken, letter dated 19 August 1935, H.L. Movius Papers #998-27, Box 127.2.

147  H.L. Movius to Dr Hugh O'Neill Hencken, letter dated 26 August 1935, H.L. Movius Papers #998-27, Box 127.2.

148   Patrick Long, 'Lawlor, Henry Cairnes', in www.dib.cambridge.org.

149   Movius, *The Irish Stone Age*, p. xvii.

150   Ibid. p. xxii.

151   Movius, *The Irish Stone Age*, p. xviii. The Americans started off having a good
      relationship with Whelan but unfortunately by 1935 things had deteriorated.
      Movius in a reference to a row over pot sherds, wrote that Whelan's 'whole attitude
      has been so frightfully adverse from the beginning'. See H.L. Movius to Dr Hugh
      O'Neill Hencken, letter n.d. but in file with letters dated 1935, H.L. Movius Papers
      #998-27, Box 127.2.

152   H.L. Movius to Dr Hugh O'Neill Hencken, letter dated 16 August 1935, H.L.
      Movius Papers #998-27, Box 127.2.

153   Movius, 'Archaeological Research in Northern Ireland', p. 7.

154   L.S. Gogan to H.L. Movius, letter dated 19 June 1936, H.L. Movius Papers #998-27,
      Box 127.3.

155   Estyn Evans, 'The Irish Stone Age', *JCLAS* vol. x, no. 3 (1943), p. 263.

156   E. Estyn Evans, 'The Irish Stone Age: Its Chronology, Development and
      Reslationships by Hallam L.Movius', *Geographical Review*, vol. xxxiv, no. 1
      (Jan.1944), pp. 168–9.

157   E.E. Evans and G.F. Mitchell, 'The Irish Stone Age by Hallam L. Movius', *UJA*, vol.
      vi (1943), pp. 145–7.

158   Joseph Raftery, 'The Irish Stone Age by Hallam L. Movius', *JRSAI* vol. xiii, no. 1
      (1943), p. 26.

159   R.A.S. Macalister, 'The Irish Stone Age by Hallam L. Movius', *JGAHS* vol. xx, no.
      3–4. (1943), pp. 190–1.

160   Woodman, *The Mesolithic in Ireland,* p. 208.

161   Ibid. p. 11.

162   Ibid. pp. 201 and 203.

163   Ibid. p. 207.

164   Adolf Mahr, 'New Aspects and Problems in Irish Prehistory, Presidential Address
      for 1937, *PPS*, no. 11 (July–December, 1937), pp. 261–436.

165   *106th Commissioners of Public Works Annual Report* (31 March 1938), p. 1;
      'magesterial survey of Irish prehistory' from Wallace, 'Adolf Mahr and the making
      of Seán P. Ó Ríordáin', p. 254.

166   O. Davies, Review Essay, 'A. Mahr, New Aspects and Problems in Irish Prehistory
      (*PPS* Presidential Address, 1937)', in *UJA* vol. ii (1939), p. 123.

167   Ibid. p. 123.

168   Ibid.

169   Ibid.

170   Ibid. p. 124.

171   Ibid. p. 125.

172   Ibid. p. 126.

173   Ibid. pp. 126–7.

174   Virginia Crossman and Dympna McLoughlin, 'A Peculiar Eclipse: E. Estyn Evans
      and Irish Studies', in *The Irish Review*, no. 15 (Belfast 1994), pp. 94–5.

175   Evans, *The Personality of Ireland*, p. viii.

176  Ibid. p. x.

177  Ibid. p. xii.

178  Ibid.

179  Hugh O'Neill Hencken to H.L. Movius, letter dated 21 July 1937, Hallam L. Movius Papers #998-27, 127.2.

180  H.L. Movius to Dr Hugh O'Neill Hencken, letter dated 4 August 1937, H.L. Movius Papers #998-27, Box 127.2.

181  Adolf Mahr to H.L. Movius, letter dated 27 May 1937, Hallam L. Movius Papers #998-27, Box 28.1.

182  H.L. Movius to Hugh O'Neill Hencken , letter dated 19 August 1937, Hallam L. Movius Papers #998-27, Box 127.2.

183  Hugh O'Neill Hencken to H.L Movius, radiogram dated 14 September 1937, Hallam L. Movius Papers #998-27, Box 127.2.

184  Editorial, *UJA* vol. iii (1940).

185  Clark, *Archaeology and Society*, p. 194.

186  Editorial, *UJA* vol. iii (1940).

187  Stout, 'Emyr Estyn Evans and Northern Ireland: the archaeology and geography of a new state', p. 18.

188  'Editorial', *UJA* vol ii (1939).

189  Aideen Ireland to author, letter dated 15 June 2009; 'Somewhere along the line Eoin O'Duffy was requested to be Patron instead of a British Royal but this need not be an indication of serious political engagement on behalf of the Society'.

190  Stout, 'Emyr Estyn Evans and Northern Ireland: the archaeology and geography of a new state', p. 23.

191  Editorial Board, 'The Celts in Archaeology', in *UJA* vol. ii (1939), p. 138.

192  Ibid. p. 141.

193  Ibid.

194  E. Estyn Evans and M. Gaffikin, 'Belfast Naturalists' Field Club Survey of Antiquities, Megaliths and Raths', in *IJN*, vol. v, no. 10 (1935), pp. 242–52.

195  Stout', Emyr Estyn Evans and Northern Ireland: the archaeology and geography of a new state', p. 22.

196  Ibid. p. 21.

197  Ibid, p. 24.

198  Ibid. p. 25.

199  Ibid. p. 24.

200  Barry Raftery, 'Celtic Ireland: Problems of Language, History and Archaeology', in *Acta Archaeologica, Academiae Scientiarum Hungaricae*, tomus lvii, fasciculi 1–3 (2006) p. 274.

201  Ann Hamlin, 'Emyr Estyn Evans, 1905–1989', in *Archaeology Ireland* vol. iii, no. 3 (Autumn 1989), p. 115. The Institute offered an interdisciplinary teaching programme including history, politics, literature, anthropology, conflict resolution, language, folklore and archaeology.

202  Stuart Piggott, 'The Coming of the Celts: the Archaeological Argument', in G. MacEoin (ed.), *Proceedings of the Sixth International Congress of Celtic Studies* (1983), p. 221.

203   Clark, *Archaeology and Society*, p. 194.
204   Trigger, *A History of Archaeological Thought*, pp. 163–170.
205   Evans, *The Personality of Ireland*, pp. 78–9.


## Chapter 7

1   Arthur D. Codling, Dept of Finance to H.G. Leask, letter dated 6 September 1938, NMI Topographical file E29:1-260, pp. 25–6.
2   Later 'Special Employment Schemes'.
3   For Lagore and Knocknalappa see Chapter 4, for Kilgreany see Chapter 5 and for Gallen see Chapter 3.
4   Mahr, 'New Aspects and Problems in Irish Prehistory'. See Appendix 2.
5   'Archaeological Excavations, 1934–1938', in *106th Annual Report Commissioners of Public Works* (31 March 1938), NAI D/TAOIS S10940, p. 50.
6   Gabriel Cooney, 'The Legacy of Seán P. Ó Ríordáin', *Archaeology Ireland* vol. xi, no. 4 (Winter 1997), p. 30; Daniel, 'Obituary, Seán P. Ó Ríordáin'.
7   Howard Kilbride-Jones, 'The excavation of a composite tumulus at Drimnagh, Co. Dublin', *JRSAI*, vol. ix no. 4 (Dec 31, 1939), p. 190.
8   H.G. Leask, 'Archaeological Excavations, 1935. Synopsis of the more Important Results', in NAI D/TAOIS S10940.
9   Ibid. *106th Annual Report Commissioners of Public Works* (31 March 1938), p. 49. E. Estyn Evans, 'Excavations at Aghnaskeagh, Co. Louth, Cairn B, Irish Free State Scheme of Archaeological Research', in *JCLAS* vol. ix (1937), pp. 1–18. It was claimed in a press release issued by the Government Information Bureau, dated 20 August 1935, that 'the results throw new light on the Early Celtic period in Ireland'. See 'Co. Louth Excavations. New Light on the Early Celtic Period in Ireland', 20 August 1935, in NAI GIS 2/2.
10   Hallam L. Movius, Report dated 8 October 1934, in NAI D/TAOIS S10940.
11   Following the discovery of this urn-burial, a survey revealed the presence of numerous similar barrows throughout the area. In 1935 excavations were carried out on twenty of these monuments. The results, according to S.P. Ó Ríordáin were 'frankly disappointing as no unmistakable burial was found in any of the barrows excavated'. However, he regarded them as important, notwithstanding the paucity of finds and compared them with urn-fields in the Netherlands and Germany: Seán P. Ó Ríordáin, 'Excavations at Lissard, Co. Limerick and other sites in the locality', *JRSAI* vol. xi (1936), p. 177 and 179.
12   Adolf Mahr, 'Quaternary Research in Ireland from the Archaeological Viewpoint', in *INJ* vol. v (January 1934–November 1935), pp. 137–44. Adolf Mahr, 'Gazetteer D: Sites examined through the Committee for Quaternary Research in Ireland', in 'New Aspects and Problems in Irish Prehistory', pp. 424–5. Knud Jessen and A. Farrington, 'The bogs at Ballybetagh, near Dublin, with remarks on late-glacial conditions in Ireland', *PRIA* vol. xliv (1937–1938), pp. 205–60.
13   President de Valera's Broadcast Message, St. Patrick's Day 1932, De Valera Papers, UCDA P150 1955.

14 Keynes was the Treasurer of the University of Cambridge Eugenics Society, 1911–1913; He gave the Galton Lecture in 1937 on 'Some consequences of a declining population'. See Veronica di Mambro, 'The University of Cambridge Eugenics Society from 1911–1913 and 1930–1933 and reasons for its ultimate demise', https://mediachecker.wordpress.com, accessed 22 March 2017. Keynes served as the *Director* of the British Eugenics Society, 1937–1944, www.eugenicsarchive.ca/discover/connections, accessed 22 March 2017.

15 John Maynard Keynes, 'National Self-Sufficiency', *Studies*, vol. xxii, no. 86 (June 1933), p. 189. See also Mark C. Nolan, *Keynes in Dublin: Exploring the 1933 Finlay Lecture*.

16 Professor George O'Brien, 'John Maynard Keynes', *Studies*, 27 April 1946, p. 193.

17 Bernard K.Means (ed.), *Shovel Ready: Archaeology and Roosevelt's New Deal for America* (The University of Alabama Press, 2013); Paul Fagette, *Digging for Dollars: American Archaeology and the New Deal* (University of New Mexico Press, Albuquerque, 1996).

18 Bernard K. Means, 'Labouring in the Fields of the Past: Geographic Variation in New Deal Archaeology Across the lower 48 United States', *Bulletin of the History of Archaeology*, vol. 25 (2), no. 7, p. 1. Published 27 May 2015. DOI: http://dx.doi.org/10.5334/bha.261.

19 Means, *Shovel Ready*, p. 8.

20 'Rate of wages paid on Minor Relief Schemes', NAI D/TAOIS S6399A.

21 Department of Finance to Secretary, Executive Council, memo dated 6 March 1933, NAI D/TAOIS S6399A.

22 Seán P. Ó Ríordáin, 'Post-war archaeology in Ireland', *Studies An Irish Quarterly Review*, vol. xxxiii, no. 132 (December, 1944), p. 478.

23 R.A.S. Macalister, 'National Museum helps the workers', in 'The New Ireland Five Years of Progress', p. 2.

24 Mahr, 'Systematic Excavations in the Irish Free State since 1932', Appendix iv, Gazeteer A., in 'New Aspects and Problems in Irish Prehistory', pp. 422–3.

25 Mahr, 'New Aspects and Problems in Irish Prehistory', pp. 268–70.

26 'Archaeological Excavations, 1934–1938', in *106th Annual Report Commissioners of Public Works* (31 March 1938), NAI D/TAOIS S10940, p. 47.

27 Ibid. 1, p. 50.

28 See letter dated 20 August 1934, NAI OPW 19734/34.

29 E.J. MacLaughlin, letter dated 30 August 1934, NAI OPW 19734/34.

30 NAI OPW 19734/34.

31 Mr. G.Ó hÍceadh to Mr. E.J. MacLoughlin, 'Relief Schemes Archaeological Excavations 1934 Short Report on Progress and Results, 8 September 1934' and 'Short Report on Progress and Results, 27 October 1934', in NAI OPW 19734/34.

32 Adolf Mahr, 'Bruree Excavations', report dated 13 August 1934, in NAI D/TAOIS S10940.

33 Ibid.

34 Adolf Mahr, 'Lough Gur, Co. Limerick', report dated 10 August 1934 in NAI OPW F/94/79/1/36: see also NAI D/TAOIS S10940.

35 Adolf Mahr, memo dated 10 August 1934, in NAI OPW F/94/79/1/36.

36 Ibid.

37 Mahr, 'Bruree Excavations'.

38 *Irish Times*, 13 August 1932.

39 Mahr, 'Bruree Excavations'.

40 Ibid.

41 Ibid.

42 Ibid.

43 T.D. Kendrick, 'Gallen Priory excavations, 1934–1935', in *JRSAI* vol. lxix (1939), pp. 1–20.

44 Mahr, 'Bruree Excavations'.

45 Mainchín Seoige, *From Bruree to Corcomohide* (Cork, 2000), p. 249.

46 Hugo V. Flinn to Éamon de Valera, letter dated 14 August 1934, in NAI D/TAOIS S10940.

47 Seoige, *From Bruree to Corcomohide*, pp. 33–4; Mary Cahill, 'Some unrecorded Bronze Age Gold Ornaments from Co. Limerick', *NMAJ* vol. xxxv (1993–4), pp. 33–4.

48 Mahr, 'Bruree Excavations'.

49 Ibid.

50 Adolf Mahr to Parliamentary Secretary, Department of Finance, letter dated 22 August 1934 in NAI D/TAOIS S10940.

51 Ibid.

52 'Black Death Victims', *Sunday Independent,* 16 May 1937.

53 Adolf Mahr to Sergeant Patrick Kavanagh, letter dated 20.5.37, NMI Topographical file E29:1–260, p. 3.

54 Ibid.

55 *106th Annual Report Commissioners of Public Works* (31 March 1938), p. 50.

56 Hugh O'Neill Hencken to Adolf Mahr, note dated 14.5.38, NMI Topographical file E29:1–260, p. 4.

57 Adolf Mahr to Mr. Mooney, letter dated 27.5.38, NMI Topographical file E29:1–260, p. 5.

58 NMI Topographical file E29:1–260, p. 1.

59 Letter from Adolf Mahr to Mr. Leask, dated 8 June 1938, NMI Topographical file E29:1–260, p. 5.

60 Harold G. Leask, Inspector of National Monuments to Manager, Employment Exchange, Dept of Industry and Commerce, letter dated 13 June 1938, NMI Topographical file E29:1–260, p. 6.

61 Letter from Inspector National Monuments to Joseph Raftery dated 16.6.38, NMI Topographical file E29:1–260, p. 6.

62 Joseph Raftery, 'Cemetery at Castleknock, Co. Dublin, 12 July 1938,' NMI Topographical file E29:1–260, p. 9.

63 NMI Topographical file E29:1–260, p. 11.

64 *Irish Press*, 13 July 1938.

65 E. Hourigan, Private Secretary to the Minister for Finance to Private Secretary to Minister for Education, letter dated 23 July 1938, NMI Topographical file E29:1–260, p. 28.

66 Eoin MacNeill to Hugo V. Flinn, letter dated 23 July 1938, NMI Topographical file E29:1–260, pp. 30–1.

67  H.G. Leask to Mr. McLaughlin, Special Works Division, letter dated 26 July 1938, in NAI D/TAOIS S10774.

68  Ibid.

69  Ibid.

70  Letter dated 28 July 1938, NAI D/TAOIS S10774.

71  Ibid.

72  Ibid.

73  Ibid.

74  E. Hourigan, letter dated 21 September 1938, in NAI, D/TAOIS S10774.

75  Ibid.

76  Adolf Mahr to A.J.E. Cave, MD, FRAI, Royal College of Surgeons of England, letter dated 9 October 1938, NMI Topographical file E29:1–260, p. 33.

77  H.G. Leask to Mr. McLaughlin, Special Works Division, letter dated 26 July 1938 , in NAI D/TAOIS S10774. Note from Adolf Mahr included with letter.

78  NAI D/TAOIS S10774, memo dated 15 August 1938.

79  John [Eoin] MacNeill to Mahr, letter dated 18 July 1938, NMI Topographical file E29:1–260, pp. 14–15.

80  Ibid.

81  'Graves reveal secret: Co. Dublin find momentous for historians', *Irish Press*, 25 July 1938.

82  Ibid.

83  Ibid.

84  Eoin MacNeill to Hugo V. Flinn, letter dated 23 July 1938, in NAI D/TAOIS S10774.

85  Adolf Mahr to H.G. Leask, letter dated 28 July 1938 NMI Topographical file E29:1–260, p. 18.

86  Ibid.

87  Adolf Mahr to Mr. Corish, 17 August 1938, NMI Topographical file E29:1–260, p. 21.

88  A.J.E Cave to A. Mahr, 12 Aug 1938, NMI Topographical file E29:1–260, pp. 22–3.

89  Adolf Mahr to Secretary, Dept of Education, 18 January 1939, pp. 35–6, NMI Topographical file E29:1–260, p. 33.

90  W.W. Howells to A. Mahr, letter dated 9 March 1939, NMI Topographical file E29:1–260, p. 38.

91  Mahr to Leask, letter dated 4 May 1939, NMI Topographical file E29:1–260, pp. 42–3.

92  Arthur D. Codling, Dept of Finance to H.G. Leask, letter dated 6 September 1938, NMI Topographical file E29:1–260, pp. 25–6.

93  Ibid.

94  'A report on the ancient burial ground at Castleknock', included in *An Foras Forbartha Teoranta, May 1981*, NMI Topographical file E29:1–260.

95  Adolf Mahr, 'Temair Érann, Co. Limerick', report, undated, but with other reports dated August 1934, in NAI D/TAOIS S10940.

96  Ó Ríordáin, 'Excavations at Cush, Co. Limerick', pp. 83–5.

97  Ibid. p. 85, n. 3; T.F. O'Rahilly, 'The Goidels and their Predeccesors', in *PBA* vol. xxi (1935), p. 15.

98    Letter dated 24 August 1934, from parliamentary secretary of the Dept. of Finance to Éamon de Valera, NAI D/TAOIS S10940.

99    Ó Ríordáin, 'Excavations at Cush, Co. Limerick', p. 87.

100   Ibid. p. 100.

101   Mahr, 'Temair Érann, Co. Limerick'.

102   H.G. Leask, 'Archaeological Excavations, 1935. Synopsis of the more Important Results'.

103   Ó Ríordáin, 'Excavations at Cush, Co. Limerick', p. 178.

104   *106th Annual Report Commissioners of Public Works* (31 March 1938), p. 49.

105   Gibbons, 'The Hunt Controversy', p. 115.

106   S.P. Ó Ríordáin to H.G. Leask, letter dated 23 July 1937, in NAI OPW F/94/157/1.

107   In Pat Wallace's opinion Ó Ríordáin's thesis was 'outlandish'. See Wallace, 'Adolf Mahr and the Making of Seán P. Ó Ríordáin', p. 261.

108   Ó Ríordáin, 'Excavations at Cush, Co. Limerick'; Mahr, 'New Aspects and Problems in Irish Prehistory', p. 179 and p. 386; Davies, Review Essay, 'A. Mahr, New Aspects and Problems in Irish Prehistory', p. 126.

109   Waddell, pp. 210–11.

110   Hallam L. Movius, report dated 8 October 1934, in NAI D/TAOIS S10940.

111   Ibid.

112   Ibid.

113   Ó Ríordáin, 'Excavations at Cush, Co. Limerick', p. 87.

114   *Irish Times*, 19 November 1934.

115   H.G. Leask, 'Archaeological Excavations, 1935. Synopsis of the more Important Results', in NAI D/TAOIS S10940.

116   Adolf Mahr, memo dated November 1939 NAI TAOIS 97/9/95.

117   'List of publications sent to Rockefeller Foundation', E.A. Hooton Papers, #995-1, in Box 21.16.

118   Trigger, *A History of Archaeological Thought*, p. 237.

119   Eoin Grogan & George Eogan, 'Lough Gur Excavations by Seán P. Ó Ríordáin: further Neolithic and Beaker habitations on Knockadoon', PRIA vol. 87C, p. 300.

120   See Bibliography.

121   Professor Harkness, 'The prehistoric antiquities of and around Lough Gur', in *Quarterly Journal of Science* (1869), pp. 387–96.

122   Bertram Windle, 'On certain Megalithic Remains immediately surrounding Lough Gur', in *PRIA* 30, Section C. no. 10 (1912), pp. 283–306.

123   Adolf Mahr, 'Lough Gur, Co. Limerick', report dated 10 August 1934 in NAI OPW F/94/79/1/36: see also NAI D/TAOIS S10940.

124   H.G. Leask to Adolf Mahr, letter dated 3 August 1934, in NAI OPW F/94/79/1/36.

125   Adolf Mahr, memo dated 10 August 1934, in NAI OPW F/94/79/1/36.

126   Seán.P. Ó Ríordáin to Harold G. Leask, letter dated 30 June 1936, in NAI OPW F/94/79/1/36.

127   Ó Ríordáin, 'Excavations at Cush, Co. Limerick', p. 180.

128   Seán P. Ó Ríordáin to Harold G. Leask, letter dated 30 June 1936, in NAI OPW F/94/79/1/36.

129   H.G. Leask to Employment Branch, Dept. of Industry of Commerce, letter dated 4 August 1936, NAI OPW F94/79/1/36.

130 Seán P. Ó Ríordáin to Harold G. Leask, letter dated 30 June 1936, in NAI OPW F/94/79/1/36. See J. Raftery, 'Excavation of two stone circles at Lough Gur (1936), *NMAJ* vol. i (1936–1939), p. 82.

131 H.G. Leask to E.J. MacLaughlin, Special Works Division OPW, letter dated 13 August 1937, in NAI OPW F/94/79/1/36.

132 H.G. Leask to Division C, OPW, letter dated July 1937, in NAI OPW F/94/79/1/36. See J. Raftery, 'Excavation of stone circle and two forts at Lough Gur (1936)', p. 82–83.

133 H.G. Leask to S.P. Ó Ríordáin, letter dated 21 August 1937, in NAI OPW F/94/79/1/36.

134 Ibid.

135 *106th Annual Report Commissioners of Public Works* (31 March 1938), p. 49.

136 Joseph Raftery, 'Excavation of Stone Circle and two Forts at Lough Gur', p. 82.

137 Seán P. Ó Ríordáin, 'Lough Gur Excavations: Neolithic and Bronze Age houses on Knockadoon', *PRIA* vol. lvi (1953–1954), p. 437.

138 Ibid.

139 The results of excavations on habitation sites A,B,C,D, E, F, G, H, I were published by Ó Ríordáin in his paper 'Lough Gur Excavations: Neolithic and Bronze Age houses on Knockadoon', pp. 297–459.

140 G. F. Mitchell, 'A Pollen-Diagram from Lough Gur, Co. Limerick' (Studies in Irish Quaternary Deposits: no. 9) in *PRIA* vol. lvi (1953–1954), p. 481.

141 Ó Ríordáin, 'Lough Gur Excavations: Neolithic and Bronze Age houses on Knockadoon', p. 298.

142 Grogan and Eogan, 'Lough Gur Excavations by Seán P. Ó Ríordáin: further Neolithic and Beaker habitations on Knockadoon', p. 300.

143 Ó Ríordáin, 'Lough Gur Excavations: Neolithic and Bronze Age houses on Knockadoon', p. 445.

144 Ibid. pp. 297–459.

145 Ibid. pp. 444–5.

146 Ibid. p. 452.

147 Ibid.

148 Ibid. p. 455.

149 Grogan and Eogan, 'Lough Gur Excavations by Seán P. Ó Ríordáin: further Neolithic and Beaker habitations on Knockadoon', p. 301.

150 Circle J, Circle K, Circle L, Circle P, Site 10, Site 12.

151 Grogan and Eogan, 'Lough Gur Excavations by Seán P. Ó Ríordáin: further Neolithic and Beaker habitations on Knockadoon', pp. 299–506.

152 Ibid. p. 300.

153 See for example papers by R. Cleary, 'The later Bronze Age at Lough Gur: filling in the blanks', in E. Shee-Twohig and M. Ronayne (eds), *Past Perceptions: The Prehistoric Archaeology of South-West Ireland* (Cork, 1993), pp. 114–20: 'Later Bronze Age settlement and prehistoric burials, Lough Gur, Co. Limerick', *PRIA* xcv (1995), pp. 1–92: 'Habitation Site and Boundary Wall', *PRIA* vol. ciii (2003), pp. 97–189: The Discovery Programme's North Munster project placed O'Riordáin's work in the context of the wider landscape: E. Grogan, *The North*

*Munster Project Volume 2: the Prehistoric Landscape of North Munster* (Dublin, 2005), pp. 47–62.

154 Gabriel Cooney, 'In Retrospect: Neolithic activity at Knockadoon, Lough Gur, Co. Limerick, 50 years on', *PRIA* vol. cvii (2007), p. 215. See also Grogan *The North Munster Project, Volume 2*, p. 47.

155 S.P. Ó Ríordáin to H.G. Leask, letter dated 10 Mar 1937, OPW F94/157/1. See Canon O'Mahony, *A History of the O'Mahony Septs* (Cork, 1913), reprinted from *JCHAS* vol. xii (1906).

156 S.P. Ó Ríordáin to H.G. Leask, letter dated 10 Mar 1937, OPW F94/157/1.

157 'Excavations at Garranes, Co. Cork', Manuscript of dialogue between the excavator (P. Ó Ríordáin) (B) and an ordinary citizen (A), p. 2, OPW F94/157/1.

158 H.G. Leask to E.J. MacLaughlin, Special Works Division, letter dated 10 March 1937, OPW F94/151/1.

159 Excavations at Garranes, Co. Cork', Manuscript of dialogue between the excavator (S.P. Ó Ríordáin) (B) and an ordinary citizen (A), p. 6, OPW F94/157/1.

160 Ibid. p. 8.

161 Ibid. p. 9.

162 Ibid. p. 11.

163 Ibid. p. 10.

164 *Antiquity* (1937), p. 7.

165 Excavations at Garranes, Co. Cork', Manuscript of dialogue between the excavator (P. Ó Ríordáin) (B) and an ordinary citizen (A), p. 12, OPW F94/157/1.

166 *Antiquity* (1937), p. 3.

167 Seán P. Ó Ríordáin, 'The excavation of a large earthen ring-fort at Garranes, Co. Cork', vol. xlvii (1942), pp. 77–150.

168 Ibid. p. 143.

169 Ibid.

170 Ibid. p. 140.

171 Ibid. p. 144.

172 Adolf Mahr, 'Megalithic Monument at Aghnaskeagh, Co. Louth', report dated 10 August 1934, NAI D/TAOIS S10940.

173 H. O'Neill Hencken, 'A cairn at Poulawack, Co. Clare, with a report on the human remains by Hallam L. Movius Jr', *JRSAI* vol. lxv (1935), pp. 191–222; 'A Long Cairn at Creevykeel, Co. Sligo', JRSAI vol. ix, no, 2 (Jun. 30, 1939), pp. 53–98.

174 Carleton Jones, *Temples of Stone, Exploring the Megalithic Monuments of Ireland* (Dublin 2013), p. 6.

175 J. Raftery, 'Excavation of stone circle and two forts at Lough Gur', pp. 82–3; E. Estyn Evans, 'Excavations at Aghnaskeagh, Co. Louth, Cairn A', *JCLAS* vol. viii (1935), pp. 234–55; Gearóid O Ó hÍceadh, 'The Moylisha Megalith, Co. Wicklow', *JRSAI* vol. lxxvii, no. 3 (October 1946), pp. 120–27; P. T. Walshe and P. O'Connor, 'The excavation of a burial cairn on Baltinglass Hill, Co. Wicklow', *PRIA* vol. xlvi (1940–1941), pp. 221–36.

176 H. G. Leask & Liam Price, 'The Labbacallee Megalith', in *PRIA* vol. xliii (1935–1937), pp. 77–104.

177 Gearóid Ó hÍceadh, report dated 27 October 1934, 'Relief Schemes Archaeological Excavations 1934'.

178  Waddell, *Foundation Myths*, p. 215.

179  Adolf Mahr, 'Baltinglass, Co. Wicklow', undated report, with other reports dated in August 1934, in NAI D/TAOIS S10940.

180  'People in Waterford History – 20th Century', www.waterford comuseum.org.

181  Adolf Mahr, 'Labbacallee Dolmen, Co. Cork', report dated 10 August 1934, in NAI D/TAOIS S10940.

182  Ibid.

183  H.G. Leask and Liam Price, 'The Labbacallee megalith, Co. Cork *PRIA* vol. xliii (1935–7), p. 7.

184  Adolf Mahr, 'Labbacallee Dolmen, Co. Cork', report dated 10 August 1934, in NAI D/TAOIS S10940.

185  Ibid.

186  Ibid.

187  Leask and Price, 'The Labbacallee Megalith', p. 95.

188  Ibid. pp. 95 and 97.

189  Jones, *Temples of Stone*, p. 243.

190  *106th Annual Report Commissioners of Public Works* (31 March 1938), p. 48.

191  Leask & Price, 'The Labbacallee Megalith', p. 97.

192  Ibid. pp. 90–1 and p. 94.

193  Ibid. pp. 77–104.

194  Jones, *Temples of Stone*, p. 7.

195  Howard Kilbride-Jones, 'The excavation of a composite tumulus at Drimnagh, Co. Dublin', *JRSAI*, vol. ix no. 4 (December 31, 1939), p. 192.

196  Howard Kilbride-Jones, 'Citizen Keane: A memoir of excavation in the thirties', *Archaeology Ireland* vol. v, no. 3 (Autumn 1991), p. 11.

197  T.G.E. Powell, *The Celts* (London, 1958). This book was reprinted in 1978 and was described in the preface as 'an established classic' by Stuart Piggott.

199  Kilbride-Jones, 'The excavation of a composite tumulus at Drimnagh, Co. Dublin', p. 192.

199  Ibid. p. 212.

200  Ibid. pp. 218–20.

201  Ibid. p. 216.

202  Ibid. p. 217.

203  Means, 'Labouring in the Fields of the Past', p. 1.

204  W. Haag, 'Federal Aid to Archaeology in the Southeast, 1933–1942', *American Antiquity* vol. l (2) 1985, p. 278.

205  Kevin Kenny, *The American Irish: A History* (Essex and New York), p. 219.

## Chapter 8

1  Seán P. Ó Ríordáin, 'Excavation in Townland of Garranes, Parish of Templemartin, Co. Cork,' 10 March 1937, OPW F94/157/1.

2  Liam S. Gogan, National University Graduates' Dining Club, 1 December 1932, Liam S. Gogan Papers, UCDA LA27/345.

3  Ibid.

4   Adolf Mahr, memo dated 10 August 1934, NAI OPW F/94/79/1/36: see also NAI D/TAOIS S10940.

5   Liam S. Gogan, speech about Conrad Arensberg's address at the National University Graduates' Dining Club dinner, 22 February 1933, Liam S. Gogan Papers, UCDA, LA27/345.

6   Trigger, *A History of Archaeological Thought*, p. 236.

7   Gogan, speech about Conrad Arensberg's address at the National University Graduates' Dining Club dinner, 22 Febraury 1933.

8   Allen, 'States of Mind: Science, Culture and the Irish Intellectual Revival, 1900–30', p. 150.

9   'Wanted – A Scientific Revival', *Sinn Féin*, 7 September 1907, p. 3.

10  Allen, 'States of Mind: Science, Culture and the Irish Intellectual Revival, 1900–30', p. 150.

11  Ibid. p. 162.

12  Hooton, 'The Harvard Study of the Irish Free State'.

13  John Collis, 'Celtic Myths', in *Antiquity* vol. lxxi, no. 271 (Mar 1997), p. 198.

14  A.D. Smith, *The Ethnic Origin of Nations* (Oxford, 1986), p. 177.

15  J.V.S. Megaw and M.R. Megaw, 'Ancient Celts and Modern Ethnicity', in *Antiquity* vol. lxx (1996), p. 180.

16  Stephen J. Gould, 'In the Mind of the Beholder' *Natural History* (February 1994); see also www. understanding race.org/history/science/debate_over.html.

17  Hooton, 'The Relation of Physical Anthropology to Cultural Anthropology'.

18  Ibid.

19  'Irish Expeditions – Clippings', Hooton Paper #995-1, Box 21.8.

20  Hooton, 'The relation of Physical Anthropology to Cultural Anthropology'.

21  Ibid.

22  Ibid.

23  Macalister, *Archaeology of Ireland*, p. 134.

24  Fagan, A Brief History of Archaeology, p. 162.

25  Mahr, 'New Aspects and Problems in Irish Prehistory', p. 262.

26  Ibid.

27  R.A.S. Macalister, 'The Excavation of Kiltera, Co. Waterford', in *PRIA* vol. xliii (1935–7), p. 14.

28  Text of broadcast, dated September 1937, in NAI OPW F/94/79/1/36.

29  Ibid.

30  Evans, 'Excavations at Aghnaskeagh, Co. Louth, Cairn A', p. 255.

31  'Co. Louth Excavations. New Light on the Early Celtic Period in Ireland', 20 August 1935, in NAI GIS 2/2.

32  Macalister, 'A Five Year Plan for Research', 11 June 1937.

33  Robert Lloyd Praeger, *The Way that I went* (Cork, 1997), p. 137.

34  R.A.S. Macalister, E.C.R. Armstrong, and Ll. Praeger, 'Report on the Exploration of Bronze-Age Carns on Carrowkeel Mountain, Co. Sligo', in *PRIA* vol. xxix (1911–12), pp. 311–47.

35  Mahr, 'New Aspects and Problems in Irish Prehistory', p. 267.

36  Praeger, *The Way that I went*, p. 140.

37   Hencken, 'A Cairn at Poulawack, County Clare', p. 191.

38   Macalister, Armstrong, and Praeger, 'Report on the Exploration of Bronze Age Carns on Carrowkeel', pp. 314 and 317.

39   Ibid. pp. 325 and 346.

40   Ibid. pp. 316–17.

41   Ibid. pp. 317 and 329.

42   Ibid. p. 337.

43   Hencken, 'A Long Cairn at Creevykeel, Co. Sligo', p. 61.

44   Charles Lyell, *The Geological Evidence of the Antiquity of Man* (London, 1863).

45   Hencken, 'Cahercommaun, a Stone Fort in Co. Clare', p. 69.

46   Jacquetta Hawkes, 'Robert Eric Mortimer Wheeler, 1890–1976', in *PBA* (1978), pp. 483–507.

47   Hencken, 'A Cairn at Poulawack, Co. Clare', p. 196.

48   Hencken, 'A Long Cairn at Creevykeel, Co. Sligo', p. 72.

49   Ibid. p. 60.

50   Hencken and Movius, 'The Cemetery-Cairn at Knockast', p. 243.

51   Ibid.

52   Macalister, Armstrong and Praeger, 'Report on the Exploration of Bronze-Age Carns on Carrowkeel Mountain, Co. Sligo', pp. 317 and 340.

53   Hencken and Movius, 'The Cemetery-Cairn at Knockast', p. 250.

54   Howells, 'The Early Christian Irish: The Skeletons at Gallen Priory', p. 104.

55   E. Estyn Evans, *Prehistoric and Early Christian Ireland* (London, 1966), p. 186.

56   Hencken and Movius, 'The Cemetery-Cairn at Knockast', p. 284.

57   Ibid. p. 258.

58   Hencken, 'A Long Cairn at Creevykeel, Co. Sligo', p. 72.

59   Hencken, 'A Cairn at Poulawack, Co. Clare', p. 206.

60   Raymond Harris Thompson et al, 'Emil Walter Haury, May 2 1904–December 5 1992', in Biographical Memoirs of the National Academy of Sciences of the United States of America, http: www.nasonline.org., pp. 151–74.

61   Hencken and Movius, 'The Cemetery-Cairn at Knockast', p. 248, n. 8.

62   L.S. Gogan, 'Carn Tighearnaigh Mhic Dheaghaidh', in *JCHAS* (July–December 1929), p. 70.

63   O.G.S. Crawford, Editorial Notes, *Antiquity* vol. i (1927), p. 1.

64   Tim Murray, *From Antiquarian to Archaeologist: The History and Philosophy of Archaeology* (South Yorkshire, 2014), p. 189.

65   Gould, *The Mismeasure of Man*, p. 54.

66   Thomas S. Kuhn, *The Structure of Scientific Revolutions* (Chicago, [1962] 1970).

67   Joseph Raftery, 'On Chronology', p. 83.

68   L. S. Gogan, 'America's Archaeologists in Ireland, The Harvard Archaeological and Anthropological Expeditions', in *Irish Travel* (December 1932), p. 60.

69   Byrne et al, 'Harvard Irish Study, 1931–1936', pp. xvii–xliii.

70   See R. Lee Lyman, Michael J. O'Brien and Robert C. Dunnell, *The Rise and Fall of Culture History* (New York, 1997).

71   J.M. de Navarro, *A Survey of Research on an Early Phase of Celtic Culture.* (London, 1936).

72   Hencken, Memories of Work and Travel, p. 21.

73   J.M. de Navarro, 'Hector Munro Chadwick 1870–1947', in *PBA* vol. xxxiii (1947), pp. 307–30.

74   Glyn Daniel, 'Editorial' [Obituary of Hugh O'Neill Hencken] in *Antiquity* vol. lvi, no. 216 (March 1982), p. 7.

75   Kenneth Jackson, 'Nora Kershaw Chadwick, 1891–1972', *PBA* vol. lviii (1972), p. 541.

76   Paul Ashbee, 'Hugh O'Neill Hencken (1902–1981) and his Archaeology of Cornwall and Scilly and Beyond', *Cornish Archaeology* No. 21 (1981), p. 179.

77   Hugh O'Neill Hencken, *Archaeology of Cornwall and Scilly* (1932).

78   Obituary on Hencken, *Antiquity* (1982), p. 6.

79   V. Gordon Childe, 'The Archaeology of Cornwall and Scilly by H. O'Neill Hencken', *AJ* vol. xii (Oxford, 1932), p. 460.

80   Ashbee, 'Hugh O'Neill Hencken (1902–1981) and his Archaeology of Cornwall and Scilly', p. 181.

81   Hencken, 'Harvard and Irish Archaeology', p. 7.

82   Ibid.

83   Fagan, *A Brief History of Archaeology*, p. 161.

84   Gordon. R. Willey and Jeremy A. Sabloff, *A History of American Archaeology* (2nd edn, London, 1980), pp. 83–4.

85   Anthony D. Smith, 'Authenticiy, antiquity and archaeology', in *Nations and Nationalisms* vol. vii, no. 4 (2001), p. 443.

86   'Fourth Harvard Archaeological Expedition in Ireland, 1935 Final Report', E.A. Hooton Papers #995-1, Box 21.9, p. 2.

87   Ó Raifeartaigh, *The Royal Irish Academy*, p. 157.

88   Hencken, *Memories of Work and Travel*, p. 22.

89   Fagan, *A Brief History of Archaeology*, p. 98.

90   C. Stephen Briggs, 'A Historiography of the Irish Crannóg: The Discovery of Lagore as Prologue to Wood-Martin's *Lake Dwellings of Ireland* of 1886', in *AJ* vol. lxxix (1999), p. 347

91   Armstrong, 'The La Tène Period in Ireland', p. 8.

92   Hencken, 'Harvard and Irish Archaeology', p. 27.

93   Hencken, 'Lagore Crannóg', p. 37.

94   Hencken, 'Ballinderry Crannóg No. 2', p. 6.

95   Ibid., p. 123.

96   'Ballinderry Crannóg No. 1', pp. 235–7.

97   Hencken, 'Ballinderry Crannóg No. 2', p. 28.

98   William Duncan Strong, 'Lagore Crannóg: An Irish Royal Residence of the 7th to 10th Centuries AD by Hugh Hencken', Review Article, in *American Anthropologist*, vol. lv, issue 5 (December 1953), p. 733.

99   Mullins, *Dublin Nazi No. 1*, p. 40.

100  Flinders Petrie, *Methods and Aims in Archaeology* (London, 1904), p. 49.

101  Hugh O'Neill Hencken, 'Archaeological Notes, The Harvard Archaeological Expedition in Ireland', in *AJA* vol. xlv, no. 1 (January–March 1941), p. 2.

102  Movius, *The Irish Stone Age*, p. xvii.

103  Ibid.

104   Ibid. p. 142.
105   Movius, 'Curran Point, Larne Co. Antrim: The Type Site of the Irish Mesolithic', pp. 115–70.
106   Hencken and Movius, 'The Cemetery-Cairn at Knockast', p. 282.
107   'Report [b] of the Second Harvard Archaeological Expedition to Ireland, 1933', p. 10.
108   Ibid.
109   Ibid. pp. 10–11.
110   Ibid. pp. 1–11.
111   Ibid. p. 12.
112   J.G.D. Clark, 'The Bann Culture of Northern Ireland', *PPS* vol ii part 1 and 2 (1936), p. 243; Sir John Evans, 'On some discoveries of Stone Implements in Lough Neagh, Ireland', in *Archaeologia*, vol. xli (1867), pp. 397–408.
113   W.J. Knowles, 'Prehistoric Stone Implements from the River Bann and Lough Neagh', in *PRIA* vol. xxx (1912–1913), pp. 195–222; J. Wilfrid Jackson, 'On the Diatomaceous Deposit of the Lower Bann Valley, Counties Antrim and Derry, and Prehistoric Implements found therein', in *MPMLPS* vol. liii (1909).
114   G. Erdtman, *INJ* vol. i (1927), p. 245.
115   C. Blake Whelan, 'The Tanged Flake Industry of the River Bann, Co. Antrim', *JRSAI* vol. x (1930), pp. 134–8.
116   'Report of the Excavations of the Third Harvard Archaeological Expedition in Ireland', p. 2.
117   Clark, 'The Bann Culture of Northern Ireland', p. 243.
118   Ibid.
119   Hallam L. Movius, Jr., 'A Neolithic Site on the River Bann', in *PRIA* vol. xliii C (1936–37), p. 24.
120   Clark, 'The Bann Culture of Northern Ireland', p. 243.
121   Eoin MacNeill, 'The Pretanic Background in Britain and Ireland', in *JRSAI* vol. lxiii (1933), pp. 1–28.
122   Ibid. pp. 3 and 28.
123   Mahr, 'New Aspects and Problems in Irish Prehistory', p. 328.
124   Ibid. p. 327.
125   H.L. Movius to Adolf Mahr, letter dated 26 July 1938, Hallam Movius Papers #998-27, Box 28.1.
126   Ibid.
127   Adolf Mahr to H.L. Movius, letter dated 7 September 1938, Hallam Movius Papers #998-27, Box 28.1.
128   H.L. Movius to Adolf Mahr, letter dated 14 October 1938, Hallam Movius Papers #998-27, Box 28.1.
129   Adolf Mahr to H.L. Movius, letter dated 26 October 1938, Hallam Movius Papers #998-27, Box 28.1.
130   Ibid.
131   For a discussion on the relationship between archaeology and documentary sources see D. Austin, 'The 'proper' study of medieval archaeology', D. Austin and L. Alcock (eds), *From the Baltic to the Black Sea: Studies in Medieval Archaeology*, 9–42 (London, 1990).

132 Adolf Mahr, memo dated November 1939, NAI TAOIS 97/9/95.
133 Adolf Mahr, memo dated 10 August 1934, NAI OPW F/94/79/1/36: see also NAI D/TAOIS S10940.
134 'Second Harvard Archaeological Expedition in Ireland'.
135 Ibid.
136 Ibid. p. 1; See also *Bulletin of the American Group, International Institute for Conservation of Historic and Artistic Works*, vol. ix, no. 2 (April 1969); www. dictionaryofarthistorians.org.
137 Movius, 'Kilgreany excavations'.
138 Richard B. Woodbury, 'Obituary: John Otis Brew 1906–1988', in *American Antiquity* vol. lv (1990), p. 453.
139 'Lagore Crannog' from 'Report of the Excavations of the Third Harvard Archaeological Expedition in Ireland', E.A. Hooton Papers, #995-1, Box 21.9, p. 1.
140 'Fourth Harvard Archaeological Expedition in Ireland. 1935 Final Report', p. 1.
141 'Report of the Fifth Harvard Archaeological Expedition in Ireland, 1936', p. 1.
142 'Lauriston Ward, 1882–1960 Papers, 1936–1960 inclusive', Harvard University Library, Oasis Online Archive Search Information, www.oasis.lib.harvard.edu./oasis.
143 Hugh O'Neill Hencken, undated letter to H.L. Movius attached in file to typed letter dated 12 July 1937, in Hallam L. Movius Papers #998-27, Box 127.2.
144 James B. Conant to Éamon de Valera, letter dated 17 June 1937, in NAI D/TAOIS 97/9/95.

## Chapter 9

1 Hencken, 'Harvard and Irish Archaeology'.
2 L. Perry Curtis Jr., *Apes and Angels The Irishman in Victorian Caricature* (Revised edition, Washington and London, 1997).
3 *Herald Examiner*, Chicago, 17 December 1932.
4 Malcolm Chapman, *The Celts: The Construction of a Myth* (London, 1992), p. 33.
5 Neil MacGregor, Director of the British Museum, Foreword in Julia Farley and Fraser Hunter, *Celts, Art and Identity* (London, 2015).
6 'Contributors to Irish Archaeological Expedition', E.A. Hooton Papers #995-1, Box 21.10. See Appendix 3.
7 'The Harvard Study of the Irish Free State'.
8 Hencken, 'Harvard and Irish Archaeology'.
9 R.E.M. Wheeler, 'The Paradox of Celtic Art', in *Antiquity* vol. vi (1932), p. 294.
10 John Collis, 'Celtic Myths', in *Antiquity* vol. lxxi, no. 271 (March 1997), p. 199.
11 J.V.S. Megaw and M.R. Megaw, 'The Mechanism of (Celtic) Dreams', in *Antiquity* vol. lxxii, no. 275 (March 1998), p. 433.
12 Barry Raftery, *La Tène in Ireland*, p. 1.
13 Joseph Raftery in Mahr, 'New Aspects and Problems in Irish Prehistory', pp. 409–10.
14 Ibid. p. 410, n. 3.
15 Ibid. p. 411.
16 James, *The Atlantic Celts*, p. 87.

17 Barry Raftery, *La Tène in Ireland*, p. 324.

18 Bremer, *Ireland's Place in Prehistoric and Early Historic Europe*, p. 30.

19 Mahr, 'New Aspects and Problems in Irish Prehistory', p. 340.

20 Dept. of Education to Dept. of the Taoiseach, memo dated November 1939, NAI D/TAOIS 97/9/95.

21 Harold G. Leask to H.L. Movius, letter dated 5 October 1934, Movius Papers #998.27, Box 128.1.

22 *Irish Independent* 10 June 1932.

23 Ibid.

24 Adolf Mahr, memo dated November 1939, in NAI TAOIS 97/9/95.

25 P.A. O'Connell, *Boston Evening Transcript*, 20 August 1936.

26 From 'Mercury, New Bedford, Mass. 12', National Press Clipping Bureau Inc. 48 West 27th Street, New York City, in 'Irish Expeditions – Clippings', E.A. Hooton Papers # 995-1, Box 21.8.

27 Name of newspaper unknown, from National Press Clipping Bureau Inc. 48 West 27th Street, New York City, in 'Irish Expeditions – Clippings', E.A. Hooton Papers #995-1, Box 21.8.

28 R. Corish to Government Information Bureau, letter dated 6 October 1937, in NAI F94/157/1.

29 Text of broadcast, dated September 1937, in NAI OPW F/94/79/1/36.

30 See 'Tara of the Kings Proposal State should undertake Excavations', in *Irish Press* 9 April 1937.

31 Glyn Daniel, 'Archaeology and television', *Antiquity* 28 (1954), p. 202.

32 Text of broadcast, dated September 1937, in NAI OPW F/94/79/1/36.

33 Anon., 'The First Ulstermen – Stone Age Discoveries, *Irish Times*, 14 February 1935.

34 Ibid.

35 Green, *Prehistorian: A Biography of V. Gordon Childe*, p. 125.

36 'Report [b] of the Second Harvard Archaeological Expedition to Ireland, 1933'.

37 Ibid.

38 Hencken, 'Harvard and Irish Archaeology', p. 8.

39 'Report [b] of the Second Harvard Archaeological Expedition to Ireland, 1933', pp. 8–9.

40 *Boston Herald*, 15 December 1932.

41 'Irish Expeditions – Clippings', E.A. Hooton Papers #995-1, Box 21.8.

42 In his memoir Hencken noted the absence of Macalister at this luncheon but accepted that Mahr 'must have invited McAllister, but McAllister [sic] didn't appear'. Why he thought this was the case remains unclear. See Hencken, *Memories of Work and Travel*, p. 23.

43 *Boston Evening Transcript*, 20 August 1936.

44 H.L. Movius, Jr. and Nelson C. Metcalf, 'A Harvard Boy tells of Five-Year Digging Course in Ireland', in *Boston Evening Transcript*, 12 November 1932.

45 *Irish Times*, 7 November 1932.

46 Hencken, 'Ballinderry Crannóg No. 1', pp. 138–9.

47 'Press Release, Harvard University, Irish Expedition 1932', in E.A. Hooton Papers #995-1, Box 21.7.

48  *Irish Times*, 29 July 1932.
49  Ibid.
50  Hencken, 'Ballinderry Crannóg No. 1', p. 206.
51  Ibid. p. 166.
52  *Irish Independent*, 29 September 1932.
53  J. Romilly Allen, *Archaeologia* vol. lvi (1898), p. 39.
54  Reginald Smith, *Proceedings of the Society of Antiquaries* vol. xxii (1907–9), p. 66.
55  T.D. Kendrick, 'British Hanging Bowls, in *Antiquity*, vol. vi (1932), p. 167.
56  Wheeler, 'The Paradox of Celtic Art', p. 293.
57  Francoise Henry, 'Hanging bowls', in *JRSAI* vol. lxvi (1936), p. 245; R. Bruce-Mitford, 'Ireland and the hanging-bowls: a review', in M. Ryan (ed.), *Ireland and Insular Art* (1987), p. 30.
58  Henry, 'Hanging bowls', pp. 213 and 245.
59  Ibid. p. 211.
60  A.W. Clapham, 'Notes on the origins of Hiberno-Saxon art', in *Antiquity* vol. viii (1934), p. 43; Francoise Henry, *Irish Art in the Early Christian Period* (1940).
61  C. Nordenfalk, 'One hundred and Fifty Years of varying Views on the early Insular Gospel Books', in M. Ryan (ed.), *Ireland and Insular Art* (1987), p. 2.
62  Waddell, Review Article, 'Vittorio Di Martino, Roman Ireland', in *JGAHS*, p. 234.
63  NAI TAOIS 97/9/95.
64  Hencken, 'A Gaming Board of the Viking Age', pp. 85–104; 'List of Publications sent to Rockefeller Foundation', E.A. Hooton Papers #995-1, Box 21. 6.
65  Hencken, 'Ballinderry Crannóg No. 1', p. 176; It is thought to have been made in either Limerick or Dublin, see Patrick F. Wallace and Raghnall Ó Floinn, *Treasures of the National Museum of Ireland Irish Antiquities* (Dublin, 2002), p. 231; J. Graham-Campbell, *Viking Artefacts: A Select Catalogue* (London, 1980), p. 23.
66  Hencken, 'Ballinderry Crannóg No. 1', p. 185.
67  Ibid. p. 188.
68  Adolf Mahr, 'Cloonfinlough, Co. Roscommon', Report dated 13 August 1934, NAI D/TAOIS S10940.
69  *Evening Telegraph and Evening Press*, 13 August 1932.
70  Macalister, 'A Five Year Plan for Research'.
71  *Boston Evening Transcript*, 20 August 1936.
72  Macalister, *The Present and Future of Archaeology in Ireland*, p. 14.
73  Mahr, 'New Aspects and Problems in Irish Prehistory', p. 112.
74  Tom Condit, Review article, 'The Iron Age Conundrum', in *Archaeology Ireland* vol. viii (Autumn 1994), p. 30.
75  Hencken, 'A Long Cairn at Creevykeel, Co. Sligo', p. 79.
76  Ibid. p. 88.
77  'Report of the Excavations of the Third Harvard Archaeological Expedition in Ireland [b]', p. 13.
78  Hencken, 'Cahercommaun: A Stone Fort in County Clare', p. 23.
79  Ibid. p. 30.
80  'Archaeological Excavations in Co. Meath, Summary', 1 August 1935, in NAI GIS 2/2.

81 Ibid.

82 Hencken, 'Harvard and Irish Archaeology', p. 9.

83 Movius, 'Kilgreany Cave, County Waterford', p. 281.

84 Ibid. p. 278.

85 Ibid. p. 81.

86 T.S.C. Dagg Department of Finance to Secretary of the Board of Works, letter dated 30 January 1936, NAI OPW F94/19/1/36.

87 H.G. Leask, memo dated 7 February 1936, NAI OPW F94/19/1/36.

88 *Séadcomartaí Náisiúnta Saorstáit Éireann The National Monuments of the Irish Free State* (Dublin, 1936), NAI OPW F94/19/1/36.

89 Ibid. pp. 6–7.

90 Ibid. p. 13.

91 NAI D/TAOIS 97/9/46.

92 The *Derry Journal* of 7 September 1936 considered it to be 'a possession valuable to everybody interested in Irish Antiquities'. The *Limerick Leader*, dated 5 September 1936, conceded that the publication 'will serve to arouse public interest in the all-important matter of the care of ancient historic buildings'. The *Tipperary Star* of 12 September 1936 regarded it as 'a very commendable booklet', which 'will help materially to impress the importance of, and the need for, preserving our national monuments'.

93 *Irish Press*, 24 September 1936.

94 *Irish Builder and Engineer*, 3 October 1936.

95 Carew, 'Politics and the Definition of National Monuments', pp. 129–39.

96 Peter Alter, 'Symbols of Irish Nationalism', in *Studia Hibernica*, xiv (1974), p. 104.

97 Peter Harbison, *Pilgrimage in Ireland: the Monuments and the People* (Dublin, 1991), p. 8.

98 'Saint Manchan's Shrine. Famous Relic on view in National Museum. Art of Irish Independence Period', press release dated 12 December 1935 in NAI GIS 2/2.

99 Brian J. Graham, 'Heritage conservation and Revisionist Nationalism in Ireland', in G.J. Ashworth and P. Larkham, *Building a New Heritage* (London, 1994).

100 Crooke, *Politics, Archaeology and the Creation of a National Museum*, p. 155.

101 PDDE 107, 118.

102 Raymond Gillespie and Brian P. Kennedy (eds), *Ireland Art into History* (Dublin, 1994), p. 145.

103 Mahr, 'Archaeology', pp. 214 and 224.

104 A.D. Smith, *Chosen Peoples* (Oxford, 2003), p. 190.

105 Whelan applies this phrase to public statuary. See Yvonne Whelan, *Reinventing Modern Dublin, Streetscape, Iconography and the Politics of Identity* (Dublin, 2003), p. 2.

106 Ricouer explores the reciprocal relationship between remembering and forgetting of historical events, showing how it affects both the perception of historical experience and the production of historical narrative in his book *Memory, History, Forgetting* (Chicago, 2004).

107 M.J. Harford, foreword, *The Pageant of the Celt*, RIA AP 1934/60.

108 Carew, 'The Pageant of the Celt', pp. 9–12.

109   Adolf Mahr, *A Century of Progress in Irish Archaeology Exhibits collected by The National Museum of Ireland* (Dublin, 1934), p. 4.

110   Ibid. pp. 9–10.

111   J V S Megaw and M.R. Megaw, 'Ancient Celts and Modern Ethnicity', in *Antiquity* vol. lxx (1996), p. 176.

112   Mahr, *A Century of Progress in Irish Archaeology*, p. 7.

113   Ibid. p. 14.

114   Ibid. p. 4.

115   Barry Raftery, 'Celtic Ireland, Problems of Language, History and Archaeology'.

116   James, *The Atlantic Celts*, pp. 1 and 141.

117   Ibid. p. 18.

118   James, *The Atlantic Celts*, pp. 142–3.

119   John Collis, 'A Brief History of the Irish Question – a Study of Ethnicity in action', in Paul Graves-Brown, Sian Jones, Clive Gamble (eds), *Cultural Identity and Archaeology The Construction of European Communities* (London and New York 1996), p. 170.

120   Colin Renfrew, *Archaeology and Language* (Harmondsworth, 1987), p. 225.

121   James, *The Atlantic Celts*, p. 81.

122   Chapman, *The Celts The Construction of a Myth*, pp. 16–17.

123   Graves-Brown, Jones & Gamble (eds), *Cultural Identity and Archaeology*, p. 1.

124   Ibid. p. 36.

125   Ashley Montagu, 'Mans most Dangerous Myth: the Fallacy of Race;' www.understandingrace.org/history/science/critiquing_race.html.

126   Anderson, *Imagined Communities*.

127   Graves-Brown, Jones & Gamble (eds), *Cultural Identity and Archaeology*, p. 19.

128   Ibid. p. 109.

129   Carew, 'Eoin MacNeill: revolutionary cultural ideologue', p. 72.

# Bibliography

## Abbreviations

| | |
|---|---|
| AJ | *Antiquaries Journal* |
| AJA | *American Journal of Archaeology* |
| AJPA | *American Journal of Physical Anthropology* |
| BIGS | *Bulletin of the Irish Georgian Society* |
| JCLAS | *Journal of the County Louth Archaeological Society* |
| IHS | *Irish Historical Studies* |
| INJ | *Irish Naturalists' Journal* |
| JGAHS | *Journal of the Galway Archaeological and Historical Society* |
| JRSAI | *Journal of the Royal Society of Antiquaries of Ireland* |
| JKSEIAS | *Journal of the Kilkenny and South East of Ireland Archaeological Society* |
| JRAI | *Journal of the Royal Anthropological Institute* |
| JRHAAI | *Journal of the Royal Historical and Archaeological Association of Ireland* |
| MPMLPS | *Memoirs and Proceedings of the Manchester Literary and Philosophical Society* |
| NAI | National Archives of Ireland |
| NMAC | National Monuments Advisory Council |
| NMAJ | *North Munster Antiquarian Journal* |
| PBA | Proceedings of the British Academy |
| PDDE | Published Debates Dáil Éireann |
| PMLA | Publications of the Modern Language Association of America |

| PBNHPS | Proceedings of the Belfast Naturalist and Historical Philosophical Society |
| PPS | Proceedings of the Prehistoric Society |
| PPSEA | Proceedings of the Prehistoric Society of East Anglia |
| PRIA | Proceedings of the Royal Irish Academy |
| PUBSS | Proceedings of the University of Bristol Spelealogical Society |
| RIA | Royal Irish Academy |
| RSAI | Royal Society of Antiquaries of Ireland |
| *TGAS* | Transactions of the Glasgow Archaeological Society |
| TRIA | Transactions of the Royal Irish Academy |
| UCDA | University College Dublin Archives |
| UJA | *Ulster Journal of Archaeology* |

## Primary Sources

### E.A. Hooton Papers

E.A. Hooton Papers, #995–1, Peabody Museum of Archaeology and Ethnology, Harvard University: Manuscripts Box 1.55, Box 1. 67, Box 21.6, Box 21. 7, Box 21.8, Box 21.9, Box 21.10, Manuscripts Box 2; Box 21.9: Box 21.16.

### Hallam L. Movius Papers

Hallam L. Movius Papers, #998–27, Peabody Museum of Archaeology and Ethnology, Harvard University: Box 28.1, Box 127.2, Box 127.3, Box 128.1.

### UCD Archives

### Eoin MacNeill Papers

UCDA LA1/D/2, UCDA LA1/D/2/b, UCDA LA1/D/5, UCDA LA1/D/20, UCDA LA1/D/33, UCDA LA1/D/48, UCDA LA1D/49, UCDA LA1/D/62, UCDA LA1/G/79, UCDA LA1/G/362, UCDA LA1/G/395.

### De Valera Papers

UCDA P150 1955.

**George Noble**

**Count Plunkett Papers**
UCDA P79/88.

**L.S. Gogan Papers**
UCDA LA27/345.

**National Archives of Ireland**
NAI D/FIN 2 E109/20/34, NAI D/FIN E103/29/39, NAI D/FIN E53/3/33.
NAI D/TAOIS S5392, NAI D/TAOIS S5935, NAI D/TAOIS S6631, NAI D/
TAOIS S6631 A, NAI D/TAOIS S10774, NAI D/TAOIS S10940, NAI D/
TAOIS S14559A, NAI D/TAOIS S9215A, NAI D/TAOIS 97/9/5, NAI D/
TAOIS 97/9/7, NAI D/TAOIS 97/9/46, NAI D/TAOIS 97/9/95.
NAI OPW F94/19/1/36, NAI OPW F/94/79/1/36, NAI OPW F/94/157/1,
NAI OPW F94/289/1/1, NAI OPW F94/289/1/2, NAI OPW F94/574/1, NAI
OPW F94/779/1/49, NAI OPW 19734/34, NAI OPW/2459/34.
*106th Annual Report Commissioners of Public Works* (31 March 1938)
NAI GIS 2/2.

**Royal Society of Antiquaries of Ireland**
RSAI MSS/IDV/26

**National Museum of Ireland**
NMI Topographical file E29:1–260

**Royal Irish Academy**
RIA SR 23/0/50
RIA AP 1933/19
RIA FH/B12/380
RIA AP 1934/60

**Newspapers and Magazines**
*An Claidheamh Soluis*
*Boston Evening Transcript*
*Boston Herald*
*Boston Mass. Evening Globe*
*Chicago Tribune*
*Connacht Tribune*
*Derry Journal*

*Dundalk Democrat*
*Evening Mail*
*Evening Press*
*Evening Telegraph*
*Gaelic American*
*Herald Examiner* [Chicago]
*Irish Builder and Engineer*
*Irish Independent*
*Irish Press*
*Irish Times*
*Irish Travel*
*Irish Statesman*
*Life* [Magazine]
*Limerick Leader*
*New York City Journal*
*New York Evening World*
*New York Herald Tribune*
*New York Times*
*New York Times Magazine*
*Sinn Féin*
*Sligo Champion*
*Sunday Independent*
*Tipperary Star*
*Tuam Herald*

**Websites**
http://www.irishstatutebook.ie/1930/en/act/pub/0002/index.html.
www.nasaonline.org.
http://www.peabody.harvard.edu/archives/hooton2.html.
www.understandingrace.org/history/science/critiquing_race.html.
www.ubss.org.uk.
http://rsbm.royalsocietypublishing.org.
http://www.britannica.com.
www.irishtimes.com.
www.oasis.lib.harvard.edu./oasis.
https://mediachecker.wordpress.com.
www.eugenicsarchive.ca/discover/connections.
http://dx.doi.org/10.5334/bha.261.
www.waterfordcountymuseum.org.

## Secondary Sources

Adams, Colin, 'Hibernia Romana? Ireland and the Roman Empire', in *History Ireland* (Summer 1996), pp. 21–5.

Aldous, Richard, *Great Irish Speeches* (London, 2009).

Allen, Nicholas, 'States of Mind: Science, Culture and the Irish Intellectual Revival, 1900–30', *Irish University Review*, vol. xxxiii, no. 1, Special Issue: New perspectives on the Irish Literary Revival (Spring – Summer 2003).

Alter, Peter, 'Symbols of Irish Nationalism', *Studia Hibernica* xiv (1974), pp. 104–23.

Anderson, Benedict, *Imagined Communities. Reflections on the Origin and Spread of Nationalism* (London, 1983).

Anon., 'Proceedings and Papers', in *JKSEIAS* vol. v (1864–6), p. 112.

—, 'Proceedings', in *JRHAAI* vol. v (1879–82), pp. 13–14.

—, 'Proceedings', in *JRHAAI* vol. vi (1883–4), p. 221.

—, 'National Monuments Act, 1930', in *JRSAI* vol. lx (1930), p. 197.

—, 'The National Monuments Act', in JRSAI vol. lxi (1931), p. 85.

—, *Dublin The Book of the Congress* (Wexford, 1934).

—, 'Obituary Notices' [Professor Kingsley Porter] in *JRSAI* vol. lxvi (1936), pp. 59–60.

ApSimon, A.M., '1919–1969: Fifty Years of Archaeological Research The Spelaeological Society's Contribution to Archaeology', Jubilee Contribution University of Bristol Spelaeological Society, in *PUBSS* (1969), vol. xii, no. 1 (1969), pp. 31–55.

Arensberg, Conrad M., *The Irish Countryman An Anthropological Study* (Gloucester, Mass, [1937] reprinted 1959).

— and Kimball, Solon T., *Family and Community in Ireland* (Clare, 2001).

Armstrong, E.C.R., 'The La Tène Period in Ireland', in *JRSAI* vol. liii (1923), pp. 1–33.

Arnold, Bettina, '"Arierdammerung": Race and Archaeology in Nazi Germany," in *World Archaeology* vol. xxxviii, no. 1 (2006), pp. 8–31.

— and Hassmann, Henning, 'Archaeology in Nazi Germany: the legacy of the Faustian bargain' in Philip L. Kohl and Clare Fawcett (eds), *Nationalism, Politics and the Practice of Archaeology* (Cambridge, 1995).

Ashbee, Paul, 'Hugh O'Neill Hencken (1902–1981) and his Archaeology of Cornwall and Scilly and Beyond', *Cornish Archaeology* No. 21 (1981), pp. 179–81.

Ashley, Scott, 'The Poetics of Race in 1890s Ireland: an Ethnography of the Aran Islands', in *Patterns of Prejudice* vol. xxxv, no. 2 (2001).

Augusteijn, Joost, *Ireland in the 1930s* (Dublin, 1999).

Austin, D. and Alcock, L. (eds), *From the Baltic to the Black Sea: Studies in Medieval Archaeology*, ix–lxii (London, 1990).

Bateson, J.D., 'Roman Material from Ireland: a Re-consideration', in *PRIA* vol. lxxiii (1973), pp. 21–97.

Beddoe, John, *The Races of Britain* (1885).

Bermingham, Kevin, *The most dangerous book: The battle for James Joyce's Ulysses* (London, 2014).

Bhreathnach Lynch, S., 'Commemorating the hero in newly Independent Ireland: expressions of nationhood in bronze and stone', in L. McBride (ed.), *Images, Icons and the Irish Nationalist Imagination* (Dublin, 1999), pp. 148–65.

Bielenberg, Andy, 'Keating, Siemens and the Shannon Scheme', *History Ireland* vol. v, issue no. 3 (Autumn 1997).

Binchy, Daniel A., 'Heirig Brunig', in *Studies* vol. xxi (Sept. 1932), pp. 385–403.

—, 'Adolf Hitler', in *Studies: An Irish Quarterly Review* vol. xxii, no. 85 (Mar. 1933), pp. 29–47.

—, 'Secular Institutions', in M. Dillon (ed.), *Early Irish Society* (Dublin, 1954).

Black, Edwin, *War against the Weak Eugenics and America's Campaign to Create a Master Race* (New York, 2004).

Blenner-Hassett, Roland, 'A Brief History of Celtic Studies in North America', *PMLA* vol. lxix, no. 4, part 2 (September 1954).

Boswell, David and Evans, Jessica (eds), *Representing the Nation A Reader Histories, Heritage and Museums* (London and New York, 2005).

Bourke, Edward, 'Stoneyford: a First-Century Roman Burial from Ireland', in *Archaeology Ireland* vol. iii, no. 2 (Summer, 1989), pp. 56–7.

Boyle, Paddy, 'Drumanagh – An exciting prospect', *Archaeology Ireland* vol. 31, no. 2, issue no. 120 (Summer 2017) pp. 12–14.

Brannigan, John, *Race in Modern Irish Literature and Culture* (Edinburgh, 2009).

Briggs, C. Stephen, 'A Historiography of the Irish Crannóg: The Discovery of Lagore as Prologue to Wood-Martin's *Lake Dwellings of Ireland* of 1886', in *AJ* vol. lxxix (1999), pp. 348–74.

Bremer, Walther, *Ireland's Place in Prehistoric and Early Historic Europe* (Dublin, 1928).

Bricker, Harvey M., 'Hallam Leonard Movius Jr. November 28, 1907 – May 30, 1987', *Biographical Memoirs*: www.nap.edu.

Brindley, A.L. and Lanting, J.N., 'Radiocarbon dates for Neolithic single burials', *Journal of Irish Archaeology* vol. v (1989–1990).

Briody, Micheál, *The Irish Folklore Commission 1935–1970 History, Ideology, Methodology*, Studia Fennica Folkloristica 7 (Helsinki, 2008).

Browman, David L. and Williams, Stephen, *Anthropology at Harvard: A Biographical History, 1790–1940* (Harvard, 2013).

Brown, Terence, *Ireland A Social and Cultural History 1922–2002* (London, 3rd Edition, 2004).

Brown, Fr Stephen, S.J., 'The Central Catholic Library: the First Ten Years of an Irish Enterprise' (Dublin, 1932).

Browne, C.R., 'Some New Anthropometrical Instruments', *PRIA* vol. xxiv (1891).

Bruce-Mitford, Rupert, 'Thomas Downing Kendrick, 1895–1979', *PBA* vol. lxxvi, pp. 445–71.

—, 'Ireland and the hanging-bowls – a review', in M. Ryan (ed.), *Ireland and Insular Art* (1987).

Burchell, J.P.T., 'Palaeolithic Man in North-East Ireland', *Nature* vol. cxxvi (1930).

—, 'Flint Implements of Early Magdalenian Age from Deposits Underlying the Lower Estuarine Clay at Island Magee, County Antrim', in *Nature* vol. cxxxii (1933), p. 860.

—, 'Some Littoral Sites of Early Post-Glacial Times, Located in Northern Ireland', in *PPSEA* 7 (1934), pp. 366–72.

— and J. Reid Moir, *The Early Mousterian Implements of Sligo, Ireland* (Suffolk, 1928).

— J.P.T. Burchell and J. Reid Moir, 'The Asturian Industry of Northern Ireland', *Man* vol. xxxi (1931), pp. 170-172.

Byrne, Anne, Edmondson, Ricca and Varley, Tony, 'Arensberg and Kimball and Anthropological Research in Ireland: Introduction to the Third Edition (2001)', in Conrad M. Arensberg and Solon T. Kimball, *Family and Community in Ireland* (Clare, 3rd edition, 2001), pp. xvii–xxx.

Byrne, F.J., 'Historical note on Cnogba (Knowth)', in *PRIA* vol. lxvi (1968), pp. 397.

—, 'Ireland before the Norman Invasion', in T.W. Moody (ed.), *Irish Historiography 1936–70* (1971).

—, 'MacNeill the historian', in F.X. Martin and F.J. Byrne (eds), *The Scholar Revolutionary: Eoin MacNeill (1867–1945)* (Shannon: IUP, 1973), pp. 5–36.

Cahill, Mary, 'Some unrecorded Bronze Age Gold Ornaments from Co. Limerick', *NMAJ* vol. xxxv (1993–4), pp. 33–4.

Cahill Wilson, Jacqueline, *Late Iron Age and Roman Ireland* (Discovery Programme, 2014).

Carew, Mairéad, *Tara and the Ark of the Covenant* (Dublin, 2003).

—, 'The Glamour of Ancient Greatness': the importance of the 1927 Lithberg Report to Irish Archaeology', *Archaeology Ireland* vol. xxii, no. 1 issue no. 83 (Spring 2008), pp. 20–2.

—, 'Politics and the definition of National Monuments: the 'Big House problem', *JIA* vol. xviii (2009), pp. 129–39.

—, 'The Harvard Mission, Eugenics and the Celts', *Archaeology Ireland* vol. xxvi, no. 4, issue no. 102 (Winter 2012), pp. 38–40.

—, 'Eoin MacNeill and the Promotion of Celtic Studies in America', *History Hub* special 2013 series on 'Eoin MacNeill: Revolutionary and Scholar', School of History and Archives, UCD, www.historyhub.ie.

—, 'The Pageant of the Celt': Irish archaeology at the Chicago World Fair', *Archaeology Ireland* vol. xxviii, no. 1 (Spring 2014), pp. 9–12.

—, 'Eoin MacNeill: Revolutionary Cultural Ideologue', *1916 Birth Pangs of a Nation? Studies* (Spring 2016), vol. cv, no. 417, pp. 67-75.

Carey, John, *The Irish National Origin-Legend: Synthetic Pseudohistory.* Quiggin Pamphlets on the Sources of Mediaeval Gaelic History i (Cambridge, 1994).

Castle, Gregory, *Modernism and the Celtic Revival* (Cambridge, 2001).

Caulfield, Seamus, 'Some Celtic Problems in the Irish Iron Age', in Donnchadh Ó Corráin (ed.) *Irish Antiquity, Essays and Studies presented to M.J. O'Kelly* (Cork, 1981, reprinted 1994).

Chapman, Malcolm, *The Celts: The Construction of a Myth* (London, 1992).

Charlesworth, J.K. and Macalister, R.A.S., 'The Alleged Palaeolithic Implements of Sligo', in *PRIA* vol. xxxix (1929–1931), pp. 18–19.

Childe, V. Gordon, *The Danube in Prehistory* (Oxford, 1929).

—, 'Scottish Megalithic Tombs and their Affinities', *TGAS* (1931–3), pp. 120–37.

—, 'The Archaeology of Cornwall and Scilly by H. O'Neill Hencken', *AJ* vol. xii (1932), p. 460.

—, *The Prehistory of Scotland* (London, 1935).

—, *Social Evolution* (London, 1951).

—, 'Retrospect', in *Antiquity* vol. xxxii (1958), pp. 69–74.

—, *The Aryans: A Study of Indo-European Origins* (New York, [1926] 1993).

Clapham, A.W., 'Notes on the origins of Hiberno-Saxon art', in *Antiquity* vol. viii (1934).

Clark, Grahame, 'Upper Palaeolithic Man in Ireland?' in *PPS* vol. ii, parts 1 and 2 (1936), pp. 241–2.

—, 'A Premium on Antiquity' in *PPS* vol. ii, parts 1 and 2 (1936), pp. 242–3.

—, 'The Bann Culture of Northern Ireland', *PPS* vol. ii part 1 & 2 (1936), p. 243.

—, *Archaeology and Society* (Suffolk, 1957).

—, *Prehistory at Cambridge and Beyond* (1989).

Cleary, R., 'The later Bronze Age at Lough Gur: filling in the blanks', in E. Shee-Twohig and M. Ronayne (eds), *Past perceptions: the prehistoric archaeology of south-west Ireland* (Cork 1993), pp. 114–120.

—, 'Later Bronze Age settlement and prehistoric burials, Lough Gur, Co. Limerick', *PRIA* 95C (1995), pp. 1–92.

—, 'Enclosed Late Bronze Age habitation site and boundary wall at Lough Gur, Co. Limerick', *PRIA* vol. ciii (2003), pp. 97–189.

Clifford, James, 'Museums as Contact Zones' in Boswell, David and Evans, Jessica (eds), *Representing the Nation: a Reader Histories, Heritage and Museums* (London and New York, 2005), pp. 435–57.

Cline, Walter, *Mining and Metalllurgy in Negro Africa*, General Series in Anthropology, no. 5 (Menasha, Wisconsin, 1937).

Cochrane, Robert, 'Notes on the 'Ancient Monuments Protection (Ireland) Act 1892' and the previous legislation connected therewith', in *JRSAI*, vol. xii (1892), pp. 411–29.

—, 'On Broighter, Limavady, County Londonderry and on the find of Gold Ornaments there in 1896', *JRSAI* vol. xxxii (1902), pp. 211–24.

Coffey, George, 'Some Monuments of the La Tène period', in *PRIA* vol. xxiv (1904), pp. 257–266.

—, 'Archaeological evidence for the Intercourse of Gaul with Ireland before the first Century', in *PRIA* vol. xxviii (1910), pp. 96–106.

— and R.L.l. Praeger, 'The Antrim Raised Beach: A Contribution to the Neolithic History of the North of Ireland', in *PRIA* vol. xxv (1904), pp. 143–200.

Coles, Bryony, 'Anthropomorphic Wooden Figures from Britain and Ireland', *PPS* vol. lvi (1990), pp. 315–33.

Collins, A.E.P., 'Excavations in Lough Faughan Crannóg, County Down', in *UJA* vol. xviii (1951–1952), pp. 45–82.

—, 'Further Investigations in the Dundrum Sandhills', in *UJA* vol. xxii (1959), pp. 5–20.

Collis, John, 'A Brief History of the Irish Question – a Study of Ethnicity in action', in Graves-Brown, Paul, Jones, Sian and Gamble, Clive (eds), *Cultural Identity and Archaeology The Construction of European Communities* (London & New York 1996), pp. 167–9.

—, 'Celtic Myths', in *Antiquity* vol. lxxi, no. 271 (Mar 1997), pp. 195–201.

Condit, Tom, Review article, 'The Iron Age Conundrum', in *Archaeology Ireland* vol. viii (Autumn 1994), p. 30.

Coon, C.S., *Races of Europe* (New York, 1939).

Cooney, Gabriel, 'Theory and Practice in Irish Archaoeology', in Ucko, Peter J., *Theory in Archaeology A World Perspectice* (London and New York, 1995), pp. 263–77.

—, Editorial, *Archaeology Ireland*, vol. x, no. 35 (Spring, 1996), p. 3.

—, 'Building the Future on the Past: Archaeology and the Construction of National Identity in Ireland' in Díaz-Andreu, Margarita and Champion, Timothy (eds), *Nationalism and Archaeology in Europe* (London, 1997), pp. 146–63.

—, 'The Legacy of Seán P. Ó Ríordáin', *Archaeology Ireland* vol. xi , no. 4 (Winter 1997), pp. 30–31.

—, 'In Retrospect, Neolithic activity at Knockadoon, Lough Gur, Co. Limerick, 50 years on', *PRIA* vol. cvii (2007).

Corlett, Christian, 'The Tara Broadcast', *Ríocht na Midhe* vol. xiv (2003), pp. 5–21.

—, 'The Royal Society of Antiquaries of Ireland and the protection of monuments (part I), *JRSAI* vol. cxxxix (2009), pp. 80–100.

—, 'The Royal Society of Antiquaries of Ireland and the protection of monuments (part II) *JRSAI* vol. cxli (2011), pp. 167–89.

—, 'The Royal Society of Antiquaries of Ireland and the protection of monuments (part III)', *JRSAI* vols cxlii–cxliii (2012–2013), pp. 166–83.

Cotter, Claire, Cahercommaun Fort, Co. Clare: A reassessment of its cultural context', *Discovery Programme Reports* vol. v (RIA, 1999), pp. 41–95.

Crawford, O.G.S., 'A Prehistoric Invasion of England', *AJ* vol. ii (1922), pp. 27–35.

—, Editorial Notes, *Antiquity* vol. i (1927), p. 1.

Crooke, Elizabeth, *Politics, Archaeology and the Creation of a National Museum of Ireland An Expression of National Life* (Dublin, 2000).

Crossman, Virginia and McLoughlin, Dympna, 'A Peculiar Eclipse: E. Estyn Evans and Irish Studies', in the *Irish Review*, no. 15 (Belfast, 1994), pp. 79–96.

Currell, Susan and Cogdell, Christina (eds), *Popular Eugenics, National efficiency and American mass culture in the 1930s* (Athens, Ohio, 2006).

Curtis, L. Perry Jr., *Apes and Angels The Irishman in Victorian Caricature* (Washington and London, 1997).

Daly, Mary E., *Dublin: The Deposed Capital.* (Cork, 1985).

—, 'Frugal Comfort or Lavish Austerity? The Economic Desiderata of Irish Nationalism', *Éire-Ireland* xxix, no. 4 (Winter 1994), pp. 78–100.

Daniel, Glyn E., 'Archaeology and Television', in *Antiquity* vol. xxviii (1954), pp. 201–5.

—, *The Idea of Prehistory in the Study of Language and Race, and in Politics* (London, 1962).

—, 'Editorial' [Obituary of Hugh O'Neill Hencken] in *Antiquity* vol. lvi, no. 216 (March 1982), pp. 1–7.

—, 'An Appreciation of Seán P. Ó Ríordáin', *University Review* vol. ii, no. 1 (Spring, 1960), pp. 59–61.'

Davies, O., Review Essay, 'A. Mahr, New Aspects and Problems in Irish Prehistory (PPS Presidential Address, 1937)', in *UJA* vol. ii (1939), pp. 123–7.

— and Estyn Evans, 'Excavations at Goward, near Hilltown, Co. Down', *PBNHPS* (1932–1933), pp. 1–16.

Delaney, Paul, *Seán O'Faoláin, Literature, Inheritance and the 1930s* (Dublin, 2014).

de Navarro, J.M., *A Survey of Research on an Early Phase of Celtic Culture.* (London, 1936).

—, 'Hector Munro Chadwick 1870–1947', in *PBA* vol. xxxiii (1947), pp. 307–30.

de Valera, R., 'The Court Cairns of Ireland', *PRIA* vol. lx, section C (1960), pp. 40–8.

di Mambro, Veronica, 'The University of Cambridge Eugenics Society from 1911–1913 and 1930–1933 and reasons for its ultimate demise', https://mediachecker.wordpress.com

Dixon, Roland B., *The Racial History of Man* (1923).

Dooley, Terence, *The Decline of the Big House in Ireland: A Study of Irish landed families.* (Dublin, 2001).

Doorley, Michael, '"The Judge" versus "The Chief" – Daniel Cohalan and the 1920 split within Irish America', *History Ireland* vol. xxiii, no. 2, p. 45.

Dowd, Marion, 'Kilgreany Co. Waterford: Biography of a Cave', *JIA* vol. xi (2002).

Duggan, John P., *Neutral Ireland and the Third Reich* (Dublin, 1989).

Dunleavy, Janet Egleson and Dunleavy, Gareth W., *Douglas Hyde, A Maker of Modern Ireland* (Oxford, 1991).

Durkheim, Emile, *The Elementary Forms of Religious Life* (Oxford University Press, 2009).

Editor's note, 'The Sligo Archaeological Discovery', in *The Catholic Bulletin* (1928), p. 369.

Editorial Board, 'The Celts in Archaeology', in *UJA* vol. ii (1939), pp. 137–47.

Erdtman, G. Studies in the Postarctic History of the Forests of Northwestern Europe. *Geol. Foren. i Stockholm Forhandl.*, Bd. 50 (1928), pp. 123 92.

Evans, Christopher, 'Archaeology in modern times: Bersu's Woodbury 1938 & 1939', in *Antiquity* vol. lxiii (1989), pp. 436–50.

Evans, E. Estyn, 'Excavations at Aghnaskeagh, Co. Louth, Cairn A', *JCLAS* vol. viii, no. 3 (1935), pp. 234-55.

—, 'Excavations at Aghnaskeagh, Co. Louth, Cairn B, Irish Free State Scheme of Archaeological Research', in *JCLAS* vol. ix (1937), pp. 1–18.

—, 'Archaeological Investigations in Northern Ireland A Summary of Recent Work', in *Antiquaries Journal* vol. xv (1935), pp. 165–73.

—, *Irish Heritage: the Landscape, the People and their Work* (Dundalk, 1942).

—, 'The Irish Stone Age' *JCLAS* vol. x, no. 3 (1943), p. 263.

—, 'The Irish Stone Age: Its Chronology, Development and Relationships by Hallam L. Movius', *Geographical Review*, vol. xxxiv, no. 1 (Jan.1944), pp. 168–9.

—, 'The Cultural Landscape of Celtic Countries: a Review', in *The Scottish Geographical Journal* vol. lxxiv, no. 3 (December 1958), pp. 189–90.

—, *Prehistoric and Early Christian Ireland* (London, 1966).

—, 'Archaeology in Ulster since 1920', *UJA* vol. xxxi (1968), pp. 3–8.

—, *The Personality of Ireland Habitat, Heritage and History* (Dublin, 1992).

—, *Ireland and the Atlantic Heritage* (1996).

— and Gaffikin, M., 'Belfast Naturalists' Field Club Survey of Antiquities, Megaliths and Raths', in *INJ* vol. v, no. 10 (1935), pp. 242–52.

— and Mitchell, G.F., 'The Irish Stone Age by Hallam L. Movius', *UJA*, vol. vi (1943), pp. 145–7.

— and Davies, O., 'Irish Court Cairns', in *UJA* vol. xxiv–xxv (1962).

Evans, Sir John, 'On some discoveries of stone Implements in Lough Neagh, Ireland', in *Archaeologia*, vol. xli (1867), pp. 397–408.

Fagette, Paul, *Digging for Dollars: American Archaeology and the New Deal* (University of New Mexico Press, Albuquerque, 1996).

Fagan, Brian, *A Brief History of Archaeology Classical Times to the Twenty-First Century* (New Jersey, 2005).

Fallon, Brian, *An Age of Innocence Irish Culture 1930-1960* (Dublin, 1998).

Fanning, Charles, 'Duelling Cultures: Ireland and Irish America at the Chicago World's Fairs of 1933 and 1934', *New Hibernia Review* vol. xv, no. 3 (Autumn 2011).

Fanning, T., 'Some aspects of the Bronze Ringed Pin in Scotland' in A. O' Connor and D. Clarke (eds), *From the Stone Age to the 'Forty Five'* (Edinburgh, 1983).

Farley, Julia and Hunter, Fraser (eds), *Celts, Art and Identity* (London 2015).

Fisk, Robert, *In Time of War: Ireland, Ulster and the Price of Neutrality, 1939–45* (Dublin, 1983).

Fitzpatrick, Andrew P., 'Celtic Iron Age Europe, the theoretical basis', in Graves-Brown, Paul, Jones, Sian and Gamble, Clive (eds), *Cultural Identity and Archaeology The Construction of European Communities* (London & New York 1996), pp. 250–1.

Fitzpatrick Dean, Joan, *All dressed up: Modern Irish historical pageantry* (Syracuse University Press, 2014).

Fleure, H.J., 'Alfred Cort Haddon 1855–1940', Obituary Notice Fellow of the Royal Society vol. iii, no. 9 (Jan 1941), http://rsbm.royalsocietypublishing. org.

Foucault, Michael, *The Order of Things* (New York, 1973).

Forsyth, William H., 'An Irish Royal Residence of the Seventh to Tenth Centuries A.D. by Hugh Hencken', in *American Journal of Archaeology* vol. lvii, no. 12 (April 1953), pp. 156–7.

Fowler, Don D., 'Uses of the Past: Archaeology in the Service of the State', in *American Antiquity* vol. lii, no. 2 (1987), pp. 229–48.

Fox, Cyril, Review Article, 'Christian Art in Ancient Ireland, vol. 1 Edited by Dr. Adolf Mahr, Keeper of Irish Antiquities, National Museum, Dublin, Dublin 1932', in *Man* vol xxxii (Sept. 1932), pp. 219–20.

Frazer, W., 'A Contribution to Irish Archaeology', *JRSAI* vol. i, no. 5 (First Quarter, 1891), pp. 391–404.

Fredengren, Christina, *Crannógs: A Study of People's Interaction with Lakes, with Particular Reference to Lough Gara in the North-West of Ireland* (Dublin, 2002).

Friedlaender, Jonathan, with contributions from Pilbeam, David, Hrdy, Daniel, Giles, Eugene and Green, Roger, 'William W. Howells 1908–2005' in *Biographical Memoirs of the National Academy of Sciences of the United States of America*, http:www.nasonline.org, pp. 3–18.

Garn, Stanley M. and Giles, Eugene, 'Earnest Albert Hooton November 20, 1887 – May 3, 1954', Biographical Memoir of the National Academy of Sciences of the United States of America, http:www.nasonline.org.

Garvin, Tom, *Nationalist Revolutionaries in Ireland* (Oxford, 1987).

Gathercole, Peter, 'Gordon Childe: Man or Myth?' in *Antiquity*, vol. lvi (1982).

Gellner, Ernest, *Nations and Nationalism* (London, 1983).

Gerig, John L., 'Celtic Studies in the United States', in *The Columbia University Quarterly*, vol. xix, no. 1 (December 1916).

Gibbon, Peter and Curtin, Chris, 'The stem family in Ireland', *Comparative studies in society and history* vol. xx, no. 3 (1978), pp. 429–453.

Gibbons, Erin, *The Hunt Controversy* (Centre Simon Wiesenthal, 2006).

Gillespie, Raymond and Kennedy, Brian P. (eds), *Ireland Art into History* (Dublin, 1994).

Glassie, Henry, 'E.Estyn Evans and the Interpretation of the Irish Landscape', in Alvin Jackson and David N. Livingstone, *Queen's Thinkers Essays on the Intellectual Heritage of a University* (Belfast, 2009).

Gogan, Liam S. 'America's Archaeologists in Ireland, The Harvard Archaeological and Anthropological Expeditions', in *Irish Travel* (December 1932).

—, 'Carn Tighearnaigh Mhic Dheaghaidh', in *JCHAS* (Jul–Dec, 1929), p. 70.

Goodman, David, 'Fear of Circuses Founding the National Museum of Victoria', in David Boswell and Jessica Evans (eds), *Representing the Nation: a Reader Histories, Heritage and Museums* (London and New York, 2005), pp. 258–70.

Gould, Stephen J., 'In the Mind of the Beholder' *Natural History* (February 1994).

—, *The Mismeasure of Man* (London, 1996).

Graham, Brian J. 'Heritage Conservation and Revisionist Nationalism in Ireland' in G.J. Ashworth and P. Larkham, *Building a New Heritage* (London, 1994).

Graham-Campbell, J., *Viking Artefacts: A Select Catalogue* (London, 1980).

Graves-Brown, Paul, Jones, Sian and Gamble, Clive, *Cultural Identity and Archaeology The Construction of European Communities* (London and New York, 1996).

Green, Sally, *Prehistorian A Biography of V. Gordon Childe* (Wiltshire, 1981).

Grogan, Eoin., *The North Munster Project Volume 2: the prehistoric landscape of North Munster* (Dublin, 2005), pp. 47–62.

— and Eogan, George, 'Lough Gur Excavations by Seán P. Ó Ríordáin: further Neolithic and Beaker habitations on Knockadoon', *PRIA* vol. 87C.

Guglielmi, Alexandra, 'My kingdom for a pot! A reassessment of the Iron Age and Roman material from Lagore crannóg, Co. Meath', in Graeme JR Erskine, Piotr Jacobsson, Paul Miller and Scott Stetkiewicz, *Proceedings of the 17th Iron Age Research Student Symposium* (Edinburgh, 2014), pp. 12–19.

Guinness, Desmond, 'The Irish Georgian Society: The First Thirty Years' in *BIGS* vol. xxxi (1998).

Haddon, A.C. and Browne, C.R., 'The Ethnography of the Aran Islands, County Galway', in *PRIA* vol. xxxix (1892), pp. 768–830.

Hale, Christopher, *Himmler's Crusade The Nazi Expedition to find the Origins of the Aryan Race* (New Jersey, 2006).

Hamlin, Ann, 'Emyr Estyn Evans, 1905–1989', in *Archaeology Ireland* vol. iii, no. 3 (Autumn 1989), p. 115.

Harbison, Peter, *Pilgrimage in Ireland: the Monuments and the People* (Dublin, 1991).

Haag, W., 'Federal Aid to Archaeology in the Southeast, 1933–1942', *American Antiquity* 50 (2) 1985.

Hawkes, Christopher, 'British Hill Forts, A Retrospect', in *Antiquity* vol. v. no. 17 (1931), pp. 60–97.

—, 'The ABC of the British Iron Age', *Antiquity* vol. xxxiii (1959), pp. 170–82.

Hawkes, Jacquetta, 'Robert Eric Mortimer Wheeler, 1890–1976', in *PBA* vol. lxiii (1978), pp. 483–507.

Hugh O'Neill Hencken, *Archaeology of Cornwall and Scilly* (London, 1932).

—, 'A Gaming board of the Viking Age', *Acta Archaeologica* vol iv (1933), pp. 85–104.

—, 'Harvard and Irish Archaeology' in *The Irish Review*, vol. i, no. 1 (April 1934).

—, A Cairn at Poulawack County Clare, with a report on the Human Remains by Hallam L. Movius, in *JRSAI* vol. lxv (1935), pp. 191–222.

—, 'Ballinderry Crannóg no. 1', in *PRIA* vol. xliii (1935–7), pp. 103–237.

—, 'Cahercommaun: A Stone Fort in County Clare', in *JRSAI* extra vol. (1938), pp. 1–82.

—, 'A Long Cairn at Creevykeel, Co. Sligo', in *JRSAI* vol. lxix, part ii (1939), pp. 53–98.

—, 'Archaeological Notes, The Harvard Archaeological Expedition in Ireland', in *AJA*, vol. xlv, no. 1 (Jan–Mar 1941), pp. 1–6.

—, 'Ballinderry Crannóg No. 2' in *PRIA* (1942) vol. xlvii, sect C, pp. 1–76.

—, with sections by Liam Price and Laura E. Start, 'Lagore Crannóg: an Irish Royal Residence of the 7th to 10th Centuries AD', in *PRIA* vol. liii (1950–51), pp. 1–247.

—, *Indo-European Languages and Archaeology: American Anthropologist*, vol. lvii, No. 6, Part 3, Memoir 84 (December 1955).

—, *Memories of Work and Travel* (privately published 1981).

— and Hallam L. Movius, 'The Cemetery-Cairn of Knockast', in *PRIA* vol. xli, Section C, No. 11 (1934), pp. 232–84.

Henchy, P., 'Nelson's Pillar', in *Dublin Historical Record* vol. x (Jun–Aug, 1940), pp. 53–63.

Henry, Francoise, 'Hanging bowls', in *JRSAI* vol. lxvi (1936), pp. 209–46.

—, *Irish Art in the Early Christian Period* (1940).

Herity, Michael, 'Roman invaders were more likely native Irish traders', *Irish Times*, 24 January 1996.

Hobson, Bulmer (ed.), *Saorstát Eireann Irish Free State Official Handbook* (Dublin, 1932).

Holmes, David G., 'The Eucharistic Congress of 1932 and Irish Identity', in *New Hibernia Review* vol. iv, no. 1 (Spring 2000), pp. 55–78.

Holmes, W.H., 'Biographical Memoir of Lewis Henry Morgan, 1818–1881, read before the National Academy of Sciences November 20, 1907', in *Biographical Memoirs of the National Academy of Sciences of the United States of America*, http:www.nasonline.org.

Hobsbawm, Eric and Ranger, Terence, *The Invention of Tradition* (Cambridge, 1992).

Hooke, B.G.E. and Morant, G.M., 'The Present State of our Knowledge of British Craniology in Late Prehistoric and Historic Times', *Biometrika* vol. xviii (1926), pp. 99–104.

Hooton, Earnest A., *Up from the Ape* (New York, 1936).

—, *Apes, Men, and Morons* (New York, 1937).

—, *Twilight of Man* (New York, 1939).

—, 'Stature, Head Form and Pigmentation of Adult Male Irish', *AMPA* vol. xxvi (1940), pp. 229–49.

—, H. Dawson and C. Wesley Dupertuis, *The Physical Anthropology of Ireland, with a Section on the West Coast Irish Females by Helen Dawson* (Harvard, 1955).

Howells, W.W., 'The Early Christian Irish The Skeletons at Gallen Priory', in *PRIA* vol. xlvi (1940–1941), pp. 103–219.

—, 'Carleton Stevens Coon 1904–1981', *Biographical Memoirs of the National Academy of Sciences of the United States of America*, http://www.nasaonline.org.

Hrdlička, Aleš, 'The Principal Dimensions, Absolute and Relative, of the Humerus in the White Race', *AJPA* vol. xvi (1932), pp. 431–50.

Hull, Mark, *Irish Secrets: German Espionage in Ireland, 1939–45* (Portland, Oregan and Dublin, 2003).

Hutchinson, John, 'Archaeology and the Irish Rediscovery of the Celtic Past', in *Nations and Nationalism* vol. vii, no. 4 (2001), pp. 505–19.

Hyde, Douglas, 'The Necessity for de-Anglicising Ireland', in Charles Gavan Duffy, George Sigerson and Douglas Hyde (eds), *The Revival of Irish Literature* (London, 1894), pp. 117–61.

Ireland, Aideen, 'The Royal Society of Antiquaries of Ireland 1849–1900', in *JRSAI* vol. cxii (1982), pp. 72–92.

Isaac, G.R., 'The Origins of the Celtic Languages: Language Spread from East to West', in Barry Cunliffe and John T. Koch (eds), *Celtic from the West: Alternative Perspectives from Archaeology, Genetics, Language and Literature* (Oxford, 2010), pp. 153–67.

Jackson, J. Wilfrid, 'On the Diatomaceous Deposit of the Lower Bann Valley, Counties Antrim and Derry, and Prehistoric Implements found therein', in *Memoirs and Proceedings of the Manchester Literary and Philosophical Society* vol. liii (1909).

Jackson, Kenneth, Obituary 'Nora Kershaw Chadwick, 1891–1972', *PBA* vol. lviii (1972), pp. 258–270.

James, Simon, *The Atlantic Celts Ancient People or Modern Invention?* (University of Wisconsin Press, 1999).

Jessen, Knud and Farrington, A. 'The bogs at Ballybetagh, near Dublin, with remarks on late-glacial conditions in Ireland', *PRIA* vol. xliv (1937–1938). pp. 205–60.

Johnson, Ruth, 'Ballinderry Crannóg No. 1: a Reinterpretation', *PRIA* vol. xcix (1999), pp. 23–71.

Jones, Carleton, *Temples of Stone, Exploring the Megalithic Monuments of Ireland* (Dublin, 2013).

Jones, Greta, 'Eugenics in Ireland: the Belfast Eugenics Society, 1911–15', in *IHS* vol. xxviii (1992–3).

Jones, Sian, *The Archaeology of Ethnicity: Constructing Identities in the Past and Present* (London & New York, 1997).

Jones, W.G., *The Wynnes of Sligo and Leitrim* (Manorhamilton, 1994).

Kane, Susan (ed.), *The Politics of Archaeology and Identity in a Global Context* (Boston, 2003).

Keith, Sir Arthur, *New Discoveries Relating to the Antiquity of Man* (New York, 1931).

Kelly, D.H., 'An Artificial Island and certain Antiquities recently discovered near Strokestown', in *PRIA* vol. v (1851), pp. 208–14.

Kendrick, T.D., 'British Hanging Bowls, in *Antiquity*, vol. vi (1932).

—, 'Gallen Priory excavations, 1934–1935', in *JRSAI* vol. lxix (1939), pp. 1–20.

Kennedy, Michael and McMahon, Deirdre, *Reconstructing Ireland's Past. A History of the Irish Manuscripts Commission* (Irish Manuscripts Commission 2009).

Kennedy, Brian P., 'The Failure of the Cultural Republic: Ireland 1922–39, in *Studies* (Spring 1992), pp. 14–22.

Kenny, Kevin, *The American Irish A History* (Essex and New York).

Keogh, Dermot, *The Vatican, the Bishops and Irish Politics 1919–1939* (Cambridge, 1986).

—, *Jews in Twentieth-Century Ireland: Refugees, Anti-Semitism and the Holocaust* (Cork, 1998).

Keynes, John Maynard, 'National Self-Sufficiency', *Studies*, vol. xxii, no. 86 (Jun 1933).

Kiberd, Declan and Mathews, P.J. (eds), *Handbook of the Irish Revival: An Anthology of Irish Cultural and Political Writings 1891–1922* (Dublin, 2015).

Kilbride-Jones, Howard, 'The excavation of a composite tumulus at Drimnagh, Co. Dublin', *JRSAI*, vol. ix no. 4 (31 December 1939), pp. 190-220.

—, 'Citizen Keane: A memoir of excavation in the thirties', *Archaeology Ireland* vol. v, no. 3 (Autumn 1991), pp. 11-12.

—, 'Macalister, Leask and Ó Ríordáin', in *Archaeology Ireland*, vol. vi, no. 4 (Winter, 1992), pp. 14–15.

Klein, Barbro, 'Cultural Heritage, the Swedish Folklife Sphere, and the Others' in *Cultural Analysis* 5 (2006).

Knowles, W.J., 'Prehistoric Stone Implements from the River Bann and Lough Neagh', in *PRIA* vol. xxx (1912–1913), pp. 195–222.

Kohl, Philip L. and Fawcett, Clare (eds), *Nationalism, Politics, and the Practice of Archaeology* (Cambridge, 1995).

Kuhn, Thomas S., *The Structure of Scientific Revolutions* (Chicago [1962], 1970).

Laswell, Harold, 'Censorship' in ERA Seligman (ed.), *Encyclopaedia of the Social Sciences* (New York, Macmillan, 1930).

Layard, Nina F., 'The Older Series of Irish Flint Implements', *Man* vol. ix (1909), pp. 81–5.

Leask, Harold G., *Séadcomartaí Náisiúnta Saorstáit Éireann The National Monuments of the Irish Free State* (Dublin, 1936).

— and Price, Liam, 'The Labbacallee Megalith', in *PRIA* vol. xliii (1935–1937), pp. 77–104.

Lee, J.J., *Ireland 1912–1985* (Cambridge; Cambridge University Press 1985).

Lee, J.J. and Casey, Marion R. (eds) Casey, *Making the Irish American, History and Heritage of the Irish in the United States* (New York, 2006).

Leerssen, Joep, *Remembrance and Imagination Patterns in the Historical and Literary Representation of Ireland in the Nineteenth Century* (Cork, 1996).

—, *Mere Irish and Fíor Ghael* (Cork, 1996).

Leone, M. P., 'Symbolic, Structural and Critical Archaeology', in David J. Meltzer, Don D. Fowler and Jeremy Sabloff (eds), *American Archaeology Past and Future: A Celebration of the Society of American Archaeology 1935-1985* (Smithsonian Institution Press, 1986).

Lyman, R. Lee, O'Brien, Michael J. and Dunnell, Robert C., *The Rise and Fall of Culture History* (New York, 1997).

Levine, Philippa, *The Amateur and the Professional. Antiquarians, Historians and Archaeologists in Victorian England, 1838-1886* (Cambridge, 1986).

Liversage, G.D., 'Excavations at Dalkey Island, County Dublin, 1956-1959', in *PRIA* vol. lxvi (1967-1968).

Lohan, Rena, *Guide to the Archives of the Office of Public Works* (Dublin, 1994).

Long, Patrick, 'Lawlor, Henry Cairnes', in www.dib.cambridge.org.

Lowie, Robert H., 'Obituary Edward B. Tylor', *American Anthropologist*, New Series vol. xix, no. 2 (April–June 1917), pp. 262–8.

Lubbock, Sir John, *Prehistoric Times* (London, 1869).

Lukes, Stephen, *Emile Durkheim: His Life and Work: A Historical and Critical Study* (Stanford, 1986).

Lynn, C.J., 'Some 'early' Ring-forts and Crannógs', *JIA* vol. i (1983), pp. 52–3.

—, 'Lagore, County Meath and Ballinderry No. 1, County Westmeath Crannógs: Some Possible Structural Reinterpretations', in *JIA* vol. iii (1985-1986), pp. 69–73.

Lysaght, Patricia, 'Swedish Ethnological Surveys in Ireland 1934-5 and their aftermath', in H. Cheape (ed.), *Tools and Traditions, Studies in European Ethnology presented to Alexander* Fenton (Edinburgh, 1993), pp. 22–32.

Maas, John, 'Letter to the Romans John Maas Replies', in *Archaeology Ireland* vol. x, no. 2 (Summer 1996), p. 38.

Macalister, R.A.S., *Ireland in Pre-Celtic Times* (Dublin & London, 1921).

—, *The Present and Future of Archaeology in Ireland* (Dublin, 1925).

—, 'Some Unsolved Problems in Irish Archaeology: an Address delivered to the Academy', in *PRIA* vol. xxxvii, section C., no. 12 (June, 1927).

—, 'On some Antiquities Discovered upon Lambay', in *PRIA* vol. xxxviii (1928-1929), pp. 240–6.

—, *Ancient Ireland, a Study in the Lessons of Archaeology and History* (London, 1935).

—, 'The Excavation of Kiltera, Co. Waterford', in *PRIA* vol. xliii (1935–1937), pp. 1–16.

—, 'The Irish Stone Age by Hallam L. Movius', *JGAHS* vol. xx, no. 3/4 (1943), pp. 190–1.

—, *Archaeology of Ireland* (London [1927] 3rd edn. 1949).

—, E.C.R. Armstrong, and R. Ll. Praeger, 'Report on the Exploration of Bronze-Age Carns on Carrowkeel Mountain, Co. Sligo', in PRIA vol. xxix (1911–12), pp. 311–47.

— and R. Lloyd Praeger, 'The Excavation of an Ancient Structure on the Townland of Togherstown, Co. Westmeath', in *PRIA* vol. xxxix (1929–1931), pp. 54–83.

MacNeill, Eoin, *Phases of Irish History* ([New York & London 1919], reissued New York & London 1970).

—, *Celtic Ireland* (Dublin 1921, reprinted 1981).

—, 'The Pretanic Background in Britain and Ireland', *JRSAI* vol. lxiii (1933), pp. 1–28.

Mahr, Adolf, 'Archaeology', in *Saorstát Éireann Irish Free State Official Handbook* (Dublin, 1932), pp. 537–549.

—, 'The Origin of the Crannóg Type of Settlement', in *Proceedings of the First International Congress of Prehistoric and Protohistoric Sciences* (London, August 1–6, 1932), pp. 1–2.

—, *Christian Art in Ancient Ireland* (1932).

—, 'Quaternary Research in Ireland from the Archaeological Viewpoint', in *INJ* vol. v (January 1934–November 1935), pp. 137–44.

—, 'Quaternary Research in Ireland from the Archaeological Viewpoint', in *INJ* vol. v (January 1934–November 1935), pp. 137–44.

—, 'New Aspects and Problems in Irish Prehistory, Presidential Address for 1937, *PPS*, no. 11 (July–December, 1937), pp. 261–436.

Mallory, J.P., *The Origins of the Irish* (London, 2013).

Martin, Cecil P., *Prehistoric Man in Ireland* (London, 1935).

Markotic, Vladimir (ed.), *Ancient Europe and the Mediterranean Studies presented in honour of Hugh Hencken* (Wiltshire, 1977).

Martin, Peter, *Censorship in the Two Irelands* (Dublin, 2006).

Maume, Patrick, *D.P. Moran, Life and Times* (Dundalgan Press, 1995.)

—, *The Rise and Fall of Irish Ireland: D.P. Moran and Daniel Corkery* (Coleraine, 1996).

McCartney, D., *UCD – A National Idea: The History of University College, Dublin* (Dublin, 1999).

McCarthy, James and Hague, Euan, 'Race, Nation and Nature: The Cultural Politics of "Celtic" Identification in the American West', in *Annals of the Association of American Geographers*, vol. lxxxxiv, no. 2 (Jun 2004), pp. 387–408.

McCormack, W.J., *Dublin 1916 The French Connection* (Dublin 2012).

McElderry, R. Knox, 'Juvenal in Ireland', in the *Classical Review* vol. xvi (1922), pp. 151–162..

McLaughlin, John Gerard, *Irish Chicago, Images of America* (San Francisco, 2003).

Means, Bernard K. (ed.), *Shovel Ready: Archaeology and Roosevelt's New Deal for America* (The University of Alabama Press, 2013).

—, 'Labouring in the Fields of the Past: Geographic Variation in New Deal Archaeology Across the lower 48 United States', *Bulletin of the History of Archaeology*, vol. xxv (2), no. 7., published 27 May 2015. DOI: http://dx.doi.org/10.5334/bha.261.

Meek, Ronald M. (ed.), *Turgot on Progress, Sociology and Economics* (Cambridge, 2000).

Megaw, J.V.S. and Megaw, M.R., 'Ancient Celts and Modern Ethnicity', in *Antiquity* vol. lxx (1996), pp. 175–81.

—, 'The Mechanism of (Celtic) Dreams', in *Antiquity* vol. lxxii, no. 275 (March 1998), pp. 432–5.

Menotti, Francesco, *Living on the Lake in Prehistoric Europe 50 Years of Lake-Dwelling Research* (London & New York, 2004).

Messenger, John, 'Literary vs Scientific Interpretations of Cultural Reality in the Aran Islands of Éire', in *Ethnohistory*, vol. xi, no. 1 (Winter 1964).

Mitchell, G.F., 'A Pollen-Diagram from Lough Gur, County Limerick' (Studies in Irish Quaternary Deposits: no. 9) in *PRIA* vol. lvi (1953–1954), p. 481.

—, 'Voices from the Past; Three Antiquarian Letters', *JRSAI* vol. cxiii (1983) pp. 47–52.

Montagu, Ashley, 'Mans most Dangerous Myth: the Fallacy of Race;' see also www.understandingrace.org/history/science/critiquing_race.html.

Morant, G.M., 'A First Study of the Craniology of England and Scotland from Neolithic to early Historic times, with special reference to the Anglo-Saxon Skulls in London Museums', in *Biometrika*, vol. xviii (London, 1926), pp. 56–98.

—, 'The Craniology of Ireland', in *JRAI* vol. lxvi (London, 1936), pp. 43–55.

Morris, E., 'A Northern Scholar in Co. Sligo': First Essays for Sligo Field Club, in Martin A. Timoney (ed.), *A Celebration of Sligo* (2002).

Morris, Ian, *Archaeology as Cultural History Words and Things in Iron Age Greece* (Oxford, 2000).

Mount, Charles, 'Adolf Mahr's Excavations of an Early Bronze Age Cemetery at Keenoge, County Meath', in *PRIA* vol. xcvii (1997), pp. 1–68.

Movius, Hallam L. Jr., 'Kilgreany Cave, County Waterford', in *JRSAI* vol. v (1935), pp. 254–96.

—, 'A Stone Age Site at Glenarm, Co. Antrim', in *JRSAI* vol. lxvii (1937), pp. 181–220.

—, 'Report on a Stone Age Excavation at Rough Island, Strangford Lough, Co. Down', in *JRSAI* vol. lxx (1940), pp. 111–42.

—, 'An Early Post-Glacial Archaeological Site at Cushendun, County Antrim', in *PRIA* vol. xlvi (1940–1941), pp. 2–84.

—, *The Irish Stone Age: Its Chronology, Development and Relationships.* (Cambridge, 1942).

—, '*Geographical Review*', vol. xxxiv, no. 1 (Jan.1944), pp. 168–9.

—, 'Archaeological Research in Northern Ireland: An Historical Account of the Investigations at Larne', in *UJA* vol. xvi (1953).

—, 'Curran Point, Larne, County Antrim: The Type Site of the Irish Mesolithic', in *PRIA* vol. lvi, section c. no. 1 (1953).

—, Knud Jessen, V. Gordon Childe and C. Blake Whelan, 'A Neolithic Site on the River Bann', *PRIA* vol. xliii (1935–1937), pp. 17–40.

Moynihan, Maurice (ed.), *Speeches and Statements by Éamon de Valera 1917–1973* (Dublin, 1980).

Mullins, Gerry, 'Letters from our No. One Nazi' in *Irish Times* 19 September 2000.

—, *Dublin Nazi No. 1 The Life of Adolf Mahr* (Dublin, 2007).

Murray, L.P., 'The Cemetery-Cairn at Knockast' in *JCLAS*, vol. viii, no. 1 (1933), pp. 65–8.

Murray, David, *Museums – Their History and their Use* (Glasgow, 1904).

Murray, Tim, *From Antiquarian to Archaeologist: The History and Philosophy of Archaeology* (South Yorkshire, 2014).

Neill, Ken, 'The Broighter Hoard or how Carson caught the Boat, *Archaeology Ireland*, vol. vii, no. 2, issue no. 24 (1993), pp. 24–6.

Nelson, Bruce, *Irish Nationalists and the Making of the Irish Race* (Princeton, 2012), p. 234.

Newman, Conor, "Ballinderry Crannóg No. 2, Co. Offaly: Pre-Crannóg Early Medieval Horizon." *The Journal of Irish Archaeology*, vol. xi (2002), pp. 99–123.

Nic Ghabhann, Niamh, 'Medieval Ireland and the Shannon Hydro-Electric Scheme: reconstructing the past in independent Ireland', *Irish Studies Review*, vol. xxv, issue 4 (2017), pp. 425–43.

Nolan, Mark C., *Keynes in Dublin: Exploring the 1933 Finlay Lecture* (2013).

Nordenfalk, C., 'One hundred and Fifty Years of varying Views on the early Insular Gospel Books', in M. Ryan (ed.), *Ireland and Insular Art AD 500–1200: Conference Proceedings* (1987).

O'Brien, E., 'Iron Age Burial Practices in Leinster: Continuity and Change', in *Emania* vol. vi (Spring 1989), pp. 37–42.

—, 'Pagan and Christian Burial in Ireland during the First Millennium AD: Continuity and Change', in N. Edwards and A. Lane (eds), *The Early Church in Wales and the West* (Oxford, 1992), pp. 130–7.

—, 'Pagan or Christian? Burial in Ireland during the 5th to 8th Centuries AD', in N. Edwards (ed.), The *Archaeology of the Early Medieval Celtic Churches* (2009).

O'Brien, George, 'John Maynard Keynes', *Studies*, 27 April 1946.

Ó Catháin, Séamas, *Formation of a Folklorist: The visit of James Hamilton Delargy (Séamus Ó Duilearga) to Scandinavia, Finland, Estonia and Germany 1 April – 29 September 1928* (Dublin, 2008).

Ó Conaire, Brendan, *Douglas Hyde, Language Lore and Lyrics.* (Dublin, Irish Academic Press, 1986).

O'Donoghue, David, *Hitler's Irish Voices: The Story of German Radio's Wartime Irish Service* (Belfast, 1998) Rory O'Dwyer, 'On Show to the World: the Eucharistic Congress, 1932', in *History Ireland* (November/December 2007), pp. 42–7.

O'Driscoll, Mervyn, *Ireland, Germany and the Nazis, Politics and Diplomacy, 1919–1939* (Dublin, 2017).

O'Dwyer, Rory, *The Eucharistic Congress, Dublin 1932: An Illustrated History* (Dublin, 2009).

O'Ferrall, F., 'Daniel O'Connell, The 'Liberator', 1775–1847: Changing Images' in Raymond Gillespie and Brian P. Kennedy (eds), *Ireland Art into History* (Dublin, 1994).

O'Flaherty, J.T., 'A Sketch of the History and Antiquities of the Southern Islands of Aran, lying off the West Coast of Ireland; with Observations on the Religion of the Celtic Nations, Pagan Monuments of the early Irish, Druidic Rites, & Co.' in *TRIA* vol. xiv (1825).

O'Halpin, Eunan, *Defending Ireland: The Irish State and its Enemies Since 1922* (Oxford, 1999).

O hIceadha, Gearóid, 'The Moylisha Megalith, Co. Wicklow', *JRSAI* vol. 76, no. 3 (Oct 1946), pp. 120–7.

O'Mahony, Canon, *A History of the O'Mahony Septs* (Cork, 1913), reprinted from *JCHAS* vol. xii (1906).

O'Mahony, Patrick and Delanty, Gerard, *Rethinking Irish History: Nationalism, Identity and Ideology.* (Hampshire and New York, 2001).

Ó Raifeartaigh, T. (ed.), *The Royal Irish Academy: A Bicentennial History 1785–1985* (Dublin, 1985).

O Rahilly, T.F., 'The Goidels and their Predecessors', *PBA* vol. xxi (1936).

Ó Ríordáin, S.P., 'Palaeolithic Man in Ireland', *Antiquity*, vol. v (1931), pp. 360–2.

—, 'Excavations at Cush, Co. Limerick (1934 and 1935)', in *PRIA* vol. xlv (1938–1940).

—, 'Excavations at Lissard, Co. Limerick and other sites in the locality', *JRSAI* vol. xi (1936), pp. 173–85.

—, 'Post-war archaeology in Ireland', *Studies, An Irish Quarterly Review*, vol. xxxiii, no. 132 (Dec 1944).

—, 'Roman Material in Ireland', in *PRIA* vol. li (1945–8), pp. 35–82.

—, 'Prehistory in Ireland, 1937–1946', *PPS* no. 6 (1946), pp. 142–71.

—, 'Lough Gur Excavations: Neolithic and Bronze Age Houses on Knockadoon', in *PRIA* vol. lvi (1953–1954), pp. 297–459.

— and C.P. Martin, 'A Prehistoric Burial at Ringabella, Co. Cork', in *JRSAI* vol. lxiv (1934), pp. 86–9.

—, 'The excavation of a large earthen ring-fort at Garranes, Co. Cork', *PRIA* vol. xlvii (1942) pp. 77–150.

— and P. J. Hartnett, 'The Excavation of Ballycatteen Fort, Co. Cork, *PRIA* vol. 49 (1943/1944), pp. 1–43.

O'Sullivan, Aidan, *The Archaeology of Lake Settlement in Ireland:* Discovery Programme, Monograph 4 (Dublin, 1998).

—, 'The Harvard Archaeological Mission and the Politics of the Irish Free State', in *Archaeology Ireland* vol. xvii, no. 1, Issue no. 63 (Spring 2003), pp. 21–3.

—, Finbar McCormick, Thomas R. Kerr and Lorcan Harney, *Early Medieval Ireland AD 400–1100, The Evidence from Archaeological Excavations* (Dublin 2013).

O'Sullivan, Jerry, 'Nationalists, Archaeologists and the Myth of the Golden Age' in Michael A. Monk and John Sheehan, *Early Medieval Munster, Archaeology, History and Society* (Cork, 1998), pp. 178–89.

O'Sullivan, Muiris, 'The Life and Legacy of R.A.S. Macalister: a Century of Archaeology at UCD', in Gabriel Cooney, Katharina Becker, John Coles, Michael Ryan and Susanne Sievers (eds), *Relics of Old Decency: Archaeological Studies in Later Prehistory Festschrift for Barry Raftery* (Dublin, 2009), pp. 521–30.

Ó Súilleabháin, Seán, 'Folk-Museums in Scandinavia', in *JRSAI* vol. lxxv (945), pp. 62–9.

—, 'Foundation Sacrifices', in *JRSAI* vol. lxxv, no. 1 (1945), pp. 45–52.

Ó Tuama, Seán, *The Gaelic League Idea* (Dublin, 1972).

Ó Tuathaigh, Gearóid, 'Cultural Visions and the new State: Embedding and Embalming', in Gabriel Doherty and Dermot Keogh, *De Valera's Irelands* (Cork, 2003).

Peate, Iorwerth C., 'The Kelts in Britain', *Antiquity* 6 (1932), pp. 156–60.

Petrie, Flinders, *Methods and Aims in Archaeology* (London, 1904).

Phillips, C.W., *My Life in Archaeology* (Gloucester, 1987).

Phillips, Philip, 'Alfred Marston Tozzer, 1877–1954', *American Antiquity*, vol. xxi, no. 1 (Jul 1955), pp. 72–80.

Piggott, Stuart, *Ruins in a Landscape* (Edinburgh, 1976).

—, 'The Coming of the Celts: the Archaeological Argument', in G. MacEoin (ed.), *Proceedings of the Sixth International Congress of Celtic Studies* (1983), pp. 138–48.

Pogatchnik, Shawn, 'Experts claim Romans may have Established Colonies in Ireland', in *Los Angeles Times*, 7 November 1996.

Powell, T.G.E., *The Celts* (London 1958).

Power, Rev. Patrick, *Prehistoric Ireland: A Manual of Irish Pre-Christian Archaeology* (Dublin, 1925).

—, 'The Problem of the Celts', in *An Irish Quarterly Review* vol. xvi, no. 6 (Mar. 1927), pp. 99–114.

Praeger, Robert Lloyd, *The Way that I Went* (Cork, 1997).

Preucel, Robert and Hodder, Ian (eds), *Communicating Present Pasts: Contemporary Archaeology in Theory* (Oxford, 1996).

Price, David H., *Anthropological Intelligence: The Deployment and Neglect of American Anthropology in the Second World War* (Duke University Press, 2008).

Radcliffe-Brown, A.R., 'The Present Position of Anthropological Studies' in *Report of the British Association for the Advancement of Science* (1931), pp. 167–8.

Raftery, Barry, 'Irish Hill-forts', in C. Thomas (ed.), *The Iron Age in the Irish Sea Province* (London, 1972).

—, *La Tène in Ireland Problems of Origin and Chronology* (Marburg, 1984).

—, *Pagan Celtic Ireland: The Enigma of the Irish Iron Age* (London, 1994).

—, 'Drumanagh and Roman Ireland', in *Archaeology Ireland* vol. x, no. 1 (1996), pp. 17–19.

—, 'Celtic Ireland: Problems of Language, History and Archaeology', in Acta *Archaeologica, Academiae Scientiarum Hungaricae*, tomus lvii, fasciculi i–iii (2006), pp. 273–9.

Raftery, Joseph, 'Knocknalappa, Co. Clare', *NMAJ* vol. 1 (1936 1939).

—, 'Miscellanea, Excavation of Stone Circle and two Forts at Lough Gur (1937)', *NMAJ* vol i (1936–1939), p. 82.

—, 'The Irish Stone Age by Hallam L. Movius', *JRSAI* vol. xiii, no. 1 (1943), p. 26.

—, 'A Backward Look', in *Archaeology Ireland*, vol. ii, no. 1 (Spring 1988), pp. 22–4.

—, 'Concerning Chronology', in Donnchadh Ó Corráin (ed.), *Irish Antiquity Essays and Studies Presented to Professor M.J. O'Kelly* ([Cork 1981] Dublin, 1994), pp. 82–90.

Renfrew, Colin, *Archaeology and Language: The Puzzle of Indo-European Origins* (London, 1987).

Rhodes James, Robert (ed.), *Winston S. Churchill: His Complete Speeches, 1897–1963*, vol. iii (New York, 1974).

Rhys, Sir John, *Celtic Britain* (1882).

Ricoeur, Paul, 2004 *Memory, History, Forgetting.* (Chicago, 2004)

R.J.G.S., 'E.K. Tratman, O.B.E., D.Sc., M.D., F.D.S.R.C.S., F.S.A.', in *PBUSS* vol. xv, www.ubss.org.uk. pp. 1–5.

Robinson, F.N., 'Celtic Books at Harvard: The History of a Departmental Collection', in *Harvard Library Bulletin*, vol i, no. 1 (1946), pp. 52–65.

Romilly Allen, J., *Archaeologia* vol. lvi (1898), p. 39.

—, *Celtic Art in Pagan and Christian Times* (London, 1904).

Rouse, Irving, 'Prehistory in Haiti: A Study in Method', in *Anthropological Publication* No. 21 (Yale University, 1939).

Ryan, Michael, 'A Long 1923', in Gabriel Cooney, Katharina Becker, John Coles, Michael Ryan and Susanne Sievers (eds), *Relics of Old Decency: Archaeological Studies in later Prehistory Festschrift for Barry Raftery* (Dublin 2009), pp. 543–8.

Rynne, E., 'The La Tène and Roman finds from Lambay, Co. Dublin. A Re-Assessment in *PRIA* vol. lxxvi (1976), pp. 23–44.

Schultz, Adolf H., 'Ales Hrdlicka 1869–1943', in *Biographical Memoirs, National Academy of Sciences* vol. xxiii, pp. 305–38.

Scott, B.G., 'Iron "Slave-Collars" from Lagore Crannóg, Co. Meath', *PRIA* vol. lxxvii (1978), pp. 213–30.

*Scroll Phi Delta Theta* vol. lvi (Oct 1931), no. 1, p. 19.

Seoige, Mainchín, *From Bruree to Corcomohide* (Cork, 2000).

Shea, S., 'Description of Human Remains found in the Cist at Annaghkeen', in *JGAHS* vol. xii (1925), pp. 13–25.

—, 'Report on the Human Skeleton found in Stoneyisland Bog, Portumna', in *JGAHS* vol. xv (1931), pp. 73–81.

Sheehy, Jeanne, *The Rediscovery of Ireland's Past: the Celtic Revival 1830–1930* (London, 1980).

Sims-Williams, Patrick, 'Celtomania and Celtoscepticism', in *CMCS* vol. xxxvi (Winter 1998), pp. 1–35.

Sklenár, Karel, *Archaeology in Central Europe the first 500 years* (Leicester, 1983).

Smith, A.D., *The Ethnic Origin of Nations* (Oxford, 1986).

—, *National Identity* (Nevada, 1991).

—, 'Authenticity, antiquity and archaeology', in *Nations and Nationalisms* vol. vii, no. 4 (2001).

—, *Chosen Peoples* (Oxford, 2003).

Smith, R.A., *British Museum. Guide to Early Iron Age Antiquities* (London, 2nd edn., 1925).

Spinden, Herbert Joseph, 'Alfred Marston Tozzer, 877–954', *Biographical Memoir of the National Academy of Sciences of the United States of America* (1957), www.nasonline.org, pp. 384–97.

Stephan, Annika, 'A bio-bibliography of Dr Adolf Mahr: his contribution to archaeology in Austria, Ireland and Germany', unpublished BA dissertation (Galway-Mayo Institute of Technology, 2000).

— and Paul Gosling, 'Adolf Mahr (1887–1951): His Contribution to Archaeological Research and Practice in Austria and Ireland', in Gisela Holfter, Marieke Krajenbrink and Edward Moxon-Browne (eds), *Connections and Identities: Austria, Ireland and Switzerland* (Bern, 2004).

Stewart, A.F., *Art, Desire, and the Body in Ancient Greece* (Cambridge, 1997).

Stocking, George W. Jr. (ed.), *American Anthropology 1921—1945 Papers from the American Anthropologist* (Nebraska and London, 1976).

—, *After Tylor: British Social Anthropology 1888–1951* (London, 1996).

Stockley, Walter, 'Hooton of Harvard', *Life* Magazine (7 August 1939), pp. 60–6.

Stokes, William, *The Life and Labours in Art and Archaeology of George Petrie* (London, 1868).

Stout, Adam, *Creating Prehistory: Druids, Ley Hunters and Archaeologists in Pre-War Britain* (Oxford, 2008).

Stout, Matthew, 'Emyr Estyn Evans and Northern Ireland: the Archaeology and Geography of a New State', in John A. Atkinson, Iain Banks and Jerry

O'Sullivan, *Nationalism and Archaeology* Scottish Archaeological Forum (Glasgow, 1996).

Strong, William Duncan, 'Lagore Crannóg: An Irish Royal Residence of the 7th to 10th Centuries A.D. by Hugh Hencken', Review Article, in *American Anthropologist*, vol. lv, issue 5 (December 1953), pp. 732–3.

Sutton, McKayla, 'Harnessed in the Service of the Nation', 'Party Politics and the promotion of the Shannon Hydroelectric Scheme, 1924–32', in Mel Farrell, Jason Knirck and Ciara Meehan (eds), *A Formative Decade Ireland in the 1920s* (Kildare, 2015), pp. 87–107.

Talbot, J., 'Memoir on some Ancient Arms and Implements found at Lagore, near Dunshaughlin, County of Meath: with a view on the Classification of Northern Antiquities', *AJ* vol. vi (1849), pp.101–9.

Taylor, Walter, *A Study of Archaeology* (1948).

Thompson, Raymond Harris and Haynes, Caleb Vance, Jr., and Reid, James Jefferson, 'Emil Walter Haury, May 2 1904–December 5 1992', in *Biographical Memoirs of the National Academy of Sciences of the United States of America*: www.nasonline.org., pp. 151–74.

Tierney, Michael, *Eoin MacNeill Scholar and Man of Action*, edited by F.X. Martin (Oxford, 1980).

Tierney, Michael, 'Theory and Practice in Early Medieval Irish Archaeology', in Michael A. Monk and John Sheehan (eds), *Early Medieval Munster: Archaeology, History and Society* (Cork, 1998), pp. 190–8.

Tratman, E.K., 'Excavations at Kilgreany Cave, County Waterford', in *PUBSS* vol. iii (1928), pp. 109–53.

Trigger, Bruce, 'Archaeology and the Idea of Progress', *Time and Traditions Essays In Archaeological Interpretation* (Edinburgh, 1978).

—, *Revolutions in Archaeology* (London, 1980).

—, *A History of Archaeological Thought* (Cambridge, New York & Melbourne, 1989).

—, 'Alternative Archaeologies: Nationalist, Colonialist, Imperialist', in Robert Preucel and Ian Hodder (eds), *Contemporary Archaeology in Theory*: (Oxford, 1996), pp. 615–31.

Turgot, A.R.J., 'A Philosophical Review of the Successive Advances of the Human Mind' (1750).

Tylor, Edward B., *Primitive Cultures*, 2 vols. ([orig. 1871] 7th ed., New York, 1924).

Van der Noort, Robert and O'Sullivan, Aidan, *Rethinking Wetland Archaeology* (London, 2006).

Waddell, John, 'The Invasion Hypothesis in Irish Prehistory', *Antiquity* vol. lii (1978), pp. 121–8.

—, 'The Question of the Celticization of Ireland', in *Emania* no. 9 (1991), pp. 5–16.

—, 'The Celticization of the West', in C. Chevillot and A. Coffyn (eds), *L'Age du Bronze Atlantique* (1991), pp. 349–66.

—, *The Prehistoric Archaeology of Ireland* (Galway, 1998).

—, Review article, 'Vittorio De Martino, Roman Ireland', in *JGAHS* vol. lvi (2004), pp. 233–4.

—, *Foundation Myths: The Beginnings of Irish Archaeology* (Dublin, 2005).

Wakeman, W.F., 'On certain recent Discoveries of Ancient Crannóg Structures, chiefly in the County of Fermanagh', in *JRSAI* (1879–82).

Wallace, Patrick F., 'Adolf Mahr and the making of Seán P. Ó Ríordáin', in Helen Roche, Eoin Grogan, John Bradley, John Coles and Barry Raftery, *From Megaliths to Metal Essays in Honour of George Eogan* (Oxford, 2004), pp. 254–63.

— and Ó Floinn, Raghnall, *Treasures of the National Museum of Ireland: Irish Antiquities* (Dublin, 2002).

Walshe, P.T. and O'Connor, P., 'The excavation of a burial cairn on Baltinglass Hill, Co. Wicklow', *PRIA* vol. 46 (1940/1941), pp. 221–36.

Warner, R.B., 'Some Observations on the Context and Importation of Exotic Material in Ireland, from the First Century B.C. to the Second Century A.D.', in *PRIA* vol. lxxvi (1976), pp. 285–6.

—, 'The Date of the Start of Lagore', in *JIA* vol. iii (1985–6), pp. 75–7.

—, 'On Crannógs and Kings (Part 1)', in *JIA* vol. lvii (1994), pp. 61–9.

—, 'Tuathal Techtmar: Myth or Ancient Literary Evidence for a Roman Invasion', in *Emania*, no. 13 (1995), pp. 23–32.

—, 'De Bello Hibernico: A less than Edifying Debate', in *Archaeology Ireland* vol. x, no. 3 (Autumn 1996), pp. 38–40.

—, 'Yes, the Romans did invade Ireland', in *British Archaeology* no. 4 (1996), www.britarch.ac.uk.

—, 'Celtic Ireland and other Fables: Politics and Prehistory', based on a talk given to the Annual Conference of the Irish Association, Carrickfergus, 2–4 November, 1999; www.irish-association.org.

Watson, George, 'Celticism and the Annulment of History', in Terence Brown (ed.), *Celticism* (Amsterdam, 1996).

Weber, Eugen, *Peasants into Frenchmen, the Modernization of Rural France, 1880–1914* (Stanford, 1976).

Wheeler, R.E.M., 'The Paradox of Celtic Art', in *Antiquity* vol. vi (1932), pp. 294–300.

C. Blake Whelan, 'The Tanged Flake Industry of the River Bann, Co. Antrim', in *JRSAI* vol. x (1930), pp. 134–8.

—, Whelan, C. Blake, 'The Palaeolithic Question in Ireland', in *Report of the XVI International Geological Congress Washington* (1933), pp. 1209–18

—, C. Blake Whelan, 'Further excavations at Ballynagard, Rathlin Island, Co. Antrim', *PBNHPS* (1933–4), pp. 107–11.

—, C. Blake Whelan, 'Studies in the significance of the Irish Stone Age: The Campignian Question', *PRIA* xliiC (1934–1935), pp. 121–43

Whelan, Yvonne, *Reinventing Modern Dublin, Streetscape, Iconography and the Politics of Identity* (Dublin, 2003).

White, Lawrence William and Foley, Aideen, 'Power, Patrick', in ww.dib. cambridge.org.

Wilde, W.R., 'On the Animal Remains and Antiquities recently found at Dunshaughlin', *PRIA* vol. i (1840).

—, *A Descriptive Catalogue of the Antiquities of Stone, Earthen, and Vegetable Materials, in the Museum of the Royal Irish Academy* (Dublin 1857).

—, *A Descriptive Catalogue of the Antiquities of Animal Materials and Bronze in the Museum of the Royal Irish Academy* (Dublin 1861).

—, *A Descriptive Catalogue of Gold in the Museum of the Royal Irish Academy* (Dublin, 1862).

—, *The Beauties of the Boyne and its Tributary the Blackwater* (3rd edn., Dublin, 1949).

Willey, Gordon. R. and Sabloff, Jeremy A., *A History of American Archaeology* (2nd edn, London, 1980).

Windle, Bertram, 'On certain Megalithic Remains immediately surrounding Lough Gur', in *PRIA* 30, Section C. no. 10 (1912), pp. 283–306.

Wilson, Peter, 'The Father of Ulster Antiquaries', in *Archaeology Ireland*, vol. xiv, no. 1, issue no. 51 (Spring 2000).

Woodbury, Richard B., 'Obituary: John Otis Brew 1906–1988', in *American Antiquity* vol. lv (1990).

Wood-Martin, W.G., *Pagan Ireland* (1895).

—, *The Lake Dwellings of Ireland Or Ancient Lacustrine Habitations of Erin, Commonly called Crannógs* (Dublin & London, 1886).

Woodman, Peter, *The Mesolithic in Ireland: Hunter-Gatherers in an Insular Environment* (Oxford, 1978).

—, 'Who Possesses Tara? Politics in Archaeology in Ireland' in Ucko, Peter J. (ed.), *Archaeology A World Perspectice* (London and New York, 1995).

—, 'Rosses Point revisited', *Antiquity* vol. lxxii (1998).

Young, Simon, *The Celtic Revolution* (Gibson Square, 2009).

# Index